Advance Praise for A.J. Gordon

'Look to the rock from whence ye were hewn' – this advice from Isaiah could well be the motto for Kevin Belmonte's excellent new biography, *A.J. Gordon*.

Belmonte, a master of historical biography, has the knack of taking you vividly into the past without leaving you there. Instead he brings to the fore just those virtues and insights in his subject which are most missing and most needed in our own generation. So in this biography of the founder of Gordon College we get much more than nostalgia, we get a call to rediscover and live from our Christian roots.

> The Rev. Dr. Malcolm Guite, author of *Mariner: A Voyage with Samuel Taylor Coleridge,* Chaplain of Girton College, Cambridge University, England

A well-written biography is a great gift from the past to the present, and Kevin Belmonte's life of A.J. Gordon is just such a gift. To read it is to learn, to be challenged, and to be inspired. Preacher, teacher, scholar, abolitionist, and activist: the life of this Christian leader from over a century ago has much to teach us today.

> —Karen Swallow Prior, Ph.D., author of *Booked: Literature in the Soul of Me* and *Fierce Convictions—The Extraordinary Life of Hannah More: Poet, Reformer, Abolitionist*

Any book written by Kevin Belmonte, I want to read. So when I discovered his new biography of A.J. Gordon, I was hooked. I knew very little of Gordon, so the book opened up a new world.

The great tragedy of modern life is how we so easily let the stories of great men and women slip through our fingers, and this is one of those stories. It's an epic journey that reminds us of faith, character, and pioneering vision. Get the book.

> —Phil Cooke, writer, filmmaker, and author of *One Big Thing: Discovering What You Were Born to Do*

A. J. Gordon

An Epic Journey of Faith and Pioneering Vision

by Kevin Belmonte

WESTBOW
PRESS®
A DIVISION OF THOMAS NELSON
& ZONDERVAN

WestBow Press books may be ordered through booksellers or by contacting:

WestBow Press
A Division of Thomas Nelson & Zondervan
1663 Liberty Drive
Bloomington, IN 47403
www.westbowpress.com
1 (866) 928-1240

Scripture taken from the King James Version of the Bible.

ISBN: 978-1-5127-9974-3 (sc)
ISBN: 978-1-5127-9973-6 (hc)
ISBN: 978-1-5127-9975-0 (e)

Library of Congress Control Number: 2017912465

Print information available on the last page.

WestBow Press rev. date: 8/16/2017

∾

Dedication

To the memory of A.J. Gordon...

with sincere gratitude to his great-grandson, Jonathan Harrell, and Dick and Carol Visser—alumni from Gordon College's Boston days on The Fenway—and with grateful remembrance of John Beauregard, a great friend from my Gordon days, who kept the flame of heritage burning brightly...

And what shall be the influence of these truths upon our daily life?

In Christ our righteousness, we see...what we are pledged to...

We understand ourselves only in Him...[1]

* * *

The happiest and most exalted moments I have ever known in this life, are those when I stand on some high outlook of my New Hampshire home, and gaze off upon the blue hills in the distance, and see those hills rising range upon range, as though they were the very portals of Beulah land....

I shall see the King in his beauty, and the land of far distances...[2]

—A.J. Gordon

Contents

Preface xiii
by D. Michael Lindsay

Foreword xvii
by Dennis P. Hollinger

Prologue. xix
A Man of Many Parts

Chapter One. 1
Upon the Blue Hills

Chapter Two 7
Yet Another Music

Chapter Three 13
The Business of a Scholar

Chapter Four 21
University Years

Chapter Five. 29
There is the Fair Vision

Chapter Six 35
Jamaica Plain

Chapter Seven 45
Clarendon Street

Chapter Eight 67
To Hear A New Song

Chapter Nine 83
The Heart of the Matter

Chapter Ten 93
Chansons du Rédempteur

Chapter Eleven 105
Messages of Grace

Chapter Twelve 123
Well Remembered Days

Chapter Thirteen 139
Among Collegians

Chapter Fourteen 147
Athens and the Arena

Chapter Fifteen 155
Toward a Distant Shore

Chapter Sixteen 173
The School in Bowdoin Square

Chapter Seventeen 197
Where the White Banner Flew

Chapter Eighteen 213
Gatherings in Summer

Chapter Nineteen 245
To See the Morningstar

Chapter Twenty 267
Years Beyond

Afterword 291
The Sacred Isle

Author's Note 295

Works of A.J. Gordon 297

A.J. Gordon: A Timeline 303

Appendix 307
*from the Funeral Tribute for A.J. Gordon given by Dr. Elisha
Benjamin Andrews, President of Brown University*

Endnotes 309

Preface
by D. Michael Lindsay

Many things mark the unique and faithful life of A.J. Gordon, but above all else he was a man committed to Jesus Christ. He lived each day for the glory of God, right up until his last breath. From a young age Gordon sought God's will for his life, and he became an ambassador of hope for his generation, worthy of a living place in our memory.

Gordon emerged as an internationally known leader during the great London Centenary Missions conference of 1888. His founding a year later of the Boston Missionary Training School (what would later be called "Gordon College") furthered his contribution to global Christianity.

As the school's first president, Dr. Gordon built a creative theological institution to prepare all kinds of people to serve in far-flung places such as Africa, Asia, and beyond. At the same time, he worked for the flourishing of his local community, in greater Boston and throughout New England. This includes his civic leadership on behalf of the area's burgeoning immigrant communities and his tireless service for the working class. He had a remarkable gift for reaching both the leaders of his era as well as entire categories of people who were often marginalized or forgotten in nineteenth-century America. Indeed, his was a life committed to improving the prospects for thousands of people, simultaneously advancing the work of Christ and the common good. In that way, Dr. Gordon serves as an exemplar for us all.

Too often Christian leaders can become enamored with what's trendy. We focus on things that are popular, and in the process, we neglect the fullness of God's vision for the flourishing of all things. As one example, A.J. Gordon worked tirelessly for two things—evangelism and social justice—noble callings that often were pitted against one another in Protestant circles of his day.

An ardent abolitionist during the Civil War, Gordon worked in the decades after for racial reconciliation, and it is a testimony to his leadership in this area that African Americans were among some of the first graduates of the Boston Missionary Training School. Gordon also believed deeply in the good that could come from the contributions of girls and women, and he cared deeply for the poor. His leadership in these areas brought other pastors and civic leaders to see the importance of women's equality and economic mobility for immigrants and the working class. These alone are remarkable achievements.

But at the same time, Gordon committed his life to evangelizing the world, to sharing the good news of Jesus Christ through preaching, personal relationship, and intentional Christian witness. He believed deeply in the imminent return of Christ, and he took seriously the mandate of the Great Commission to reach the world with the Gospel. From his preaching to his institution-building, Gordon's life work was oriented around the need to bring others into a saving relationship with Jesus Christ. He had a special ability to bring together social justice and evangelism, and that became a hallmark of the institution that came to be known as Gordon College. Gordon is a place that I have come to serve with deep love and admiration for our founder, in part because of his and the institution's legendary ability to bring seemingly disparate ideals together.

Even though Gordon was educated at Brown University and served there for many years as a trustee, his educational vision was for a place that could reach the masses. His was a revolutionary idea: educate those who were underserved by existing institutions of theological instruction, and in so doing, draw many more laborers into the Lord's work and help transform a generation. By founding this school, Gordon opened up novel vocational pathways for many left out of existing educational avenues, and created ways for them to offer meaningful service in their hometowns and around the globe. It was a pioneering vision.

Finally, we should remember A.J. Gordon's ability to build strategic alliances and relationships with co-laborers. From his great friendship with D.L. Moody to collaborative ventures in greater Boston, Dr. Gordon modeled an irenic approach to ministry that created partnerships for good. It's a helpful reminder to us all that the Lord's work is best accomplished when we build partnerships for the Gospel.

A.J. Gordon's life is both an inspiration and a challenge. As we reflect on his legacy of ministry and service, we see for ourselves the fruit of a life well lived.

May we follow his example, and pursue a life worth leading.

Foreword
by Dennis P. Hollinger

Though gifted, well-educated, and well-connected, most of his cohorts in the late 1800s could not imagine the significant impact and legacy of A.J. Gordon more than a century later. This pioneering pastor, educator, and leader exemplified a breadth and depth rivaled by few of his peers or successors. Global missions, evangelism, social concern/justice, urban church ministry, education, hymnody—A.J. Gordon exemplified all of them in a holistic expression of Christian Faith.

In this book, Kevin Belmonte captures Gordon's life and impact with clarity and vitality. I was deeply touched by it. The genius of Gordon was not merely his giftedness, or even his vision—it was rather his deep devotion to and passion for his Lord and Savior Jesus Christ. Gordon responded to the many physical, social, and educational needs of his time as a reflection of biblical faith. But ultimately he understood, as quoted in this book, "What is needed is not a revival of ethics, as some are saying, but a revival of vital piety. For men will not recognize their stewardship to Christ until they recognize Christ's Lordship over them."

It was A.J. Gordon's abiding faith in Christ, and reliance on the power of God's Spirit, that led to his vision and the enduring legacy of his work that was to follow. Gordon College and Gordon-Conwell Theological Seminary are results of his vision and wisdom. But ultimately, they exist because of his devotion to Christ. As Gordon's timeless hymn states: "My Jesus I love Thee, I know Thou art mine."

In the pages that follow you will be stirred by Gordon's impact in pastoral ministry, world missions, evangelical ecumenicity, and contextualized education to meet the needs of his day. But even more importantly you will be stirred by a man devoted to Christ, before being devoted to the causes of Christ.

Prologue
A Man of Many Parts

They spoke in his praise, they sang his hymns,
they prayed to be made like unto him in Christian character and work.[1]
—*The Boston Globe,*
February 11, 1895

In July 1896, eight years after he graduated with distinction from Harvard, Ernest Barron Gordon marked another, more treasured milestone: the release of his memoir about his father, A.J. Gordon—known throughout the world as an author, educator, preacher, poet, philanthropist, and spiritual leader.[2]

Ernest Gordon was ideally suited to write such a book.

To be sure, he had the great advantage of a lifelong, near view of his father. But he was also a gifted writer. During his days at Harvard, he won academic laurels in history, and authored a Bowdoin Prize-winning essay.[3]

These were exceptional honors. But Ernest Gordon must have been more deeply gratified to see his memoir win critical acclaim. His father was taken far too soon, at age fifty-eight. That this new book found an audience, and was widely reviewed, meant that something of his father's work would go on.

These reviews began with *The Outlook* magazine, whose contributors later included Theodore Roosevelt. "An admirable life of an admirable man," the magazine said, and Ernest Gordon was an author who had "inherited his father's spirit;" the book "is full of filial love for all that his father stood for."[4] A second review, in much the same vein, appeared in *The Literary World*—close to the notice for a book featuring President Grover Cleveland.

The Literary World, created as "A Fortnightly Review of Current Literature," praised Ernest Gordon for writing "a loving portrait of [a] beautiful, gifted, and highly graced character...Dr. Gordon's face, which shines forth from the frontispiece, bespeaks the man. A rare man he was, in many ways."[5]

The New York Examiner, for its part, said that "in the field of literature, there is nothing that can compare with a good biography," and *The Examiner* heralded this new life of A.J. Gordon as "one of the best biographies that have been written during the last twenty-five years."[6] The review closed by saying Ernest Gordon's "powers of description are extraordinary," as shown in the opening chapter. And last, the picture of "the quiet New England hamlet" where A.J. Gordon was raised was itself "a masterpiece of delicate art."[7]

* * *

Long years ago, William Shakespeare vividly described what it was like to see one's father "in his habit, as he lived."

Ernest Gordon's book bestowed that kind of gift.

In one passage, he spoke of his father reading aloud, "with rich intonation, *High Tide on the Coast of Lincolnshire* to his sick child, while the butterflies came in the windows and the leaves rippled in the breeze." Another portrait spoke of Gordon, "standing, watch in hand, in the perspective of the long bridge over the Pemigewasset, timing his little sons as they raced to the other side after their evening's bath in the river." Then too, in later years, he loved to climb a hill path, a "St. Christopher of the mountainside...his eldest grandson astride his shoulders."[8]

Ernest Gordon's memoir was a copious and grateful return for seasons he had known with his father. In time, other biographies would come. That was very much in the nature of things. But only he could write, as an elder son, of scenes that caught the touch of life—

> [Father] possessed—oh, rare delight of youngsters!—an
> almost Helvetic skill in wood-carving. To recount the various

amusing and play-provoking things which his deft fingers whittled out would be to give an inventory of the contents of a well-stocked toy-shop. Miniature farming tools, houses, barns, churches, animals, were released one by one from the enveloping thraldom of a pine block by his emancipating penknife, as Ariel was released from the riven oak.

Besides this, he would make watering-carts out of tomato cans mounted on wheels, transparencies for campaign purposes out of old soap-boxes, and "keroogians," an invention of his own—bits of glass of various lengths strung on strings, and arranged in the order of the notes of the scale—on which he would play long "kinder symphonies."[9]

Given moments like these, it is little wonder Ernest Gordon wrote a memoir of the father he had lost too soon. Throughout his book, he painted a wide and eloquent canvas, bestowing great care to help readers see things he had seen: the many sides of A.J. Gordon's life, character, and legacy.

*   *   *

Meanwhile, in March 1895, another tribute to A.J. Gordon had appeared.

Presented in *The Granite Monthly,* it was written by Alice Rosalie Porter, a graduate of Mount Holyoke, a former Associate Principal at D.L. Moody's Northfield Seminary, and the wife of Civil War General Howard L. Porter.[10]

The Porters were widely known for their philanthropy, and work with fine cultural institutions. With their ties to Northfield Seminary, and A.J. Gordon's prominent place there as a leader in the famous Northfield Summer Conferences, the Porters had come to know him well.

In her essay, Alice Porter said Gordon, though only fifty-eight when he died, had become a leader in many fields. She wrote of his achievements in each sphere—and things she had seen in years of close friendship with the Gordon family.

It all made for a telling portrait.

From his student days at Brown University, and later Newton Theological School, friends spoke often of Gordon's "consecration of purpose, [his] beautiful faith, and loyalty to God's word." These traits, Alice Porter said, "increased as the years went by, characterizing not only his own career, but the life of the churches to which his ministry was given in Jamaica Plain and Clarendon Street, Boston.[11]

Often quiet and unassuming, though not at all a retiring man, Gordon had a gift for tact, and a quick wit "that was often of service to himself and others."[12]

Alice Porter saw, first hand, that Gordon was also "a man of wide culture, [much] interested in the cause of education," serving as a trustee of Brown University, and lending strong support to Newton Theological School.

Well versed "in literature and history," Gordon's fine preaching, "like that of [C.H.] Spurgeon, was *first and last Biblical.*" Weighing all this, Porter said her friend "seemed to me a man whom the truth had made versatile enough to fit into any age of the world."[13]

Porter turned next to Gordon's gifts as a preacher. "His whole bearing," she stated, "deepened the impression of his masterful grip of the truth, and his clarity of thought...Dr. Gordon spoke as an eyewitness of the Christ, as one who sat and supped with Him, hearing the words of life."[14]

In memory, Porter concluded, A.J. Gordon was "a man after God's own heart." And New Hampshire's hills, she believed, played a great role in fashioning this man "with simplicity of heart," yet one "so conversant with the varied forms of feeling" that he was a brother to people "in every plane of life."[15]

Parishioners in two Boston-based churches, Jamaica Plain Baptist Church, and Clarendon Street Church, knew this to be true, no less than the first students to attend the Boston Missionary Training School, which Gordon founded with his beloved wife Maria (pronounced "Muh-rye-ah"), in 1889.

Not far from their home at 182 West Brookline Street, the Boston Missionary Training School was the kind of place where students were often dinner guests in the Gordons' home, and mentored "by their advice and assistance."[16]

Gordon College and Gordon-Conwell Theological Seminary are kindred institutions to carry this vision forward today. Since the days of A.J. and Maria Gordon, students in the tens of thousands have cultivated their gifts, and discovered their callings in life.

A beacon they set alight still burns brightly.

* * *

Books by and about A.J. Gordon have travelled the world in the years since his passing—held in repositories like The Bodleian Library, Oxford, and Harvard. His legacy has carried to places he might little have imagined. It is often so with those who bring good gifts to the world.

Many such gifts rest in words A.J. Gordon gave posterity.

Alice Rosalie Porter rightly understood this.

As her essay drew to a close, she remembered Gordon as an author. She turned to one of the finest lines from his book, *In Christ*. Here, as with all the books he had written, Gordon pictured the great hope that endows all Christians.

"It is this hope," he said, "that bridges the chasm of death, and enables the heart to bound across it in triumph."[17] For him, heaven was "the Long Home of Forever," the blessèd realm of the Savior he so dearly wished to see. All his life, he brought others to the place where this hope became theirs too.

He bequeathed a goodly heritage.

Chapter One
Upon the Blue Hills

In his boyhood home...the geniality of his disposition came out most clearly...rambling over the rough pastures... excursions to far-away hilltops and to distant lakes, in riding homeward at dusk, singing the evening hymns of Lyte and Keble—while the glow was still living in the west, and the whippoorwills were beginning their chant in the hollows...[1]

—Ernest Gordon

Adoniram Judson Gordon was born on Tuesday, April 19, 1836, the son of John Calvin Gordon and Sally Tilton Gordon, whose maiden name was Robinson.

They made their home in New Hampton, a rural village ringed by the hills and mountains of central New Hampshire. It was "a land of upland pastures," with dozens of lakes nearby, along with great forest tracts of maple and birch trees. These, when touched by the frost-filled days of autumn, brought mingled, resplendent colors "of scarlet, orange, crimson and yellow."[2]

When John and Sally Gordon welcomed their eldest son to the world, they couldn't know the day of his birth would be a day sacred to American history—for it was the day when Ralph Waldo Emerson's "Concord Hymn" was sung publicly for "the completion of the Battle Monument" in Concord, Massachusetts.[3] On that occasion, words now a part of our literature first echoed in the air of springtime—

> *By the rude bridge that arched the flood,*
> *Their flag to April's breeze unfurled,*
> *Here once the embattled farmers stood,*
> *And fired the shot heard round the world.*

As it happened, A.J. Gordon's great-grandfather, Levi Robinson, fought in the American Revolution so vividly celebrated in Emerson's verse.

Born in Exeter, New Hampshire, in 1753, Robinson served several enlistments from 1775 to 1778. At the age of eighty, he was "placed on the pension roll of Strafford County...for service as a private in the New Hampshire Continental Line."[4] When he died, on October 22, 1849, his then thirteen-year-old great-grandson, A.J. Gordon, would have remembered him well.

Family lore celebrated Robinson as a stouthearted patriarch—a man who "shouldered his flint-lock, and tramped through wood and stream, one hundred miles to Boston." He arrived too late to fight in the Battle of Bunker Hill, but served with honor throughout much of the Revolutionary War.[5]

The Gordon family lineage was no less storied or eventful.

Alexander Gordon, A.J. Gordon's ancestor, was born in Scotland and fought in the Scottish army that clashed with forces under Cromwell in the early 1650s.[6] In several decisive engagements, the Scottish army was routed, and young Alexander was one of hundreds of prisoners deported to America as indentured servants. He eventually settled in the colony of New Hampshire, and his story is given briefly in the *Genealogical and Family History of New Hampshire* as follows:

> Alexander Gordon, the first of the name in New Hampshire, was a member of a Highland Scottish family which was loyal to the cause of the Stuarts. While a soldier in the royalist army of King Charles the Second, he fell into the hands of Cromwell as a prisoner. After being confined in Tuthill Fields, London, he was sent to America in 1651, and held a prisoner of war at Watertown, Massachusetts. In 1654 he

was released and went to Exeter, New Hampshire, where
the town gave him a grant of twenty acres of land ten years
later, and he became a permanent resident. He engaged
in lumbering upon the Exeter River, and was a successful
and exemplary citizen. In 1663 he was married to Mary,
daughter of Nicholas Lysson, and they had six sons and two
daughters.[7]

Yet there is far more to this story than what has been said above.

Before coming to New Hampshire, history reveals that Alexander
Gordon "was a victim of ill treatment."[8] Seeking redress, he brought
a petition before the Deputy Governor and Magistrates of the County
Court at Charlestown, in November 1653. Alexander Gordon may not
have been literate, and able to write this petition himself. However, given
what is recorded there (even if it was dictated) we have something of his
story, as he would have told it.

"By the wise providence of the Almighty God," the petition said,
"your poare petitioner (with many others of his countrymen) was
taken a prisoner...and with many more prisoners brought into Tottell
fields."[9] Gordon then told the Deputy Governor and Magistrates of his ill
treatment at the hands of an American colonist, John Cloise of Watertown,
Massachusetts. Cloise, Gordon said, "moved your petitioner to go along
with him by sea to [America,] without any agreement for time or wages,
only his promise to be as a father in all love and kindness."

Honoring this agreement for what was called an "apprenticeship," but
what really amounted to indentured servitude, Gordon told the Deputy
Governor and Magistrates: "Your poare petitioner obtained his passage
[to America] *by his labour,* without any charge to [John] Cloise—as Mr.
John Allen, the Master of the said Ship, hath under his hand given [i.e.
testified]."

In all these things, Alexander Gordon acted in good faith.

How great the grief must have been when John Cloise refused, after
Gordon's "faythfull service" in America "for about a year," to give him
any wages.

Further, Cloise compounded this offense by planning to sell Gordon to Samuel Stratton, "a planter in Watertowne." Not only had Cloise refused to pay Gordon wages he had rightly earned, he was trying to get more money by selling Gordon's so-called "apprenticeship" to someone else. The young Scot's servitude would be perpetuated.

As Gordon told the Deputy Governor and Magistrates, "your poare petitioner apprehendeth himself to be much wronged…yet being a poare exile and friendless." Then, he did "humbly intreate this Honored Court" for relief.[10]

In a word, Gordon's petition was a request for release from his "contract" with Cloise, and a request to stop Cloise's plan to sell him to Samuel Stratton.

This petition was shamefully denied, and Gordon was forced soon after to sign a letter of indenture to Samuel Stratton, which read—

> This indenture witnesseth that I, Allexander Gorthing, Scotchman, Lately being arrived the coasts of New England, do covenant agree and promise to Serve Goodman Stratton, Planter of Watertowne the full space of six years, wherein I do promise to do him true and faithfull service not to absent myself day or night out of his family during the time of Apprentiship aforesaid without his Licence or consent, that I will not entangle or engage myself in any way of Contracts of marriage during the aforesaid time, all his Lawfull demands and injunctions I do promise to fulfill to my uttermost power and abilities…
>
> All this I the aforesaid Allexander do likewise promise, bynd and ingage myself to serve my full time to some of his sonnes untill it be fully expired if providence should take away my present master by death, witness my hand
>
> Allexander Gorthing
> His marke & a seale
> [October 15, 1652].[11]

Surviving evidence then suggests that for one to two years, Gordon endured another time of forced servitude. Then in 1654, he was brought to Exeter, New Hampshire, when he was either hired or–more likely—his indenture was purchased by Nicholas Lysson, who owned and operated a sawmill on the Exeter River.[12]

Alexander Gordon had no idea what to expect, but from this time on, his fortunes changed for the better. Nicholas Lysson was clearly a man of character and kindness, taking young Gordon to heart. It cannot have been otherwise, for Gordon wed Lysson's daughter Mary in 1663.

Gordon had by this time been several years a freeholder, and, as stated above, the town of Exeter gave him a land grant of twenty acres. As a tradesman, he engaged in lumbering upon the Exeter River, and was regarded as "a successful and exemplary citizen." In the years to come, Alexander and Mary Gordon "had six sons and two daughters."[13]

At long last, he'd found a life; one he never thought to have.

One of Alexander and Mary Gordon's descendants was Enoch Gordon, who came to New Hampton, New Hampshire, about 1765. He settled on high land to the west of Carter Mountain, and his son, Benoni Gordon, built a woolen mill which grew into an extensive business. It was Benoni's son, John Calvin Gordon, who became A.J. Gordon's father.[14]

One local historian, F.H. Kelley, described where this mill was, and what it was like. In New Hampton, he said, "on the south and east sides of the Pinnacle, are some very remarkable springs which deserve mention. That on the south and overlooking the village is never affected by droughts, and furnishes a considerable part of the water which forms the brook running through the village, [finding] its way into the Pemigewasset River. On this stream was the only grist-mill in town, a saw-mill, and a clothing mill, the latter run fifty years ago by John Calvin Gordon."[15]

As he was growing up, A.J. Gordon likely heard many stories of the family patriarch, his great-grandfather Enoch (who died in 1839), as well as his grandfather and other relations as they made a life for themselves in and around New Hampton. There were times of clearing land, building houses and a woolen mill, being with and around sheep as they grazed highland pastures, the birth of children, hard winters, summer seasons and autumn. There must have been so much to tell, and remember.

This said, A.J. Gordon likely knew little of the trials Alexander Gordon had endured before coming to Exeter, finding a home and family.

But perhaps some memories survived—echoes of what had been.

Alexander Gordon's struggles had been harrowing—a call to war, desperate hand to hand fighting, death and bitter defeat, the loss of brothers in arms, imprisonment, and a long, cruel voyage to a land he had never seen—far from the Scotland he would never see again. Then too, he suffered much in servitude, like the biblical patriarch Jacob—many times indentured, many times deceived and mistreated. Wages denied, some never given.

And yet…

Had Alexander Gordon not endured these trials as he did, A.J. Gordon, to say nothing of his many ancestors, would never have been born in America.

It was a mysterious providence—but perhaps it was also a severe mercy.[16]

Chapter Two
Yet Another Music

Threading its way like a stream of quicksilver...the Pemigewasset carries seaward the contributions of unnumbered mountain brooks. The hill-country is a land of idyllic beauty, with a charm of its own...[1]

—Ernest Gordon

Given all that Alexander Gordon suffered, it is fitting to recall that his descendants, within a century of his time, settled in the highlands around the Carter Mountains, in the near vicinity of New Hampton, New Hampshire.

Something of the highlands' mist and music would always stir A.J. Gordon profoundly. Later years meant leaving New Hampton; but it never left him. Its foothills, mountains, and rills struck deep roots. They were a part who he was.

Words he once said of his friend D.L. Moody were true for him as well: "Moody cannot endure the sea-shore. His green fields and ever-shadowing hills and deep-rolling Connecticut are his paradise. So my native hills and quiet shades at New Hampton are to me. I long to be back thereto."[2]

Gordon's early education took place in the village public school—learning "the three R's," reading, writing, and arithmetic—and likely work with a slate, or pouring over textbooks similar to McGuffey's Readers, first published in 1837.[3]

He grew fond of children's fiction too. "In the days of boyhood," he would remember, "[I read] the story of the alchemist who spent his life and fortune in trying to discover the philosopher's stone; that by which he might have the power of the fabled Midas—that whatever he touched might turn to gold."[4]

Still other things came outside the home and classroom.

In youth, Gordon also learned first hand about something he wryly described as the "agricultural curriculum on a farm."[5] Each day, he worked with his hands at any number of commonplace farm chores—tasks like cleaning horse stalls, feeding pigs, or ploughing garden furrows. He described another kind of field work in vivid language: "the great problem in my boyhood was how to pull the stumps whose strong, deep, gnarly roots have struck down into the earth and grasped it with giant fingers. Only by a tremendous convulsion can these be uprooted."[6] And always, in the spring, "work in the fields" was often exchanged for hours of hard and grimy work in his father's woolen mill.

Understandably, it wasn't work he relished; and there were times, he later admitted, when he helped his father and brother in the mill "with grudgings and chafings."[7] One family member put it another way, saying he "eagerly left his ordinary task of washing greasy wools in the big iron kettle."[8]

It was all part of the family business, preparing wool to create "yarns and heavy cloth." Young A.J., or "Judson," as his family called him, was expected to do his share of work.[9] Not everything in New Hampton was idyllic.

Recollections too of rustic folkways in New Hampshire lingered in young Gordon's mind. Life was challenging in these highlands. "I remember," he said—

> my boyhood in the country, where the winters were long and heavy, that it was the policy of the farmers to gather their cattle and begin to tread down the snow as soon as it fell. For they said,
> "If we do not break a road through it, we shall be blocked in by it."
> And so they stepped upon the snowflakes as they

descended, and these became a smooth white pathway beneath their feet, when otherwise they would have blockaded their homes by their huge drifts piled high in air.[10]

Gordon knew baseball too in boyhood, and later drew on his recollections to frame a fine article illustration, saying: "Good ball players are skilful at catching the ball on its rebound."[11] Still, one wishes for more from him about this pastime, as any such memories would harken to a very early time of baseball in America—from the 1840s and 50s. But sadly, the record is silent beyond this brief sentence.

At the same time, facets of the man A.J. Gordon became were present in his childhood, and they were encouraged as he grew older. Music was one of them.

All his life, he had a deep love of music—an affection, and a gift, shared by many in his family. They often gathered in the parlor to sing hymns. During such times, the children would sing solos, or play solos, for their parents.[12]

It was during these years Gordon learned to play the piano, and one wonders what it would have been like to see him sitting there as a boy, in the parlor of his home—learning, practicing—and finding his love for music deepen.

The world may be grateful such hours unfolded.

Gordon's gift and his skill were such that he later composed the verses or the melodies for many fine hymns, even though he was not classically trained. Moreover, he very capably edited four widely used hymnbooks.

The plaintive, stirring music for "My Jesus, I Love Thee," may well be his finest composition.[13] To listen to its melody is to hear something like a Scottish air, yearning set in song, a longing for home. Perhaps, though it is only speculation, this melody had its beginnings in remembered moments—when he looked on the highlands of home, and saw cloud-gilded mountains in the morning light.

"There is something indescribable in these mountain-top experiences," he once said, "they never fail to lift me out of myself and bring me nearer to God."[14]

The music of his stirring hymn seems to summon such imagery.

*   *   *

When he was fifteen, A.J. Gordon heard yet another kind of music.

All his life, things of faith had been taught in his home—devotional readings from his father, heartfelt prayers he heard his mother speak, times of home worship when the weather was too inclement for travel to church services.[15] And of course, he heard many sermons as well.

These things set the stage for a time when he deeply considered what faith meant for him, personally. One evening, all his questions came to the fore, and he spent a long night—a young seeker's vigil—calling upon Christ with a penitent heart and embracing the sterling promise of redemption.

All through the night, his father was there. When the first light of morning came, John Gordon saw his son give his life, and his heart, to the Savior.

One family member later wrote of this "great change" beautifully: "calm as the sunshine which flooded the hills the next day [he] found peace with God through our Lord Jesus Christ."[16]

For himself, A.J. Gordon cast something very like these feelings in verse—

I shall see the King in His beauty,
In the land that is far away,
When shadows at length have lifted,
And the darkness has turned to day.[17]

Christ was now the beloved Sovereign of his soul.

*   *   *

On June 6th, 1852, as warmer weather allowed, A.J. Gordon was baptized "on a lovely Sabbath" in the waters of an old millstream.[18] And even as he emerged from the waters, in mystic newness of life, other things, previously unlooked for, were set free. As his son Ernest wrote—

[Father's] conversion was a new impulse in all directions. Books had been an aversion, study...almost [punishment].

> With what avidity did he now go back to these distasteful tasks! …they [became] the necessary preparation for a future, the anticipation and hope of which he was now treasuring in his heart…
>
> This hope and purpose he did not long keep to himself.
>
> Shortly after his sixteenth year had opened he confessed before the church his determination to enter the ministry[19]

One person present when A.J. Gordon stated his wish to enter the ministry was still living when Ernest Gordon wrote his filial memoir. Thus, from first-hand recollections, he was able to set the scene when his father told his family of the call God had placed on his heart.

On "a warm evening in late spring [1852]," Ernest Gordon said, with "the sounds of the wakeful world coming in the open doors and windows; a shy, awkward boy, yet with a light on his face, announced, with much difficulty and stumbling, his purpose to devote his life and best powers to his Savior's work."[20]

Welcome as this news was—Gordon's parents were deeply gratified—one reputedly sage observer doubted the prospects for such a seemingly shy, contemplative boy in the ministry. An old deacon said portentously: "Judson is a good boy, and would make a good minister, *if only he had energy.*"[21]

Ernest Gordon knew his father far better, and rightly noted that the old deacon wasn't the first person to mistake "noisiness for force," nor to "disregard the latent power which lies hid in the quietest mill-pond."[22]

Those latent powers soon emerged in memorable ways.

At sixteen, A.J. Gordon was two years older than most students sent to preparatory academies with a view to the ministry; but he ardently resolved to make up for lost time. He was enrolled, forthwith, in The New London Scientific and Literary Institution, or Colby Academy, located in New London, New Hampshire.[23] Setting out for school, he wore a new suit of clothes, made by his mother, from cloth spun in the family woolen mill.

And far from lacking energy, young Gordon *walked the entire thirty-four miles* from home to this new school, carrying all his belongings with him. These included a change of clothes, a copy of Virgil, and an algebra textbook.[24]

If this seems an unduly arduous trip, Ernest Gordon suggested his father would have taken a different view. The countryside along the way was "peculiarly beautiful, past Cardigan and Ragged mountains, round the base of Kearsarge and by Sunapee Lake," into the plain where Colby Academy was situated.[25]

A hardy young man, A.J. Gordon had always liked to walk alone in the forests and fields near his home.[26] He likely looked on this trek to start a new phase of his life as something like an adventure—thinking all the while of what lay ahead. He was travelling to follow the call he had been given.

That counted for much.

Chapter Three
The Business of a Scholar

Colby Academy…was founded in 1853 [and named] in honor of the late Governor Anthony Colby. Many leading men [across] the United States have been students - A.J. Gordon. D.D.; John Quincy Adams Brackett, Ex-Governor of Massachusetts; and Benjamin Wheeler, President of the University of California…

Colby Academy owns four well equipped buildings…a carefully selected library of 4,000 volumes, and aims to present the influences of a well regulated Christian family with the advantage of skillfully directed intellectual discipline.[1]

—*Who's Who in New England* (1909)

When A.J. Gordon entered Colby Academy in autumn 1853, he found a setting that must have seemed a world away from anything he had known. The school had a fine 20-acre campus on New London Hill, in Merrimack County, New Hampshire. It was 30 miles northwest of Concord, 90 miles north of Boston.[2]

Colby Academy opened as New London Academy in July 1837. Its name was subsequently changed to The New London Literary and Scientific Institution—still later to The Colby Academy.[3]

Colby's first principal was Dr. George W. Gardner, then a recent graduate of Dartmouth, and he served during A.J. Gordon's time there.[4] Colby was a large school for its region and time. During its first term 120 students enrolled—and the second term had nearly double that number, with 210 students.

Promotional literature touted other elements of Colby Academy's appeal: including its near proximity to the Sunapee, Ascutney, Cardigan, Ragged, and Kearsarge mountains. Nearby were "many charming bodies of water, among which is the famous Lake Sunapee." And last, this literature stated, "an altitude of 1,350 feet gives this region a dry, cool, and invigorating air."[5]

On his arrival at Colby, Gordon was given a room in Colby Hall, the academy residence that afforded "twenty rooms for the boys and [male] teachers." Each room was supplied "with a double bed, a table, two chairs, washstand and mirror, and a box stove." Students like A.J. Gordon were expected to "care for their own rooms and provide fuel." But more than this taxing expectation, they had to take still greater care, for "the danger of fire was great with red-hot stoves and whale oil lamps." "Somehow," one chronicler said with a dash of wit, "the years went by without a conflagration."[6]

For some seventy years, Colby Hall was home to hundreds of young men like Gordon. Here, "they found new associations and cemented ties of friendship that lasted for a lifetime." And here, they "learned habits of study that served them well when they went on to college and professional school."[7]

School discipline was said to be "strict but kind." As to regulations, the catalogue stated there would not be many, "but that they must be observed." Manners and morals were dealt with in turn. The list of "prohibited indulgences" included smoking, or drinking intoxicating liquors. But one tenet was as time bound for rural America as it is wont to bring a smile: there was to be *"no carrying firearms, or keeping gunpowder."* Here, the wry chronicler above gave another rejoinder rich with unintended humor. Since students, he said, "were accustomed to these practices at home, this was something of a hardship."[8]

As customary, the school was "divided into male and female departments." English and classical courses were provided for the young men, each covering three years. For the young women a preparatory as well as a three years' course of study was offered; within a short time

(1856) the trustees voted that the regular course for young women should extend over four years.[9]

The young men took the classical course if they were preparing for college, with "plenty of Latin and Greek." The English course was strong in mathematics and was designed to qualify for civil engineering, mechanics, or the scientific courses in college. Young women studied Latin, French, and Italian, a term of rhetoric and another of English literature, and the usual amount of mathematics. Their course also included several subjects then called sciences: political economy, moral philosophy, and natural theology.[10]

Then there were the "ornamental branches," or music, painting, drawing, and the making of wax flowers. The trustees tasked an examining committee of nine to visit the school to see students were getting what they came for. The young women were then given diplomas if their examinations were satisfactory, and the full course of study completed. A careful record was kept of individual attainment on a score of one to five. Reports were sent to the parents of each student.

Students attended church both morning and afternoon on Sunday. Such was a part of a church tradition "not yet vitiated by Sunday movies and ball games, and students did not have a gasoline nag at the back door of Colby Hall, or the Ladies' Boarding-house for a trip to Newport or Claremont or the White Hills."[11]

Chapel attendance on weekdays was also compulsory and there were no cuts. And while it was true that chapel services "did not constitute religion in the minds of those who formulated the resolutions," they were regarded as "conducive to those inner attitudes of the soul which are vital to religion."

Students seemed genuinely interested in religion, judging from the events. For a time the Sunday evening meetings of the church were held at the Academy, and a school prayer meeting, which was voluntary, was held on Friday evenings. Once a week, Principal Gardner held an inquiry meeting which was well attended.

Several of the students professed conversion and "conducted themselves as if they meant it." So pervasive was the interest in personal religion that even class sessions were interrupted for prayer and conference, and twenty persons, most of them students, joined the church. This gladdened the heart of the new minister, Reverend Henry Lane, who had recently commenced his pastoral ministry. Church and school were close, and the pastor and teachers worked together cordially.[12]

It is possible to catch a glimpse of student life as it was then in New London. Men and women toiled from sunrise to sunset on the farm, but the children were given "time enough to go to school until their labor was too valuable in summer." Villagers plied their trades. Shopkeepers stocked dry goods and other necessities. Students were everywhere about the community. Many of the homes gave them lodging, for the academy dormitories could not house them all. Students "gave a bustle" to the community, and became much a part of its life.[13]

At festive times, Colby Academy gave a "colorful appearance" to town streets. Commencement Day was such an event.

There were eight candidates for graduation in 1855. Those responsible for the program "were not content with a simple ceremony and the townspeople would have been disappointed without something more." There had to be "a procession of students and a band of martial music" with displays of student oratory.

People thronged the streets, with peddlers and hawkers quick "to turn a penny." It was all very much like a college Commencement, and "the people were as well satisfied as if it had been." It was "the gala day of the year."[14]

Several graduates went on to further study. In 1855 three young men, "Butterfield, Cilley, and Gage" went to Dartmouth. Another three, "Cowles, Plumer, and Porter" entered Brown University. "Two young women graduates, Elizabeth H. Browne of New London and Susan M. Tracy of Concord," completed the regular course and received their diplomas.[15]

* * *

As for A.J. Gordon, his first year at Colby was a fortunate one. His elder sister Julia was a faculty member of "the Female Department," teaching drawing and painting. She thus shared his artistic nature. But on a practical level, she could help ease his transition to such a new, perhaps rather intimidating setting.[16]

It wasn't long, though, before Gordon showed himself a very fine student: especially in classics under the teaching of Dr. Gardner. Bright and diligent, Gordon steadily became fluent in ancient Greek.

As Gardner recalled, "he liked the language, and pursued it with a genuine zest...He studied his long and tedious lessons in the Greek paradigms as though in pursuit of game...In later years...I have noted in his writings specially fine and discriminating renderings of difficult texts [and] thought I could detect an apt and skilful use of the principles of the Greek language first learned in New London."[17]

At the same time, Gordon dispelled any idea that he lacked "energy," or initiative—to use the old deacon's language from home. During his first term at Colby Academy, he was elected First Recording Secretary of the school debating society, "The Euphemian Association."

In this setting, he learned to speak effectively when making prepared remarks, or when speaking spontaneously—and he was subject to peer evaluation. There was a certain rigor in this verbal form of fencing and declamation, and however hesitant he may have been at first, Gordon's desire to be there, and to succeed, said much for his character and determination at this time.[18]

Outside the classroom, seeking to offset school expenses, Gordon also demonstrated what people in his day called "pluck," a mingling of courage, grit, and resolve. He showed these traits when he decided to "take the contract of painting the exterior of the main school building" there at Colby, a large building, some four stories tall. His son Ernest later described it all, the hours of hard work "on high ladders with paint pots and brushes," saying: "the whole spring recess was spent in work on corner boards, and cases, and window sashes."[19]

And in this considerable task, young Gordon had the welcome company of his roommate—a young friend of greater financial means, who generously offered to work alongside Gordon without being paid. Gordon always remained grateful for this show of kindness, and their friendship endured for many years thereafter.[20]

Ultimately, the promise George Gardner saw in Gordon was fully realized. He worked diligently to hone his intellectual gifts, and when he graduated in July 1856, he did so with honors, was one of only seven students from his graduating class who were bound for college.[21]

After leaving Colby Academy, Gordon returned to New London on several occasions to renew his acquaintance with the school that had done so much to help him develop as a scholar. He later wrote of how indebted he was to Colby's influence in shaping his career.[22]

H.K. Rowe, writing in *The Centennial History* of Colby Academy, said that "high on the roll of honor" among those the academy "would not forget"

> is the name of Adoniram Judson Gordon…a New Hampton boy with the stamp of the country upon him…fitted for college with the class of '56. Bearing a name honored in missionary history, he turned to the theological seminary after graduation from Brown University, and completed his course at the Newton Theological Institution with the class of '63.
>
> A pastorate of six years followed in the flourishing suburb of Jamaica Plain, and then Boston called him into the city where he served as minister of the Clarendon Street Baptist Church for twenty-five years.
>
> His preaching and pastoral service endeared him to the people of a large parish, his books of a devotional character made him widely known and beloved, and the [Boston Missionary Training School], which he organized at the church in 1889 for the training of religious workers, perpetuated his influence…
>
> Closely [allied with] missionary enterprises, [Dr. Gordon] was President of the Executive Board of the American Baptist Missionary Union, and editor of *The Watchword*. He founded the Industrial Home for needy men in Boston. His own college, [Brown,] conferred on him the degree of doctor of divinity.[23]

In 1904, a notice ran in the January 1904 issue of *The Watchman* magazine, describing "the A.J. Gordon Memorial Fund of Colby

Academy," saying: "donations or inquiries may be sent to C.L. Page, 13 Rockville Park, Boston, Mass."[24]

Some might have seen this as a rather standard advertisement; but in truth it was far more. C.L. Page established a scholarship to insure that promising students of humble means—as A.J. Gordon once was—could be educated in the very place that shaped his character and intellect. Through this welcome door of opportunity, he would always be remembered.

Chapter Four
University Years

Neath the shade of these time-honor'd walls...
Then, as in memory, backward we wander...
Often, we'll ponder and smile,
As we murmur the name of Old Brown.[1]

When A.J. Gordon began studies at Brown University in autumn 1856, that venerable Ivy League institution was just eight years shy of its centenary. Founded in 1764, Brown was the third college established in New England, and the seventh in colonial America. Since 1770, its campus had been on College Hill, overlooking the city of Providence, Rhode Island.[2]

An engraving from 1840, just over fifteen years before Gordon's arrival, shows the university's College Green and Halls as a cluster of handsome buildings with elements of Greek architecture, fronted by a fine quadrangle and several young trees. The streets beyond were cobblestone or packed earth. The overall effect was impressive: yet it was very much a university still coming into its own.[3]

For a time, there was some question of whether A.J. Gordon would attend Brown. Ernest Gordon said initially his father was "drawn to Dartmouth College, the noble and richly historic university of his native state."[4] Very likely this reflected the influence of his Colby Academy instructor in Greek, Dr. Gardner, who attended Dartmouth. But Dartmouth was also the finest college in New Hampshire. Both factors would have been strong inducements to seek undergraduate education there. In the end, though, Gordon opted for Brown; and there were several compelling reasons why.

First, Brown was then a Baptist university, the faith tradition of his family. Also, as Ernest Gordon observed, Brown was home to President Francis Wayland, "the Thomas Arnold of America," who had just concluded his career as a reforming educator, but "whose fame and the immediate influence…were still strongly felt in the Christian circles of New England."[5]

Last, Wayland would have been still more highly regarded within the Gordon family; for in 1853 he had published a famous and widely read biography of the very missionary pioneer A.J. Gordon was named for: Adoniram Judson.[6]

Gordon's dormitory room at Brown—at least from the fall of 1858 until spring 1860, was "no. 44 University Hall"—a large brick building of handsome proportions, designed in the Georgian-Colonial architecture style, with a columned cupola atop its roof.[7] It was, and remains, a venerable edifice. Built in 1770, it is the oldest building on the Brown University campus.

From the window of his top-floor room, Gordon had a fine view and could watch passers-by walking along College Street, perhaps returning from a trip to the nearby Athenaeum. Over time, he gained a great fondness for "no. 44," which he called "my lofty lookout in this old ante-Revolutionary building." And from there, he said, he often found himself "gazing into the future."[8]

* * *

The future Gordon contemplated was preparation for pastoral service in Christian ministry, his sole purpose in coming to Brown University.

And here, the personal example and reputation of Brown's president, Francis Wayland, was highly important—for he was as famous a spiritual mentor of young men as he was the leader of a prominent school. Wayland had only just ceased to be Brown's president, in 1855—but the university, and its current leaders, bore the stamp of Wayland's tenure.

Ernest Gordon described this facet of his father's education, saying—

The output of the New England college before the present era of expansion and specialization was…wonderfully true, tempered, and substantial. It was hand-made, of selected raw material, with the personal touch of such masters as Wayland, Mark Hopkins, and Timothy Dwight ineffaceably inwrought.

These distinctive qualities, this peculiar timbre, which can be imparted only by human contacts, is more rare as universities become assimilated to the wholesale, factory tone of our civilization.

The successful president now is the one who secures the most numerous legacies, the most sumptuous dormitories for his college. He no longer draws and moulds and shapes young men. He no longer visits and counsels, and, if need be, prays with them. He has not the sense of accountability which made the great president of Brown say, quoting [Thomas] Arnold, that "if ever I could receive a new boy from his father without emotion, I should think it was high time to be off."[9]

Aside from Brown University's stature as a school shaped by a gifted leader, there were many other excellent resources there to help A.J. Gordon prepare for his pastoral calling—chief among them the opportunities he had as a Classics major.

The study of Greek could help him translate the Scriptures from their original language; while the study of Latin would enable him to read widely among the great writers of the Christian tradition through all centuries of church history.

But before he could delve deeply into subjects of scholarship, he had to contend with other, less welcome things during his early days at Brown.

As one of the "sturdy, self supporting" students from "the back farms," Gordon was often considerably challenged in his efforts to cover the modest sum of sixty-seven dollars needed to meet his yearly expenses. His parents weren't able to offer assistance from home, and while he worked when he could—and church friends he made in Providence "helped much"—there were still times when he had little or no money. Oatmeal became a staple of his meals, and there were moments he fought hard to overcome the dejection he felt. Sometimes, "it seemed hardly possible to continue for want of money."[10]

At the same time, he experienced some of the less welcome traditions of college life: for "there was much obnoxious hazing of freshmen." And in Gordon's case he was the more likely to be hazed, as he was "a student for the ministry."[11]

Just weeks into his freshman year, Gordon was "smoked out" of his room by a ring of upperclassmen who demanded he "mount the table [to] preach a sermon." Older than most of them, and used to trying circumstances growing up, Gordon wasn't cowed by this attempt at hazing. He stood up on the table, and said to them: "A certain man went down from Jerusalem to Jericho—*and fell among thieves!*"[12]

Angered by these defiant words, the upperclassmen rushed forward and pushed the table over. Getting quickly to his feet, Gordon sprang at the ringleader, and "tore his coat in halves." A fight followed, in which Gordon had unexpected help from a fellow student who happened on the scene: John Hay, who later became the Private Secretary and biographer of Abraham Lincoln.[13]

* * *

Gordon's years at Brown "were years of diligent application." His "special aptitude in composition" was singled out for praise.[14]

He had a "warm interest in the classics" as well, and was among the students "fortunate enough to read the Greek tragedies with Professor Harkness, and the Satires and Epodes of Horace with John L. Lincoln."[15]

Professor Lincoln, in particular, was known for his "accurate scholarship, delicate humor," and "fine, discriminating literary sense." These traits, combined with genuine warmth for students, made him "for two generations the especial favorite of young men." Gordon was among the students grateful to hear Lincoln say *Bene!* or *Optime!* "after an unusually felicitous translation" in class: a welcome and ample reward "for hours of night study."[16]

Gordon and his peers learned rich, enduring lessons from Professor

Lincoln. For him, "Latin was literature, and the classics 'humanities.'" As an appreciation for the classics deepened, Gordon and his classmates strove to please "Johnny Link," as he was endearingly called, and so grew in their own scholarship and taste.[17]

Gordon's spirit, as well as his scholarship, was evident when he decided, at the last moment, to vie for the second year prize offered for "the best Latin essay."

He had no thought of doing so initially, but a classmate's boasting of prowess in Latin prompted Gordon to put the fellow in his place. So decided, he "went to work, wrote out his theme, passed it in to the committee," and won the prize. Gordon took pains to appeal to "Professor Lincoln's inordinate love of Horace" by filling his paper with "as many Horatian expressions and turns of thought as he could." He later learned this strategy carried the day. No record of the boastful student's thoughts has survived.[18]

* * *

Gordon's scholarship at Brown yielded riches that stayed with him the rest of his life. His reading in these years was "extensive, and, within certain limits, multifarious in character."[19]

Gordon's copy of Todd's *Index Rerum,* or a scholar's commonplace book, was "close packed with quotations," as though Gordon kept them for use in later years, "like water in a mountain pool." As he read the first pages of this book, learning its system for crafting a well-sourced repository of eloquence and wisdom, Gordon learned more about leaders, philosophers, and writers like William Wilberforce, Socrates, Cicero, and David Hume.[20] One line from essayist Francis Bacon was a favorite: "He is the wisest man who is most susceptible of alteration."[21]

Other writers transcribed into Gordon's copy of *Index Rerum* included Thomas Carlyle, Lord Byron, Samuel Taylor Coleridge, Elizabeth Barrett Browning, John Ruskin, Archbishop Robert Leighton, Edward Irving, Pascal, St. Augustine, John Foster, and August Tholuck. As Ernest Gordon said, on reading through his father's book, these were "names that recur again and again."[22] Poetry, philosophy, theology, literary criticism, and architectural history—all these fields of study were part of A.J. Gordon's compendium of personal reading.

Among the philosophers he read, and later quoted in his writings, were Henry David Thoreau, and Ralph Waldo Emerson. Gordon had read Thoreau's correspondence, and had a special appreciation for one line Thoreau had written to Harrison Blake in 1848: "Be not simply good, but good for something."[23]

As for Emerson, whom Gordon called "our American philosopher," one proverbial line from the sage of Concord became a phrase Gordon often cited, as a longing for light, or a prelude to prayer—

> Mr. Emerson used an expression which has become a proverb, *"Hitch your wagon to a star."* Oh, Thou Star of Bethlehem, who hast become now the bright and morning Star, help us to fasten our souls on Thee.[24]

Ernest Gordon also observed that during these years at Brown University, his father's "love for devotional reading" increasingly grew. His favorite writers in this literary genre were two 17th century writers: the Anglican divine Thomas Fuller, and Sir Thomas Browne, the author of *Religio Medici*.[25]

Reading Thomas Fuller, A.J. Gordon found many hallowed and eloquent passages, like the following, written in praise of "the true church antiquary"—

> He desires to imitate the ancient fathers, as well in their piety as in their postures; not only conforming his hands and knees, but chiefly his heart, to their pattern.[26]

The Religio Medici of Sir Thomas Browne, for its part, was a work that breathed the air of holy mystery and devotion, as in the lines: "I remember I am not alone, and therefore forget not to contemplate Him and His Attributes Who is ever with me, especially those two mighty ones, His Wisdom and Eternity."[27]

With such sage and consecrated guides, Gordon's faith could hardly help but deepen and flourish during his time at Brown. But then, fine books and classic authors were—and would always be—an abiding passion.

"Were I to buy all my favorite books," he wrote, "I am sure my library would be of quite an antique cast. St. Augustine's *Confessions* afford delineations of almost seraphic raptures. They give one an idea of what Christianity is able to impart to him who is willing to bear its sternest self-denials...I feel, with him, what we most of all need is the power to commune with God. I know of no greater attainment than the ability to hold unbroken communion with the Savior, closing up those avenues through which sinful thoughts and vain desires steal in, and, as [Thomas] à Kempis says, making of the soul a tabernacle with but one window, and that for Christ."[28]

Others among Gordon's favorite books were volumes written by Martin Luther, whom he quoted all his life, as in this citation cast in vivid imagery:

> But he that is loved and forgiven, "accepted in the Beloved," has nothing to fear. Beautifully did Martin Luther express his sense of safety thus—
>
> *"As I was at my window, I saw the stars and the sky, and that vast magnificent firmament in which the Lord has placed them. I could nowhere discover the columns on which the Master has supported this immense vault, and yet the heavens did not fall."*[29]

* * *

On Wednesday, September 5, 1860, Gordon received his Master of Arts degree at the ninety-second commencement of Brown University. He graduated fifth in his class, as a member of Phi Beta Kappa, the prestigious national academic honor society.[30] And last, about midway through his college years, a "new and important tributary" came. It led him to someone who would change his life.

Her name was Maria, and their story unfolds in the chapter to follow.

Chapter Five
There is the Fair Vision

Till heart with heart in concord beats,
And the lover is beloved...[1]

—William Wordsworth

Maria Hale won A.J. Gordon's heart, and it was the great blessing of his life that he'd won hers. "Never man had such a helpmeet," he said, and he could count the reasons. She was, all friends and family knew, his "most valued treasure."[2]

Born on August 19, 1842, Maria was six years younger than her husband, and her upbringing was very different from the early life A.J. Gordon had.

The home she was raised in wasn't the home of a woolen mill owner in rural New Hampshire, but rather a handsome residence in the "College Hill district" of Providence, Rhode Island. It was built in the Greek Revival architectural style, with a pedimented gable roof, corner pilasters; a five bay façade; and a colossal portico above three central bays.[3] It stands to this day, and is now part of the National Register of Historic Places.

Amid such a cultured setting, Maria was "a gregarious and lively young girl," the second of seven children born to Isaac and Harriet (Johnson) Hale.[4] Through her father's side of the family she was related to novelist Sarah Orne Jewett, a younger cousin, best remembered for writing *The Country of the Pointed Firs*, published in 1896.[5]

Harriet Hale also had a storied family history. She was the granddaughter of Colonel Thomas Johnson of Newbury, Vermont—who fought in The Revolutionary War—and was present at the surrender of Fort Ticonderoga. Such was his stature during this conflict that his wartime correspondence with George Washington was later published.[6] Doubtless as a girl, Maria heard oft-told stories of her famous grandsire, and the struggle to win independence for America.

Isaac Hale, a prosperous watchmaker and jeweler, was actively involved with church life and social causes, among them abolition. Wendell Phillips, the famed anti-slavery orator, was a family friend.[7]

Isaac Hale's ardor for abolition, and his involvement with the "underground railroad" for escaped slaves, was apparently too much for some staid citizens in Providence, and he was asked to withdraw from the local Congregational Church. He then began attending a Baptist fellowship.[8]

Harriet Hale, for her part, was also an abolitionist. She also supported the preaching of women, as her husband did—rare views indeed for mid-nineteenth century America. When her daughter Maria was twenty-two, Harriet voiced these sentiments memorably by letter. "Last Sunday evening," Harriet said—

> I succeeded in walking...to Dr. Hall's church, where E[lizabeth] Comstock was invited to preach...The silence of the immense audience was breathless when that small woman came forward in her plain garb & commenced to speak. She spoke without notes or premeditation and as did the apostles of old "as the Spirit gave her utterance..." She spoke with an unction which proceeded from & reached the heart. Her discourse came nearer up to my idea of what the preaching of the Gospel should be than anything I often hear from the pulpits.[9]

Elizabeth Comstock was a prominent English Quaker émigré to America with a great gift for public speaking, and held ardent abolitionist views. In 1864, she was part of a Quaker delegation that met with President Abraham Lincoln. During the Civil War, she traveled great distances to visit army hospitals, prisons, and minister to refugee slaves. During the 1870s she spoke out powerfully on behalf of the Women's Christian

Temperance Union, an organization Maria Gordon would later become actively involved with.[10]

Given this context of faith-based social concern, the Hale family challenged "acceptable" Christian behavior in the eyes of some. Isaac Hale's clash with the Congregationalist Church was one instance of that. As one scholar has noted, "strength of conviction characterized the family."[11]

And what of Maria Gordon's early years and education?

She learned at home early on, studying piano, violin, singing, and three foreign languages: French, German, and Latin. For her sixteenth birthday, while in the classical course of study at the Girls' Department of Providence High School, she was given a beautiful rosewood pianoforte, that she might give piano lessons to others. To this day, the pianoforte is a treasured heirloom among her descendants.[12]

Following Maria's graduation from Providence High School in 1860, her intellectual and artistic interests remained ardent all her life.

Reading was especially important. "How do people live without books?" she once remarked. "Every good book introduces you to a new world of *thought,* which is the *only abiding* world."[13] Music too was an abiding interest. She loved to sing and play at church events.

Isaac and Harriet Hale gave their daughter every opportunity they could to become a vibrant, cultured young woman. And she was. Had nearby Brown University admitted women at this time, it is almost certain she would have gone there. As it was, she had received a fine education in its own right.[14]

At the time of her high school graduation, brown-haired Maria was said to be beautiful, full of fun and energy, light-hearted, and charming. She had a keen sense of humor also. Sometime after she had met A.J. Gordon in 1858, (she was then seventeen, he twenty-two), she wrote: "Yankee, I regard you as so nearly perfect that I take a malicious pleasure in picking at the least intimation of a mistake."[15]

She admired her handsome beau's scholarship, and loved him, but she was not above good-natured ribbing. He knew it, took it in good stride, and took to calling her "dear friend." He had a fine sense of humor as well, writing about this time: "I wish Artemus Ward would bring out something new. What should we do without those benefactors of the human race, the humorists? Wouldn't society stagnate? Wouldn't sanctimoniousness become soon the presiding genius...?"[16]

They courted five years, and corresponded when Gordon left Providence to begin studies for the pastoral ministry at Newton Theological School in Andover, Massachusetts. Yet getting these letters was an event in itself, as his handwriting was sometimes indistinguishable from hieroglyphics. Years later, this side of Gordon's character was memorably described in *The Outlook* magazine—

> The handwriting of the late Rev. Dr. A.J. Gordon was singularly difficult to decipher. In the biography by his son, the story is told of his answering some correspondent who wanted to know his views on some eschatological question. He wrote briefly, expressing his regret that he had no time to amplify. Some months later he received another letter saying: *"It is certainly fortunate for me that your time was so limited. I have already spent nine weeks in attempting to decipher the handwriting of your note, and am not nearly done yet."*[17]

But Gordon's letters to Maria, if marked by cumbersome penmanship, were worth taking trouble over. One letter especially captured his love for her, and why she'd won his heart. It was a charming letter, written years after their marriage, but recalling days when he first knew her, and everything for him changed—

> Brown University, Providence, R.I.,
> June 21, 1860
> [Actual date, June, 1882]

> *Miss Maria T. Hale*
> Dear Friend:
> I am sitting in my room for a few moments after the commencement dinner meditating. I just saw you come down Prospect Street and turn down College Street, and I almost thought you cast a glance upward to my window, as if to say,..."I would not object to your joining me in a walk."

Excuse my presumption in suggesting such an idea, but you know that I have now and then run down to join you, and you never were greatly opposed to my doing so. Well, I have just finished my studies in this honored university, and from my lofty lookout in this old ante-Revolutionary building I am gazing into the future and dreaming of what it shall be.

I know you will pardon me for repeating my dream, since it is only a dream. It seemed to me that twenty-two years had passed, and the pale-faced, slender student had become a portly man of forty-six. He had become, moreover, a minister of a large city parish with a wide field and great responsibilities. Through the dim mists of futurity, I see his house and his family. I count his children—five ruddy and splendid children…

And there is the fair vision of the wife; I cannot name her here, but she looks strangely like one whom I just saw passing. I dream that people say of her that she is wonderfully efficient, and that a large share of her husband's success is due to her; that she has inspired him, who used to be rather slow and backward, with much of her energy and enthusiasm. They say, indeed, that, between his hold and her push, the result is a pretty strong team; that they are the center of no mean circle of activities. And I dream that she sometimes interprets his natural reserve and stolidity and abstractedness as indifference, and she says that he doesn't appreciate her.

Then his heart opens, and he says, 'Nay; never man had such a helpmeet, and if she bears many burdens and does much hard work for him, he thanks her in his heart, and prays that the Lord may spare her for many years to walk by his side.' And the thought became so emphatic and the emotions so strong that he repeated the last words aloud—*walk by his side*—and that woke him up.

Yes; here I am in the window of 44 [University Hall], looking down College Street, and you are just coming back with a book in your hand, from the Athenaeum, I suppose.

And so I have written it all out. When will you take
another of those moonlight walks out toward the Red
Bridge and round by the Friends' College?[18]

It was little wonder, on reading letters like this, that Maria said yes
when her beau proposed marriage. After Gordon graduated from Newton
Theological School, and accepted a call to pastor the Baptist Church in
Jamaica Plain, Mass., they married on Saturday, October 13, 1863. For
nearly thirty-two years, they walked together, side by side. [19]

Chapter Six
Jamaica Plain

We get an idea of [father's] appearance from a portrait painted about this time, a wealth of chestnut hair brushed across a high forehead, grave though kindly eyes of an indeterminate blue-gray...

His height was above the medium...His voice was full, rich, flexible, yet a little roughened...as a Cremona violin before it attains the mellow timbre of maturity...In manner he was shy and reserved, though delightfully genial when once the restraints of new acquaintance were well melted.[1]

—Ernest Gordon

A.J. Gordon looked younger than his twenty-seven years, as for several months prior to graduation from Newton Theological Seminary, he traveled on Sundays to give "pulpit supply" for churches in eastern Massachusetts. At times, he came away disheartened, as with this recollection of one church visit—

> The people...were quite astonished to see such a boy in the pulpit, and made various conjectures about his age, none of them going above seventeen or eighteen...Passing down the middle aisle to-day after meeting, I was accosted by an estimable, near-sighted lady, who was apparently considering the current opinion as to my age, with the

somewhat confusing question, "Do you suppose that that young man _really_ wrote the sermon himself?"[2]

Hence Gordon's consternation. Seeking a pastoral call—after years of careful academic training to give his best, and honor the pulpit—he poured himself into writing sermons, with hours of study. Chatter about his boyish appearance, and speculation as to whether he really had written his sermons stung. Little or no comment about the *actual message* of his sermons was most discouraging of all. "There seems to be so little real appreciation of what has cost so much," he wrote, "and so little apparent good from the words spoken."[3]

This made a visit to Jamaica Plain Baptist Church on January 11, 1863 all the more meaningful. Invited there, his "gentle, open face, and thoughtful sermon" won many hearts.[4] Within weeks, on February 17, he was called to the pastorate. He accepted on March 20, providing he "not enter upon his duties until the close of his studies at Newton, in June."[5]

Soon to be wed, his future was now far brighter: he and Maria would have a home all their own, the church manse.

Gordon's arrival at Jamaica Plain was a festive event. On Monday evening, June 12, 1863, the church at the corner of Centre and Myrtle Street was hung with greenery, and all the parishioners gathered for the ordination service. A program was printed, which read: "For the Installation of Mr. Adoniram Judson Gordon as Pastor of the Jamaica Plain Church, West Roxbury."[6] Here a formal sermon was given, and pastoral charge, with a blessing by the elder ministers who were present. Then everyone sang lines of a familiar, fervent hymn by Samuel Smith—

> *Gird thou his heart with strength divine;*
> *Let Christ through all his conduct shine...*[7]

The venerable edifice Gordon would now call home was a large stuccoed Gothic Revival church, completed in 1859.[8] Handsome, with an appearance of light freestone, Jamaica Plain Baptist Church had a seating capacity of 600. It also had two vestry rooms, suitable for smaller meeting use.[9]

All in all, it was a fine place for beginnings.

* * *

Gordon commenced his ministry at Jamaica Plain during auspicious days. The Civil War was almost two years from ending, and the Battle of Gettysburg had yet to be fought. Gordon spoke out ardently against slavery and for the Union cause. True, he could at times be reserved in a one on one setting; but when he stepped into the pulpit, many witnessed a holy boldness when it came to matters of deeply held conviction.

And such convictions had been with him all his life.

For example, Gordon's abolitionism, his son Ernest recalled, had been very much in evidence during his years of study at Newton Theological School.

From there, on one occasion, "walking into Boston to browse among the old book-stores of Cornhill," he saw "a vast crowd [milling] about the entrances to Tremont Temple." Asking the cause of the gathering, he was told that the people were mobbing the entryway to hear Wendell Phillips speak.[10]

He went to Boston once more "to see the immense night parade organized during the first Lincoln [presidential] campaign." What he saw left a stirring memory. Standing at the wrought-iron gates of Boston Common, he witnessed "an unending stream of torches" pour past him.[11]

It was a display of political fervor the like of which he had never seen. During these years, he also eagerly read Agénor de Gasparin's antislavery writings, and closely followed the trial and execution of anti-slavery insurrectionist John Brown.[12]

Gordon himself would later pen a very eloquent and moving statement of his profound belief in equality among the human family. "The image of God," he said, "be that image Saxon ivory or African ebony, is a wonderful thing to look upon."[13]

Faith taught active sympathy, and common cause with the oppressed. Their plight could be ours, under other circumstances. Gordon phrased it this way:

> Only to be so united to the Man of Sorrows that we should be joined in indissoluble union with our sorrowing humanity! If it then were so, we should sometimes be waked at night

by the frightened cry of the slave-child in Africa whom the slave-hunters are seizing and binding with chains, even as we are startled at the cry of our own little ones in the crib at our bedside, when some troubled dream scares them in their sleep.[14]

And this was not to be wondered at, said Ernest Gordon, for his father "had been bred in the strictest sect of the abolitionists, his father [John Gordon] being an antislavery debater and lecturer in the local lyceums of New Hampshire." At the same time, A.J. Gordon's letters to Maria Hale in Providence were letters to the home of a family which had for many years "been visited by [William Lloyd] Garrison and his confrères."[15]

So it was that in one sermon, not long after he settled at Jamaica Plain, Gordon reproached the idea of "ministers who start with ghostly horror at the thought of taking weapons against the iniquities which infest our land, who refuse to speak out against such sins as slavery and corruption in high places, but, with wonderful dexterity of conscience, dodge behind the shadow of what they call the dignity of the pulpit, and spend their days writing metaphysical disquisitions on long-forgotten theological jangles."[16]

Here was a robust clarion call. America had been sundered over the question of slavery, and Gordon did not mince words over what he felt was right. His actions here, inspired by faith, recall those of William Wilberforce, who had once said of the abolition of slavery: "If to be feelingly alive to the sufferings of my fellow-creatures, and to be warmed with the desire of relieving their distresses, is to be a fanatic, I am one of the most incurable fanatics ever to be permitted at large."[17]

It was much as Gordon's son Ernest later observed: "[my Father] did not hesitate then, more than in later life, to 'preach politics' when 'politics' was but the synonym for righteousness. In the dark days of '63, his voice rang out constantly and unequivocally in behalf of freedom and the Union."[18]

This, however, "was much to the disgust" of many parishioners. And once, during the climax of one of Gordon's ardent appeals, a leading church member rose portentously in his pew, and drew forth, with utmost deliberation, his hymnbook, Psalter, and Testament. Books in hand, he marched slowly down the main aisle and out of the church. So he thought to shake the dust off his feet as a witness against this "commingling of the sacred with the secular, of the things of the Bible with those of the newspaper."[19]

The parishioner was never seen again.

Years passed. Gordon left the scene of his early ministry, and was settled in a new church. But one day, he received a request to attend a funeral in the suburbs. Street and house number alone were given. On entering the home, he was surprised to learn that the dead man was none other than "the stiff dissenter of war times." This gentleman had insisted that no one else should conduct his funeral than the young pastor of former days, "who never feared to preach what he believed."[20]

Then too, Gordon's thoughts at the end of the Civil War were also stirring and memorable. "Some of you," he said—

> remember well what happened on the 3rd of April, 1865. Suddenly the bells began to ring, and throngs of people poured into the streets, and gathered round the news office; and there were shouts going up from the exultant crowd, and glad congratulations between friends...
>
> A message had come across the wires, from the President, announcing that the capital of the Confederacy had fallen, that the war was ended, that peace had come. What wild delight and exultation filled all hearts![21]

And to be sure, Gordon's newly established home with Maria gave much cause for gratitude. "The village of Jamaica Plain," his son Ernest said, "was at that time perhaps the most delightful spot" on the outskirts of Boston—

> It was a suburb of close-shaven lawns, well besprinkled, across which querulous robins ran, and over whose walks spirea, flaming rhododendrons, and gorgeous, golden forsythia hung in profusion.

Bending elms and thick-foliaged chestnut-trees lined the roads. Pleasant homes, deep bedded in shrubbery, and filled with books and all the comforts of an ample, affluent life, welcomed the new pastor in his round of calls. His own house stood just at the edge of a sedate little pond, not far from the place where [scholar Francis] Parkman, battling with disease, raised incomparable roses and wrote incomparable histories...[22]

These new surroundings were idyllic for "a man of quiet tastes," and Gordon's marriage, which took place "soon after his settlement at [Jamaica] Plain," heightened the joy of his new home. With these circumstances went a deep sense of gratitude to God—reflected in letters Gordon wrote to Maria when he was called away from his own church to speak. In one of them, he said—

I look back on the time when I first realized that we were one in Christ, and a higher gratitude fills my heart...Dear wife, I wonder now, when the thought of our life in Christ so fills my soul, that we do not talk more about it. Oh, what is it to be joined together in the Lord...[23]

In one aspect of Gordon's new duties as a pastor, Maria was especially a valued guide and help. By nature, especially in settings when he was just getting to know people, Gordon could be reserved, even shy—though he was always warm and cordial when meeting others.

But giving counsel to couples who were soon-to-be-wed, or performing a marriage ceremony, weren't things that came easily at this time, and he wondered if he really would be able to speak to such couples in ways that would benefit them most. He knew *what* he wanted to say, he just wasn't sure *how well* he might be saying it. And he often second-guessed himself.

He spoke of this in one letter to Maria—

I have just been interrupted by another couple to be married...It is painful to stand in the presence of such...

with no possibility of getting up a conversation. I greatly wished you had been here to speak your piece beginning, "I trust you may be as happy in your married life as I," etc.

I really missed it, and was so embarrassed after I got through the service in thinking to myself, "Well, there is something I have forgotten; I am sure it does not seem quite complete." I couldn't for the life of me think what it was till they had gone; then it flashed upon my mind, *"Why, it's my wife's speech!"*[24]

Of "the quaint experiences incidental to every pastor's life," Gordon "had his full share." Marriages always "recall to a minister's family much that is amusing." Many whom he married gave him "silk handkerchiefs and walking-sticks" as "legal tender" for the customary wedding-fee. And once he received "a fifty-cent piece," out of which he was asked *"to take what he thought right."*[25]

In seven cases out of ten, his son Ernest recalled, "he made over the fee to the bride," a fact deeply appreciated by many. Indeed, this so impressed one whom Gordon married that the young man "returned in a day or two with a friend and suggested that the minister might like to pay the latter's fare to New York, whither he had been unexpectedly summoned!"[26] Gordon's place as a young pastor was of a piece with the kindness, warmth, and good humor expressed here.

As Ernest Gordon also remembered, "[father's] relations with his people were most familiar, tender, *intime.*"[27] Formality had here no place. He was wont to gather his little flock around him in the Friday evening prayer-meetings, conferring, instructing, opening the Word, encouraging all in "the practice of the presence of God...The second year he preached a series of sermons on the development of the higher life, [showing] the trend of his opinions and of his aspirations."[28]

* * *

He took particular pains over his sermons—wrestling, as many a young pastor has, with ambition to do well, but hoping that such ambition flowed from proper motives—and was not an impediment to what mattered most: fidelity to scripture, and bringing a well considered, prayer-guided "word in season" to his parishioners.

He wrote of this to Maria, forthright about his sense of shortcomings, and the weight of the responsibility he felt to honor the Lord in all he said.

In this letter, it was clear how much he relied on Maria as the one who knew him best, and could give good counsel in kind. "I find," Gordon told her—

> it is so hard to preach as I desire, so many little ambitions thrusting themselves in to influence and shape my sermons. A right heart has, I believe, as much to do with the matter as anything.
>
> I think yesterday's sermon was well received. I only hope the doctrine was according to the mind of the Spirit, and that God was not displeased with it. I feel more and more the worthlessness of man's applause, and I have a deepening desire to please Christ in all such works. I send you a little notice of it (very flattering). It is only for you, dearest, not for myself.[29]

* * *

At this time, Gordon was also becoming established as an author, and one of his finest early essays was published during his pastorate at Jamaica Plain. It touched on the subject of "mere Christianity," and appeared in the July 1865 issue of *The Congregational Review*. Here, Gordon gave perhaps his most important statement on the charity and conciliation that should guide relations among Christians, saying: "Whatever brings the church into nearer accordance with the spirit of Christ and His gospel, whatever exalts the central and centralizing truths of our common faith, will do most toward promoting that unity for which we all hope and pray."[30]

Immediately thereafter, Gordon showed his great debt to the British writer Dora Greenwell, whose description of mere Christianity he much admired. He could do no better to convey his feelings on this subject than cite "beautiful words" from one of her books, which was called *The Patience of Hope*—

> The bosom of Christ is the grave, the only grave, of religious acrimony; we learn secrets there which render it possible for us to be of one heart, if we may not yet be of one mind, with all who lean upon it with us. For, slightly as we may think to heal long-festering hurts, there is no cure for religious dissension except that of spiritual acquaintance with God, as revealed to us in the mind and spirit of Christ Jesus. To acquaint ourselves thus with God is to be at peace, for it is to learn how far more strong than all which separates is that which unites us in Him.[31]

Such was the spirit and atmosphere Gordon hoped to foster among his parishioners, a spirit well-captured in a story he liked to tell in later years—

> Hazlitt, the essayist, says, I remember, in his mature age: "I have been struck, lately, in looking into the glass, with my strong resemblance to my father. I never in youth was thought to resemble him, but in age my father's features seem to be coming out more and more each year."
>
> And so, a Calvinist and an Arminian, a Baptist and a Presbyterian, a Churchman and a Dissenter, may not look much alike; but let them grow in grace, year after year, and be filled with the Spirit more and more, and it wouldn't be strange if in old age they should say to each other, as they chance to meet—
>
> "Why, how much we look like each other, I shouldn't have thought it."
>
> We must be growing to look like each other, if we are growing in the grace of the Lord.[32]

* * *

The Gordons now settled into their new life, and the next six years seemed to fairly fly by. The little church in Jamaica Plain grew in numbers. "Pastor and people," their son Ernest recalled, "were bound together in the bonds of a heart-deep affection [and] three children were born into the home by the pond."[33]

Gordon and his young bride were happy in their home. How happy they were can be seen in a tender letter Gordon wrote while Maria was away on a visit. "You will naturally ask, with your jealous disposition," he began teasingly—

> if I have paid attention to any lady in your absence. I answer solemnly, none! Only your old dress fell at my feet as I was brushing through the closet, and in picking it up I involuntarily embraced it, and even clutched a kiss from the eloquent emptiness that protruded from the neck.
>
> I gazed this morning, (I confess lovingly for a married man in his wife's absence), on one sweet face that crossed my path; but it was [a framed picture] in gilt, [your photograph,] therefore I plead no guilt for myself, or at least a suspension of judgment. I will make a clean breast of it. I have stopped several times a day before a certain window, and gazed perhaps too admiringly on a beautiful maiden face that has looked out therefrom.[34]

Clearly, when Gordon thought of Maria, love had bestowed many blessings. To count them was a cherished gift.

Chapter Seven
Clarendon Street

As completed [the church] is substantially built of brick, with light free-stone trimmings in Gothic style; it has a tower and spire rising to the height of some two hundred feet; with a bell and clock, the former being the munificent gift of one of the members of the church. The interior is finished in black walnut, with light and pleasing frescoing. There are two hundred pews, furnishing seats for nearly twelve hundred...[1]
—*A History of the Churches of Boston*

In his lifetime, no place was more closely connected with A.J. Gordon than Clarendon Street Baptist Church, the handsome house of worship at the corner of Clarendon and Montgomery Streets. Over time—some twenty-five years of Gordon's life, it became a storied setting of still-remembered blessing. Thousands in Boston, and beyond, were better for the ministry he faithfully established there.

But at the outset, it wasn't like that at all. By Gordon's own account, few decisions were ever as difficult—or less likely to be made—than for him to accept a call to become the pastor of Clarendon Street Church. To be sure, at the time there was no way he could know the history that would be, only the genuine challenge of leaving Jamaica Plain he faced in the present.

It began one evening in the fall of 1867 with "a sharp pull" at the door-bell of the manse in Jamaica Plain. That evening Gordon was seated "alone in his study, writing on his Sunday sermon, and rocking now and then the cradle of his last baby," little Ernest Gordon, who slept placidly beside him.[2]

When Gordon went to the door to see who had called, he was met by a small group of delegates from Clarendon Street Church. Their errand: "to tender him a call, hearty and unanimous," to become the next pastor of their church.

Gordon was thunderstruck.

To be sure, he was moved by the kindness this represented. It was an honor for these gentlemen, and their church, to repose such confidence in him. But no thought was more unwelcome that the idea of leaving the home he and Maria had made for themselves there by the little pond in Jamaica Plain. No home was dearer to him as a father and husband than the one where he was sitting.[3]

Honored as he was, it just wasn't to be thought of. Respectfully, he told his guests he had to decline their offer out of hand—and, when they pressed him to reconsider shortly thereafter, he gave them "a more formal and decisive refusal."[4]

One year passed. Still Clarendon Street was without a pastor. Kind yet ever more persistent delegations kept calling at the Jamaica Plain manse. Doubtless, they continued to tell him how they would do all in their power to make such a move one Gordon would not regret.

He began to feel terribly conflicted. What was being held out for him was a call many young pastors would have run to—relocating to the heart of one of America's first cities, with a newly-built church and fine new parsonage.

"Why will they not let me alone," he said to Maria in one letter—

> and not press their suit? I wish I were out of it. If you will go to them, and get me off in my absence, and agree that they shall never trouble me again, I will give you half of my kingdom. I am well-nigh insane over the matter.
>
> Tell all my flock how I love them, and how I loathe the pastures of Boston and the bulls of State Street, which are worse than those of Bashan. Thank God, their call cannot divide me from you, though it may thrust me forth from my

Paradise. What a comfort it must have been to Adam that,
though expelled from Eden, Eve went with him!⁵

Yet not long after this, amid such alluring entreaties, Gordon yielded,
and wrote out a letter of acceptance to Clarendon Street. But he'd no
sooner written it than he felt a deep revulsion of feeling. He destroyed
the letter, "with many expressions of self-recrimination for his disloyalty
to the church of his first love."⁶

Several months passed, and still delegations from Clarendon Street
came. They held out an opportunity Gordon was finding it hard to resist.
After two full years, and much prayerful seeking, he at last consented to
become their pastor.

In December 1869, "amid the universal mourning" of his flock,
Gordon left Jamaica Plain. He would now begin a time of ministry that
"was to constitute the capital achievement of his life."⁷

* * *

The first sermon Gordon gave at Clarendon Street Church was on the
Sunday following its festive dedication on Thursday evening, December
9, 1869.

Horse-drawn coaches had arrived that morning, and parishioners
alighted. Still others had walked to the new church on that first Sunday.
Clusters of conversation took place on the sidewalk, and people pointed
to the tall spire. They were no less excited to enter through the graceful
arched doorway and see the handsome interior within. Few occasions
would have been more genuinely welcome and anticipated. It was a day
people had looked to for years.

As for A.J. Gordon and Maria, with three little children, four and
under—Harriet, Ernest and Elsie—there was much to discover and
become accustomed to as they began to make a new home in the
parsonage at 182 West Brookline Street. They were now in the heart of
a great city.

One vignette of this new home brings Boston in the late Victorian
era to life. Gordon often chose such scenes to help his parishioners grasp

a larger truth, such as resurrection hope—when darkness came before the dawn. Here Gordon said—

> As I wake in the twilight of the morning, I often see the glimmer of the street-lamps falling upon the walls of my chamber; but in a little while the lamp-lighter passes by, and turns out one after another of these gas-jets, leaving the room in deeper darkness than it has had at any time during the whole night. But I know that he is only putting out the street-lamps because the sun is about to rise.[8]

Other stories about 182 West Brookline Street have survived, both rooted in the hospitality the Gordons always observed, and their neighbors came to know. Many times, those who were destitute came to their front porch. Always, they were treated "with an unfailing courtesy and tenderness." As Gordon was fond of saying, "Remember them that are in bonds, as bound with them." Then, he added: "If you are temperate and prosperous and fortunate, you are called upon to share the sorrows of the drunkard's wife and the trial of the widow's poverty and the pain of the sick man's couch. *As bound with them!*"[9]

Some little time after the Gordons and their children settled into "no. 182," Gordon met with two tramps on their way to his home, who had no idea who he was. As he walked by, he heard them speaking of the home address they were going to, and one of the men sang out in a thick Irish brogue: *"It's wan eighty-two."*[10]

On a different evening, also when walking home, Gordon met another man in need, tottering and confused after too much drink. He stopped Gordon, asking as well as he might, *"where the institooshun on Brookline Street"* was.[11]

So it was the Gordons had given home, and hospitality, a name people knew. It spoke volumes of their Christian witness.

* * *

Much the same was true of Gordon's study at Clarendon Street Church.

Set in the back of the church, in the second story above the rear entrance, many came to seek him out for counsel or assistance. Once, the Rev. O.P. Gifford came on such an errand. "Wishing to see him one day," Gifford recalled—

> I shook and rattled the door. The window of the study slowly opened, his face appeared, and when I told him what I wanted, he took his key from his pocket and tossed it down with the words, *"Come up."*
>
> He lived above the rest of us, but was always ready to share the heights with any who wished, and tossed the key to his secrets to any who sought them. He always worked with door open for all...to seek, knock, and climb...No book in his library was too good to be loaned, no experience too deep to be shared, no hour too busy to be yielded to the life in need.[12]

Outside Gordon's study window was a marvel of modern technology, and while it intermittently brought some of the noise common to trolley cars, it caught Gordon's fascination. As he said: "Just in front of the study window where I write is a street above which it is said that a powerful electric current is constantly moving. I cannot see that current: it does not report itself to hearing, or sight, or taste, or smell, and so far as the testimony of the senses is to be taken, I might reasonably discredit its existence. But I see a slender arm, called the trolley, reaching up and touching it, and immediately the car with its heavy load of passengers moves along the track as though seized in the grasp of some mighty giant."[13]

Other vignettes of this kind came from magazine writer Marion Howard, who penned a prose portrait of A.J. Gordon as he was during his Clarendon Street pastorate. She'd seen him speak in person, and came away with telling impressions.

For a start, she said, "a scholarly, intellectual, and faithful pastor is not always a man of great personal popularity." But with Gordon, there was "no question as to the fact." Based on time in his company, Howard also considered him "a thoroughly good, wholesome, big-hearted, Christian man—and a remarkably fine preacher."[14] When she published her article, Howard said Clarendon Street Church was a place "now called Dr. Gordon's."[15]

During his time there, Howard told readers of *The Granite Monthly*, Gordon had been instrumental in the formation of The Boston Industrial Home, helping destitute men and women—often homeless and without work—receive food, shelter, and employment. Dr. Gordon, Howard said, "is interested in all reforms."[16]

In all these endeavors, Howard observed, Gordon was "ably assisted and sustained by his wife," Maria Gordon, a native of Providence, Rhode Island.

Then followed a compliment both Gordons would have deeply appreciated. "Mrs. Gordon," Howard wrote, "shares with her husband many of the honors conferred upon him."[17] Many beautiful tributes, Howard said in closing, are "paid to both Dr. and Mrs. Gordon for their noble utterances and work, both at home and abroad."[18]

*   *   *

In the holdings of Harvard University Library is one book by A.J. Gordon that shows, perhaps more than any other, what he aspired to as the pastor of Clarendon Street Baptist Church. Its subtitle underscores how central the book was to his Christian witness, "The Pastor's Dream, A Spiritual Autobiography," while the book's title, *How Christ Came To Church*, reveals his deep desire to foster church life in close keeping with the teachings of Christ in the New Testament.

The heart of this book was set in the twin devices of recollection and parable. For, as Gordon told his readers, "I recall a lecture,"

> which I heard some years since from a scholarly preacher, in which he aimed to show that Christ's second coming—so far from being personal and literal—is a spiritual and perpetual fact; that He is coming all the time in civilization, in the diffusion of Christianity, and in the march of human progress.
>
> He closed his argument by questioning seriously what practical influence upon Christian life the anticipation of

an event so mysterious, and so uncertain as to time and circumstance can have.[19]

After this preacher had finished speaking, Gordon was asked to offer a reply. He agreed, and crafted a homespun parable from his own experience to do so. "I related a little household incident," he began, "which had recently occurred"—

> Having gone into the country with my children for a few weeks' vacation, I had planned with them many pleasant diversions and engagements for the holidays, when almost upon my arrival I was summoned back to the city on an important mission. In the disappointment of the children I said to them:
>
> "Children, I am going to the city to-day. But I shall soon be back again. I may come to-morrow, or the next day, or the day after, or possibly not till the end of the week, but you may expect me any time."
>
> It so happened that I was detained until Saturday. But when I returned, I learned that in their eagerness to welcome me back the children, contrary to their natural instincts, had insisted on having their faces washed every day, and upon having on their clean clothes, and going down to meet me at train time.[20]

When Gordon finished speaking, his colleague smiled and said— "A good story—*but it is not an argument.*"

"Ah, but is it not?" Gordon answered. He then proceeded to explain: "Human life is often found to be the best expositor of Scripture." Jesus cast his most sublime doctrines "into parables drawn from common experience."[21] If we would honor the Lord until His return, Gordon declared, *the promise of His coming* ought to guide every aspect of our lives.

Now it is true, Gordon hastened to say, that "if we believe that He will not return till hundreds of years have elapsed," we might "reasonably delay" preparations for His coming. There is time enough, some might say, for us to make things, to make ourselves ready for that advent.[22]

But, Gordon said, there is one question that might change everything. *"What,"* he asked, *"if His coming is ever imminent?"*[23]

Such, Gordon believed, was the clear and unmistakable teaching of scripture. It changed everything for him; and he hoped it would change everything for others. "Let this truth be deeply realized," he stated, "and let the parables in which [Jesus] affirms it become household words to us." Who then, he said, "shall say that it will be without effect?"[24]

Gordon then described how much the teaching of Christ's immanent return meant for him, saying in third person voice, "One at least may, with all humility, testify to its influence in shaping his ministry."[25]

That left no room for doubt.

The close of Gordon's reply to his scholarly friend was set with an eloquence all its own. "Our hearts," he said, "should rejoice evermore," and "it is enough to say that when *'the solemn Maranatha'* resounds constantly through the soul, the most powerful impulse is awakened toward our doing with all diligence what [Christ] would have us do, and our being with all the heart what He would have us be."[26]

* * *

Apart from this "recollection and parable," A.J. Gordon's rich knowledge of Clarendon Street's history shone in an October 1877 memorial address, published as *The Fiftieth Year: A Sermon Preached on the Semi-Centennial Anniversary of the Clarendon Street Baptist Church.*[27]

Very appropriately, Leviticus 25:10 was his sermon text: "And ye shall hallow the fiftieth year…It shall be a jubilee unto you…"

"We find ourselves," Gordon began—

> constantly repeating ancient customs, because those customs are founded in what is natural and fitting…We keep our anniversaries because it is natural for us to pause on our return to a given point in the revolving year, and look back upon our progress and our attainment. And it is just as natural for us to keep the fiftieth year, the half-way station of the century,—and from it to survey the past, and look out with hope and expectation into the future.[28]

This 50th anniversary year, Gordon said, was hallowed "by a special and gracious effusion" of the Lord. How so? God made "a year of jubilee" because "scores of ransomed sinners" had come to faith. Redemption was a recurring gift at Clarendon Street Church.

At the same time many church members, past and present, returned to mark this anniversary. Gordon spoke directly to them, saying: "you gave your money and your toil and your prayers to build up this church; you have, therefore, a treasure and possession in it still. It was your Christian home for years, and its people were your people. We welcome you back."[29]

Gordon then reflected on the very nature of a church—what it was biblically, and what church members should always aspire to. Such was *his* resolve.

"The Christian church," he said—

> is a living organism. It is simply the sum and aggregation of a certain number of Christian lives. Its history, therefore, if properly written, would be a series of biographies all interrelated and bound together.
>
> A church of Christ, if you will stop to think of it, is the most wonderful thing on earth. It was a fable among the old warriors, that the spirit of each soldier falling on the field of battle entered into their chieftain and became a part of his life. It is true concerning the church of Christ, and no fiction.
>
> The life, the character, the spirit of each departed saint has entered into the life of the church. The glorified ones live with us still; their piety and prayers and consecration form a part of the inventory of grace...
>
> We turn over the leaves of our church manual; here is a fresh page, just written over with the names of the new-born children of the family, and there is a page that opens and shuts in eternity...Yet it is all one book, a single volume in the great library of redeemed life. And it is this book that we are called upon to study and review to-day.[30]

Next Gordon recounted key events of Clarendon Street's early history, up to the time when its cornerstone was laid, October 31, 1868. He described the honor it was to begin his ministry by preaching the dedication sermon "on the evening of December 9, 1869." The events, he continued—

> which have succeeded during the intervening eight years are too fresh in your minds to require rehearsing. They are too recent events to be invested with the halo of historical interest. They are too personal to make it proper that I should speak of them, and so I leave them to be set forth by the historian of the next half century. Only permit me to express the honor I esteem it to be called to hold succession in such a ministry; to be a follower in the line of such a pastorate.[31]

One event Gordon hadn't described in his address took place near this time. On Saturday, January 3, 1874, *The Cambridge Chronicle* newspaper reported Gordon took part in an august gathering at Old Cambridge Baptist Church. There on Harvard Street, the previous Wednesday evening, a Service of Recognition had taken place for Rev. Franklin Johnson, newly installed as pastor.

Some of the most respected clergymen in New England were present for the occasion. Rev. Dr. A.P. Peabody, Chaplain of Harvard College, gave the Invocation, and the sermon came from Rev. Dr. E.G. Robinson, President of Brown University, speaking on 2nd Corinthians 19:9 – *"Most gladly, therefore, will I glory in my infirmities, that the power of Christ may rest upon me"* (KJV).

For his part in this collegial setting, Gordon offered the Installation Prayer.[32] It was just the kind of event that he deeply appreciated; seeing another pastor commence a new sphere of ministry.

But just after this special evening, a terrible thing occurred.

For, as Gordon stated in his anniversary sermon, a "trial by fire" came, "our church being partly destroyed by...flames on the morning of the first Sunday in January, 1874."[33] Papers throughout America covered the story, and although the church itself was severely damaged, there had mercifully been no loss of life.[34] "Clarendon Street Baptist Church," *The New York Times* reported—

> the Rev. Mr. Gordon's, took fire shortly before the hour of morning service [yesterday], it is supposed from imperfect furnace flues, and large portions of the roof were burned. The steeple—one of the handsomest in Boston—and the brick walls appear to have suffered little damage. The organ was ruined, but the Sabbath-school library was saved. The church, which was a quite new and costly edifice, will be immediately repaired. The loss is between $50,000 and $60,000, on which there is an insurance of $70,000.[35]

The fire had occurred just five years after the church was built. Yet here, an unlooked-for mercy came. As Gordon remembered: "Every church of every name in the vicinity proffered us its hospitality." The Union Congregational Church, so long a neighbor on Chauncy Street, "was accepted as offering us the best facilities for carrying on our work; and the months spent there will ever be gratefully remembered for the opportunity which they offered us of fraternal fellowship with brethren owning the same Lord." Rebuilding quickly commenced, and as Gordon remembered, "we returned to our renovated house of worship on the first of May, 1875—where by the blessing of God we still abide."

He then said: "It becomes us...on the fiftieth anniversary of our existence to count up our mercies, and to inquire in what [ways] God has signally and especially blessed us as a church."[36]

There were, thankfully, far more gratifying milestones to recount, and some of these centered on noteworthy parishioners who once called Clarendon Street home. They held "an eminent name without, as well as within the church."[37]

Before the move to Clarendon Street, the church had borne the name, "Rowe Street Baptist Church." Still earlier, "South Baptist Church of Boston."

This is the more significant in that during the 1820s and early 1830s, the years of the South Baptist Church, Lydia Malcom, the wife of Pastor Howard Malcom, had taken an "active interest in the education of the blind," displaying remarkable "energy and ability."[38] Her pioneering philanthropy stemmed from a trip to Europe, during which time she "visited a number of asylums for the instruction and cure of the blind, which were unknown in [America]." She was "so impressed with these facilities that upon her return to the United States, she enlisted the interest of several wealthy people in Boston and in cooperation with Dr. J.D. Fisher, organized the Blind Asylum, which resulted in the establishment of the famous Perkins Institute for the Blind."[39] We know this institute today for its storied association with the life and work of Helen Keller.

Then too, there was publisher William D. Ticknor, of Ticknor and Fields, "who as a young man wrought with such zeal in the office of Sunday School Superintendent." [40]

Founded in 1832, in Boston's Old Corner Bookstore, on Washington and School Streets, Ticknor and Fields would someday publish *The Atlantic Monthly* and *The North American Review*.[41] And in 1842 W.D. Ticknor showed the depth of his character when he became the first American publisher to pay foreign writers for their works, beginning with Alfred, Lord Tennyson.[42]

This was amply rewarded down the years. Ticknor and Fields became the publisher for, among others, Charles Dickens, Ralph Waldo Emerson, Harriet Beecher Stowe, Lydia Maria Child, Nathaniel Hawthorne, Oliver Wendell Holmes, Henry Wadsworth Longfellow, and Henry David Thoreau.

Gordon also fondly remembered Richard Fletcher, "a judge standing in the very highest rank of his profession, and yet combining with his eminent judicial wisdom the piety and stern purity of a saint." All through a busy life, Gordon recalled, "at the bar and on the bench, like the old Puritans, he kept a daily journal of his spiritual exercises, whose pages since his death I have read with a rare and wondering interest." Fletcher was a learned legal scholar, yet "almost as learned in theology; and in his large and well-selected library, the works of the saints and the theologians were as numerous and well studied as those of the lawyer and the jurist." Thus Gordon was not surprised to find Fletcher was "ranked among the intimate friends" of Daniel Webster, Charles Sumner, and Francis Wayland, president of Brown University.

"I count it among the highest privileges of my life," Gordon said, "to have known this man in his mellow and beautiful old age, and to have ministered at his bedside in his dying hours."[43]

Rounding out a triumvirate of celebrated Clarendon Street parishioners was Augustus A. Gould, "the eminent physician, and not less eminent naturalist." Gould, as Lecturer in botany and zoology at Harvard, authored many scientific works, and was "a co-laborer of Professor Louis Agassiz in important investigations."

As a churchman, Gordon said, Gould "was honored in his life and sincerely mourned in his death." And last, there had also been Dr. Gould's brother, Charles D. Gould: "known equally well as a publisher and senior partner in a house honored both in America and England for the character of the literature to which it set its imprint."[44]

Gordon spoke also of Clarendon Street's storied involvement with foreign missionary endeavors—an abiding commitment he ardently shared.

"Among the especial blessings of this church," he said, was "her perpetual interest in the great work of foreign missions and her intimate connection therewith." Indeed, Clarendon Street's history nearly overlapped "the era of American Baptist missionary effort."[45]

He spoke of "revered missionaries who have gone forth from this church," John Taylor Jones, Lyman Jewett, Elizabeth Lincoln Stevens, and Mary Rice.

"May the chain of sympathy," he observed, "that has bound us to this great cause be strengthened by added links in years to come," through consecrated men and women who "give their lives to this noble service!"[46]

Nor could Gordon omit memories of relucent days of spiritual renewal that Clarendon Street had known in the past.

"By the grace of God," he said, "divine favor has been frequent and marked in the history of the church. What gracious years were 1831, and 1838, and 1842, and 1852 and 1858! Scores of Christians are still with us, who remember these seasons as their spiritual birthdays. They were the returning Pentecosts of the church...to refresh the saints."[47]

Last, looking to more recent events, Gordon recalled the only just concluded Boston Tabernacle gospel meetings led by D.L. Moody.

More will be said of this in a later chapter, but here Gordon's reflections were deeply meaningful, and they pointed to the future. These remarks brought his Fiftieth Anniversary Sermon to a close. Nothing could have been more fitting.

"I speak," he said—

> with the profoundest gratitude to God…when I add that the present year, 1877, has witnessed the largest addition of any in the history of the church, one hundred and twenty-three having been added to our number since it opened. I repeat what I said in the beginning, that the Lord has stamped this truly as a year of jubilee. He has hallowed it as a year of His right hand.
>
> And now…as we look out into the future, let it be our prayer and our endeavor to make that future worthy of the past in which such history and such inspirations lie. Young men and young women, I have shown you your exemplars and forerunners…Follow them as they followed Christ.
>
> Elders and fathers in the Lord, I have spoken—alas, how imperfectly!—of your brethren and companions in the service and fellowship of Christ. Long may you abide with us to bless and gladden us by your presence; and when you go hence, carry this message to the sainted ones who have departed.
>
> Tell them that, by the grace of God, we will keep untarnished the heritage of peace which they have left us; and that all we have of life and strength and talent we pledge to the service of "Him that loved us."[48]

Such were passages from Gordon's stirring account of Clarendon Street's history. But how had it been when he began his time of ministry there?

Just before, it was a church in obvious transition, building an impressive new edifice, while seeking to secure a young pastor of fine reputation and widely acknowledged gifts. Gordon fit that bill.

The new Clarendon Street Church, as completed, stood on a lot measuring one hundred by one hundred twenty-five feet. It was substantially built of brick, with light free-stone trimmings in Gothic style; it had a tower and spire rising to the height of some two hundred feet; with a bell and clock—the former a munificent gift from one of the members of the church.[49]

The interior was handsomely finished in black walnut, "with light and pleasing frescoing." There were two hundred pews, to seat nearly twelve hundred people. Elsewhere within the church, "arrangements for religious meetings and social gatherings in the basement were ample and complete." A very fine organ and baptistry had been installed. The cost of the land and church, completely furnished, was $173,000—about half of which, $86,736, was acquired from the sale of a former house of worship. This amount was supplemented by generous subscriptions, totaling $61,839. This left a temporary mortgage on the land of $25,000.[50]

This was an impressive outlay of funds, and attended with high expectations. Converted to modern currency values, $173,000 was a sum equivalent to $2,800,000 dollars today. The amount generated from the sale of the former house of worship, with subscriptions, $148,575.85, would be $2,400,000 dollars today. And last, the mortgage that the church carried on its land, $25,000, would be equivalent to $400,000 dollars today.

In a word, A.J. Gordon was now pastor of a church with very substantial resources, and more than a few wealthy parishioners. This brought benefits—but also challenges connected with high expectations, and firm ideas of right practices.

The first indication Gordon had entered a setting with staid traditions about church culture occurred within two weeks of his arrival. For on Tuesday evening, December 28, "the sale of pews took place." This, as church records indicate, "was very successful; all but a few, about four, of the highest priced pews being taken."[51] However, Gordon had no love for this practice; and the setting it created was one described by his son Ernest who—though a graduate of Harvard and genuinely appreciative of culture—nevertheless remembered:

> The church which [father] was entering for a quarter-century's incessant work was, from some points of view, the most important of [its] denomination in Boston. It was a "family" church of an approved type, somewhat exclusive, with a generous sprinkling of rich men in its

pews. It was a church in which the line of separation between the Haves and the Have-nots, so fatal to the best type of church development, was defined with more or less conscientiousness.

The *optimates,* the "nice" people, the "best" people, were distinctly in evidence. A line of substantial merchants and bankers ran up and down the ends of the most desirable pews. If you had gone in any Sunday morning, you would have seen well-dressed ladies and gentlemen, singly or in groups, passing down the center aisles to their seats.

The more common folk in the fringe of gallery and rear seats were, as befits the outer edge of a *parterre,* in more subdued dress. Numerous carriages at the doors lent a pleasant suggestion of capitalism to the [church] exterior...[52]

Still other things brought concern.

Gordon, who cherished congregational singing, now pastored a church that only condoned "performance singing." Why so? Clarendon Street had one of the finest pipe organs in America, played each Sunday, in tandem with a highly trained professional quartet. *Classical music, and that alone,* was what well-to-do parishioners wanted—"faultless" performances each Sunday, and every Sunday.[53]

No one loved fine music more than Gordon did, but he was increasingly grieved over a worship setting guided solely by fashion and "cold, correct formality." How could parishioners rightly experience worship when singing wasn't something *they did,* but always something done *for them?*

Accomplished performances certainly had their place, rightly honoring God with artistry and talent. Gordon was in no way opposed to that. Indeed, some hymns he would later write had ties to classical music that he greatly treasured.

But to have *only* accomplished performance music, and nothing else— to the exclusion of any singing by all parishioners—few things unsettled him more.

This was not, he keenly felt, what the Bible intended.[54]

Most of all, this practice pointed to something far more pervasive and worrying: an air of exclusivity and entitlement. Clarendon Street was showing itself *a church for the chosen,* not a place for any and all who might enter its doors.

At heart, this wasn't really about music. Once more, Ernest Gordon knew of this first hand. At this time, he said, Clarendon Street Church—

> was indeed a church of a well-defined and easily recognized type—a church which has its counterpart in every city of Protestant Christendom. It summarized, as all of its class, the admirable traits of Protestantism—comfort, order, intelligence, affluence, reserve, a not too aggressive religiousness. A church of this sort [might] be called the Church of the Disciples, the Church of the Covenanters, the Church of the Pilgrims. A more nearly correct and more modernized sobriquet would be, perhaps, the Church of the Bank Presidents. This was the apprehension, evidently, of many who attended the church in Clarendon Street during the early seventies.
>
> The feeling of exclusiveness congealed finally into a condition of things akin in some degree to that prevailing in close corporations with elected membership. An officer of the church was [once] rebuked by one of the deacons for attaching the words *"Strangers Welcome"* to some circulars for public distribution.
>
> The theory which prevailed, apparently, was that which, in the field of economics, goes under the name of Gresham's Law. Base metal will drive out better currency; people of humble social status will scare away the more "desirable" families. The result may easily be imagined.[55]

Nor was this atmosphere of resolute exclusivity confined solely to *the interior* of Clarendon Street Church. More than a few who lived close by—non-church members—coined a term of undisguised ridicule to describe what they encountered in their public dealings with some parishioners.

The church, they felt, should be called *"The Saints' Everlasting Rest."* As Ernest Gordon recalled, this was a reputation, and a by-word, "not altogether undeserved."[56]

This contrasted starkly with Gordon's ardent belief in what faith should be. "Christianity," he said, should be like a fine, handsome carriage, "in which there is always room for more, and from which you are always reaching out to urge others to come in with you." The church, he concluded, should "be ever inviting."[57]

Amid these patterns of strident exclusivity, A.J. and Maria Gordon must have wondered many times just what they had gotten themselves into.

New England congregations were often called, proverbially, "a stony field"—hard to cultivate and seek a harvest from. Gordon knew places like that in the rough, stony pastures he had tended as a youth in rural New Hampshire. He little thought to find them in the cultured environs of Boston. Wasn't this supposed to be a place where people rightly understood and strove for better things?

Here was a sober and necessary truth for any young pastor, in any kind of setting, to learn: human nature is the same everywhere, whether a city or village. Besetting sins do not discriminate. "As surely," Gordon said, "as darkness follows sunset, will the alienation of the masses follow sanctimonious selfishness in the church. If a Christian's motto is, 'Look out for number one,' then let him look out for estrangement and coldness on the part of number two."[58] It came down to this, Gordon believed: "what we need is not a revival of ethics, as some are saying, but a revival of vital piety. For men will not recognize their stewardship to Christ until they recognize Christ's lordship over them." There can be, he said, "no clear sense of responsibility except we stand in *'the light of the knowledge of the glory of God.'*"[59]

Here, he also recalled a passage from Francis Wayland of Brown University. "President Wayland," Gordon observed, "used to condemn strongly what he called 'a long-tailed benevolence.' It is the least effective form of charity, for the circulation is always feeblest at the extremities. If the Christian is to bless humanity with a warm flesh-and-blood sympathy, let him extend to men the help of a living hand, and not merely touch them with the cold tail of a residuary legacy."[60]

* * *

Early on, Gordon saw that to strive for better things—to help bring about a church more Christ-like in character—all this had to begin with *him*—in his home, his family, his sermons, and his dealings with parishioners. He had to model what he was commending, no less than speak of it.

Moreover, the subtle miasma of spiritual exclusivity could slowly envelope a church, and that is why Gordon was so concerned. "Ecclesiastical corpses," he said, "lie all about us. The caskets in which they repose are lined with satin; they are decorated with solid silver handles and with abundant flowers, and, like other caskets, they are just large enough for their occupants, with no room for strangers. These churches have died of respectability and are embalmed in complacency."[61]

Yet sobering as things were, it wasn't as though, to use Ernest Gordon's phrase, Clarendon Street was "beyond resuscitation."[62] True, those committed to their exclusivity were a vocal and powerful minority. Yet there were many at Clarendon Street who were open to church growth—welcoming new members from all walks of life, growing together as a community of faith, and learning all facets of what it meant to be faithful. This was a foundation to build on, though Gordon no longer had any illusions about how hard the task might be.

For years, Ernest Gordon wrote, his father worked persistently and patiently to further these ends. "His reward," Ernest observed, "was to see [Clarendon Street], in his own closing days, the ruddiest, healthiest church in the city, bending all its strength for the salvation of others."[63]

In 1890, reviewing twenty years of his pastorate, Gordon said himself—

> We believe we have learned much, through divine teaching, as to the true method of conducting the affairs of God's church; have proved by experience the practicability of what we have learned; and have largely united the church in the practice thereof. *Innovations* have from the beginning been strongly urged. 'Innovations'?
>
> No! that word implies newness; and God is our witness

that in theology, in worship, and in church administration it
is not the new to which we have been inclined, but the old.

Renovation, rather, is what we have sought. With a deep
feeling that many of the usages which have been fastened
upon our churches by long tradition constitute a serious
barrier to spiritual success, it has been my steady aim to
remove these…And with the most deliberate emphasis we
can say that every step in our return to simpler and more
scriptural methods of church service has proved an onward
step toward spiritual efficiency and success.[64]

So Gordon's program of reform "extended over many years." Ernest Gordon wrote of each one, "in order as they were suggested and consummated."[65]

First among his father's aims was to foster a sense of church that could be likened to the image of a hospital. Properly understood, and "to use the old English phrase," churches were to offer "a cure for souls"—settings where brokenness could encounter loving, compassionate witness, thence healing and restoration.[66]

This ethos, or guiding spirit, was at first "alien to the early life of Clarendon Street," and yet it was "one of the best fruits of the [D.L.] Moody meetings of 1877," held in close vicinity to the church. These gospel gatherings led many, who formerly led sin-ravaged lives, to join Clarendon Street. Many who had battled alcoholism or known poverty, for example, were among them. Working as part of the outreach team that Moody, Gordon, and others assembled, many at Clarendon Street were discovering how grace drew near for people needing love and compassion. They could be ambassadors of grace, see lives transformed, and be transformed themselves.[67]

* * *

It is worth taking time to reflect on the challenges A.J. Gordon had faced to this point of his ministry at Clarendon Street.

The church's leaders had clearly wanted him. Why else would they constantly petition him to come, for two years, refusing to take no for an answer? Clearly, they thought he was just what they needed: an eloquent, caring, and cultured young pastor—with credentials from the best schools, and a fine young family. In a word, he was someone who could, as the phrase had it, "take them places."

And Clarendon Street's leaders had persuaded Gordon to come; though in short order they must have begun to wonder just what *they* had on their hands.

In truth, Gordon was all the things they thought him to be. But he also had deep reserves of principled determination. They underestimated this, thinking he was just the kind of fine young man they could mold, or rather fit into their mold.

They were wrong.

Gordon had no wish to be unnecessarily difficult. Nor was he a headstrong young pastor who lacked a teachable demeanor. But when he discovered a deeply entrenched culture of exclusivity, and hardness of heart, he felt he'd be shirking his duty if he didn't do what he thought right to commend a better way. Simply put, there was a conflict of visions. Here his devotion to biblical teaching guided his actions. At the same time, there's a tendency—especially with someone well known to history like Gordon—to think he went through life largely from strength to strength. But people celebrated in history seldom do so—if ever.

The reality is that Gordon was a gifted and conscientious young pastor who met with bracing challenges at Clarendon Street Church.

How he dealt with them says much of his character.

Gordon's road was never one of pre-determined success. Though marked by blessing, and events time would remember fondly, his journey wasn't always easy. Yet difficulties, as Epictetus said long ago, "are things that show what men are."[68]

Chapter Eight
To Hear A New Song

Richard Storrs Willis [of Yale,] treating of what he calls "the music of the people," informs us upon reliable authority that "this is the oldest style of music in the Christian Church. During the first three hundred years after Christ there was no other. The singing of the early Christians was wholly congregational." [1]

—A.G. Stacy

In many ways, one of the most pressing concerns of A.J. Gordon's early years at Clarendon Street Church was congregational singing—or rather, a dearth of it. He held, and would always say, that this type of singing was vital as a shared spiritual experience. He phrased it emphatically, saying: "The worship of song *has generally been the measure and expression* of the spirituality of the Church." [2]

But there was more to consider. "If you, the people," he told parishioners—

> expect the minister to stir you to duty by his sermons, ought you not to put yourselves in the best possible condition to be stirred?…If any fact has been made clear to me…it is this: that *the people that enter heartily and enthusiastically into the worship as earnest participants* can be inspired with interest, and moved to duty with half the labor which would otherwise be required. [3]

Gordon said these things in a now little-known book published early in his time at Clarendon Street Church, called *Congregational Worship*. It was a *cri de coeur*, a pastor's plea for his parishioners, and parishioners everywhere, to discover myriad blessings they were missing.

In the book's Preface, Gordon described what led him to put pen to paper. "The question," he said, "has been seriously resting on the author's mind for a long time, whether it is not possible to secure a more general participation of the people in our Lord's-day worship."[4]

Here he stated that this question had been "suggested by various facts," such as *the non-attendance* "of the great majority of the children and young people of the Sunday school upon the services of the church." He thought it tragic that children and young people were missing out on singing with their parents, and others their own age—as it was a moving and meaningful way for faith to deepen.[5]

At the same time, many other churches used a liturgy, and clearly, in those settings, people cherished "taking part in the services." In contrast, churches like his own allowed "praise to be rendered vicariously by quartet choirs," and praying to be done largely by the minister, "instead of joining in it ourselves."[6] This went to the last of the great concerns Gordon felt. There were far too many churches, his own among them, with an "almost total lack...of anything that can be properly called worship on the part of the people."[7]

So Gordon had written his book, or rather, published a set of five sermons he had given about congregational singing at Clarendon Street.

Why do so? To set out "what scriptural and reasonable methods could be found to popularize our worship, and save it from [the] tendency to exclusiveness." And if this little volume, Gordon said, "shall conduce to the honor of God, by encouraging His people to a more hearty and unanimous participation in His praise, the end of its publication will have been answered."[8]

* * *

Well before he published *Congregational Worship*, indeed, after only three months at Clarendon Street Church, Gordon invited Professor Eben Tourjée, founder of the New England Conservatory of Music, and

Dean of the College of Music at Boston University, to deliver a lecture on "Church Music." Clearly, the intent was to introduce a widely respected and cultured guest who shared his views, and it didn't hurt matters one whit that Tourjée's lecture was followed by what was described as "a good sing."[9] Here was a beginning to win people over.

By 1874, when *Congregational Worship* appeared, there had been moments of congregational singing for some time during morning and afternoon services at Clarendon Street. Yet in 1877, when Gordon sought "to replace the hired anthem-singing quartet with congregational singing," his proposal met "stiff opposition by the [Church] Standing Committee." For several more years, he kept trying. And for several more years, this reform failed to carry the day.[10]

One incident symbolized how frustrating this could be. Once, when a church member died suddenly, Gordon sent a Saturday request to the hired quartet for a change in the opening hymn—to show kindness, and rightly honor the departed.

This request met with something far different than sympathy.

The quartet leader was "outraged that he had been given short notice." He protested to the chair of the music committee, who "advised him to ignore Gordon's request." To Gordon's dismay, as he announced the hymn he had chosen, the quartet stood and defiantly sang the hymn he had discarded.[11]

Gordon studiously ignored them till the service ended. One could hardly blame him. He had made a just request, and a caring one. How could the quartet leader not grasp the fact that someone passing away *suddenly* meant, by definition, that there would be little or no notice as to a change of hymn?

Everyone in the quartet was highly trained, and could read music. Singing a new hymn required very little, other than brief practice before the Sunday service. And if compassion called for an extra effort, wasn't that what faith was all about?

*   *   *

By 1881, Gordon had moved a compromise idea: "a chorus choir" in place of the ill-tempered quartet. This reform had come to many churches, and Gordon was deeply gratified when the Clarendon Street Standing Committee agreed. Five years later, this had paved the way for the chorus choir itself to be dispensed with. In 1886, singing at Clarendon Street became entirely congregational at last, led by a twelve-member volunteer choir.

Within eight years, by 1894, a sea change had taken place. Clarendon Street was now "one of the leading Baptist churches in congregational worship." Words from one visitor were something Gordon had long waited to hear—

"A spirit of true worship pervades everything, and possesses all hearts."[12]

*　*　*

Gordon's tenure at Clarendon Street was many times difficult, especially in his early years. But one facet of his ministry that shone, and most people greatly appreciated from the first was his sermoncraft. Each Sunday, his messages conveyed fluent, accessible scholarship, and fine expository preaching.

To see what these sermons were like, we need look no further than a collection that was published in 1880, *Grace and Glory: Sermons For The Life That Now Is, And That Which Is To Come.*

As the book's title suggests, forgiveness and redemption were its recurring themes—and likewise, these sermons were pervaded by a deep sense of holy majesty. Two Latinate phrases capture Gordon's purpose. Here Jesus was Christus Creator – *"all things were created by Him... and by Him all things consist"* (Colossians 1:16-17), and he was Christus Redemptor – *"In whom we have redemption...according to the riches of His grace"* (Ephesians 1:7).

As a book, *Grace and Glory* took its title from the first sermon to appear. And the phrase "grace and glory" was part of the verse Gordon chose as the point of departure for his sermon: *"For the Lord God is a sun and a shield; the Lord will give grace and glory. No good thing will he withhold from them that walk uprightly"* (Psalm 84:11).

Straightway here, Gordon showed his gift for a conversational style.

"It is not," he began, "for the sake of rounding out the sentence, and rendering it sonorous, that the Psalmist uses these words, sun and shield." They appear in tandem, Gordon said, because they show how "two sides of Jehovah's character are thus strikingly exhibited,—His majesty, which is as the sun shining in his glory; and His mercy, which is as that sun, tempered and assuaged by the intervening shield of clouds."[13] And as for the Psalmist's phrase, *"the Lord will give grace and glory,"* it was, for Gordon, "simply a continuation of the same thought." The sun lends glory to the day, as in the phrase "a glorious sun," while it also imparts grace, as with the idea of a "life-giving sun," a benison to the world.[14]

Aside from conversational style, Gordon's sermons were also marked by a fine use of metaphor. "Grace and Glory," as a sermon, was a prime example of this. For in one passage, he stated—

> How profound is this saying, as well as how apt in its imagery, "The Lord is a sun"! The sun is the source of all life as well as of all light. The food which sustains the body, the colors which delight the eye, the flavors which regale the senses, are all woven with the same shuttles,—the sunbeams.
>
> The pattern is different, the warp is various, but the filling is the same; the sunlight woven and wrought together into all the countless fabrics which the body needs for food and clothing and pleasure.
>
> The thousand trades by which man gains a livelihood, the sun is carrying on all the time. He is the great farmer, who grows and ripens the grain for the millions of the earth; he is the great mechanic, who, by means of steam and vapor, lifts the water-floods to the sky, and so feeds the rivers, and showers the plains, and turns the wheels; he is the great architect, who builds the trees which the carpenter only hews and polishes; and he is the great artist, who tints the flower and colors the landscape, and paints the sunset with a beauty which the highest human skill can only imperfectly copy.
>
> It is the most potent and everywhere present object in nature which the Spirit has here selected as the image of the invisible God. And I have thus sketched his offices in order

to remind you that the sun is the fountain of life as well as
the fountain of light.[15]

At the same time, Gordon was deft in his use of contrast to commend
a truth to his parishioners. Often he did so by way of a question, as when
he asked: "Is it not one of the most fatal errors of unbelief that it has
separated what God has joined together, and presumed to feed man's
moral and spiritual nature without the light of God's word, or the light
of His Son?"[16] For, as a Christ-follower, it was Gordon's ardent belief that
"we understand ourselves only in Him."[17]

In *Grace and Glory,* Gordon phrased it this way: "I am the Way," says
Christ; "but how little of hope there would be in that revelation had He
not also added, "and the truth and *the life!*" It is life, Gordon taught, that
restores our brokenness, and life that "far-off wanderers from God need in
order that they may get home. And blessed be God," Gordon concluded,
who *"hath shined into our hearts to give us the light of the knowledge…"* (2nd
Corinthians 4:6).[18]

Other sermons in *Grace and Glory,* such as "The Two-Fold Ministry
of Christ," were places where Gordon drew on his scholarship of ancient
languages. His text for this sermon was Psalm 103:3, which speaks of God
as the One "who forgives all thine iniquities; who heals all thy diseases."

With these inspiriting words of solace and restoration, Gordon
maintained, "we have a striking instance of what is known as the
Hebrew parallelism." These words, he continued, form "one of the most
rhythmical and beautifully balanced sentences in the whole Book of
Psalms." But, he was quick to add, "we see in the words something more
than the rhythm and cadence of poetic measure. There is parallelism of
thought and doctrine here."[19] Here, he likened the text of Psalm 103:3 to a
divine fountain, from which flow "two streams of blessing—forgiveness
and health; recovery for the soul and restoration for the body."[20]

These streams, moreover, "are not merely consecutive in God's plan,
forgiveness now and healing hereafter,—they are parallel; they move side
by side as a double manifestation of the same divine power. They are not
two facts even, but the twofold expression of one fact—the life of God
communicated…invigorating and repairing by the same energy."[21]

Given such eloquence, insight, and compelling scholarship, it is little wonder Gordon's sermons won their way with parishioners, or were published. They were among some of the finest pulpit addresses in America during the late 1800s.

Prominent Christian leaders elsewhere also knew this, and some time after *Grace and Glory* was published, no less a figure than C.H. Spurgeon asked Gordon to be ready to preach in his absence at London's Metropolitan Tabernacle. It turned out in the event that Spurgeon, who had been sick, had recovered sufficiently to preach himself, but that in no way diminishes the high trust and regard he reposed in Gordon.[22]

Others saw that too.

* * *

A second hallmark of Gordon's years at Clarendon Street was the deep commitment the church developed for foreign missionary endeavors, as chronicled by scholar Dana L. Robert in her essay, "The Legacy of Adoniram Judson Gordon." Here, Gordon emerged as a true missionary statesman.

"Gordon," Dr. Robert has said, "was one of the major speakers during the Northfield Bible Conference at Mount Hermon School in 1886 when the *'Mount Hermon 100'* volunteered to become foreign missionaries." These young men were the first gathering of the Student Volunteer Movement that would send thousands of college graduates to the mission field in the years to follow. Many of these first volunteers "looked to A.J. Gordon as their spiritual mentor."[23]

Gordon's singular commitment as a missions leader in Northfield was tied to many endeavors long underway at Clarendon Street Church. Its vision of mission "was global as well as local in scope." Time and again, the church exceeded previous benchmarks in raising money for Baptist foreign missions. At one particularly pressing time, "a year of special need for the American Baptists," Clarendon Street raised $20,000 for foreign missions, equal to half a million dollars today.[24]

Aside from Gordon's leadership in missions fundraising, he'd served on the Executive Committee of American Baptist Missionary Union

(ABMU) since 1871. He played a key role in the expansion of American Baptist missions to Africa.[25]

Nowhere was this more in evidence than with Gordon's involvement with what had been the Livingstone Inland Mission along the Congo River.

The stage for this chapter of Gordon's life and work was set when, in 1871, Henry Stanley of *The New York Herald* undertook his famous search through the jungles of Africa for missionary explorer David Livingstone. Taken in tandem, the travels of Livingstone and Stanley had shown these regions of deepest Africa were accessible. In the months following international coverage of Stanley and Livingstone, various mission societies and European governments set out for the African interior.

By 1876, the Rev. Dr. and Mrs. H. Grattan Guinness, well-known English Baptists, had started the Livingstone Inland Mission. It was "one of the earliest Protestant missions to Africa," and by 1884 the LIM had "sent fifty missionaries, opened seven mission stations, spent $150,000, and reduced the Ki-Kongo language to writing; it also owned a steamboat named the *Henry Reed*."[26]

All this was indeed groundbreaking, but the LIM had grown so fast and become such a considerable undertaking that it was simply "too large for the Guinnesses, and in 1883 they proposed that the American Baptist Missionary Union take it over as their Congo Mission."[27]

Enter A.J. Gordon, who as stated above, served on the Executive Committee of the ABMU. Gordon's leadership vis-à-vis the adoption of the Livingstone Inland Mission proved crucial. True, the ABMU "had already passed general resolutions in favor of opening an African mission," and the organization "had surveyed the coastline of Africa to find a suitable location." But all this was in its way rather preliminary. The Guinnesses' offer of the Livingstone Inland Mission "forced the issue of African missions for the American Baptists."[28]

Even when the AMBU formally adopted the Livingstone Inland Mission in 1884, "many Baptists continued to raise their voices against it." There were strong concerns "about the death rate in the Congo, volunteers were in short supply, and Baptists doubted that the Missionary Union, already hard-pressed for funds, could raise enough money for the risky venture."[29]

A.J. Gordon was never more stalwart than in his determined support for the AMBU to fully shoulder this new opportunity. He "lobbied incessantly for the Congo Mission" and was in large part responsible for its eventual acceptance by American Baptists.[30]

In 1886, for example, he began travel throughout the northeast with "the first Congo missionary to visit the United States." Gordon personally arranged for this gentleman to speak before influential groups of Baptists, and he did one thing more: he penned a powerful pamphlet called *The Ship Jesus,* which did much to influence public opinion.[31] The small book's title was taken from the purported name of the first slave ship to bring captives to America.

In this pamphlet, Gordon wrote something very like "a tract for the times," invoking a chapter from America's recent past: "American guilt over African slavery," and its complicity in the African slave trade. Now that so many former slaves and descendants of slaves had become Christians, Gordon said, it was America's responsibility to ensure that they could return to the Congo, if called of the Lord, to share heaven's hope in their ancestral lands. In a word, "the ship Jesus was ready to go back to Africa."[32]

"Next to the disgrace," Gordon wrote, "of having for centuries taken the wages of Africa's unrequited toil, will be the disgrace of refusing to refund those wages for Africa's redemption as God now calls for them." Americans who had grown "rich from the work of slaves, or from the industries spawned by the Civil War," owed something to every African. "The ship *Jesus* is ready to sail," Gordon concluded, "the mariners are eager to depart; what will you do to furnish the [journey]?" Gordon asked his fellow American Baptists.[33]

What shaped Gordon's abiding concern in this matter? He described it this way: "There are dialects to be mastered on the foreign field beside the linguistic—the mother tongue of sympathy and fellow-feeling; the universal speech of suffering and pain. He who can conjugate these through all their sorrowful moods and tenses has the highest requisite for successfully preaching the Gospel."[34]

Then too something extraordinary unfolded when, in August 1886, "a revival broke out at the Banza Manteke Station of the Congo Mission." In the space of just a few weeks, "a thousand Africans became Christians."

On hearing these new brothers and sisters were in need of a chapel, Gordon's Clarendon Street Church mobilized into action. $2,500 was raised, and "a complete prefabricated chapel" sent to Africa by steamship. When this new chapel arrived, the Christians resident in Africa "divided the chapel into 700 loads and carried it piece by piece on their heads over sixty miles." It was remarkable altogether, and nothing like it had ever taken place. It was, in its way, a beautiful and deeply meaningful confirmation that Gordon's faith in the Congo Mission had not been misplaced. Indeed, it could now look to a bright future.[35]

Gordon's lifelong "fervency for evangelistic missions" was best captured in his address before the American Baptist Missionary Union in 1893—

> The church which is not a missionary church will be a missing church during the next fifty years, its candle of consecration put out...As ministers and churches of Jesus Christ, our self-preservation is conditioned on our obedience to The Great Commission...
>
> Evangelize or fossilize! Be a saving church, with girded loins and burning lamp, carrying a lost world on the heart day and night; or be a secularized church, lying on the heart of this present evil world, and allowing it to gird you and carry you whithersoever it will. *Which shall it be?*[36]

For all the challenges Gordon faced during his tenure at Clarendon Street Church—and there were many—his sermoncraft and legacy as a nationally acclaimed leader in Christian missions commend him to our living memory. Serving a church that had been in many ways exclusivist, and spiritually cold, he persevered. Thousands of lives were transformed during his pastoral ministry, and through his stalwart commitment to missions.

* * *

In 1887, Gordon gave an address in Minneapolis which set forth a "strikingly suggestive" contrast, as his son Ernest said, between "the life of old and new Clarendon Street."[37] To consider the reflections and themes of this address is a fitting way to close this chapter.

Gordon began with a use of biblical metaphor and imagery.

"As soon as Zion travailed," he said, "she brought forth children. It is the law of God that renewed souls should come forth through the birth-pangs of prayer and faith in the church of Christ."[38]

Often, though it was rather like a paradox, Gordon said, some of the best things—prayerfulness, allegiance to the teachings of scripture, longsuffering commitment to all facets of Christian charity, sharing reasons for hope—required ardent devotion, often born of adversity or in humble circumstances. Indeed, in a setting like this, the "first things of faith" often shone brightest. So they ought to be kept by Christians in all seasons of life.

Just here, however, Gordon gave a telling *caveat*.

For history—both a reading of biblical times, and chapters throughout the era of the church—showed nothing was more difficult than to rightly cherish and retain the first things of faith.

Gordon drew on biblical metaphor once more, saying the tendency is for the church, as soon as it becomes wealthy and aristocratic, "to shirk the responsibilities of child-bearing," preferring "the luxuries of worship, the music, the oratory, and the architecture of an elegant sanctuary, to the bringing forth and nursing of children."[39]

Fashionable religion, Gordon said with concern, "frowns on prayer-meeting exhortations as sanctified baby talk, and on [forthright] gospel preaching as weak pulpit milk," while "lifting the hand, and rising for prayers," are considered "nursery exercises in which cultivated Christians do not care to engage."[40]

But such disdain, Gordon averred, went terribly awry—and was at cross-purposes with the best practices of scripture. Had not the apostle John repeatedly addressed Christ-followers in his letters as "little children," indicating the simple, abiding trust in God that ought to be normative? And did John not ardently commend the "first things" of orthodoxy, namely "this is the love of God, that we keep his commandments" (1 John 5:3), and "love one another" (1 John 3:23), saying in essence: adhere to them always, with all fidelity?

And hadn't John learned all this from Christ Himself, who said "of such is the kingdom of heaven," referring to "little children," or those child-like in their devotion, trust, and obedience? Indeed all these things were true, and Gordon commended them to his listeners.

He put it this way: "But the church that knows its calling as the mother and nurse of souls will use all these things because God has enjoined milk for babes, and the rudiments of faith for children." He went still further, saying, "All honor to the church that accepts the function of child-bearing and nursing."[41]

At the same time, Gordon mourned over other church settings he had seen, and he continued to draw on the maternal, caring language so resonant in scripture to explain what he meant. How sad it was, he said, to see a church "which prefers barrenness to maternity, in order that she may be at ease in Zion."[42]

It was an ever-present temptation, Gordon said, for churches to become "formal, self-contained" congregations, bastions of fashionable conformity, with parishioners who'd forgotten the very first things of faith that brought the Christian church into existence.[43] Here, perhaps, Gordon recalled "the Saints' everlasting rest" epithet that outsiders had formerly applied to Clarendon Street Church.

Moreover, Gordon was grieved to know "scores of churches in my own city, planted in orthodoxy, but now fallen from the faith." Again, he used the imagery of scripture, saying "when they ceased to bring forth children," that is, to share the hope of heaven, and nourish new believers in the first things of faith, they began to lose their way. If one didn't commend these first things, commitment to them began—perhaps insensibly at first—to wane.

Such was the heart of Gordon's 1887 Minneapolis address.

It was a message prompted by hope for better things.

* * *

Growing up, and through his years at Harvard, Ernest Gordon watched the trajectory of his father's time of ministry. He believed he knew why this ministry ultimately flourished.

"The preaching of spiritual truths," he said, "and the insistence on spiritual methods had a sifting effect." The results, he continued, were twofold—

The restless, the worldly, the unfriendly, gradually dropped off and went elsewhere. This was in some ways a great relief to the pastor. Indeed, during a period of friction he prayed earnestly a whole summer long for the departure of a leading member whose presence he felt to be fatal to the church's best interests. In the autumn this man left in a most unexpected way without trouble or irritation. On the other hand, there gathered around the church a large [company] of earnest, devout souls, whose views of church life corresponded with those set forth from the pulpit. Hundreds were converted, too, bringing with them the vigor which goes with fresh and powerful religious experiences.[44]

Clarendon Street, Ernest Gordon honestly felt, "was no church built up by attracting the comfortable and well dressed from other churches with oratory and subtle, dexterous rhetoric."

A.J. Gordon hadn't shied away from "uncomfortable truths and unpopular causes," as when he opposed the prejudice against congregational singing, or persistently argued for the abolition of pew rents that had the net effect of segregating his parishioners.

Nor had he run to embrace "all parties and all beliefs, however opposed they might be." He had shown fidelity to orthodox, creedal Christianity. And last, he constantly admonished his Clarendon Street parishioners to care for "the drunkard, the outcast, the vagabond, [and] the opium-slave." Christ, their Savior, had always sought out "the least, the last and the lost,"[45] they could and should do no less.

"So," Ernest Gordon stated, "the Spirit of God carried on His redeeming work in Clarendon Street Church." And this good work carried still further—

The impulses gained vitalized [many other] Baptist churches of Eastern Massachusetts. For years, Clarendon Street stood as a religious [nexus] between the city and surrounding towns. Young people from the country and from the provinces would spend five or ten years here, and

> then, when married, go to establish homes about suburban churches—staunch, reliable men and women with the stamp of the city church upon them.[46]

By the 1890s, Clarendon Street was "no longer a select congregation of pewholders." Rich and poor met together, "the Lord as the Maker of them all."[47]

Many pastor's sons are discomfited by much that they see in their formative years. More than a few turn away from faith. What Ernest Gordon saw drew him to what his father believed, and asked others to believe. "A noble type of Christianity," he said, "is regnant in these hearts."[48]

Why would he feel this way? Words A.J. Gordon spoke held the answer.

"The source of unity and love," he said, lay in Christ's words, *"If two of you shall agree on earth as touching anything that they shall ask, it shall be done for them."*

That word "agree," Gordon said—

> is a beautiful one in the original, meaning to be in symphony or musical accord. But it is not possible for two to be in holy agreement among themselves unless each is attuned to a third—the Holy Comforter. The harp strings must be keyed to a common pitch in order to chord with each other.[49]

* * *

Ultimately, signs of life and health at Clarendon Street had only come about "with much labor and toil," or "travail," to recall the first words of Gordon's 1887 Minneapolis address. His son Ernest later described some of the ministries that originated, grew, and flourished over time. "Local missions of the church," he said—

> included, in addition to the work among Jews and Chinese, a mission for colored people, which became in time

self-sustaining; [there was also] the work of the [Boston] Industrial Home, administered largely by members of the Clarendon Street Church; an important rescue work for women; the various evangelistic enterprises of the young people at the wharves, car stables, and hospitals; and the evangelistic work of the deacons in weak churches.

[As for foreign missions,] in addition to the support tendered the missions of the [Baptist] denomination, an independent mission in Korea was organized by a member of the church, with five workers in the field. This number is to be increased...

[Last,] on the walls of the vestry, where the prayer meetings are held, are inscribed the names of missionaries and evangelists connected with the church. The number... averaging anywhere from ten to twenty.[50]

How were these "deep and comprehensive changes" effected?

Ernest Gordon borrowed an image from Asian culture to offer an answer. "Like the Japanese sword-smith who spends a lifetime on a daimio's single blade, [Father] worked at his church for twenty-five long years. No wonder it became an effective instrument. He loved his people. When at home, he bound them to him by the tenderest ministries, at the side of the sick, comforting the bereaved, burying the dead."[51] And when he wasn't in Boston—away on travels or vacationing—Gordon wrote frequently to his parishioners.

"I am resting powerfully," he told one, "and have much time for communion and quiet talking with the Lord. I feel that my busy and hurried life in Boston robs me too much of this. How much we need the times of refreshing to fit us for toil, lest we become mere superficial and routine servants!...I have written to many in the parish, having time now to think of all their wants and sorrows, and all I wish to say to them...I have written long letters, and am going to write scores more."[52]

To another correspondent he said, "I am using great diligence in the midst of my country work, in writing letters to such as need a word of comfort or counsel. Yet I begin to feel quite anxious to get back again to my parish, and to all the interests and labors that are so dear to me. I cannot entirely cast off the burden of it, even while so far away, but am constantly sending back my desires and longings toward those whom God has given me to watch over and care for. I really desire, above all things, to go back to a more devoted ministry for the good of souls."[53]

Chapter Nine
The Heart of the Matter

It is really a book of 'vital' religion, and at the same time 'sound' in doctrine. We make the distinction, because doctrinal soundness is often accompanied with spiritual dryness. Mr. Gordon is all alive. He is intensely 'Orthodox,' but he is also intensely human.[1]

—*The Boston Globe*

In June 1872, A.J. Gordon published *In Christ,* a book often called his finest. It was published by the Boston-based firm, Gould and Lincoln— still later in London, by Hodder & Stoughton, using "American plates by special arrangement." Many times re-published, and critically acclaimed, fine copies of this book are now kept in The Bodleian Library, Oxford, and Princeton University Library, among other famous academic repositories.[2]

To be sure, this book was one Gordon had close to heart, for as he had written in its Preface: "If this little book should be to any in reading it, what it has been to the author in writing it…it will have served the end of its publication."[3]

Further, of all Gordon's books, *In Christ* was the most carefully wrought and considered. It was at once literary and cast with profound spiritual insight.

For as his son Ernest wrote—

> *In Christ* was the fruit of much deep meditation, the distillation of many late hours in the Jamaica Plain manse.

It is, perhaps, the most nearly perfect in form and content of any of [my father's] works, quintessential in its compression, rich, finished, and imbued with mysticism, the mysticism of the New Testament.[4]

From the first, reviewers took note of the book's special qualities. Apart from the fulsome *Boston Globe* review above, *The Sunday Courier* also gave an important commendation, saying—

This book comes well up to its divine theme.

We do not remember, since Thomas à Kempis, a book so thoroughly imbued with great personal love of Christ, and such longing desire to bring men into like love of our Lord and Master as this…This book has beside its spiritual beauty, great literary merit. It is written in that full, rich, old style, which once was common among good divines, but now is unhappily so rare anywhere.[5]

To read a book like *In Christ* is to read a text in some ways reminiscent of *Mere Christianity* by C.S. Lewis, who was deeply aware that his understanding of the first things of Christianity was shaped by earlier writers—not least Richard Baxter, who was the first to use the term, "mere Christianity."[6]

Likewise, A.J. Gordon stated in the Preface for *In Christ* that his book laid "no claim to originality in doctrine, having sought in every line to be in humble subjection to the word of God, and constantly to reflect whatever lesser light might fall upon it from the thought and experience of good men, since as has been fitly said, *'only with all saints'* can we comprehend what is the depth and length of that which is presented to us in Jesus Christ."[7]

The concept of mere Christianity was a central theme of Gordon's book. Though eighty years separate Lewis's book and Gordon's, lines from the Preface of *In Christ* are of a kindred nature to things Lewis had written.

"If subjects have been touched upon," Gordon had written—

still in the list of disputed doctrine, they have been brought forward [in] the love of the truth as it is in Jesus, and not in the interest of any sect or party; while to controversy, "whose rough voice and unmeek aspect" have perhaps oftener repelled from the truth than won to it, no place has been given.[8]

Gordon closed with a "humble prayer" that the perusal of his book might "help some to rest in Christ with a deeper assurance [and] to abide in Him."[9]

Moving forward, though, Gordon started down a path different from Lewis's *Mere Christianity*. That book was one of apologetics, or a survey of concepts that undergird the intellectual case for faith. The guiding theme of *In Christ* centered on the ways of grace, and how a loving God seeks redemptively to draw all people to Himself. From that one truth flows all others, as Gordon said—

> *And what shall be the influence of these truths upon our daily life?*
> *In Christ our righteousness, we see…what we are pledged to…*
> *We understand ourselves only in Him…*[10]

Gordon told readers that salvation brings a reunion of our soul with God, "that through this union He may communicate to it [His] divine life and energy." Gordon called this "the method of grace," and because it is the first great reality—the starting point of the Christian life, we can thereafter begin to learn the ways of holiness.[11]

Here, readers of *In Christ* discovered a book that was literary and profound. Yet it also breathed a deeply devotional spirit, with a conversational tone that many found winsome and compelling. The following lines, from Chapter One, show why.

"God's taking upon Himself humanity," Gordon said—

> and yet remaining God, is hardly more inexplicable to human thought than man's becoming a "partaker of the divine nature," and yet remaining man.

Both are of those secret things that belong wholly unto God.

Yet, great as is the mystery of these words, they are the key to the whole system of doctrinal mysteries. Like the famous Rosetta stone, itself a partial hieroglyph, and thereby furnishing the long-sought clew to the Egyptian hieroglyphics, these words, by their very mystery, unlock all mysteries of the divine life, letting us into secrets that were "hidden from ages and from generations."

True, we may not find in them an answer to the question, "*How* can these things be?" but we shall see clearly that they *can* be.

For through this "Emmanuel knot of union," as one has quaintly called it, those great facts of the Christian life, regeneration, justification, sanctification, and redemption, are drawn up from the realm of the human and the impossible, and made fast to Him with whom "all things are possible."[12]

Once believers enter the realm of faith, Gordon explained, their "daily life should become 'a good conversation in Christ.'" And here he quoted the great British commentator, Matthew Henry, who had written: "A good conversation in Christ is a holy life, according to the doctrine and example of Christ."[13] Gordon treasured Henry's spiritual insight, as one of the good company of the wise. His writings helped shape Gordon's understanding of faith, as when Henry had written: *The sentences in the book of providence are sometimes long, and you must read a great way before you understand their meaning.* To this, Gordon responded: "Very true, good commentator; for God's book is very large, and it makes up many volumes—a chapter here and a chapter there, and the plot running through many chapters before it is fully manifest."[14]

Midway through *In Christ,* Gordon returned to the theme of communing with the Savior. "As between man and man, thought is the medium of life, and the words of intimate conversation serve to transmit the subtle essence of intelligence, affection, and feeling, from one to another; so between the renewed soul and God. Spiritual converse is the means to a community of spiritual life."[15]

Kindred traits of meditation and contemplation, facets of medieval spirituality, held the key here for Gordon. "From the devout contemplation of the character of Christ," he told readers, "[the Savior's] image is insensibly reproduced in the life of the believer. And so, as by communion one enters into fellowship with Jesus Christ, by meditation he enters into conformity to Him. And these two are the principal requisites to our attainment of the fullness of the stature of Christ, his life constantly imparted, and his character constantly reflected."[16]

Meditation and contemplation, Gordon concluded, yield resplendent things of faith—hopes of pilgrimage—paths much to be sought.

"Through the one," he wrote—

> obedience tends more and more to become the spontaneous law of our being, and service the unconstrained fulfillment of God's word; and through the other, likeness to the Lord Jesus grows more and more towards realized oneness with Him, while, "beholding as in a glass the glory of the Lord, we are changed into the same image from glory to glory, even as by the Spirit of the Lord."[17]

When *The Sunday Courier* had stated in its review that *In Christ* was a book reminiscent of Thomas à Kempis, a book of "spiritual beauty," it discerned elements like the sacramental themes Gordon evoked so skillfully in his writing.[18] In one such passage, he had written—

> Our Lord's whole earthly career is one continuous and living sacrament, of which his disciples partake through faith. And if their eyes are not holden, they will discern, in each great event of that life, not only the earnest and symbol of what He works in them, but they will see that only by feeding upon this Bread, can they have any life dwelling in them.[19]

Literary allusions also infused Gordon's prose, as here, when he cited one of England's finest poets to illumine facets of faith—

> "God manifested in the flesh," says Coleridge, "is eternity in the form of time." Christ crucified is an eternal fact realized at a certain date, but touching all time with equal closeness.[20]

Gordon's debt to Coleridge also ran to another passage, which he cited with admiration: "never yet did there exist a full faith in the Divine Word…which did not expand the intellect while it purified the heart."[21]

Like so many in his day, Gordon owed a deep debt as well to the writings of John Bunyan, the British prisoner of conscience whose book, *The Pilgrim's Progress,* was written within the confines of his cell. Somehow, Bunyan had been able to capture moments of that trying sojourn in the pages of his text, and turn them to golden lines of allegory that conveyed first things of faith. No one has ever written more eloquently of the passage from this life to the realm of eternity that awaits believers. Gordon acknowledged this, and drew upon Bunyan's work to describe the blessèd hope that Christians possess—

> And so we may tell the story of the Christian's burial no longer in that brief, hollow phrase which to the ancients seemed the tenderest allusion that could be made to the deceased, *"Non est,"* he is not; but in words like those of Bunyan's, so fragrant of heart's-ease and immortelle,— "The pilgrim they laid in *a chamber whose window opened towards the sun rising;* the name of that chamber was Peace, *where he slept till the break of day."*[22]

The writings of other dissenters also found a place in Gordon's book.

"We never," he said, "get so near the heart of our sorrowing humanity, as when we are in communion with the heart of the Man of Sorrows." And to further illumine this thought, Gordon quoted George Fox, the founder of the Quakers, who had written: "I prayed to God that He would baptize my heart into a sense of all conditions, that so I might be able to enter into the needs and sorrows of all."[23]

Samuel Rutherford was a divine (or spiritual writer) Gordon admired all his life. In letters he wrote during his years of study at Newton

Theological Seminary, references to "sweet Rutherford" recur again and again.[24] It is the less surprising, therefore, that Gordon paid tribute to Rutherford's spiritual wisdom and eloquence in the pages of his own book, as in this passage—

> [God] has put our title-deeds to salvation so high that we may not mar them, having hidden them "with Christ in God." As "holy Rutherford" says, "Unbelief may perhaps tear the copies of the covenant which Christ hath given you; *but He still keeps the original in heaven with Himself. Your doubts and fears are no part of the covenant, neither can they change Christ.*"[25]

Gordon's reflections here, vis-à-vis Rutherford, were an anticipatory echo of words C.S. Lewis would later write in *Mere Christianity*: "But the great thing to remember is that, though our feelings come and go, His love for us does not. It is not wearied by our sins, or our indifference; and, therefore, it is quite relentless in its determination that we shall be cured of those sins, at whatever cost to us, at whatever cost to Him."[26] Then too, Gordon's prose itself was inset with many literary qualities. Cadence, phrasing, and imagery—all were elements he'd mastered, carefully sought and interwoven. "What a place then," he asked,

> does the sepulcher of Jesus occupy! It is the border line and meeting place of law and grace. It is the solemn pause, "the divine ellipsis" in the work of redemption, whence we look back upon the old nature, the old sin, and the old curse, and forward upon the "all things" that "are become new." Standing here and looking either way, we see how Christ's work divides itself into what he did as the Sin-bearer, and what he did as the Life-giver.[27]

Last, showing the depth of his reading, and that his home library was indeed "of quite an antique cast,"[28] Gordon drew on the wisdom of an early church father to fathom the mystery of baptism—

And so we look back to that solemn moment when, in the name of the Trinity, we were immersed beneath the water, and then raised again from the parted wave, and we see in the act the divine credential which our Lord gave to our consenting faith of our union with Him in his dying and rising; or in the expressive phrase of [John] Chrysostom, "the sign and pledge of our descent with Him into the state of the dead, and of our return thence."[29]

And nowhere was Gordon's gift for commending the heart of faith more in evidence than in the passage below, which hallowed the resurrection and its purchase of heaven's hope for believers—

It is the resurrection that gives us back our belovèd, looking and speaking as they were wont; that gives us back our bodies parted from us awhile, but endeared to us by the very sorrows we have borne in them; and that restores us wholly to the lost image of God, in which we were created, by making us to awake in the likeness of Christ, new created.[30]

In lines like these, readers saw Gordon had a rare gift for describing Christian teaching in ways poignant and profound, yet readily understood. This was certainly true of Gordon's thoughts about "the union of the believer" with Christ. Here, he said: "the union of the believer with his Lord is a *reciprocal* union. 'Ye in me, and I in you.' Through it Christ both gives and takes,—gives the Father's life and blessèdness, and takes the believer's death and wretchedness."[31]

To compliment this thought, Gordon cited Martin Luther, who had written: "All that Christ has now becomes the property of the believing soul; all that the soul has, becomes the property of Christ. Christ possesses every blessing and eternal salvation; they are henceforth the property of the soul. The soul possesses every vice and sin; they become henceforth the property of Christ."[32]

So Gordon's book unfolded.

Along the way, he gave readers a guided tour of collective wisdom from great spiritual leaders of the past, even as he introduced reflections from his own study of scripture. It all made for a stirring, reverential book—one thousands of readers, down the years, have been grateful to take up and contemplate.

Chapter Ten
Chansons du Rédempteur

As with Luther, love of music was one of [father's] most striking characteristics. Though without a musician's training, he edited with peculiar discrimination two hymn-books, and wrote admirable and much-used tunes for fifteen or more hymns.[1]

—Ernest Gordon

Within fifty years of A.J. Gordon's passing, a slender anthology was published—one he would have deeply appreciated. Replete with a frontispiece photo and signature facsimile, it bore a simple title, *Hymns by Adoniram Judson Gordon*. Running to just fifteen pages, it contained all the hymns for which he had written either the music, text, or both.

It makes for fascinating reading.

The second hymn given, "I Saw One Toiling in the Way," had text written by Gordon, and was set to music by none other than Sir Arthur Sullivan, the great Victorian Era British composer of light opera and sacred music, one half of the duo we know today as Gilbert and Sullivan. One wonders just what the circumstances were that led Gordon to this choice of music; but clearly, he had a fine appreciation for Sir Arthur's compositions.

The first verse of Gordon's text expressed deep sympathy for the destitute and care-worn—from his reading of Matthew 11:28-29—

I saw one toiling in the way
'Neath heavy burdens pressed,
"Take thou My yoke," I heard Him say
"And bearing it find rest."

This hymn had been preceded by "Cast All Thy Care;" set with text by Gordon, and music by D.B. Towner.

Here, Gordon collaborated with one of the finest, most prolific hymn writers of the late nineteenth and early twentieth century. Daniel Brink Towner had for many years traveled with D.L. Moody, leading music for thousands in the great gospel gatherings Moody held throughout America. For over twenty-five years, Towner served as the Music Director at Moody Bible Institute. In his lifetime, he composed music for over 2,000 hymns, including the classic, "Trust and Obey."[2]

A third hymn in the Gordon anthology was titled "Where Art Thou, Soul." Once more, Gordon had written the text. But here he'd collaborated with a different composer, W.H. Doane, the composer of music for many classic hymns, "To God Be The Glory" and "Jesus, Keep Me Near The Cross" among them—both written with Fanny Crosby, the greatest writer of hymn texts in American history, composing more than 9,000 hymns in all.[3]

Gordon's theme was God's purpose in redemption, and his hymn was rich with lines like, "I have brought thee life," and "I formed thee for a child of light." Many souls are lost, Gordon knew, and walk in a kind of wilderness. Borrowing imagery from John Bunyan's *The Pilgrim's Progress*, Gordon wrote of those who wander through "wild and wood and moor."

To all such, the Lord of heaven calls, through moving lines like these—

Where art thou, soul? I hear God say...
For long, long years I've called to thee
Where art thou, soul? I'm calling yet,
I cannot give thee o'er...

* * *

Fourth in the Gordon hymn anthology was "In Tenderness He Sought Me." Here, Gordon had written the music, while the text was written by an Englishman, W. Spencer Walton. This collaboration touched on Gordon's lifelong commitment to foreign missions, for Walton was a missionary with the South Africa General Mission in the late 1800s, and the founder of "The Sailors' Rest," Capetown's well-known mission station. During The Boer War, Walton faithfully distributed Bibles, warm clothing, and food to soldiers. He was a deeply dedicated man, after Gordon's heart.[4] Lines from Walton's text and refrain read—

> *With adoring wonder, His blessings I retrace*
> *It seems as if eternal days*
> *Are far too short to sound His praise*

> *O the love that sought me...*
> *O the grace that brought me to the fold*
> *Wondrous grace that brought me to the fold*

For a fifth hymn, Gordon took up a plaintive German melody, setting a text to it that bore the title, "Thy Way And Not Mine." Here, Gordon drew on the theme of Mark 14:36 to write a hymn of consecration. In part, his lines read—

> *Thy way and not mine,*
> *O Saviour divine*
> *I yield to Thy gracious direction.*

> *Thy merit, not mine,*
> *In this I shall shine—*
> *The robe of Thy spotless perfection.*

"O Blessèd Paraclete" was the title Gordon gave to a sixth hymn, writing four verses for music composed by Sir Joseph Barnby.

Here, Gordon's abiding interest in hymnody met the world of classical and high church music. For Barnby had studied at the Royal Academy of Music, and was later conductor of The Royal Albert Hall Choral

Society, and as such, "a choral conductor of the highest attainment." And during his student days, Barnby was narrowly defeated by none other than Sir Arthur Sullivan in a competition for the first Mendelssohn Scholarship. Among Barnby's most important conducting achievements was a performance with full orchestra and chorus—memorable in the history of church music in England—of Bach's 'St. Matthew Passion' in Westminster Abbey, in April 1871. Barnby was knighted on August 5, 1892, and was a fellow of the Royal Academy of Music. A prolific composer of hymn-tunes, Barnby was one of the editors of the *Cathedral Psalter* published in 1873.[5]

Gordon's hymn text, as its title suggests, honors The Holy Spirit—

O Blessèd Paraclete
Assert Thine inward sway;
My body make the temple meet,
For Thy perpetual stay.

* * *

All these above are among Gordon's contributions to American hymnody. But the most famous hymn, by far, is a classic piece for which he wrote the music, "My Jesus, I Love Thee," long within the canon of American sacred song. Generations have come to treasure its opening lines—

My Jesus I love Thee, I know Thou art mine,
For Thee all the follies of sin I resign,
My gracious Redeemer, my Saviour art Thou,
If ever I loved Thee, my Jesus, 'tis now.

* * *

To show the place of this hymn in American music, The Library of Congress, in its collection of historic recordings, has curated a 1907 Victor-Victrola disc, a vocal performance with orchestra, of A.J. Gordon's most famous hymn, which was published in 1872.[6] The 1907 recording, featuring a solo by the renowned English tenor Frederic Freemantel, is also archived with The Discography of American Historical Recordings, part of The National Endowment for the Humanities.[7]

"Hymnology," as Ernest Gordon quaintly called it, was, indeed, his father's "only diversion, a spring of refreshment and a means of relaxation after tension, as fiction is to most." His fondness for walking was likely also a time when thoughts of music came to him, especially in "the summers of his life," when "as regularly as the day of rest settled down on the quiet hills" of his native town, New Hampton, he could be seen, with Bible under his arm, "walking the long, maple-shaded village street to the little white meeting-house," with its "resonant bell." Its music tolled out over the land: a summons to things of eternity.[8] In keeping with this, Gordon read a fellow hymn writer and poet famous for pastoral verse: Henry Kirke White, and kept a volume of White's *Complete Works* in his personal library.

Always for Gordon, there was music in the land, in scenes he had known all his life—"oxen bearing the yoke, sheep straying on the mountain-side, [and] seed thrown into the fresh furrow."[9] Likewise, he asked: "Have you never searched for the little creature which chirrups such shrill music from the trees on an August night?"[10]

Writing of *The Pilgrim's Progress,* biographer Ola Winslow once stated that John Bunyan's youth was "nourished by country fact." She told of how well he knew "the sound of bells across the valley…wide spaces, secret dells, rocky slopes, [and] fields stretching far away. There is dew on the grass, the music of brooks…the footprint of animals at dawn."[11]

This was no less true of A.J. Gordon, for he had once memorably observed: "A hundred dewdrops may hang on the grass blades in the morning; and each one can reflect a full orbed sun as completely as though there were not another."[12]

Wonder was woven in other things, too.

"I have just revisited many scenes of my early walks in this so familiar place," Gordon once said, "I remember a tree where I used to go as a boy to pray. Only the stump of it remains; but I could call it to witness, while kneeling there, that God had done exceeding abundantly above all that I thought or asked. What a change! Who could have dreamed it!"[13]

Trees, like those of his highland home, would always hold a fine and lyrical place in Gordon's imagination, leading him to say: "A tree gathers up into itself all the growths of former years, and makes them part of its present substance."[14]

Flowers too held many charms.

"Nature," Gordon said, "has given to the rose its exquisite fragrance, but she has also armed it with thorns; so that while the delicious odors attract, these little sentinels stand guard with their drawn bayonets to defend the flower, which is endangered by its very beauty and sweetness."[15]

Elsewhere, he wrote of lilies, and how they beckoned to deep things of scripture: "*As the lily among thorns, so is my beloved among the daughters.*' The beauty of Christ's Church is guarded...Her graces are hedged about with self-denial, her gifts are compassed with crosses, and her triumphs are crowned with thorns."[16]

Asked to preach during his visits home, Gordon's "parables of the gospels" were "translated into the homely correspondences of New England country life," drawing forth his "great gifts of illustration and of story-telling." In services at the Dana Meeting House, with folk "in old-fashioned box pews, facing in all directions," Gordon would lead them in song: time honored anthems ringing beneath hand-hewn rafters past generations knew.[17]

At all times, he was fond of "matching in spare moments old hymns to new tunes," and "writing either hymns or tunes as the case required, humming into being new melodies as he went to sleep." At other times, he loved to sing old hymns with his family "till all throats were hoarse and all lungs weary save his own."[18]

Gordon was also "so responsive to music that a few chords would often suffice to bring him downstairs to the side of the piano, as if an invisible, yet no less potent, spell were working."[19] Few loved music as he did.

Doubtless, the place of his hymn-books and hymn recordings in America's music history would have brought Gordon genuine astonishment and deep, unaffected gratitude. But one suspects that nothing would have meant more to him than three stories Ernest Gordon recorded—stories A.J. Gordon witnessed.

During his lifetime, he saw that "My Jesus, I Love Thee," had become familiar "wherever hymns [were] sung by men and women of the English tongue." He was profoundly honored to learn that it was "sung by thousands in jerseys and bonnets" on the sad day when Catherine Booth, "the mother of the Salvation Army, was laid away to rest."[20]

Still later, after a largely attended gospel gathering in New York City, he met "a handsome and stately young woman…a singer of distinction in opera." Disillusioned, and "sick at heart of the pride of life," filled with "a yearning for she hardly knew what," she had sat down at the piano in the reception-room of the hotel where she was staying. Opening haphazard a hymnal, which lay on the rack, she played the first song she turned to.

It was "My Jesus, I Love Thee."[21] She sang verse after verse—and something extraordinary took place. Before she had finished singing, she had known an entire spiritual experience—"tears, repentance, forgiveness, [and] peace." Gordon listened in astonishment as she told him that "for more than a year, now," she had given herself "to mission work in the metropolis."[22]

* * *

Yet another time, after Gordon spoke to "a large meeting in a Canadian city" where the provost of the town presided, "My Jesus, I Love Thee" was announced for the closing hymn. It was "sung with great power and fervor" by the congregation.

It was then, when looking over to the chairman, Gordon saw him give way to emotions of deeply held grief. The services closed, and Gordon went with this gentleman to his home.

There, in "the quiet of his library," he told Gordon how "his only son had passed away some weeks before, in his arms," singing the same hymn.[23]

What a fulgent testimony to the power of sacred song.

Colby Academy in 1899

Brown University in 1867

Jamaica Plain Baptist Church in 1895

Clarendon Street Baptist Church, Clarendon Street

Clarendon Street Baptist Church in 1887

A.J. Gordon in his mid-thirties

A.J. and Maria Gordon with their family

The Boston Industrial Home in 1893

The Boston Missionary Training
School, Class of 1892

A.J. Gordon, about age 50

Round Top, the Northfield hill where A.J. Gordon spoke on the resurrection

Chapter Eleven
Messages of Grace

The handsome church building on the southeast corner of Madison-Avenue and Thirty-First Street was opened yesterday. The Madison-Avenue Baptist Church pulpit was occupied by Rev. A.J. Gordon, of the Clarendon-Street Church in Boston. He preached in the morning from Ephesians 2:17 – "and came and preached peace to you which were afar off, and to them which were nigh."[1]

—The New York Times

On Friday, December 30, 1877, A.J. Gordon gave the inaugural sermon for the newly reopened Madison Avenue Baptist Church in New York City.

It was then one of the most beautiful churches in America—architecturally rich in that its superbly crafted brickwork achieved a rare, inspiring harmony of Italianate and Gothic design. Its stained glass windows, rendered in vibrant colors of azure, crimson, and gold, were highly reminiscent of pre-Raphaelite paintings. Among churches of the era, Madison Avenue Baptist Church was something very like a cathedral in the heart of the city. That Gordon had been asked to give the inaugural sermon here spoke to his stature as one of America's most prominent Baptist clergymen. *The New York Times'* coverage of his sermon was noteworthy in itself, as the text of his sermon was copiously cited for the *Times'* readers. They could see how fine elements of sermoncraft were present in his words.

Invoking Christ's redemptive work, Gordon spoke meaningfully of the need to see that work in perspective, as with "a Chinese picture," where "all the elements are in the foreground." In the same way, he said, "Christ's peace and pardon are the prominent things in the gospel."[2]

Gordon turned next to the pathos and hope of faith, his words recalling the "amazing grace" of John Newton's timeless hymn—grace to "save a wretch like me." For Newton, once a slave ship captain, was a great study in the work of redemption. Many, knowing only his crimes against the sons and daughters of Africa, might have sent him forever to prison and destroyed its key. But God sundered that cell with unrelenting grace: no one was beyond redemption.

Gordon captured this in his sermon.

"God," he said, "is infinitely more merciful than man. He can pardon where man can only punish. He can make heaven's doors swing open to men whose prison doors we dare not open."[3]

Here no one was beyond redemption, no one beyond hope. Salvation, the benison beyond price, could be theirs—if they only repented their sins and sought pardon in Christ.

This was the heart of Gordon's message. The one thing each of us need, he said, "is peace with God." No other thing was more to be desired.

"That peace," he continued—

> may be yours now, at this very hour, if you will only accept it. It is not a peace that is fenced about by hard conditions. It is yours if by the simplest exercise of faith you will receive it…
>
> When it is said of Christ that He is our peace, it is an expression that comprehends all else about Him…in His gloried person we have the summary and certificate of His whole redemption work…the archive in which all He has done and suffered for us is treasured up…the sacrifice never to be forgotten, and never to lose its power in all the endless years.[4]

The *New York Times* had printed some of the finest lines Gordon ever spoke.

* * *

None knew these facets of Gordon's sermoncraft better than his wife Maria. Writing in the Preface to *Yet Speaking*, one of his posthumously-published books, she said: "No Christian ever listened to his preaching without being stimulated to holier living; and no unsaved one ever turned away from the service, without having heard in simplest, tenderest phrase, the way of life explained."[5] Maria's touching tribute captured the essence of her husband's pastoral gift.

That gift, with Gordon's place in American pulpit oratory, was remembered long after his passing. In 1950, the distinguished house of F.H. Revell published an influential series of books called "Great Pulpit Masters." Volume Eight was devoted to a rich selection of sermons from A.J. Gordon. Other volumes held sermons from D.L. Moody, C.H. Spurgeon, F.B. Meyer, and T. DeWitt Talmage.

Looking through the A.J. Gordon volume for *Great Pulpit Masters*, one sees many choice things, including lines from authors he admired. The Scottish writer George MacDonald was one such writer. Gordon chose lines of MacDonald's verse inspired by the timeless image of Jesus, the carpenter's son. He then quoted these lines in his sermon, "The First Thing in the World"—

> *Lord, might I be as a saw,*
> *A plane, a chisel, in thy hand!*
> *No, Lord, I take it back in awe—*
> *Such prayer for me is far too grand.*
> *I pray, O master, let me lie*
> *As on Thy bench the favored wood;*
> *Thy saw, Thy plane, Thy chisel ply*
> *And work me into something good.*[6]

Words from the 18th century leader Count Zinzendorf also brought inspiration, as Gordon deeply respected the pioneering Moravian commitment to missionary endeavor.[7] Zinzendorf had written four poetic lines Gordon cherished as "grand, sweet words," translated from German by John Wesley—

Midst flaming worlds, in Thee arrayed,
With joy shall I lift up my head;
Bold shall I stand in that great day,
For who aught to my charge can lay?[8]

Zinzendorf's prose writings, apart from poetry, were also cited by Gordon, who sensed in him a consecrated, kindred spirit. In one sermon, called "Grace and Reward," he spoke of Zinzendorf at length—

> We need not wonder if Zinzendorf, who exclaims from a glowing heart, "I have one passion; it is He, He alone," should soon find himself the object of bitterest contempt in a world whose one passion is self and self alone...
>
> Slander and detraction followed Zinzendorf as dark shadows follow a brilliant light. He who [said] "that place is our proper home where we have the greatest opportunity of laboring for our Saviour," found his residence for years in exile...Bearing the heavy cross of obloquy, he could yet [say of his] journey—
>
> *"All the way I swam in peace and joy in the Lord."*[9]

Still other writers Gordon extolled, and quoted, include the English poets George Herbert, Isaac Watts, and Adelaide Anne Procter, along with English divines John Newton, Thomas à Kempis, Joseph Alleine, John Bunyan, William Gurnall, and Jeremy Taylor.[10]

One quote from Gurnall that Gordon treasured was this: "It is storied of Cato, who was Caesar's bitter enemy, that when he saw Caesar prevail, rather than fall into his hand, and stand his mercy, he laid violent hands on himself; which Caesar, hearing of, passionately broke out into these words: *'O Cato, why didst thou grudge me the honor of saving thy life?'*" And to this moving passage Gordon responded: "So Christ sorrows with exceeding sorrow that we will not allow Him to forgive us, or permit Him to save us."[11]

Here Gordon showed himself a writer of fine skill, as in the pages of *Great Pulpit Masters*, when he wrote about "The Love of God," a sermon still anthologized today, in a collection of classic sermons edited by Warren Wiersbe.[12]

In this classic sermon, Gordon began with a text reading of Galatians 2:20 – *"The Son of God, who loved me and gave Himself for me."* He then observed—

> Some of us never get beyond the vague notion of a benevolent power working in and through the world, which somehow overrules all things for good. The above text expresses a more satisfying viewpoint, as it sets forth the love of God in Jesus Christ. It reminds us that that love is individual.
>
> *"Who loved me"*—We could never be content with a love that had no focus. A good will that is so infinitely diffused that it touches everywhere in general and fails to touch anywhere in particular is no more than an ineffectual sentiment. Yet just here lies the difference between that "eternal goodness," so much on the lips of [some], and the personal love for individual souls which the gospel declares to us.
>
> Love is a real, measurable, comprehensible thing. A ray of light may be analyzed. It is composed of several distinct and recognizable colors—red, violet, orange, and the rest. So love may be resolved into its constituents, and shown to include such elements as sympathy, yearning and good-will.
>
> If these do not show themselves we may conclude we are dealing with something else than real love.[13]

At the same time, Gordon's stature as a herald of heaven wasn't confined to America's shores. C.H. Spurgeon, of London's great Metropolitan Tabernacle, had a keen appreciation of Gordon's talents as an author.

Reviewing *Grace and Glory,* a collection of sermons Gordon issued in 1880, Spurgeon said it was a text full of "thought, living and earnest, expressed in forcible language; the doctrine orthodox, evangelical, [and] practical." Nor would he be surprised, he said, "if these discourses [were] reprinted by an English house."[14]

And indeed they were.

Once, to illustrate the gift of grace, Gordon tapped his training in the classics to cast a vivid parable set in ancient Rome. "When Caesar," he said—

> had bestowed a rare present upon one of his friends, the recipient of the gift said to him, "This is too costly a gift for me to receive."
>
> "But it is not too costly for _me_ to give," said the emperor. The peace of God may be too costly a gift for us to receive, for the mere taking of it; but it is not too costly for Christ to give. He earned it…we are not required to earn it. He paid enough for it, though it is without money and without price…[15]

Apart from crafting parables, Gordon also showed himself adept in framing aphorisms that helped bring truth home, to give it a place in the reader's memory. "A very lovely song," he once said, may be made "from the preludes of a Paradise regained."[16] And, to strike a tone much like G.K. Chesterton, Gordon had written: "The world will never get over wondering at this paradox,—this divine enigma of Christ crucified, the 'power of God.'"[17]

Other lines, no less telling, were the fruit of much reflection. Among them were lines that were, by turns, moving and insightful, pithy or reverent—

> *[Christ] returned from the conquest, having "led captivity captive."*
> *There is no question touching our peace that is not answered there.*[18]

> *Applause is not an infallible proof either of the truth,*
> *or the eloquence of the speaker to whom it is given.*[19]

> *The most real and precious things to us are often those*
> *which cannot be reckoned up in figures, or valued in dollars and cents.*[20]

> *Every genuine nature has a hidden reservoir of sorrow…*[21]

> *Our true life has come down from heaven.*[22]

At other times, Gordon drew on his study of church history to unfold the tapestry of redemption. St. Augustine and Martin Luther, paragons of earlier ages, were cited in one telling illustration, evoking the power woven in words of scripture. "It is so wonderful," Gordon said—

> how a strong, holy life will build itself...out of a single grain of Scripture truth accepted and believed...The history of God's church bears incontrovertible testimony to the fact."
>
> "Augustine and Luther," Gordon continued, "were regenerated by a single word of Scripture...and their regeneration meant a new age for their respective countries. They were not only new men, but mighty sons of God..."[23]

Last, Gordon's cast of mind, with his gift for eloquent, forceful expression, recall these same traits in the writing of C.S. Lewis. Here Gordon's thoughts took a philosophical turn, to merge arresting imagery with reasons for hope—

> Christ is dwelling in a fixed and well-defined place...He is always and fully accessible there to all who will come to Him for grace.
>
> I think this truth is of vast importance.
>
> Men cannot pray into the air. They cannot worship towards the vague immensity. It may do well enough for schoolmen and philosophers to tell us that the home of God is "a circle, whose centre is everywhere and whose circumference is nowhere." But there is nothing inviting or attractive to us in such a home as that. The soul's cry is, "Where dwellest thou?"
>
> And I bless God, who has not hidden his presence-chamber from us, that I can tell you, first, that Christ lives as a real person, with a form the same as that He wore on earth,—the same face, the same features, the same nail-pierced hands; and, secondly, that He lives in a real place, just as definitely fixed and bounded as Boston or London.[24]

In the pages of *Mere Christianity,* Lewis had spoken in much the same way, saying nothing was more indispensable than a map of the cosmos, and why we would do well to consult the very map God gave humanity.

To prepare the way for this point, Lewis described the sad flaw present in "vague religion—all about feeling God in nature." True, such a mindset held a certain attraction. But, Lewis said, it offered no more than that. "It is all thrills and no work: like watching the waves from the beach." Yet, as Lewis continued—

> you will not get to Newfoundland by studying the Atlantic that way, and you will not get eternal life by simply feeling the presence of God in flowers or music. Neither will you get anywhere by looking at maps without going to sea. Nor will you be very safe if you go to sea without a map. In other words, Theology is practical: especially now.[25]

Theology, or the study of God's nature, lends profound solace and strength. At times Gordon struggled, as so many do, with discouragement, even despondency. The recurring study of God's nature, he said, brought a balm of peace—and he drew on a metaphor of the painter's art to convey his meaning—

> To those who have experienced it, it is no mystery. There are times when, from depression and self-condemnation and momentary despair, the soul throws itself back on the righteousness of Christ, set to the sinner's account, with the quieting effect which finiteness has in trusting in Infiniteness...His righteousness is set to our account, His infinite merit is put to our credit. When the soul discovers this, will not quietness and calm succeed despair and agitation?
>
> I have read of a young painter, a pupil of one of the great Italian masters, how for weeks he labored wearily and hopelessly to produce a certain result on canvas. The outlines were there, but to fill them out and bring forth the picture of which he dreamed, he strove in vain. But one day,

in his absence from his studio, his teacher stole in, and with his skilled and practiced hand, brought out the lines and tints of beauty which the pupil had striven so hopelessly to produce. As the young man returned and his eye caught sight of the canvas, he exclaimed, "The Master, the Master has been here!"[26]

*   *   *

Fast forward to October 1889, when Gordon learned he had been profiled in a new anthology from Morgan and Scott, then the British publisher for D.L. Moody. The book, over 400 pages long, was called *The Christian Portrait Gallery*, with one hundred profiles of "highly-esteemed Christian Men and Women."[27] These finely detailed essays, familiar to readers internationally, had originally run in *The Christian* newspaper, published in London, and edited by R.C. Morgan.[28]

The Christian Portrait Gallery covered an array of notable figures from many fields: politicians and reformers, hymn writers, academic leaders, members of the clergy, pastors, philanthropists, reigning monarchs, and missionary pioneers. Among them were the peers like Lord Shaftesbury and Lord Cairns (a former Chancellor of the Exchequer), Frances Ridley Havergal, James McCosh (the former President of Princeton University), F.B. Meyer, D.L. Moody, Lord Mount-Temple, George Müller, C.H. Spurgeon, Queen Sophia of Sweden, and J. Hudson Taylor.

Published in Demy quarto, and "attractively bound with beveled boards and gilt edges," pre-release advertisements for this anthology ran in prestigious venues like *The Bookseller,* which featured British and Foreign Literature.[29] One early review of *The Christian Portrait Gallery* stated the book "may be said to represent the leading philanthropists of the world in many departments of Christian enterprise."[30]

The Christian Portrait Gallery held a long essay on A.J. Gordon as a clergyman and preacher. Since England was a country widely known for pulpit oratory, these reflections were the more significant and revealing. "His public ministry," it was said, extended "to about a quarter of a century, has been confined to cultured Boston and its suburbs; but his name is a household word in evangelical circles throughout the United

States. Though only in middle life, there is probably no man in the American pulpit today whose ministrations are more appreciated, or who is more highly esteemed for his own sake."[31]

The Christian Portrait Gallery also described what it was like to see and hear sermons from Gordon—as he had crafted them in his early fifties. Here, in the mind's eye, he stood before readers. "Dr. Gordon," the book said, has a "well-proportioned, somewhat portly form"—

> rather above the ordinary height; a large, square head, set firmly on his shoulders…light hair, now tinged with grey…a smooth face, with clear and pleasant eyes, and expressive mouth; an alert step and graceful bearing…one which cannot easily be forgotten. It has the sweetness and openness of a child, with the strength and intellect of a man. There is something quite boyish in it, revealing a suppressed but not extinguished capacity for fun…a marvelously bright, beautiful, benign face, revealing the man…[32]

The Christian Portrait Gallery drew attention also to Gordon's discernment, decisiveness, and tact—saying he was "a man of action… clear-eyed and quick to comprehend, and as quick to act; courteous, yet frank; always with the word ready which needs to be said." Next came an interesting comparison to Martin Luther: "As to his manner, Dr. Gordon illustrates Luther's maxim to young preachers: 'Stand up cheerily; speak out manfully; leave off speedily.' He has literally a speaking countenance. He enters upon his service in a sunny way, 'rejoicing like a strong man to run a race.' It gives no impression of a task to be performed. He evidently enjoys the Gospel that he preaches."[33]

Gordon's voice and delivery were other things *The Christian Portrait Gallery* described. His voice was said to be "clear, rich, and powerful," one that captured and kept attention. At times, there were moments when a hush seemed to fall over congregants as he spoke, "due not only to the way in which truth was brought to bear upon the individual soul of the hearer, but to the perfect adaptation of the speaker's tone and manner." In sum, he was a preacher who had a rare gift: "the faculty of making the Gospel at once imperative and inviting."[34]

In addition, *The Christian Portrait Gallery* noted Gordon's gift for crafting sermons that were both accessible and content-rich. He could "hold his own in any conclave of scholars and thinkers, [yet] neither young nor old could fail to be held by the interest which is imparted to the simple story."[35] Here Gordon emerged as a painter of vivid word pictures, images rich in simile and insight.

"From this," *The Christian Portrait Gallery* stated—

> it will be understood that Dr. Gordon's services are in great request…His Boston congregation has generously recognized the claims of the public [and] provided an assistant, so that the Doctor may be set free for frequent outside service…Several visits paid to the far-famed Princeton University have been seasons of much spiritual reviving among the students there. As a speaker at Christian Conferences he is always most welcome [with] a freshness of thought and felicity of expression that make his addresses linger long in the memory. Mr. Moody, we imagine, would not think a Northfield Conference half complete without the presence and testimony of his friend from Boston.[36]

As for charity's place in his preaching, *The Christian Portrait Gallery* stated Gordon was "a man of large-hearted view and catholic sympathy… No subject comes amiss to him. Whether in reverently seeking to fathom the mysteries of the Trinity…proclaiming the simple Gospel message; [or] pressing home the paramount privilege and duty of the believer to a complete consecration of life."[37]

In closing, this fine compendium described Gordon as a writer, noting that "some other works of his are published on this side of the Atlantic: all are well worthy of study, as the product of a cultured and deeply-taught mind."[38]

* * *

Telling as it was, *The Christian Portrait Gallery's* essay about Gordon wasn't the only important contemporary account of his life and ministry.

The American essayist J.B. Houser had also written a fine study, in February 1887, for a prominent New York City--based magazine called *The Pulpit Treasury*. In some ways, Houser's study anticipated the one published in *The Christian Portrait Gallery*.

At the outset, Houser said Gordon, "by common consent, stands in the front rank of the leaders of his denomination in this country, both as a preacher and as a man of varied attainments and influence." As to appearance and manner, Houser described Gordon as "a man of large physique with a full, sonorous voice, who fills his pulpit physically as well as mentally."[39]

Houser then gave reflections on Gordon's intellect and spirituality.

To be sure, the pastor of Clarendon Street Church was "strong in native abilities, and in the exactness and graces of good scholarship," yet Houser thought it was clearly "the deep spiritual power" present in Gordon's sermons "that wins most upon the hearer, and accomplishes the greatest results."[40]

Why so? Houser said Gordon's sermons flowed from a mind "saturated with Bible truth" and phraseology. Both gave color "to every thought and expression" in his sermons—and also his prayers—which were "composed almost exclusively of Scripture passages and phrases."[41]

Houser also said Gordon's sermons were "chiefly exegetical in character." Generally, they contained "a few choice thoughts" from some verse or passage, presented with "a natural fluency," and observations that "a quick and rather quaint [or colorful] fancy suggest."[42]

And rather than "deal with doctrines as abstract questions," Houser noted that Gordon sought "to present the more spiritual truths of the Gospel in such a way as to make holiness deeply attractive and induce a deep desire for such intimate union with Christ." Seldom, Houser stated, had he ever heard "a man who knows so well how to kindle high and holy aspirations."[43]

Thus many a pithy phrase, or metaphor, found its way into Gordon's sermons, as when he reflected on Christ's phrase, *"Take, therefore, no thought for the morrow"* (Matt. 6:34), which had been ably paraphrased in the old New England proverb: "don't borrow tomorrow's trouble today." To help that wisdom linger in the memory, Gordon spoke of a favorite summer pastime—

When I have been fishing in a mountain stream, I have found that so long as I kept a short line I could manage very well. But when I let my line run out, the stream took it along… there I was, at the mercy of every stick in the water and every rock that jutted from the banks. I lost my fish and I tangled my line; very likely I lost my footing too and fell in.

Now many people cast their line into life forty years long, when it ought to be no longer than a day. In consequence they are unable to manage their tackle at all, but are pulled about after it, stumbling first into one hole and then into another…[44]

From these reflections flowed a wise truth. "Walk through today as well as you can," Gordon concluded, "and God will take care of the future."[45]

Then too, one of his finest sermons evoked walks in the English countryside, showing grace by way of a parable. "In a country town," Gordon said—

in the South of England, about midway up a long and steep hill, stands a tavern, outside which is displayed a sign with this very inviting motto,

"Rest, and Welcome."

And up the rough, hard hill of life,—and to the most of mankind it *is* hard,—the God of much mercy, the "only true God," has put out his sign, that the toiling sons of men may be eased and refreshed, and it bears substantially the same inscription, "Rest, and Welcome."[46]

Houser also observed that when Gordon spoke, he used notes, but more frequently appeared without them. He used, "almost exclusively, the conversational tone and style in his delivery." And often, there was "a short flight of eloquence, [with] an occasional touch of humor, or more frequent illustration—in the use of which he is remarkably felicitous."[47]

The Boston Globe caught another side of Gordon as a humorist. One feature in a Sunday edition of *The Globe*, June 19, 1892, stated: "Rev. Dr.

A.J. Gordon is celebrated for his quiet humor and wit. But few people, however, know of his natural abilities as an artist of the caricature school."[48]

Just above, *The Globe* reproduced a fine sketch captioned, "Under the Rose," showing three august gentlemen, in close proximity, falling hapless victims to a fit of sneezing—rose pollen ostensibly the culprit. Gordon's sketch revealed a gift for terse caricature much like G.K. Chesterton's of a generation later: whimsy mingled with satire—in just a few deftly drawn lines. Here was an artist who relished laughter.

*   *   *

Many times as well, Gordon led hallowed times of prayer.

Here, Houser said, Gordon's "power and skill as a spiritual leader" were shown. "Models of their kind," they were "emphatically meetings for the people."[49] With wisdom and tact, Gordon began these gatherings with a guiding line of thought, then urged those present to offer prayers for one another and share thoughts as led. Thus no two meetings were alike, and care for others was fostered in a setting of genuine friendship. A sense of common purpose grew.

The result, as Houser noted, was that the "people are interested in the [prayer] meetings and make them interesting to all who attend. They are known and spoken of over the city, and many strangers are attracted to them."[50]

Many hearts were drawn to faith through these gatherings. It was little wonder that Gordon set such store by them and gave so much time to them. Here fellow travelers, many weary and care-worn, could find a haven—and hope.

As his essay closed, Houser focused on two key facets of Gordon's life and ministry: his work as an author and his leadership in the kindred spheres of foreign and home missions. Gordon, Houser maintained, "is an author of repute. He is [also] the editor of a monthly periodical—*The Watchword*—devoted chiefly to short Scripture studies and striking illustrations and anecdotes."

Memorable among such anecdotes in *The Watchword* were vignettes of the president Gordon admired above all others: Republican James

Garfield, who died tragically of an assassin's bullet in mid-September 1881. Gordon mourned his loss deeply, and paid eloquent tribute to his memory.

"For once," Gordon said, "we have had a President who could shine in the most illustrious position in the nation...a leader of the people, and a follower of Christ." In Chicago, during the contested Republican presidential convention of 1880, Gordon described how Garfield's conduct had been exemplary. Amid the "strain of rivalry between contending factions," he had emerged as "a leading figure."[51]

Character here was key, for on the Sunday that fell during the convention, Garfield quietly left the proceedings to attend church. Asked why, Garfield gave a reply Gordon treasured: *I have more confidence in the prayers to God which ascended in the churches yesterday, than in all the caucusing which went on in the hotels.*[52]

Garfield had barely assumed office when his life was taken. To hallow his memory, Gordon told another story in *The Watchword* soon after his passing.

"What is the highest blessing we can have in this world?" Gordon asked at the outset. "Our late beloved President gave the following beautiful answer to the question when asked to write in the [autograph] album of a lady." This answer had given Gordon great solace and inspiration—

> *If the treasures of ocean were laid at my feet,*
> *And its depths were all robbed of its coral and pearl.*
> *And the diamonds were brought from the mountain's retreat,*
> *And with them were placed all the wealth of the world—*
> *Not silver, nor gold, nor the spoils of the sea.*
> *Nor the garlands of fame that the world can bestow,*
> *But a purified heart that from sin was made free,*
> *I would ask for thee, friend, on thy journey below.* [53]

Apart from such telling magazine vignettes, J.B. Houser said Gordon had written several books which "circulate even more widely abroad" than in America: *The Ministry of Healing* (1882), *The Two-Fold Life* (1883), a volume of sermons titled *Grace and Glory* (1880), and the earliest of his books, "a work more theological in form" called *In Christ* (published in 1872).[54]

Notably, Gordon also wrote frequently for *The Christian Herald,* "a leading weekly religious illustrated journal" which had "half million readers, in every State of the Union, [and] influence possessed by no other weekly religious newspaper." Edited by Rev. T. DeWitt Talmage, of Central Presbyterian Church in Brooklyn,[55] *The Christian Herald* issued press releases stating "Dr. A.J. Gordon of Boston," was one among "other preachers of world-wide eminence," whose writings regularly appeared with pieces from C.H. Spurgeon of London, Rev. Dr. R.S. McArthur of New York, and Talmage himself.

Gordon was also featured on the cover of the November 11, 1886 issue, which stated: "Dr. Gordon has become known to English-speaking Christians the world over."[56] All these things pointed to his stature as a writer. In this and kindred settings, he was becoming "a household name," as a then current phrase had it.[57]

*   *   *

As to foreign missions, Houser told his readers that Gordon was "a leading office bearer and supporter of all the great missionary enterprises carried on by the [Baptist] denomination of which he is a member, and of late has been specially interested in the great work going forward along the Congo [in Africa]."[58]

These were, in their nature, noteworthy public spheres of endeavor.

But Gordon's influence extended beyond them to a lesser-known setting just as urgent and important: home missions. Here too, Gordon gave guiding leadership for, as Houser said, among "house-to-house visitors and the unknown toilers in the many missions of the city—no other minister of Boston is so well known, nor is any other so frequently appealed to for sympathy and help."[59]

Gordon knew faith commends itself in acts of compassion abroad; but philanthropy, or love for others, was no less vital for near neighbors, often recent immigrants, who were all too often destitute: the homeless, families ravaged by alcoholism, and those too poor to obtain enough food, clothing, or shelter. And if Gordon was "an intellectual and moral force...felt far and wide," his passion for souls brought blessings closer to home, "inside and outside of his church."[60]

Nor had Gordon's ministry gone unnoticed in the halls of academe.

Brown University had conferred an honorary degree of Doctor of Divinity upon him in 1878, "and many other Institutions of learning and Theological seminaries delight to do him honor," such as, Houser noted, his "course of lectures before the students and professors in Princeton Theological Seminary, which were greatly enjoyed by all who heard them, and left deep impressions for good upon many minds and hearts."[61] Houser then concluded: "Dr. Gordon has only passed his semi-centennial, [he] is full of life, vigor and godly zeal, and if spared by the Master for many years, may we not hope for rich harvests of souls yet to be gathered by him for the Savior whom he loves to serve?"[62]

Chapter Twelve
Well Remembered Days

Peace with God...may be yours now, at this very hour...It is yours if by the simplest exercise of faith you will receive it... Christ is our peace...an expression that comprehends all else that it said about Him...In His glorified person we have the summary and certificate of His whole redemption work.[1]
—A.J. Gordon, *The New York Times*,
Monday, December 31, 1877

Some tales catch us on the sudden—even in faraway places. Still others are moments from elder days; stories we might never think to find.

A century ago, Dr. J.H. Franklin, of the American Baptist Foreign Missionary Society, discovered this. Touring Asia, he boarded a train in Japan. His attempts to speak Japanese were halting at best, and he was much relieved when a young Japanese national kindly offered help in fluent English. When Franklin said he was from Boston, he saw a sudden light in the young man's eyes.

"I studied science at Boston University," he said, smiling. He then asked quickly: "Do you know the Rev. A.J. Gordon? Have you ever visited Northfield? I heard Dr. Gordon there, and D.L. Moody, and Henry Drummond."[2]

Franklin marveled. So far from America, an unexpected story. A.J. Gordon's influence, and his words—with those of Moody and Drummond—had travelled the world. More than this, Gordon and Moody were united in the memory of the young man J.H. Franklin met.

This scene was both a symbol and a tribute.

Gordon and Moody had a remarkable friendship and kindred legacies. They worked together often, and they relied on each other. Moody's eldest son Will saw this first hand, as Gordon was a "confidential advisor" for many projects in consultation with his father. Gordon, Will Moody said, gave "assistance at the Northfield Conferences...of inestimable value." Will Moody knew his father "relied much" on Gordon—and always, Gordon had shown a "readiness to do any service, to take any place, to stand in any gap."[3]

Each summer the famous Northfield Conferences drew thousands, primarily collegians—from the Ivy League, and many far flung places in the world. Planning for each gathering proved a formidable task. Skilled leadership was also needed to coordinate a small legion of volunteers and scores of events.

One summer, Gordon had "the whole charge" of the Northfield Conference while Moody was overseas. "I cannot thank you enough," he said, "for your great help at Northfield. All the letters I have got from there speak in the highest terms of your generalship. I know of no one who could have taken your place. It will now answer the question, *What is going to become of the work when I am gone?*"[4]

This was Moody's forthright declaration that A.J. Gordon should assume leadership of the Northfield Summer Conferences if he were to pass away. Moody's steadfast respect for Gordon, and his trust, ran deep.

* * *

The two friends met in 1877, in the run-up to Moody's transformative and unprecedented series of gospel gatherings in Boston.

At this time, Moody was just two years removed from his celebrated mission to Great Britain, where he had preached to millions over a stay that extended from June 1873 to July 1875. The resulting movement for spiritual renewal had become internationally famous, and reached its zenith between March 9th and July 21st, 1875, when Moody addressed, in total, "over 2½ million people at four venues: the Agricultural Hall, Islington; the Royal Opera House, Haymarket; Camberwell Green; and Bow Common."[5]

Seeking A.J. Gordon's support, with other prominent leaders, Moody now thought to hold a series of city mission meetings in Boston, in a great "Tabernacle" specially built to house several thousand people. So it was that from late January to the close of April, 1877, Boston was the site of gospel gatherings unlike anything "the Athens of America" had ever seen.[6]

Here proximity was literally everything—for the Tabernacle stood within three hundred feet of Clarendon Street Church,[7] and indeed, the Church was used for overflow and spiritual "inquiry" meetings. Both buildings were constantly in use, and Moody had myriad reasons to rely on Gordon's crucial support and leadership, not least the fact that "the Tabernacle was thronged night after night by audiences of from five to seven thousand."[8] Clearly, the challenge here was a daunting one.

As a contemporary account stated—

> Trains brought in thousands from all parts of New England… Meetings were organized…for all classes in the community that were ready to help or be helped.
>
> And at the centre of all these operations stood the Clarendon Street Church…What experiences of grace, what widening vistas of God's power, what instruction in personal religion, resulted…A new window was built into the religious life of the church…The true purpose of [its] existence began to be emphasized. Drunkards and outcasts were daily reclaimed, and brought into fellowship. Christian evidences of the best sort, evidences which had to do with the present potency of a saving Christ, were multiplied… strengthening the faith of believers.[9]

Volunteerism on a massive scale shaped the work Moody and Gordon led. More than 2,000 volunteers undertook door-to-door visitation to each of Boston's 90,000 households in March 1877. This in turn had a marked effect on public awareness and press interest.

The Boston Tabernacle meetings had become a genuine phenomenon.

Held over thirteen weeks, Moody preached more than 100 sermons— while his song leader and featured singer, Ira Sankey, sang over 300 solos.

More than one million people, men and women from all walks of life, heard them speak and sing. Some 6,000 new converts were reported.[10] Daily stenographic accounts of Moody's sermons ran in most major newspapers, other news outlets provided substantial summaries. Heretofore, as *The Boston Globe* observed, "a religious article of any length was a phenomenon…Now all the papers are brimful with religious news."[11]

Indeed, we get a rich sense of what went into these gospel gatherings from contemporary press reports. They show preparations began in early May 1876.

On the 28th of June, Moody visited Boston and "held a conference with the representatives of about three hundred churches." By mid-September, a fifty-member planning committee had been appointed, led by the Rev. Dr. E.B. Webb. On November 6, Dr. Webb could report that "the sum of thirty thousand dollars had been given or pledged for the construction of a building," something like $600,000 in modern currency. Construction began immediately, and finished by the second week of January 1877.[12]

The Boston Tabernacle was "a substantial brick edifice on Tremont Street, with eight entrances, and capable of seating about six thousand." It had an ample platform to seat about eight hundred people, in addition to the choir, together with rooms for inquirers and needs. Far from being a warehouse-type structure, it was "well lighted, warmed, and ventilated." As one observer wrote, the tabernacle presented "without, as well as within, a tasteful, neat, and inviting aspect."[13]

As workmen constructed the tabernacle, earnest prayers were being offered in churches, ministers' meetings, Christian conferences, Sunday Schools, and individual homes. "Evangelical ministers," it was said, "were united, spiritual forces were combined, and Christians, forgetting the denominational lines dividing them, held union meetings, and freely gave their talents, time, and money, to help [with] the preparations."[14]

Part of these included rehearsals for "a choir of about two thousand singers" under the direction of Dr. Eben Tourjée, a longtime friend of A.J. Gordon, and one of America's finest choral conductors and music educators. In 1873, on the establishment of Boston University, Tourjée became Dean of its College of Music. In 1867, Tourjée and Robert Goldbeck had founded The New England Conservatory of Music, which was, and remains one of the leading conservatories in the United States.

Throughout the gospel gatherings held in the Boston Tabernacle it was said, "the singing by Dr. Tourjée's large choir was grandly effective."[15]

Anticipation was palpable throughout the city as the Boston Tabernacle was dedicated on Thursday evening, January 25. Addresses were given by leading clergy: Bishop Randolph S. Foster (of the Methodist Episcopal Church), the Reverend Robert R. Meredith (the Congregationalist Minister of Phillips Church, Boston), and the Rev. Dr. E.B. Webb (of Shawmut Congregational Church).[16]

A.J. Gordon was given the honor of offering the dedicatory prayer.

One can only imagine his thoughts as gospel gatherings so long in the planning were finally about to begin. He, and Clarendon Street Church, were about to experience something extraordinary.

* * *

Even as Gordon had given the dedicatory prayer for the Boston Tabernacle, lending very public support to the gospel gatherings D.L. Moody was undertaking, many parishioners at Clarendon Street "were engaged in the supervisory, evangelistic, and supportive work of the revival." Deacon George Dexter was one of them, and he played a key role in the days ahead—that of "Chief Usher of the Tabernacle for several weeks." This meant he took responsibility for "the general operations" of the Tabernacle gatherings, along with "the seating of the thousands who thronged to the meetings daily," and "arrangements for out-of-town visitors."[17]

Gordon meanwhile, had charge of what was called "the inquiry room." There, with other volunteers, he told people who were spiritually seeking what it meant to "trust in Christ." Maria Gordon and several Clarendon Street members were also there with him, commending the hope of heaven.[18]

Gordon's responsibilities went still further. Even as he served on the Boston Tabernacle Executive Committee, he opened meetings in prayer, spoke in them, and led "prayer meetings for the grocers" of Boston. As he did, he saw something singular unfold: Clarendon Street was "so connected with the Tabernacle" that church members felt themselves a vital part of it.[19]

Thus the Tabernacle gatherings became "a turning point for the ministry of the Clarendon Street Baptist Church." And it meant the church grew substantially. By May 1877, fifty people became new members. Ninety-one people were baptized by year's end, with an additional thirty-four new members—for a total of one hundred twenty-five. This trend continued and grew. From this time, until 1895, "no less than fifty [people] were added to membership" each year.[20]

Significantly, most new members weren't from the upper middle class, as many parishioners in the church had been before this time. Recovering alcoholics, former prostitutes, with others among working class men and women—all these comprised the new membership at Clarendon Street.

Two new members held a special place in Gordon's memory, as their lives had been shattered through opium addiction. Their deliverance, amid the storied gospel gatherings of 1877, was something he never forgot—

> An opium-eater of the most desperate stamp came into Mr. Moody's evangelistic meetings in Boston in the spring of 1877. His case was one of long standing, in which the coils of habit had closed about him tighter and tighter each year—every medical help, every human remedy having utterly failed. None present will forget his pitiful cry as he rose up in the meeting, and begged to know if there was any hope for him in Christ.
>
> Prayer was offered in his behalf, and he was led to accept Jesus as his Saviour and Healer. He came the next day with the glad tidings that his appetite was gone.
>
> Mr. Moody, knowing how much more powerful is experience than assertion for proving that Christ is "mighty to save," put this man upon the platform night after night, to tell the story of his healing. It was "a palpable confirmation of the Word," not to be gainsaid, and the effect was irresistible upon the great audiences who listened.
>
> Another case was almost identical. A stranger, rising up at a revival meeting in our own church, the marks upon

his person confirming the testimony of his lips, confessed that he was a long suffering victim of the opium habit, who had spent all his living upon physicians, and was nothing bettered but rather made worse.

Here also, upon the offering of prayer and the surrender of the sufferer to Christ, the cure was instantaneous—at least, so the patient has always claimed.

Fifteen and ten years have passed since these respective experiences. The men on whom the cures were wrought are exemplary members of the church, with whom I have maintained a constant acquaintance, and they solemnly testify that from the moment of their appeal to the Great Physician they have been absolutely delivered from their former plague.[21]

Gordon, and many at Clarendon Street, saw all this as a profound blessing: broken lives and homes transformed for the better. But inevitably, the coming of these new members "caused tensions with the old guard." And it was during the height of the Boston Tabernacle meetings one wealthy deacon, Levi J. Brandish, decided to take matters into his own hands.[22]

Brandish wasn't just wealthy (which meant some in the church placed great reliance on his weekly giving), he was a powerful, long-term member, who had been a deacon for twelve years prior to A.J. Gordon's pastoral ministry. He was "a pillar of the church," and just as immovable in his likes and dislikes.[23]

From the start, Brandish "was consistently against" any changes that Gordon proposed. When he wished to make church pews free to any and all who visited, and abolish "pew rents," fees not everyone could afford— Brandish opposed him. When Gordon wished to allow congregational singing and have church members take part in worship through music, rather than listen only to a paid quartet sing—Brandish objected strongly. Brandish liked the largely upper middle class enclave Clarendon Street had been at the start of Gordon's ministry. He devoutly wished Gordon would toe the line, and not make waves. The church was meant to be a cultured setting, with pew rents (and choice seating for the highest bidder), paid quartet choirs, decorous church bazaars, and fine oyster suppers.[24]

Everything had been duly fitting as it was.

Gordon was in a trying situation. There were other leading church members who differed from Brandish, but "they urged tolerance so as not to offend him." Clarendon Street simply couldn't do without his financial support. Further, at every turn Brandish visibly and divisively turned a deaf ear to anything he might suggest.[25]

Maria Gordon remembered it all only too well.

Her husband, she said of this time, "had as severe testings of his forbearance" as any pastor ever had.[26] "In the early days of his connection with the Clarendon Street Church," she continued—

> a leading member, one of the wealthiest, and as such supposed to carry considerable influence, seemed determined to oppose every measure the pastor proposed, which was contrary to the traditions in which he had been trained.
>
> Did Dr. Gordon want an evangelist to come and visit with the people and hold extra services, [this deacon] always managed to veto any such movement. He reproved one of the officers who put "Strangers Welcome" at the end of some circulars announcing the meetings of the church.
>
> [This deacon] had evidently reversed the exhortations of the apostle James concerning the rich and the poor, for those in poor apparel received scant welcome at his hands. While other prominent members disagreed with him, they would always counsel "patience" on the pastor's part, since "it would not do to offend Brother X; he might leave the church and his financial assistance was necessary."
>
> Despairing of stemming the tide which seemed setting against him, the young pastor put the whole case in the Lord's hands, and made it a definite subject of daily prayer [that] "He would *convert* or *remove* this man."
>
> In the course of a few months, a letter of dismission was

requested by him, and it was unanimously granted without remonstrance or explanation.[27]

Only later, Maria said, did Gordon learn "the circumstances which led to this action." Deacon Brandish, who she discreetly called "Brother X," had invited "the deacons and standing committee to his house one evening." When these church leaders arrived, Brandish "there laid before them, drawn up in due form, a long list of grievances against the church administration of the pastor, with the assertion that if allowed to go on as he wanted to, the church would be wrecked in a couple of years...[He] ended with the suggestion that the pastor be asked to resign."[28] Brandish sought to get Gordon discharged, and put things back on proper course.

He was wrong.

Instead of "the favorable response which he had hoped for," the other church leaders, to a man, were greatly angered to be "brought together on any such business." They told Brandish that given his conduct, *he* "must withdraw himself, and that immediately."[29] And so, Brandish left Clarendon Street in April 1877.[30]

Maria Gordon's closing thoughts of this stormy season spoke volumes—

> The result was that the church was satisfied to have this "pillar" removed; peace was preserved, [and] the pastor was in no way involved...A new [openness] in spiritual matters was developed, when there no longer existed any hindrance to unity of action.[31]

* * *

All the while, even as the troubled episode with Deacon Brandish unfolded, the Boston Tabernacle "was thronged night after night by audiences of from five to seven thousand." As Ernest Gordon remembered, "A new window was built into the religious life of the church, letting in floods of light. The true purpose of a church's existence began to be emphasized. Drunkards and outcasts were daily reclaimed, and brought into fellowship."[32]

In the event, A.J. Gordon also recorded memories of this season of renewal, and his close collaboration with D.L. Moody. To read his recollections is to travel back in time to a Boston where gas lamps illumined city streets, and horse carriages plied its narrow thoroughfares. "In 1877," Gordon recalled—

> during Mr. Moody's meetings in Boston, there was an inquiry meeting in our church. The house was full, and Mr. Moody sent me around to find workers to help. I came upon a woman with a baby. She was anxious to find Christ; for when I approached her and asked if she wanted to be saved, she said—
>
> "That is what I came here for." I stepped over to a gentleman on the front seat, a fine-looking man, and said,
>
> "Are you a Christian?"
>
> "Yes, sir," he answered.
>
> "I want you to go over there and talk to an inquirer."
>
> "I never talked to an inquirer," he replied.
>
> "But you are a Christian?"
>
> "Yes."
>
> "Here is a woman just ready to be led to Christ."
>
> "Excuse me, I should not know what to say to her."
>
> Well, because I could not get him to go, I went over myself and sat down beside the woman. But the baby was so restless that she could not give me her attention. The man kept watching us, and saw the situation.
>
> By and by he crept softly down and gave the baby some sweets, and took her in his arms and carried her to the other side of the church and held her for an hour, while I led the woman to Christ.
>
> He found that, if he could not lead a soul to Christ, he could hold the baby while someone else did. I think a special blessing rested upon that work; for not only was the mother saved, but that little girl came to Christ when she was twelve years old, and I haven't a more [dedicated] Christian in my church than that baby has grown to be.[33]

This vignette was much like one D.L. Moody recalled from gospel gatherings in England. As he told the story—

> When I was in London, one of the wealthiest young men of the city, an only son of [a] leading London banker…a young man who was coming into possession of millions, a student at Cambridge University, felt that he could not go into the inquiry meetings and [volunteer] in that way, but he went out to a cabman one night and said: "I will pay you your regular fee by the hour, if you will go in and hear Mr. Moody preach. I will act as cabman, and take care of your horse."
>
> On that cold, bleak night, that gentleman stood by the cabman's horse, and let that cabman go and hear the Gospel. He was gone about two hours…all the while that young man stood there, confessing Christ silently. [34]

As for happenings during the Boston Tabernacle meetings themselves, one afternoon, February 15, 1877, was well remembered. It was then Moody preached "a very practical sermon on Faith." Along the way, he gave a flash of his famous sense of humor, involving his good friend A.J. Gordon.

"Some," Moody began, "say they're so constituted they cannot believe God. Away with that! *What's your constitution got to do with it?*"

He then turned to Gordon, seated nearby, and said with a sly wink—

"Suppose Dr. Gordon here asked me to take dinner with him tomorrow, and I said, "Doctor, I'd like to, but I don't know that I can.""

To this, Dr. Gordon might say, "Why, are you busy?"

"No," I reply, "but I don't know that I feel just right."

"Don't feel just right! What do you mean?" says Dr. Gordon.

"Don't you want to come to dinner with me?"

"Oh, yes!" I say, "*but I am so constituted I can't believe you want me to come.*"

At this, the audience broke out in laughter.

"Ah!" Moody said quickly, "you laugh. But yet that is what people do when they say they're so constituted that they can't believe the Eternal God."

"God invites you to His feast," he concluded, "and it is a real invitation."[35]

Amid such moments, and many lives touched in the Boston Tabernacle gatherings, new members, as stated above, came to Clarendon Street Church in large numbers. So a committee was formed "to look after and welcome strangers." Yet when cards stating *"Strangers Welcome"* were printed, some "elite members" balked. Still, "the momentum for change had already begun," and the actions of Deacon Brandish notwithstanding, those who opposed the coming of new members decreased over time.[36]

Over time was indeed the key phrase, and until things turned course for the better, Gordon's reserves of perseverance and patience were constantly tried.

At the height of the Boston Tabernacle meetings, the Clarendon Church membership presented the Standing Committee with a motion to open unoccupied pews "to those of the church who could not afford to pay for the same." All too conveniently, the motion was "lost in committee."[37]

By 1882, as Sunday morning crowds continued to grow, another motion passed, requesting that "the seats in our house of worship shall be retained for the holders until 25 minutes of 11 only, on Sunday, and that, if not occupied by that time, they shall be fully at the disposal of the ushers for the seating of Strangers." It failed, and ownership of the pews remained. Meanwhile, at the same meeting, a further request was introduced to make pews in the side galleries of the church "entirely free to the public." But here the Standing Committee stood in the way again, voting that it was "inexpedient" to do so.[38]

In a word, "resistance to free pews ran deep in the life of the church." Ultimately, "the battle Gordon waged to free the pews lasted for twenty-three years."

Yet he would not be dissuaded.

Finally in 1892, a full fifteen years after the Boston Tabernacle meetings, the church voted at last "to make the pews free, and raise the necessary income through voluntary subscriptions."[39]

* * *

Resistance from yet another quarter also reared its head when Gordon, who found his pastoral duties ever increasing with so many new members, requested an assistant. Quite understandably, he felt Clarendon Street "had grown beyond what he considered manageable for one person."[40]

Once more, the Standing Committee denied his request. But Gordon was resolved, and not above thinking "outside-the-box" when it came to a solution.

He reasoned that just because the Standing Committee said *they* wouldn't hire an assistant, nothing prevented *him* from doing so, and paying this assistant "from his own salary."[41]

He did just that.

This set down a curious marker, yet church leadership didn't take exception. How could they really? Gordon was shouldering the expense after all. And perhaps a growing sense of just embarrassment came into play, for "after a few months" the Standing Committee "officially employed his assistant."[42]

Gordon's resolve in this matter could not have been better rewarded, nor could he have made a better choice than the man he hired: John A. McElwain.

A man of remarkable gifts and abilities, McElwain felt "a call to the ministry" in his youth, but a period of poor health prevented it. Instead this gentle man had, once his condition improved, taken a lucrative management position in business, where he flourished. In time he felt a call to ministry once more, and left his career in business "to learn about Christian work as an assistant to Pastor W.W. Boyd of the First Baptist Church of Charlestown, Massachusetts."[43]

McElwain's thirty-five year association with Clarendon Street Church began in 1877, the very year of the transformative Boston Tabernacle gospel gatherings. He strove to lighten Gordon's workload by undertaking home visitation for the sick, assisting the poor, sharing his faith among them, and handling tasks more strictly administrative in nature.[44]

Then crucially, in later years, McElwain "superintended the daily operations" of the Boston Missionary Training School, founded by A.J. Gordon—about which more will be said below.

But here it will suffice to say that had Gordon not persevered in his resolve to hire an assistant—with or without the Clarendon Street Standing Committee's permission—many things in the years to come would have been decidedly different.

* * *

As for the Boston Tabernacle gatherings that prompted McElwain's hiring, they "continued into 1878 and beyond." After the autumn and winter services of 1877, "evangelist D.W. Whittle came in February 1878 and Moody and Sankey returned for a short series in March."[45]

During "traditionally slow summer months," Gordon organized special services, aided by evangelist George F. Pentecost and musician George C. Stebbins. McElwain and Clarendon Street members now continually visited "the surrounding district and personally, or by card" invited families to attend church meetings. The huge sanctuary was full every evening. By 1883, a season of spiritual renewal came once more to Boston. The church "welcomed ninety-seven members that year."[46]

* * *

Long after the Boston Tabernacle gatherings became part of Boston's storied spiritual history, A.J. Gordon's friendship with D.L. Moody deepened. In time, Gordon's name became closely tied to the most hallowed place in Northfield: the high hill called "Round Top." For many years, hundreds of students—from places like Harvard, Yale, and Brown—grew to know Round Top well.

Gordon spoke to them often there.

"Round Top," recalled J.W. Chapman, "has ever been a place of blessing. Each evening, when the Northfield Summer Conferences are in session, as the day is dying out of the sky, students gather to talk of the things concerning the Kingdom. The old haystack at Williamstown figures no more conspicuously in the history of missions than Round Top figures in the lives of a countless number of Christians throughout the whole world."[47]

Here Chapman's thoughts grew poignant.

"A.J. Gordon, of sainted memory," gave many telling addresses from the crest of Round Top, which overlooks the beautiful Pioneer Valley—further on to mountains that edge the horizon.

One evening, Chapman said, Dr. Gordon "spoke of the Lord's return" and just as he finished, he stood for a moment, his kind face aglow with the power of his theme. Then, looking toward the west, he spoke of the Savior, saying—

"I wish He might come now."[48]

Chapter Thirteen
Among Collegians

At 2 p.m. the first public meeting of the day was begun. The chief features [included] an address by the Rev. A.J. Gordon, D.D., of Boston. Dr. Gordon [cited] the Epistles of Timothy and Titus, taking as his subject "The Word of God and the Man of God." The address was very interesting, and an unusually large number of students were present.[1]

—The Harvard Crimson,
23 February 1885

In 1884, "a door to new opportunities and new activities" was opened for A.J. Gordon.[2] Dr. James McCosh, the President of Princeton, had heard of his work among collegians during the Northfield Summer Conferences, and wrote with a request that he visit the university, "to undertake special religious work among the students."[3] Gordon agreed.

Yet such an invitation, though most welcome, had a challenge.

President McCosh had chosen to make these gatherings compulsory, and many students resented being "packed off *en masse* to college chapel." Any speaker, however gifted or engaging, had to overcome this. So A.J. Gordon, age forty-seven, rose to address a gathering of "discontented, angry youths," compelled to hear an "unknown preacher from Boston," instead of the time off they'd looked forward to. In a letter home, Gordon described the daunting reception he met with—

Princeton, N. J.,
February 4, 1884

My Dear Wife:

I will give you a little account of the work, thanking God for what He has graciously given. The first day was the toughest experience I have ever had. The students have been free, hitherto, to come to the prayer-day services or not—they have largely chosen not to come—till this year their attendance was made compulsory.

My first address was to this compelled crowd, many of them disgusted that their holiday had been turned into a holy day. They sat before me facing at all angles, ogling and squirming and showing plainly enough that they did not propose to be solemnized.

I was never so taken off my pins in my life. I sweat and floundered about and made an utter fizzle. All the grave and dignified faculty sat ranged on either side. I came home and dried my clothes and went back to the evening service with fear and trembling. That was not compulsory, and I got on much better. Still, I was so discouraged that I determined to start for home on Friday morning.

But I feel that the Lord overruled my rash purpose. A large delegation of students, who appreciated exactly the trial under which I had labored, came to see me, and insisted that I should stay. I consented, and began to visit the young men at their rooms. Sunday morning I preached again before students and faculty. There was a great change; no compulsion, but all were out and very attentive. In the afternoon again [there was a] deeply solemn meeting.

The good old president arose and made a most solemn appeal, saying, "Young men, you have heard the gospel to-day so plainly declared that you are without excuse if you do not accept Christ."

In the evening the students who were Christians

planned for meetings in their rooms, inviting those in their respective halls to come in. I started at seven o'clock to visit these meetings. I found them all crowded.

In the first one I struck, ten rose at my invitation to indicate their purpose to follow Christ. I went from building to building among the meetings, finding in almost every one those who were ready to stand up. I visited six of these, and I judge there must have been twenty who confessed Christ in different rooms.

My reception among the students was most cordial and affectionate. I think the Lord has given me their hearts, and my first discouragement has been turned into great joy.

I have addressed the theological students, and have met many of them in private for prayer and conference. A good work has certainly begun. I shall stay to-day at least to see it furthered. It has been a peculiar and valuable experience.

Much love to you, and to all. The Lord bless you. Pray, all of you, that I may not labor in vain, or run in vain...[4]

The effect Gordon had on these students may be gathered from notes taken at the time by a member of the senior class at Princeton. This was almost certainly Robert Wilder (of whom more will be said below), though Gordon's son Ernest, who published these notes, did not name their author.[5]

This unidentified Princetonian had written—

The beautiful Marquand Chapel was filled with students, professors, people from the town, and students from the theological seminary. The sermon was excellent... but [Dr. Gordon] was far from being himself. I remember very distinctly, in talking with him several years later regarding that service, he said it was one of the most trying experiences of his life...

In spite of the earnest request that he stay and continue the good work which had sprung up among the students during his brief visit, he felt obliged to return to [Boston]. For the next week or two we carried on special religious services with some degree of success; but finally it was decided that we must have Dr. Gordon return.

At our earnest solicitation, indorsed by [President] McCosh, he came back and was with us for perhaps ten days. He preached each evening in Murray Hall, and from nine till eleven o'clock went from dormitory to dormitory to conduct prayer and inquiry meetings. All the students that could be induced to attend were summoned from the section of the hall in which the meeting was held—a dozen, twenty, or more. A great many in those meetings made a profession of faith in Christ...

Those who are familiar with such matters know how hard it is to suit an audience of undergraduates...The professors as well as the students were pleased. Professor [George Lansing] Raymond, of the chair of oratory, said the quality of Dr. Gordon's voice was unsurpassed; indeed, he had heard but one speaker who equaled him in this respect.

* * *

These meetings proved a stirring time of spiritual awakening. Dr. McCosh, Princeton's president, "was in most hearty sympathy with the work." He was present at many of the meetings, and "always urged their importance upon the students."[6]

When each evening service was over, Gordon often went to Dr. McCosh's house for overnight lodging. "Of course you will live with me while in Princeton," McCosh had kindly written when he had invited Gordon to campus.

And Gordon, for his part, remembered—

When I returned to the president's house at the close of these midnight meetings Dr. McCosh would invariably be found waiting, with a warm fire on the hearthstone and a table spread with refreshments, always eager to hear what new names had been added to the list of [spiritual] inquirers.

There could hardly have been greater joy in heaven over repenting sinners than there was in his heart as the names were read to him from my note-book night after night; and then he would talk them over and lift them up before the Lord, that [God] would by his Spirit make thorough work in their hearts...[7]

What of the Princeton senior who recorded all these events?

He thought them the more noteworthy, as Dr. McCosh "had absolutely no gift as an evangelist." He was, rather, "wholly lacking in that tact, grace, and delicacy which one must possess" to undertake such meetings as Dr. Gordon led.[8]

Still, McCosh did what he could.

Frequently, at the close of a meeting, he had "something to say by way of commendation of the work," and Dr. Gordon.[9] Indeed, he often "seemed unable to find words to express his appreciation" for Gordon as a preacher. With his broad Scottish accent, which for many was "well-nigh unintelligible," McCosh would say—

"Dr. Gourdon is the looveliest mon I iver had in me house. And if I iver h'ard the gospel preached in me life, it has been from the lips of Dr. Gourdon."[10]

* * *

In this venerable academic setting, A.J. Gordon never had a finer hour.

The religious awakening here "lasted a number of weeks," and was soon assisted by "some of the most noted preachers."[11] Among these clergymen were "Drs. John Hall and Charles Cuthbert Hall, of New York, Drs. Pierson and Mutchmore, of Philadelphia, and Professors Hodge, Patton, and Paxton," of Princeton Theological Seminary.[12]

But none of these fine and venerable speakers, the Princeton chronicler said, not even D.L. Moody, "who had been at the college some years before," was as well received as Gordon had been.[13]

* * *

In many ways, this era of Gordon's life rightly symbolized his work more generally among collegians. In later years, over and above his role in the Princeton meetings, he spoke many times at Yale, Amherst, Rutgers, Mount Holyoke, Williams, and his alma mater, Brown University— "always with great acceptance"—and in several of these colleges, he "conducted a series of religious meetings" with results much like those at Princeton.[14]

Nor did Gordon's work among college students cease there.

"At the Northfield college conferences," one writer said, "his influence upon young men was always marked." And Robert Wilder, "the original and most prominent leader in the Student Volunteer Movement"—later of international renown—declared in a letter that "to A.J. Gordon and to J. Hudson Taylor" he was more deeply indebted "for the development of [my] spiritual life than to any others, living or dead."[15]

* * *

Harvard was yet another university setting where Gordon was welcomed.

In February 1885 he was featured, along with Phillips Brooks (the Rector of Boston's prestigious Trinity Church), at a gathering of over one hundred students for the Third Annual Meeting of the College Young Men's Christian Association at Harvard. Farewell exercises for this event were held in Harvard's Holden Chapel. These gatherings were described as "interesting and profitable, and earnest…tending to the advancement of the work in which the associations were engaged."[16]

And, in March 1886, *The Harvard Crimson* reported: "the Fourth Annual Meeting of the Young Men's Christian Association of the New England colleges was held at Brown University last Friday, Saturday and Sunday. Twenty colleges and academies were represented, by about one hundred and thirty delegates. Some twenty-five men were present from Harvard."[17]

As he had been one year earlier, A.J. Gordon was a featured speaker at this gathering, and he then gave a noteworthy address "on the use of the Bible in Christian work."[18] Among these collegians, he clearly had fruitful times of ministry.

* * *

Sometimes, things otherwise lost to history can be recovered.

One seemingly typical alumni letter published by Harvard's Class of 1877 showed how this may be so. Its story bears an eloquent connection to the life and ministry of A.J. Gordon.

Nathan Harding Harriman was born in Prospect, Maine—a small village in Waldo County, along the west bank of the Penobscot River. Following his graduation from Harvard in 1877, Harriman was Sub-master of Brookline High School. He studied theology at Bangor Theological Seminary, and served as the pastor of three churches, among them The Pilgrim Congregational Church of Providence, Rhode Island. He was there for three years, from 1886 to 1889.

No written record offers confirmation, but it was almost certainly in this setting that Harriman met A.J. Gordon: for Gordon frequently traveled to Providence in his capacity as a Trustee of Brown University— and visits to his wife Maria's family often took place there as well.

What is known from Harriman's posting to his Harvard Class Secretary is that he "became a Baptist, and was baptized in May 1890, by Rev. A.J. Gordon, D.D., of Boston." Several years later Harriman's son, Frederick Gordon Harriman, was "named for Dr. Gordon."[19] And in time, Frederick Gordon Harriman also graduated from Harvard, with the Class of 1915.

Throughout his childhood, Frederick Harriman was doubtless told many times why the surname Gordon was chosen for his middle name. It was a treasured part of family lore, no less than the reasons why Nathan Harriman left the Congregational tradition where he'd been ordained to become a Baptist. He had a profound sense of indebtedness to A.J. Gordon as a spiritual mentor.

Still later, when the *Harvard Alumni Bulletin* published Harriman's obituary, in October 1922, it revealed some telling vignettes from the years after A.J. Gordon became Harriman's friend and counselor.

As an evangelist, Harriman "travelled extensively," from the east coast to places as far west as Bozeman, Montana—where he became a "frontier pastor" for some time in that town's First Baptist Church.[20] Like his fellow Harvard alumnus, Theodore Roosevelt, Harriman heard a compelling call to the west. It changed his life, and the lives of others whom he met.

That Harriman ever went west as a Baptist clergyman, or touched people's lives there, could be traced directly to A.J. Gordon's role in his life. This story was one instance, among many, of how Gordon's ministry among students at Harvard, or collegians from other universities, had far-reaching influence.

Chapter Fourteen
Athens and the Arena

As early as 1867, the [Boston YMCA] obtained a permit from the mayor, and held open-air meetings on the Common. They were usually careful to obtain the best clerical talent in the city and elsewhere, and conducted their services in a manner creditable to religion and good government. There never was any disturbance. The Association had no trouble in obtaining permits until 1882, when their application was denied. They applied in 1883, and were refused. In 1884 they applied, and The Committee on the Common did not deign to make any answer.[1]

—Rev. M.R. Deming

On Wednesday, May 20, 1885, Dr. Adoniram Judson Gordon, a trustee of Ivy League bastion Brown University, and for sixteen years pastor of "the prestigious Clarendon Street pulpit," was arrested for preaching on Boston Common.[2]

His arrest had not been mere happenstance.[3]

And a storm of controversy erupted.

For several years, events had been leading to this.

Near the epicenter was the Evangelical Ministers' Association of Boston, which had grown increasingly alarmed that "an obscure city ordinance" was being cited by "The Committee on the Common" to refuse permits for open-air preaching—a long tradition traced to the

1700s and sermons by George Whitefield. Gordon knew and revered "more than a hundred years of unchallenged custom."[4] For fifteen years, he had regularly conducted open-air preaching. His parishioners, and people beyond Clarendon Street, knew this well. So when the Boston YMCA, urged by the Evangelical Ministers' Association, invited Gordon to preach on Boston Common, he "willingly accepted."[5]

He had been asked to engage in civil disobedience. He agreed.

*   *   *

The rationale of the Boston YMCA, a "well-established organization with impeccable Christian and middle-class credentials,"[6] and the Evangelical Ministers' Association, was "to test the authority of the city government to prevent preaching by responsible parties."[7] As for the "obscure city ordinance" in question, it read: "no person shall, except by permission of the appropriate committee, deliver a sermon, lecture, address or discourse on the Common or other public grounds."[8]

The Boston YMCA and Evangelical Ministers' Association contended that "the ordinance requiring a permit was intended to give the city government power *to regulate* speaking on the Common, but not absolutely to prohibit."[9]

*   *   *

When Gordon arrived at Boston Municipal Court on Thursday morning, May 21, he, along with two others who had been arrested— H.L. Hastings, the editor of *The Christian* magazine, and W.H. Davis, superintendent of a mission in Boston's North End—were met outside the court by a thronging crowd, "reported to be between four thousand and five thousand."[10] True, those who had gathered were "principally of the middle-class, well-dressed and well behaved," but they were no less outraged over what had unfolded.[11] They felt the issue was one of free speech, permit or no permit required.

As this hearing began, Judge George Z. Adams was chagrined to see a noted civic leader in his courtroom. He stated that "the by-law concerning a permit was *never intended to prevent responsible clergymen like Dr. Gordon* from obtaining one, but only to preclude objectionable persons; and that any responsible person could obtain a permit."[12] However, the Boston YMCA believed this only "showed that The Committee on the Common had used the ordinance for three years as a means to invest themselves with arbitrary power."[13]

After the hearing, the Boston YMCA paid Gordon's fine, and immediately asked for a permit to hold services on Boston Common for the remainder of the summer. Yet here, another setback quickly arose, for as Gordon's long-time friend at the YMCA, the Rev. M.R. Deming wrote—

> [the permit wasn't] forthcoming. I inquired of a member of The Committee on the Common why we did not receive it, and he said that we had stirred the city up so much, and got the newspapers down on the committee, that the probability was, that the committee would not grant the permit.
>
> In my capacity as general secretary of the Boston Y.M.C.A., I engaged the services of a highly esteemed member of The Boston Bar, and authorized him to take all legal measures necessary to enforce Judge Adams's ruling on the committee on the Common. This, or something else, produced an immediate and favorable response from the committee.[14]

Gordon's conduct in this episode, amid arrest and heavy-handed treatment by The Committee on the Common, showed strength of character and conviction. He had undertaken open-air outreach among Bostonians before—he would do it again. Though the risk he had run in this act of civil disobedience had been less than it might have been—no confinement in jail, and only a fine to be paid—a powerful and very public point had been made. Thousands had rallied around it. The Committee on the Common took note of that, getting far more than they bargained on by way of public outcry against their actions.

And Clarendon Street Church supported their pastor wholeheartedly. More than a decade after his arrest, a study of Boston's South End reported that the church was still busily engaged in "systematic house to house visitation," holding meetings in "wharves and cheap lodging houses," and "carrying tracts and flowers to the sick in hospitals." The church also, according to one historian, "found missionary minded Protestant allies across the city of Boston." Throughout the summer of 1885, a veritable legion of open-air preachers went into parks, beaches, and urban neighborhoods. Beyond this, during the 1880s and 1890s, they set up "gospel tents," held an evangelists' conference at Crescent Beach, and sent a steady array of preachers to Boston Common, "often in knowing defiance of the city ordinance." The Committee on the Common took no action against them.[15]

Gordon's role in making a principled public stand was well taken.

* * *

But not all that unfolded in 1885 was as contentious or taxing.

Gordon's duties as editor of *The Watchword*, which he'd founded in 1878 as "a Christian monthly," gave him the opportunity to write and reflect on many things of interest. By 1892, *The Watchword*, with offices at 120 Tremont Street, had a fine circulation for a regional city periodical, with 2,850 subscribers.[16]

As he crafted each issue of *The Watchword* for the press, Gordon introduced choice excerpts from writers he admired, under the heading "Words of the Wise." This recurring feature of the magazine was a window on the breadth of his reading, and his respect for authors of many Christian traditions, past and contemporary.

Through four issues of *The Watchword*, for example, Gordon cited Canon Edward Hoare (Church of England), C.H. Spurgeon (Baptist), François Fénelon (Catholic), François de Sales (Catholic), Thomas Boston (Scottish Presbyterian), Augustus Toplady (Church of England), and Thomas Manton and Thomas Brooks (both Puritans). As for Gordon's writing itself, he typically prepared at least two full-page articles for each issue of *The Watchword*, often three. Each contribution offered a chance to speak from his wide reading—namely his familiarity with church history, art, music, ancient cultures, and "divinity" (or older religious writing).

In the May 1885 issue, Gordon spoke of the complementarity of faith and reason, yet noting the distinct benefits each could bestow—a brief, cogent foray in the realm of apologetics. "Faith and demonstration," Gordon said—

> stand at quite the opposite poles. It is the highest triumph of reason to prove a thing true because it is logical: it is the highest achievement of faith to believe a thing true because it is written. And yet faith and demonstration are friends, not foes. A strong belief in the truth of a given proposition does much to help one in demonstrating it; and an incontestable proof goes far to strengthen the faith.
>
> "We walk by faith, and not by sight," says the Scripture.
>
> But a glimpse of permitted sight now and then is vastly helpful for strengthening one's faith. It is like a burst of sunshine which enables the mariner to take an observation by the heavenly bodies, who has been sailing many days by the compass.[17]

Elsewhere, Gordon turned to St. Augustine to expound John chapter 1, verse 16: *"And of His fullness have all we received, and grace for grace."*

He began with a literal rendering of this verse from the original Greek, saying: "From His fullness have all we received," the words mean exactly. We have *all* received of His fullness, but we have not received *all of His* fullness. How could we, with our narrow and limited capacity?"[18] Here, to explain his meaning, Gordon turned to the sage of early African Christianity and walked shores of profundity—

> St. Augustine was walking on the seashore in earnest thought concerning the Trinity. He saw a child playing with its little cup; and taking it and filling it with water from the sea, he said, "Can I dip up the whole ocean in this cup? Neither can I comprehend the infinite with my finite understanding."
>
> That is true; and yet it contains a double illustration.
>
> The cup-full which he dipped did contain all the ocean in miniature; that is to say, all the constituents were there.

Everything that is in the sea, the salt, the oxygen, the hydrogen, was in that cup. And so it is written, "He that believeth on the Son hath eternal life"—hath it, that is, in its nature and substance, though not yet in its fullness.

This explains what is so hard to comprehend. "Hath eternal life!" How can the finite heart contain the infinite? How can the mortal hold the immortal in its embrace? It can hold it only in germ [or seed], in principle…[19]

Gordon also wrote about consecration, or living wholly and unreservedly to God. "If we want to be consecrated," he said—

if we want to be useful, if we want to bring glory to God, we must learn from the Master the true secret. We have but one heart, and two worlds cannot fill it at the same time. Give ourselves wholly to God, and he will give himself wholly to us. Every self-denial, every act of humiliation, every yielding-up of selfish desires and will, means so much more of the indwelling of the Spirit, even as every indenture of the coast means so much fullness of the incoming tide.[20]

Gordon's gift for a brief, lissome phrase was also shown in *The Watchword,* as when he wrote the following line for an article published the May 1885 issue: "Mutual burden-bearing is the true secret of strength and fellowship in the Church of Jesus Christ."[21] So too, the light of creation led him to say, with fine concision: "No power or might of man can sweep the stars from the sky, or blot the sun from the heavens, or efface the splendid landscape from the universe."[22]

Yet Gordon was versatile as well, moving with facility from such moments of brief wisdom to more extended passages, rich with erudition and devotion. Writing in July 1885, he showed this through a long reflection on the place of petition, and the mystic truth that prayer "moves the hand which moves the world."[23]

Why should we pray? Gordon asked. "Can the finite move the Infinite? Can the human will bend the Divine? It is sometimes urged by those who question the propriety of prayer."[24]

Thus setting the scene, he moved to the heart of the matter—

> We answer that the relation of the human and the Divine is mutual.
>
> God's willingness to give is exercised through our willingness to receive; and, in the order of divine providence, the Lord needs the action of our will just as much as we need the action of His will. In the old-fashioned watch there is the main-spring and the hair-spring. The hair-spring does not move the main-spring, but is moved by it. And yet the main-spring depends on the hair-spring to take off the power that was stored up in it. By tick after tick of this little spring, the motion that was coiled up in the great central spring is released, and communicated to the machinery.
>
> So we say our will does not move God's will: it is moved by it. At the same time, God's will is dependent on the submission and choice of our will, in order that He may bless us and give us the things which we need.
>
> And this is what prayer is. It is the expression of our will, our desire, our consent, concerning the things which our Father in heaven is willing to give us.[25]

Metaphors inspired by the sea also guided Gordon's pen, as here, when he spoke of love and its ultimate source—

> We can only give back to God that which is His own.
>
> The river hastening on to the sea, is returning to its source. We say, indeed, that its source is the mountain spring. But, in truth, the mists and vapors from the ocean make the spring. So it is God's love that creates ours; and God's choice of us, that is the spring of our choice of Him.[26]

With stirring passages like these, it was little wonder *The Watchword* became welcome reading for thousands in Boston, and also places "from many parts of the world."[27] It was rich things of faith, taught by a learned and compelling writer.

Chapter Fifteen
Toward a Distant Shore

May 26, 1888 – Saturday. Our first day at sea has been exceptionally pleasant. Though the mists were drizzling when we started, in less than an hour they cleared away; the sun shone with delightful warmth, tempering the cool breeze, and the sea has been as smooth as Boston Harbor...[1]

—Maria Gordon

In 1888, when A.J. and Maria Gordon took ship from Boston for England to attend The London Centenary Conference on Foreign Missions, they were given a fine and festive send off.

"The long demonstration of friends at our departure," Maria Gordon told her diary, "was quite overwhelming." They received "a most lavish bouquet of roses, tied with a broad white ribbon," and were moved that "hosts of friends came down to have their adieus."[2] Anticipation fairly filled the air, as a steamship journey then held a romance all its own. It was the eve of the great steamship era, one that could boast comfort and speed for overseas travel unheard of just a few years before.

Their ship was the *S.S. Cephalonia,* a Cunard Line steamship built in 1882. Four hundred thirty feet in length, and nearly fifty feet wide, she was typical of the transition from sailing vessels to steamships, with one steam funnel and three masts. As the first vessel built on the Mersey for The Cunard Company, she was then the largest ever launched from a Liverpool yard.[3]

A.J. and Maria Gordon, with their fellow passengers, must have marveled to see the *Cephalonia* moored dockside in Boston. There was so much to see, and take in, aboard this marvel of modern sailing.

The ship was substantial, yet it had "much of the clipper as well as of the carrier in her lines." Then too, the *Cephalonia* could berth some 1,500 passengers for a voyage. Barque rigged and straight stemmed, she had "wide alleyways under the promenade deck, open to seaward." And given "her immense proportions," it was said the ship "handled like a yacht." As with her sister ship, the *Pavonia,* she could easily maintain "a speed of 14 knots an hour," quite a feat for this time.[4]

Pride of the ship's interior was its dining saloon, "on the lower deck forward of the engines," which extended the entire width of the vessel, and was 32 feet long. It held five great tables, each of which ran fore and aft, with revolving chairs. Saloon panels and ceiling were made "of the handsomest polished woods."[5] Maple, walnut, rosewood were largely used for panelings and pilasters, with white and gold on the ceiling. Throughout "the want and requirements of passengers" had been carefully studied, and "the comforts of a first-class hotel" were to be found on board.[6]

An aperture graced the dining saloon ceiling, and let down light through a stained glass window in the hurricane deck. A companionway led from the saloon to the upper deck, where passengers could enter the music parlor, or drawing room. This was elaborately furnished, and from it, one could look down into the dining saloon. The music parlor had an upright piano,[7] and one imagines the Gordons, loving music as they did, would have found this most appealing. Likely they often listened to selections performed on this fine instrument.

As to accommodations, the staterooms, "nearly all aft of the saloon," were "roomy, well lighted and ventilated." Several companionways went from different areas of the passenger rooms to the upper and hurricane decks.[8] This last deck, some 228 feet long, made "an excellent promenade for cabin passengers."

Lighting throughout the ship was provided "by the Swan electric light." Each state room had "one of these lamps, which can be turned on or off according to the will of the occupants."[9]

Modern amenities indeed.

* * *

On May 27, the "first Sunday at sea," A.J. Gordon began writing a travelogue letter describing the voyage for his parishioners at Clarendon Street Church.

"I send you greetings today, across the waves," he wrote, "for 'though taken from you for a short time in presence, not in heart,' my thoughts go out to you on this first Lord's Day upon the deep. Beautiful weather greeted us on rising this morning; and after breakfast we were called to worship."[10]

According to long-held custom, one of the officers aboard the *Cephalonia* "read the English Church Service," Gordon said, but "few chose to attend." Sadly, it was a rather staid affair, as "the ordinary ritual of the Episcopal Church" was gone through "in a mechanical way," and "the officer read it with little animation.[11]

Still, one prayer, Gordon wrote, had been "so appropriate and beautiful," that he reproduced it in his letter. At its conclusion, he said, "our hearts responded to it with a most hearty amen."[12] The prayer read—

> Almighty God, who art the confidence of all the ends of the earth and of them that are afar off upon the sea; under whose protection we are alike secure in every place, and without whose providence we can nowhere be in safety; look down in mercy upon us...who are called to see Thy wonders upon the deep...Let Thine everlasting arms be underneath and round about us.
>
> Preserve us in all dangers, support us in all trials, conduct us speedily and safely on our voyage, and bring us in peace and comfort to our desired haven. Be pleased to watch over the members of our families and all the beloved friends whom we have left behind. Relieve our minds from all anxiety on their account by the blessèd persuasion that Thou carest for them...
>
> Grant that our souls may be defended from whatever ills or perils may encompass them; and that abiding steadfast

in the faith we may be enabled to a pass through the waves and storms of this uncertain world, that finally, we may come to the land of everlasting rest through Jesus Christ our Lord. Amen.

Very early the next morning, Monday, May 28, Gordon told his Clarendon Street readers how he had been "a little restless," and couldn't sleep. "I rose at two," he said, "and walked the deck until the sun rose out of the waters." Deeply moved by this "magnificent sight," he recounted his impressions of it all—

> How many suggestive lessons we may learn, even on the sea.
>
> At four o'clock I heard the stroke of a bell, and then the cry sounded out by the officer on the bridge, and taken up by man after man along the whole length of the ship, "All's well."
>
> Asking a sailor what it meant, he told me that it was the third watch of the night, and that the cry "All's well" is the watchword which the men on duty give to indicate that they are awake and at their posts.
>
> This gave an excellent text from which to preach a few words to my informant on *"Blessèd are those servants whom the Lord, when He cometh, shall find watching. And if He shall come in the second watch, or come in the third watch, and find them so, blessed are those servants."*[13]

These were words Gordon had shared often with his parishioners, and they seemed to gain added meaning aboard a ship at sea.

"Three days out," he continued, "we encountered, contrary to the season, quite tempestuous weather, which lasted four days." Many were sick, he said, but he and Maria "by the good favor of God...were both entirely exempt...enabling us to cheer and help our fellow-voyagers."[14]

On the second Sunday at sea, June 3, there was "a most interesting service among the steerage and intermediate passengers."[15] Many nations and languages were represented.

"We found," Gordon said, "many men and women of warm and earnest evangelical piety. Australians, Americans, Swedes, Norwegians, Welch, Scotch and English were there, a goodly company, who took up *Nearer, My God, to Thee* and *Jesus, Lover of my Soul,* and made it sound out grandly over the waves."[16]

It was, he continued, "two o'clock when we held our service, but, looking at Boston time, I found it was just the hour that morning worship was commencing in our own dear church in Boston. And so, while praying and preaching with others, I was holding service with you."[17]

Gordon then found his thoughts ran to scripture…

"The sea has calmed," he wrote, "the waves are at rest, and the peace of God is on the deep." And he marveled at the idea that "the Psalmist, *though never at sea,* so far as we know, should yet have given so wondrous a picture."[18]

The next morning, Monday, June 4th, brought "an incident of rare interest." As Gordon and his fellow passengers "were coming out from breakfast," word was received of a ship in distress. He described it in present tense, and vivid detail—

> The great throbbing heart of the *Cephalonia* stops beating, and a ship is dimly visible with sails torn and two masts gone. A boat is lowered, and four men are seen rowing toward us. They come alongside; a rope is thrown out to them, and, while holding fast to our vessel, the spokesman pours out his tale of distress, though in an unknown tongue.
>
> It is a Norwegian ship, stormbound and delayed for many weeks; short of provisions, and for three days having had nothing to eat. Among the steerage passengers is one who can interpret. Then our great steamer gives out stores, a cask of bread, a barrel of water, a barrel of pork, a barrel of biscuit, meat, great loaves of bread, tossed down, and bags of fruit and vegetables, till the little boat is full, and the grateful sailors row away.
>
> The flag on the torn ship makes a signal of gratitude, the sailors wave their caps, and cheers go up for all on

board, and we move on: and I find myself singing as the ship disappears on the horizon:

> *"Let the lower lights be burning,*
> *Send a gleam across the wave,*
> *Some poor fainting, struggling seaman*
> *You may rescue, you may save."*[19]

This incident, etched in memory, brought Gordon a profound insight about the whole of life—the voyage, as it were, we all undertake.

"God make us all as ready," he said, "to lend help to our suffering, storm-tossed fellow voyagers on the ocean of life, as our good ship was to aid these."[20]

Within a day of making port, there could be few things more meaningful as a close to his pastoral letter for Clarendon Street Church. "All are getting ready to send off their letters," he said, "so I close. The Lord be with all, and cause His face to shine upon you."[21]

* * *

Concurrently, Maria Gordon had been writing eloquent letters homeward. One of them, written "300 Miles out at sea," was dated Sunday, May 27. Addressed to her children in Boston, hers was a richly detailed, narrative counterpart to what her husband shared in his pastoral letter. We have," she said—

> just finished a delightful service in the steerage. Papa went down in the cabin to speak to about 75 or more down there, while Dr. Pengra and I led the singing of Gospel hymns, and gathered a large company from the second cabin, steerage, and forecastle on the foreword deck, till he could come and address them.
>
> It was a most interesting audience and many sweet Christian faces, testified by their expression and by voice of their sympathy with the hymns sung and the word spoken.

There was the usual English service of Morning Prayer conducted by the doctor of the ship, in the dining room, and one prayer especially touched my heart and drew tears.

We are having an exceptionally pleasant passage. The sun came out warmly when we had left Boston twenty miles behind us yesterday, and the air has been deliciously cool and clear ever since—wrapped in our rugs, reclining on our steamer chairs, the waves giving us only a gentle rocking motion, we have slept and read, and rested most lazily. We have not had a touch of sea-sickness. We have had a few qualms of homesickness, especially in watching the babies on board. There is one sturdy little fellow of 15 mos. who is wheeled about the deck by his nurse in an ingenious contrivance and makes friends with everybody; and another chap, about four, who rooms opposite us and makes just enough chattering to remind us of sweet Theodora.

We have many pleasant people on board. We occupy seats at table with Mr. Fritz and family, Mr. James Gordon and wife, Mr. Robert Morse and wife of Jamaica Plain, among old friends; and we are forming acquaintance with some new ones. The appearance of the deck is like a huge picnic.

Steamer chairs are thickly set on the leeward side, at every angle, and the picturesque wrappings and costumes of their occupants…reading or chatting or dozing is most suggestive of comfort. Our steamer cleaves the water with a perceptible motion, but that given by the mighty engine. We were much interested yesterday in seeing how the steering was done.[22]

Ernest Gordon then added to this account by citing a letter his father had written about the Sunday service Maria had described, there in the steerage section of the *Cephalonia*—

Sunday afternoon we got permission to hold service among the steerage passengers. They were of all nationalities and all creeds, and were not ready at once to gather for a religious and Protestant service. So I went down into the hold, and preached to the men and women in their bunks, or as they sat lounging and smoking on the floor. Though disinclined at first to hear, they soon became attentive, and listened with deep interest as I preached to them of the Good Shepherd going after the lost sheep.

Meanwhile Mrs. Gordon had started singing on the deck among the same class, and, with the help of a few Christian friends, had held their attention till I came up and preached to them also. This service was quietly listened to, though with some interruptions.

When I announced to the people that 'there is none other name under heaven given among men, whereby we must be saved,' a Catholic Irishman, with just enough of his national beverage aboard to make him mellow and religious, stepped out and crossed himself very devoutly, exclaiming,

'That's so, your Riverance! Jesus Christ is the Savior, and St. Peter is head of the church—St. Peter, whom he commanded to walk on the water. Think of that, my friends'—pointing out over the waves—'think of St. Peter walking on the sea.'

And so he went on in a very noisy but friendly way to vindicate the primacy of St. Peter, the head of the apostolate, till the crowd insisted that he be quiet, that the preacher might finish his sermon.

Then I proceeded, urging the people that they were sinners in need of pardon, till a socialist, sitting on the bulkhead with his pipe in his mouth, cried out, 'Preach to Jay Gould. He is the sinner that needs praying for.' And so he gave us something of a talk on the tyranny of capital, and the oppression of labor.

Thus we closed, but not without finding warm-hearted Christians, Swede and Scotch especially, and a Welsh Methodist, who led the singing and became thereafter my faithful helper and co-laborer among his shipmates.[23]

And last, it was to his son Ernest that Gordon penned an affectionate letter closing the story of his voyage to the United Kingdom.

"As we are nearing Queenstown," he said—

> I send off this record of our voyage. The wind has been against us the entire distance…so we are more than a day later than the usual arrival. But on the whole it has been a very pleasant voyage. As soon as we arrive and hear from you that you are all well and prospering, we shall settle down to a contented sojourn in the old world…We have enjoyed the voyage better than any previous, though it has been so rough as to make it a winter passage in severity…[24]

* * *

The *Cephalonia* arrived in Queenstown, Ireland, on June 5, 1888.[25] Thereafter, it was a very busy time of gathering belongings and finalizing travel arrangements for London. On Thursday, June 7, Maria Gordon resumed the narrative of this journey by recording their arrival in Liverpool.

From thence, it wasn't more than a day's journey to London, when she and "Mr. Gordon" visited Westminster Abbey. Afterward, she recorded her impressions of some stirring memorials they saw, among them places of honor for abolitionists Thomas Fowell Buxton and William Wilberforce, the poets William Wordsworth, John Keble, and Isaac Watts, clergymen John and Charles Wesley, novelists Charles Dickens and William Makepeace Thackeray, and heroes of the British Empire like Major John Andre and David Livingstone.[26]

From Westminster Abbey they walked through St. Paul's Cathedral, taking time to view its moving memorials to Samuel Johnson and Sir Christopher Wren. England, Maria told her diary, "is certainly the mother of great men."[27]

* * *

Saturday, June 9, was also a day Maria Gordon long remembered. It began with a visit to an internationally famous repository for religious art: The Doré Gallery in the center of Bond Street, London—which opened twenty years earlier to exhibit and publicize the work of the French artist Gustave Doré, long renowned for his classic illustrations of biblical settings and characters.

Among the works Maria saw was "The Vale of Tears," which she said, was the "last production of the artist, representing Jesus with the cross beckoning with his hand as if saying 'come unto me' and wretched of every condition and nation responding to his call." She also saw "Christ leaving Praetorium," "Christ entering Jerusalem," "Moses before Pharaoh," "The Dream of Pilate's wife," "Ecce Homo," "The Massacre of Innocents," and "Christian Martyrs."[28]

After such an eventful and inspiring afternoon, she and her husband rode at 5pm to Exeter Hall "to the Reception and meeting of welcome" for the Centenary Conference on Foreign Missions. The Earl of Aberdeen presided, giving an address of welcome. Maria thought him "a gracious young man," and she deeply appreciated the opening prayer offered by D.L. Moody's friend, the Rev. H.W. Webb-Peploe, Prebendary of St. Paul's Cathedral. A "hearty amen," followed this prayer—witness to the glad truth that all hearts on this evening "were of one accord."[29]

A.J. and Maria Gordon had long awaited this gathering; for during their time at Clarendon Street Church, its vision of missionary endeavor was global as well as local in character.[30] And in this august setting, A.J. Gordon would emerge as an international apologist for missions,[31] though neither he, nor Maria, suspected this might unfold. Their desire—given their lifelong commitment to Christian missions—was to attend this London Centenary Conference, and bring things they had learned home with them—to better serve the cause of missions in Boston, and encourage parishioners at Clarendon Street toward a deeper commitment for missions.

Gordon, "an executive in the management of extended missionary interests," listened to every speaker he heard with rapt attention. Here was a chance to gauge the current state of international Protestant missions, a subject of more absorbing interest as he had for seventeen years been a member of the Executive Committee of the American Baptist Missionary Union. During this time, he had played a key role in the expansion of American Baptist missions to Africa.[32] On his return to America he would be elected chairman of this committee, and serve there six years.[33]

* * *

In hallowed memory, A.J. Gordon called the Centenary Conference on Foreign Missions "the greatest privilege of my life."[34] Held in Exeter Hall, London, from June 9 to 19, it was a vast undertaking—with more than 1,500 delegates from around the world, representing 140 agencies.[35] A.J. and Maria Gordon attended this event under the aegis of the American Baptist Missionary Union and the Women's Baptist Foreign Missionary Society, two of the fifty-eight societies represented from the United States.[36] And here, *The Watchman* magazine predicted Gordon would "doubtless be recognized as one of the prominent men" at the meetings.[37]

It proved a prescient insight.

During the London Centenary Conference, Gordon spoke in vivid detail about missionary endeavors in Japan, Africa, and China. As a long-time member of the Executive Committee of the American Baptist Missionary Union, he was well placed to give content-rich presentations that others would have valued.[38]

Aside from overviews of current missionary efforts in these places, two other themes marked Gordon's talks: he urged his fellow delegates to be Christians "making haste to obey the call of God," and he placed great emphasis on the need for all those undertaking missionary service to "be filled with the Holy Spirit." Indeed, he went one step further, asking that a time be set aside at the convention for delegates to seek this special, consecrated blessing.[39]

Gordon's plea, and his compelling reflections made a deep impression.

Ten years after the Centenary Conference, Eugene Stock, Editorial Secretary of Britain's Church Missionary Society, recounted his memories of Gordon and other American delegates. A greatly respected elder statesman of British foreign missions, the author of a magisterial 3-volume *History of the Church Missionary Society*, his memories of Gordon and other compeers carried added weight.

"Many of the papers and addresses were of the highest value," Stock said. "The American delegates were quite in the front for ability and culture and eloquence. England had scarcely anyone to put alongside such men as Dr. Gordon, Dr. Ellinwood, Dr. Pierson, Dr. Post, Dr. Judson Smith, [and] Dr. W.M. Taylor."[40]

The Centenary Conference impressed Gordon no less. In one session, the sheer number of missionary minded believers, in concert with a warm and cordial air of "mere Christianity," led him to draw lengthy attention to them. His eloquent thoughts were heard with deep appreciation, so much so that they later appeared in the official *Report of the Centenary Conference*.

Here, Gordon had stated—

> I, for one, may say that I have never witnessed such a scene, and my heart goes up forth this wonderful blending together of those who are one in Christ Jesus of various names. We never know how beautiful a ray of sunlight is until it is divided by passing through a prism, and so separated into its beautiful colours, and I think we should never have known how beautiful the Church of Christ is, had not the pure light of the Gospel been permitted to be refracted. But we have seen its various rays here, blending once more into the pure white light, a token that the Lord is near them that gather together unto Him.[41]

Nor were these seminal incidents the only noteworthy scenes to unfold during the Gordons' stay in Great Britain. Some of the most memorable moments of Gordon's fine friendship with Charles Spurgeon took place during this sojourn in Great Britain.

As for the nature of that friendship, it was stamped by mutual regard. Spurgeon, for his part, knew Gordon's printed sermons well, and described him as "a preacher of high excellence…a sound evangelical divine [who] lays himself out to win souls by the truth of God."[42]

Spurgeon's high regard for Gordon brought an invitation to preach in his stead, as Spurgeon was slowly recovering from a serious cold he had caught at his mother's funeral in May 1888. The story was told in Spurgeon's now classic *Autobiography,* one of the most popular works of the late 1800s.

On Sunday morning, June 17, many delegates to the London Centenary Conference gathered at Spurgeon's church, London's vast Metropolitan Tabernacle. Spurgeon now felt himself able to preach, though "obliged, through great weakness, to sit during a considerable portion of the sermon."

It had all been rather a close call for Gordon, who, honored though he was by Spurgeon's kind invitation, was more than mindful that he had only just missed the daunting task of preaching before a church filled with 5,000 to 6,000 people.[43]

In the event, Gordon "took part in the service," happy to lend a mite of homage to the ministry of his friend. Afterward, he wrote a spirited letter to Spurgeon, recalling the "deliverance" from having to preach in his place—

> Charing Cross Hotel,
> London, June 19, 1888
>
> My Dear Brother,
>   I sincerely trust that you were in no wise injured by your effort on Lord's-day morning. It seems to me that the Lord's help given to you then was the most powerful commentary on your text, "Let Him deliver him *now*."
>   ...*I also experienced a great deliverance,* for there were hundreds of visitors,—our whole Missionary Conference, indeed,—who had come to hear you...I can conceive of no embarrassment greater than that of having to preach to such a disappointed congregation as it must have been in your absence...
>   I greatly desire, with Mrs. Gordon, to call on you for a few moments at your home. I should be thankful to know when we can see you. If you are too ill to desire callers, please do not for a moment think of my request, and I shall entirely understand the reason.
>
>   Sincerely yours,
>   A.J. Gordon[44]

Some years earlier, Gordon had also expressed high regard for Spurgeon in print, through a long and revealing Introduction written in November 1883 for George Needham's book, *Charles H. Spurgeon: His Life and Labors.*

Gordon's Introduction was a literary sketch, but also a window on things he deeply respected in Spurgeon. At the same time, this essay displayed many of his gifts as a writer, underscoring why he was widely read in his lifetime.

Gordon began with a fine turn of phrase, saying the blessing that attended Spurgeon's ministry came from a close communion with God.

"To have the ear of the people is a great thing," he said, "and much to be coveted...*if only it be certain that God has the minister's ear.*"[45]

Gordon spoke too of Spurgeon's fidelity to the entirety of scripture—things construed as "the hard sayings of the Bible,"—as well as the more "tender and winning aspects" of Holy Writ. "Among the popular preachers of this generation," Gordon confirmed, "Mr. Spurgeon has been singularly distinguished for his plain and pungent declaration of the whole gospel."[46]

Nor had Spurgeon, Gordon believed, ever sought personal notoriety through his ministry. In truth, it was quite the contrary. "The high merit of his preaching," he said, lay in the fact it was "evidently shaped to attract men to God, rather than to the servant of God;" and it was "manifestly the utterance of one who, like plain John Woolman the Quaker, is '*jealous over himself, lest he should say anything to make his testimony look agreeable to that mind in the people which is not in pure obedience to the Cross of Christ.*'" In keeping with this, Spurgeon "constantly declared the doctrines of the Cross, with rare fidelity, sharp distinctness, and exemplary boldness."[47]

Gordon was the more grateful to write this introduction, he said, as it was an opportunity to commend Spurgeon's ministry to a wider American audience—

> How great is the debt...we all owe to...The Metropolitan Tabernacle of London. In an age that is running greedily after theological novelties, the steady, conservative anchoring power of that pulpit has been felt wherever the English language is spoken...May [Mr. Spurgeon] long be spared to the pulpit, that the pulpit may long be spared to the truth.[48]

* * *

Apart from Gordon's fellowship with C.H. Spurgeon during his sojourn in Great Britain, other aspects of this time were deeply rewarding. Ernest Gordon, on the eve of graduating from Harvard when his parents sailed for England, gave first hand accounts of things his father spoke of.

The first memory Ernest Gordon described centered on the constellation of luminaries from world missions attending the London Centenary Conference.

"It was," he stated, "a gathering in the best sense ecumenical"—

> Every Protestant missionary society in the world gave to it its adherence. Every evangelical church, having any agency for the extension of the Redeemer's kingdom was represented. Distinguished missionaries from abroad— Hudson Taylor, Bishop Crowther, John Wilkinson, Dr. Post, Murray Mitchell—gave to the gatherings the results of years of observation and experience.
>
> There were laymen, too, friends of missions, whose names command attention in the East as well as in the West—Sir William Muir, Sir Monier Williams, Sir Richard Temple, Sir W.W. Hunter, General Phayre, Sir Robert Cust, and Lord Northbrooke, the ex-Viceroy of India.[49]

The support of prominent delegates was doubtless important to the success of the conference, and certainly had its place; but what lingered most in Gordon's memory had less to do with considerations of that kind than with direct reports from the mission fields, which "filled him with delighted enthusiasm."[50]

Hearing them, he said, was much like "the great review which closed our Civil War, as veteran after veteran came to the front and related his struggles and victories in Africa, in Asia, or in the islands of the Pacific."[51]

Amid these moments, Gordon met a Moravian brother, whom he described as "a man of humble bearing, and broken English." Here, Gordon's wide reading about the missionary pioneer Count Zinzendorf and "remembrances of Herrnhut" in the 1700s suddenly became very real. Tears "welled up into his eyes, and rolled out on his cheeks" as he clasped the Moravian brother's hand.[52]

Auxiliary meetings followed the London Centenary Conference, and these also were important for Gordon. Among them was a tour of H. Grattan Guinness's East London Institute, with gospel gatherings at the Association Hall and Mildmay—where Gordon "was listened to by great throngs." With "brimming eyes" he listened to "the wonderful expositions of Hebrews by Adolph Saphir." Others were no less moved during Gordon's "beautiful address" on "Union with Christ."

Last, recalling the rancor and the arrest he had experienced for preaching on Boston Common just three years before, Gordon was deeply gratified when he was able to preach "in the streets and parks of London, without interference."[53]

Gordon's own account of this part of his London visit was vivid—

We were spending the Sunday [July 1st] as the guest of Lady Kinnaird in Trafalgar Square, one of whose daughters invited us to go to a street meeting at about 6 o'clock in the afternoon. The spot selected was a side street, near a public park.

A portable organ was placed in the street sufficiently near the sidewalk to give room for carriages to pass. [Miss Kinnaird] seated herself at the instrument and began a familiar hymn, and immediately the crowd commenced to gather from every direction.

After a few hymns, and a fervent prayer by a working-man, who opened the services, I began my address. What a congregation!

The most respectable and well dressed had stopped to listen—a few only—and the most wretched and outcast in great numbers. Poor women with beer-bloated faces, stood eagerly attentive through the entire address.

Many boys and girls, with such marks of poverty and squalor as one rarely sees in Boston streets; old topers with their pipes still puffing under noses whose lurid redness told how terribly the furnace fires of intoxication had burned within; women with the painted face, who stopped for a moment to hear of the divine love, tenderer than a mother's, and then suddenly moved on as though it was more than they could bear—all these sorts and more were represented [and] listened respectfully.

Policemen now and then drew nigh, but never with the look of suspicion of disapproval as of those who were spying out our liberty.

The address finished, another hymn was sung, in the midst of which, at a given signal, the little organ was taken up and we moved on singing, and drawing the bulk of the crowd after us into a hall, which became completely filled. There were further services, and then a going among the crowd by Christian ladies and gentlemen in order for personal talk and to find out the sorrows, wants and distresses of each, if by any means they might be helped.

As we finished our evening work and came out, we said to ourselves: "Surely we had never addressed a congregation who more deeply needed the helping hand of the gospel than these, and, alas, for the law makers of American or in England who shall put obstacles in the way of that hand being freely extended to them."[54]

* * *

After the London gatherings ended, A.J. and Maria Gordon traveled to Paris "to look into the work of The McAll Mission." Gordon spoke several times during this visit, and his addresses at the various halls had "a powerfully moving effect" on the audiences of French men and women.[55]

Even as Gordon addressed these Paris meetings, "an urgent message" came from representatives of several Scottish churches, who'd heard him in London, earnestly asking him to address a series of meetings which had been scheduled in Edinburgh for July 14 to 17. These dates had been chosen "in order to reach the university students before their dispersion for the vacation."[56]

This meant a "complete alteration of plan," yet the Gordons resolved to leave for Scotland with Dr. A.T. Pierson. In the days to come, people throughout Scotland had much cause for gratitude. The meetings were duly advertised as the "Centenary Conference on Foreign Missions Visit of Delegates to Edinburgh."[57]

The Edinburgh meetings were said to be "of great power," and the commodious Synod Hall, which could seat 2,000, "was filled to its utmost capacity." As the meetings progressed, it was clear that something remarkable was unfolding.[58]

Before the conference ended, an appeal came "importuning Dr. Gordon and Dr. Pierson to make a tour" of principal cities and towns of Scotland "on behalf of the missionary interests of Scotch churches." This was heard with great fervor, some "two thousand people rising *en masse* to express their approbation" as soon as the letter was read. Then followed, as Ernest Gordon said, "a laborious but fruitful missionary campaign."[59] Though called together hastily, "largely attended meetings" were held in Edinburgh, Oban, Nairn, Elgin, Inverness, Aberdeen, Strathpeffer, Dundee, and elsewhere.

"Everywhere," Ernest Gordon wrote—

> the American ministers were received with enthusiasm; everywhere their words made a deep impression. [Dr. Gordon's] allusion to his Scotch name and ancestry excited warm response. [As he wrote:] "We are getting much enjoyment, too, along with this unexpected service, into which we have been drawn by the importunity of our Scotch friends."[60]

These gatherings, as missions scholar Dana L. Robert has written, were a watershed event: "Not since the Moody-Sankey revivals of 1875-76 were the Scottish Christians so aroused. The mission tour of Gordon and Pierson was a huge success that inspired increased contributions and numerous young Scots to volunteer for foreign missions."[61]

In early August, after this storied and welcome whirlwind, the Gordons set out on their return to America. From Aberdeen, they traveled down to Liverpool to board the *Pavonia* on August 9th, the fine sister ship of the *Cephalonia*. They sighted Boston ten days later.[62]

All these experiences marked the journey of a lifetime.

Chapter Sixteen
The School in Bowdoin Square

Many tender memories now cluster about the teachings given in this school. Opened in the fall of 1889, the school lost its Founder in 1895 and its Dean [my father,] in 1900; but the work goes on, and the teachings of those years live.[1]

—Harriet Chapell,
Mount Holyoke, Class of 1888

In the late 1890s, Frederick Leonard Chapell took up his pen to commit memories of a stirring event to paper. He was a gifted writer, clergyman, and academic—graduating from Yale, with the Class of 1860, and a few years later from Rochester Theological Seminary, Class of 1864.[2]

When Chapell wrote his account, he was Dean and Resident Instructor for a newly founded institution: the Boston Missionary Training School.[3] It had been founded by A.J. Gordon, and Chapell was there from the beginning.

"The first gathering," he remembered, "was held on Wednesday afternoon, October 2nd, 1889, in the rooms on [Seven] Chardon Street in the rear of the Tabernacle Church in Bowdoin Square."[4]

Therein lies a story.

As an institution, The Boston Missionary Training School owed much of its initial inspiration to England, and the work of Dr. H. Grattan Guinness, who founded the East London Institute for Home and Foreign Missions in 1873.[5]

In summer 1888, as A.J. Gordon attended the London Centenary Missions Conference, he toured Guinness's missionary training school. Set in the slums of East London, the Institute was from its inception a school among the downtrodden, bringing light and hope to a place that had known little of either.

Gordon saw this, even as he saw students in their morning and afternoon classes, learning "a trade or craft, mechanics, building, [or] carpentry." They also learned elements of "basic medicine, cookery, botany, and reading the compass and sundial."[6] Everything made a deep impression.

Indeed, it is possible that during this time Gordon and Guinness discussed the idea of establishing a similar institution in Boston. But it wasn't until the spring of 1889, when Guinness visited America, that the idea of a Boston Missionary Training School became a reality.[7]

During his stay, Guinness saw the Bowdoin Square Tabernacle Church—led by Gordon's friend, Rev. M.R. Deming, since 1887. He saw two former houses of prostitution—purchased and renovated to serve as settings for Christian ministry. In one, a "Young Men's Institute" had been created, a place where "working men of the city" could find "lodging, religious training, and biblical instruction."[8] What Guinness saw was much like the East London Institute.

He took note, and he did more.

As A.J. Gordon recalled: "Dr. Guinness, seeing the earnest, soul-saving work going on constantly under the ministry of Pastor Deming in the Bowdoin Square Tabernacle, suggested to him and myself that we open in that church, and in the adjoining buildings, 'a recruiting-station for lay missionary workers.'"[9]

The precise date of this pivotal conversation isn't known, but it took place in the spring of 1889. In a letter dated May 24, 1889, Gordon recounted his discussion with Guinness to Dr. Alvah Hovey, President of Newton Theological Seminary.[10] In October 1889, with new classrooms in the two buildings bought and renovated by the Bowdoin Square Tabernacle,[11] and instructors retained, the first notice for this newly fledged school was given in *The Baptist Missionary Magazine*—

A MISSIONARY TRAINING SCHOOL will be opened at the Baptist Tabernacle, Bowdoin Square, Boston, Mass., Oct.

1, under the presidency of Rev. A.J. Gordon, D.D...The number of persons is becoming very large who wish to devote themselves to special religious work, but have not the opportunity or the means to secure a full education. It will be the aim of this school to assist such as wish to enter the missionary service.[12]

One month later, in November 1889, *The Missionary Review of the World,* edited by A.T. Pierson, chronicled the opening of Dr. Gordon's new "Missionary Training School"—

A Missionary Training School was opened at the Baptist Tabernacle, Boston, Mass., Oct. [2nd], under the presidency of Rev. A. J. Gordon, D.D. The object is not to interfere with existing educational institutions, but to supply to those who are called to missionary labor, but are unable to avail themselves of the usual advantages, the best possible training to fit them for the work which they feel God intends them to do.

Evidences of piety, earnestness, and a reasonable degree of fitness for religious work will alone be required of those desiring to enter. Both ladies and gentlemen will be admitted, and boarding facilities are provided adjoining the Tabernacle. The course of study will be chiefly exegetical and practical.

Rev. F.L. Chapell of Flemington, N.J., is to be the resident Instructor; but, aside from his classes, the services of a number of teachers and lecturers have been secured, whose instructions will be of great value. Further information can be had by addressing Rev. R.M. Deming, Secretary, Baptist Tabernacle, Bowdoin Square, Boston, Mass.[13]

* * *

The launch of the Boston Missionary Training School coincided with another public spirited philanthropy started by the Bowdoin Square

Tabernacle, a charity that met a most basic human need: cool, clean water for destitute families.

The "Bowdoin Square Ice-water Fountain" became a literal oasis for people who knew the squalor of tenement living, and worked amid sweat shop factory conditions. It also bore testimony to Christ's timeless words: "I was thirsty and you gave Me drink" (Matt. 25:35).

An early public notice of the Bowdoin Square ice-water fountain appeared in a Board of Alderman Report issued by the city of Boston in July 1889—

> Report and order—That a license be granted to the [Bowdoin] Tabernacle Young Men's Institute, the owners of the estate known as the Bowdoin Square Baptist Church, on Bowdoin Square and Chardon street, to construct and maintain on Chardon street, at the corner of Bowdoin Square, an ice box and ice-water fountain...in the street and sidewalk in front of their said estate...[14]

A more lengthy and detailed account of the ice-water fountain, and the great boon it was to the city, appeared in *The Arena* magazine in 1891—

> It may be of interest to our readers to know that $75 has been spent for a large, public, cold water fountain, situated at a point easy of access by the most wretched dwellers in the West End. This fountain was erected a year ago. At stated intervals several tons of ice are packed in a large receiving vault, around and through which thousands of feet of water-pipe pass.
>
> Thus the water is cooled, and for the first time in the history of Boston the sick among the very poor have been able during the torrid nights to enjoy anything other than the hot water in the city water-pipes. This fountain last summer proved a wonderful boon to the fever-parched bodies of hundreds of poor invalids, as it did to a still larger number of poor factory girls and others who have suffered in hot, close quarters during June, July, and August.[15]

Though unintended, another unlooked-for benefit came from this ice-water fountain. As *The Arena* magazine reported, "it has also, in numbers of instances saved men from patronizing the saloons, who otherwise would have done so to quench their thirst."[16] Given the temperance movement then so prevalent in the late 1800s, and the sad ravages of whisky among inner-city families, more than a few failed to mourn a less frequent patronage of saloons. But one group did decidedly, as *The Arena* magazine noted with wry humor: "Quite a number of men, who after a hard day's work were in the habit of taking one or more glasses of beer in neighboring saloons, regularly patronized the free, cool fountain, *much to the disgust of the saloon-keepers…their revenues considerably lessened.*"[17]

Other stories of the Bowdoin Square Ice-water Fountain led to word pictures of the trying lives many knew, and places where they worked.

> One day last summer, one of the earnest men engaged in the work of the Bowdoin Square Tabernacle [the sponsor of this fountain] noticed a small boy attaching a short hose to the fountain, the hose [leading to] a wooden pail.
>
> "What are you doing, Johnny?" asked the gentleman. "Do you intend to sell that water?"
>
> "Oh! no, sir, this is for the [factory] girls; there are fifty of them cooped up in [there], and they have had nothing to drink but the hot water in the pipes; but now they have each chipped in a cent and bought this bucket and hose so they can have some good water."
>
> An investigation proved that the lad spoke truly. More than half a hundred poor girls were working in small, stifling quarters. The cool water was to them a wonderful boon.

Beyond the stifling air of this factory, there was yet another sequel, no less moving or meaningful. One night, a staff member at the Bowdoin Square Tabernacle "noticed a ragged little urchin filling several old cans with water." He approached the boy, wondering what the reason might be for this—

> "You cannot drink *all* that water," he said, "what are you going to do with it'?"

"I'm gittin' it fur the ole woman."

"Who do you mean?"

"My mother; she used to strike the beer every night until she found out about this spring, and now she does without the beer, and ain't so cross."

How much that little dialogue (subsequently verified) told of the wonderful possibility of environment and opportunity. If only an equal opportunity could be enjoyed by this vast multitude of society's outcasts…

We must do something more…relieving the great misery, and lessening the degradation of [those] who suffer so much and have so little…[18]

* * *

But to return to the Boston Missionary Training School.

For a start, tuition was free, as "the expenses of the school [were] met by free-will offerings." And A.J. Gordon played no little role in helping to meet the school's expenses, from his personal income. "How busily," his son Earnest said, "his pen wrought in those days to earn money for continuing the modest work…For during the first year more than eight hundred dollars of his own [pastoral] salary was turned over to the school, and in succeeding years all the proceeds from copyrights and articles, as well as his entire income as co-editor of *The Missionary Review*.[19]

At the same time Gordon's generosity in support of higher theological education also stood as a reproach to those who, like *The New York Examiner,* wrongly accused him of being antagonistic to the kind of schools where he had been educated. Such charges were a farce, and easily brushed aside by a cursory inquiry.

For fifteen years inclusive (1874-1888), Gordon was a trustee of Brown University, and thereafter a Fellow of the University. As Dr. E.B. Andrews, the President of Brown, said at the time of Gordon's passing—

Quite early in his ministry to [Clarendon Street Church], he was chosen to be a member of the Governing Board of Brown University, and I cannot tell you how faithful he has always been in that relation...not only in attending the meetings whenever possible—and the occasions when it was not possible were very few—but in attending to the matters that were brought before the Board from time to time. He always showed an uncommon grasp of commercial matters from one year's session to another, and I felt very proud of Dr. Gordon.[20]

And in December 1890, Gordon wrote to tell his friend Charles R. Brown of Newton Theological Seminary he would send the school fifty dollars a year (something like $1,200 dollars now)—even as he was leading a great capital campaign for The Missionary Union, then much in need—and Clarendon Street Church was pledged to raise $5,000 to $10,000 within a month's time.[21] This was a telling sum, ranging between $120,000 and $240,000 dollars today.[22]

* * *

From its inception, the Boston Missionary Training School was distinctive. "Thoroughly inter-denominational," it stood "unequivocally for the great vital truths of Redemption," emphasizing "the supreme authority of the Holy Scriptures; the necessity of the enduement of the Holy Spirit, the Lord's Coming, the nature and need of the times in which we are living; and the urgent duty of heralding the Gospel throughout the whole world."

As to teaching at the BMTS, classes were given in "New Testament Greek and Christian Song," with "lectures on various Biblical and Missionary subjects," and "evening lectures for those who cannot attend during the day."[23]

The roster of BMTS leaders and faculty also said much of its character.

A.J. Gordon served as founder and president of the BMTS, while Maria Gordon served ably as the school's Secretary, and later, its Treasurer. F.L. Chapell, selected personally by A.J. Gordon, was the school's "resident instructor," and later, its first Dean.[24] As Chapell's daughter Harriet fondly recalled—

> When in 1889, Dr. A.J. Gordon was projecting the Boston
> Missionary Training School...he sought out [my father,] Rev.
> F.L. Chapell, as the man best fitted to conduct the instruction
> of the school, and as a result of conference between them, a
> scheme for the curriculum...was formulated...[25]

So it was that in Gordon and Chapell—graduates of Brown and Yale respectively—the BMTS had an Ivy League pedigree. And Maria Gordon, with her myriad gifts, was a school administrator both men greatly relied on. She was a true role model and mentor for young women undertaking their course of study.

Looking at the BMTS, as it was in 1897, the names of early teachers and the courses they offered appear. F.L. Chapell led student classes in Biblical and Practical Theology and Exegesis. They later became the basis for Chapell's posthumous book, *Biblical and Practical Theology,* published in 1901.

Dr. J.M. Gray, many years pastor of Boston's Reformed Episcopal Church, gave "valuable instruction on the Synthesis, History, Inspiration, Interpretation and Use of the Bible." He was widely respected throughout New England, receiving an honorary Doctorate from Bates College in 1896.[26] He later served with great distinction as President of Moody Bible Institute in Chicago.

Gray's colleague, Dr. Julia Morton Plummer, was a true pioneer, teaching "two courses of lectures—one on Physiology and Hygiene, and one on Obstetrics."[27] Her reputation preceded her, for as *The Cambridge Tribune* stated: Dr. Plummer is "known in Boston and vicinity in the work of promoting the social and moral condition of young women."[28]

Plummer was among the leaders of the New England Moral Reform Society to create the Talitha Cumi Home of Jamaica Plain, "a maternity home for unmarried girls," or crisis pregnancy center.[29] "Talitha Cumi" was itself a biblical phrase meaning, "Arise, young woman," and it expressed the Home's mission to offer "God's open door of forgiveness and hope."[30] Thousands of young women were cared for in this way, and Dr. Plummer later wrote a poem expressing the faith-based compassion of the Talitha Cumi Home—

Oh, pour forth the name of Jesus,
   In its tender, wonderful grace,
   Till all the darkness of the way
   Is lost in the light of His Face.[31]

*   *   *

Impressive as these early days and faculty of the Boston Missionary Training School were, this new institution, as noted above, had its detractors.

"Nothing A.J. Gordon did," historian Dana L. Robert has written, "stirred more controversy than opening the [Boston] training school. Bitter criticism poured in from Baptists and from the religious press. Gordon was accused of doctrinal fanaticism and of abetting 'short-cut' routes to the ministry."[32]

One might have foreseen a welcome for the BMTS—a groundbreaking school giving fine training to young men and women, including African-Americans, Hebrew converts to Christianity, and Chinese students from the immigrant community of believers Clarendon Street Church long supported.[33]

Yet such was not the case, and a firestorm of criticism broke over the new school. As Gordon's son Ernest recalled—

> Hardly were the doors of the unobtrusive and modest institute opened before [an] assault began...great men of the press did furiously assail the champion of the "little man." To [see] the bitterness with which the school was attacked one has only to turn back the files of *The New York Examiner* to the winter of '89.
>
> "The short-cut plan," a [derisive name] pleasing to these critics, was denounced as "a method fraught with grave perils to our [Baptist] denomination." It was questioned whether such schools "could be established without both brains and money, and a great deal of both." It was doubted whether "the strong common sense of the Baptist laity, from whom

the money was to come, could be brought to support" this novelty. It was claimed "that the new school could do a great deal of harm, and that the sooner denominational opinion was decisively expressed against it, and its abandonment secured, the better for every cause that Baptists have at heart."

[Thus] "The Bowdoin Square craze" was denounced as "a movement for reversing educational qualifications among the Baptists, and as an accusation of incompetence against our seminaries." The demand for "half-educated but self-confident men" was ridiculed...[34]

Initially, A.J. Gordon gave no reply to these baseless and scathing attacks. But when "the chorus of indolent reviewers" turned on H. Grattan Guinness, the reply from his pen was decisive and immediate.[35]

Early in 1889, Gordon wrote, "Dr. Guinness, of London, became my guest. I found that he was deeply burdened for Africa, literally bearing it on his heart night and day with tears."[36] It was during this stay, as noted above, Guinness had suggested the creation of the BMTS.

"The enterprise," Gordon said, "was designed to give practical experience in evangelistic work, and a course of systematic biblical study." There was no intent, and never had been, "to interfere with any higher schools of biblical learning, or to encourage a short cut into the ministry." Indeed, the BMTS prospectus explicitly stated: "All students whose gifts and age warrant them in taking full college and seminary courses of study will be strenuously encouraged to do so."[37]

At heart, the BMTS was established "solely for the benefit of such as could not by any possibility avail themselves of these advantages."[38] In a word, the BMTS sought to serve underprivileged young people who would not otherwise receive any formal education in preparation for missionary service. Here Gordon wrote words that must have brought a smile to Guinness, as they so evidently recalled the work of the East London Institute for Home and Foreign Missions.

"The applicants for admission," Gordon said—

> have come from the carpenter's bench, from the painter's pot, from the tailor's shop, some of them confessing to a

desire which had burdened them for years to give themselves to foreign missionary service, but seeing no chance till this door opened. They are all poor, and have undertaken, while engaged in study, to work for their board in such places as the Tabernacle Employment Office may furnish...[39]

Last, Gordon closed with a clarion defense of the BMTS, set in a telling challenge: "With the superb opportunities for higher culture which our denominational colleges and schools afford, is it quite gracious to grudge these poor [students] this very humble opportunity for instruction in the Word of God?"[40]

Gordon hadn't sought controversy, only to give underprivileged young men and women a well-guided education to allow them to serve as missionary volunteers. Yet if others sought to destroy this new Boston Missionary Training School, or denigrate the philanthropy of friends like Guinness, he would enter the lists.

A.J. Gordon was a gentleman scholar by nature—but here, he showed himself a man of principle and deep determination.

* * *

Often, troubled waters precede making port in a better place.

Such was now the case, for "the attack on the school," said Gordon's son Ernest, "served to advertise it." Students began to come in from all parts of the country. Contributions to its support followed. "One lady," Ernest Gordon said, "wrote to the head of the school that she had read the *Examiner* articles, and that, though she had no knowledge of the working of the new project, was sure it must be a 'good thing,' else the *Examiner* would never have assailed it." She sent a large cheque, and "each succeeding year gave generously toward current expenses."[41]

Soon, well-trained graduates were entering the mission field.

In March 1895, for example, the Boston Missionary Training School reported four volunteers had done so. E.C. Pauling sailed for Korea; J.D. Matthews sailed for China, in company with Wong Tsin Chong his interpreter and helper; Emil Linde, who was Hebrew, sailed for Russia, to "preach to his own race;" and Miss M. Estella Magee sailed for Swatow,

China, under the direction of the Woman's Baptist Foreign Missionary Society of the West.[42]

* * *

Of these BMTS pioneers, Wong Tsin Chong had for many years been one of Gordon's great friends and was, in his estimation, "a remarkable man." For Gordon and the other parishioners of Clarendon Street, he was also "our Chinese deacon," inspirationally faithful in "looking after his country-people and fellow-Christians in the church."[43] There were 100 such members of the Chinese "Sabbath School" class at Clarendon Street, and they had a deep commitment to missions: supporting "three of their countrymen as preachers" in China.[44]

No Sunday, Gordon observed, "passes without finding [Wong] preaching the gospel to his countrymen in the Chinese quarter. As he stands in the street speaking in his native tongue, crowds of English-speaking people will often gather. Then, changing his language, he will plead with these to be reconciled to Christ."[45]

What kind of Christian was Wong Tsin Chong? Gordon held him up as an exemplar for all his parishioners to emulate—

> Would that there were scores of such! His sole thought day and night is how to reach his country-people at home and abroad…For some years he has provided for the maintenance of a native missionary to preach to the people of his own village in China. Association with Christians is a delight to him.
>
> When he stood up to receive the right hand of fellowship on admission into the church, the pride and satisfaction with which he accepted such high honor were visible in his entire bearing.
>
> At the next communion, when other members were to be received, Wong innocently took his place in the line again. Though an unusual thing to repeat the ceremony, we did not pass him by. "How I like this church!" said he. "They shake hands every month."[46]

At one point during Wong Tsin Chong's years at Clarendon Street, there were four successive Sundays when a Chinese émigré was among the new members admitted to the church. "Isn't it remarkable," someone observed to Wong, "that we have had a Chinaman [welcomed] on each of the last four Sundays?"

Wong turned to his fellow parishioner with "the most radiant look," saying, "Not at all remarkable. I asked the Lord for ten this year; you have got four of them. Hold fast, and you will get the other six before the year is over."[47]

Nor could Gordon ever forget the way Wong Tsin Chong showed love and Christian charity to Yee Gow, one of the older men in the Chinese Sunday School which had been established at Clarendon Street.[48]

Yee Gow was an elderly, good-hearted man who often struggled with mental clarity. He often came across to some superficial observers as "a blundering fellow." But Wong Tsin Chong saw Yee Gow as a cherished brother.[49]

One winter Yee Gow fell sick, and quickly fell victim to consumption, or "a wasting away of the body, especially from tuberculosis of the lungs."[50]

He was carried to a nearby hospital, but sadly there wasn't much to be done. However, Yee Gow was a Christian, and was faithfully visited in his final days by parishioners of Clarendon Street.

On the last day of his life, he was found by Wong Tsin Chong, who had come to pray with his friend. Yee Gow was saddened at this time and physically very weak. At first, Wong did his best "to cheer him with hopes of heaven." Yet the old man's lethargy was slow to lift, now shrouded by confusion and dismay.

"I don't know whether I want to go there, after all," he said, speaking of heaven. "I won't know anybody there; nobody will care for me."

"Never mind, Yee Gow," said Wong; "I shall be there before long; and when I get there I will look first for the Lord Jesus, *and when I find him I'll bring him to you.*" At these words, Yee Gow found comfort, and "closed his eyes in peace."[51]

* * *

By 1896, when Ernest Gordon's filial biography was published, he could report that graduates of the Boston Missionary Training School were "now working in all parts of the globe—in Algeria, in China, in India, on the Congo, in Barbadoes, in Oklahoma, and in the Soudan." Many became "efficient and prized city missionaries and pastors." One had "charge of a chapel car and has founded a hundred or more new churches." Ernest Gordon described other graduates as "apostolic," true pioneers who had given their lives in the mission field.

Their names were a roll of honor: David Miller in Sudan; Richard Jones and Banza Manteke in "the Free State of Congo," and Idalette Mills in Barbados.[52] "They died," it was said, "for the testimony of Jesus, after much toil and suffering [and] their praise is on all lips." Still other graduates worked among the poor, undertaking "summer work" in "the destitute parts of Maine, and among the hills of Vermont and New Hampshire."[53]

Letters from early graduates were "full of gratitude and affection for the school, for the instructors, and for the founder." What's more, the educational model established by A.J. Gordon and his confrères was widely followed elsewhere, as "the numerous institutions of a like character...have sprung up all over the country." They pointed to "a recognition of the need of such schools."[54]

* * *

And yet...

The BMTS consumed much of Gordon's energy in the last years of his life.[55] It also brought great worry, and sobering thoughts of whether it was all too much. As Gordon's friend and colleague F.L. Chapell remembered—

> Funds were not always as promptly in hand from outside as could have been wished. There was no suitable home for the young women. A few of the students had been disappointing in their conduct; so that burdens and perplexities of various kinds accumulated on Dr. Gordon to that degree that he wrote me in the summer of '91 that he was in doubt about continuing the school, and asked me to meet him at Northfield to talk the matter over.
>
> I went, and at a little lull [during the conference,] we

descended into the basement of Stone Hall, and seating ourselves on two broken chairs, discussed the situation. I urged that much of the difficulty for him arose from the fact that the school was not in connection with his own church, and that if it were brought to Clarendon Street, which neighborhood would soon need something of the kind, all would go more smoothly. To this he assented, and said that the house next door to him was for rent and could be procured as a home for the young women. The financial situation was somewhat relieved by my taking the regular supply of a church at Bridgeport, Connecticut.

[Thus] the first turning point in the story of the School took place and is described. At the time it was announced simply as follows, in the leaflet which took the place of a catalog in 1891: "For the first two years it (the School) was held at No. 7 Chardon Street near the Tabernacle Church; but now, more conveniently for the President, it is in connection with the Clarendon Street Church."[56]

Gordon's meeting with F.L. Chapell proved crucial, and indeed, after two years of operation, the BMTS moved to Clarendon Street Church—though as Chapell noted, "the church was made in no wise responsible for the support."[57] Further, as agreed, a residence home was opened next door to Gordon's home at 182 Brookline Street.[58] This was called "Carey Home," after missionary pioneer William Carey, and created as "a home for lady students coming from a distance, and a resting place for out-going and returning missionaries."[59]

We know little of Carey Home now, but we may imagine something of what it was like: fellowship among residents, conversations on the landing of the stairway, times for gathered prayer and song in the parlor, letters written home or to far-away mission fields from bedside tables in each room, meals and repartee at a boarding-house style dining room table, reading books and sacred texts by the hearthside.

Always, Maria Gordon was there to lend counsel, or a listening ear to those burdened with concern, and do any number of things that made this new facility feel like a welcome home.

Two accounts of Carey Home near to A.J. Gordon's time have survived. The first dates from October 1895 issue of *The Watchword* magazine, touching in its brevity and gentle allusion to A.J. Gordon's recent passing—

> THE GORDON TRAINING SCHOOL opens this year with the promise of a large attendance. The old teachers are in their places and Dr. Pierson [the new president] will give all the attention possible to the work, Carey Home is open and Mrs. Gordon still lives next door to it, where she will still keep in touch with the School and with the students.[60]

The second brief account dates from October 6, 1896, and concerns missionaries sent out under the auspices of The Board of the Women's Baptist Missionary Society of the West. Two young women were to travel to foreign lands, Misses Sumner and Daniels. They "sent back words of cheer" on their day of sailing, and said they had "greatly enjoyed the hospitality of the Carey Home in Boston," taking "sad, glad farewells in Clarendon Street Church."[61]

Other encouraging developments followed the establishment of Carey Home at the Boston Missionary Training School. "A larger teaching force was gradually secured," Chapell wrote. "Students and money came unsolicited. And thus the work has gone on...Scores of workers have been put into the field, who perhaps would have never gotten there but for the School."[62]

By the time A.J. Gordon died in 1895, the BMTS had graduated twenty-five foreign missionaries, fifteen ministers, twenty evangelistic workers, twenty home missionaries, and fifteen persons into higher theological education.[63]

* * *

Another feature of the Boston Missionary Training School was the decided preponderance of women there. Because women were "often denied seminary training and had heavy family obligations," missionary training or Bible School was often the only avenue open to them. A.J.

Gordon's "support of a woman's right to preach, prophesy, and teach men in the church" was reflected in the student composition of the BMTS.[64]

Indeed, "a generation of women responded to Gordon's concern for the theological training of laywomen and registered for courses in the Boston Missionary Training School."[65]

Gordon believed in the full utilization of women as missionaries, and he held that the need for workers in God's harvest fields also extended to them. In the political arena, he "fully supported the suffrage movement and believed that women should be enfranchised and given equality under the law."[66]

"Defending women's rights to be missionary evangelists," Gordon wrote a biblically-based call for an expanded role for women in the church. It was based on a close study of the seemingly most negative Pauline injunctions against female leadership roles. The resulting article, "The Ministry of Women," was published in *The Missionary Review of the World*.

Here, Gordon stated the spiritual equality under the current dispensation of the Holy Spirit gave women "equal warrant with man's for telling out the Gospel of the grace of God."[67] Through Greek exegesis of various Pauline passages, Gordon identified places where "Scripture had been deliberately mistranslated in order to limit women's sphere." Though "stopping short of arguing for the ordination of women," Gordon sought to show in his careful study "that women acted as deacons, teachers, and even as apostles."[68]

In August 1891, writing as Editor of *The Watchword,* Gordon had said—

We count it among the most significant signs of the times that so many women are moved by the Spirit of God to tell out the story of redemption, and to lend their help in the work of gathering in the harvest of souls.

At home and abroad, as missionaries and evangelists, as Bible readers and tract distributers, the number of Christian women who are doing the Lord's work is constantly increasing. The Psalmist's prediction seems to be literally fulfilling before our eyes: *"The Lord gave the word, and great was the company of the women that published it"* Psalm 68:11.

We believe…that the Spirit of God calls and commissions

women to be evangelists and to tell out the story of the cross. What else can be the meaning of the words of Joel reiterated by Peter on the Day of Pentecost. "And it shall come to pass in the last days, saith God, I will pour out of my Spirit upon all flesh, *and your sons and your daughters shall prophesy...and on my servants and on my handmaidens I will pour out in those days of my Spirit and they shall prophesy."* "Prophesy" means not to foretell, necessarily, but *to forthtell,* to witness for Christ unto the people.[69]

This was a theme and biblical emphasis Maria Gordon sounded in her writings. Indeed, several months before A.J. Gordon published his scholarly article in *The Missionary Review of the World,* Maria had given an address at the Northfield Summer Conference on "Women As Evangelists." It was later published in *Northfield Echoes,* a book read widely throughout the English-speaking world.[70]

"There has sprung up in response to the demand for trained workers," Maria told those gathered for her talk—

a number of schools where women as well as men are being taught the Scriptures, that they may be prepared to answer any call of the Spirit through the church. *And from our own Training School in Boston* about twenty young women have been sent out by two and two into the rural districts of New England, to visit from house to house, to gather the people into schoolhouses and churches, and give out the message of eternal life. One pastor has proved his confidence in the young women sent to his parish, by taking his summer vacation during their visit to his town, and leaving them in full possession of parsonage and church. Another lady, who undertook to supply a little church in New Hampshire, has sent for her former pastor to come and baptize twelve converts who are awaiting the ordinance."[71]

In her Northfield address, Maria Gordon also spoke movingly of China missionary Adele Fielde, and A.J. Gordon took a cue from Maria rhetorically in his own essay, "The Ministry of Women," recounting Fielde's story at length.

Gordon told his readers that

> in the early days of woman's work in the foreign field…that brilliant missionary to China, Miss Adele Fielde, was recalled by her board because of the repeated complaints of the senior missionaries that in her work she was transcending her sphere as a woman.
>
> "It is reported that you have taken upon you to preach," was the charge read by the chairman; "is it so?" She replied by describing the vastness and destitution of her field-village after village, hamlet after hamlet, yet unreached by the Gospel—and then how, with a native woman, she had gone into the surrounding country, gathered groups of men, women, and children-whoever would come-and told out the story of the cross to them. "If this is preaching, I plead guilty to the charge," she said.
>
> "And have you ever been ordained to preach?" asked her examiner.
>
> "No," she replied, with great dignity and emphasis—*"no; but I believe I have been foreordained."*
>
> "O woman!" Gordon concluded, "you have answered discreetly; and if any shall ask for your foreordination credentials, put your finger on the words of the prophet: "Your sons and your daughters shall prophesy," and the whole Church will vote to send you back unhampered to your work, as happily the Board did in this instance."[72]

Closer to home, and in August 1891, A.J. Gordon wrote in *The Watchword* magazine about the "two weeks' mission with the Clarendon Street Church" conducted by Emilia Louise Baeyertz of Australia. Of Hebrew ethnicity and faith, she had become a Christian evangelist of international renown—so much so that today, the National Library of Australia has paid tribute to her life and work, and houses papers relating to her legacy.

Baeyertz had been the featured speaker for gospel gatherings at Clarendon Street Church in July 1891, and the story she had to tell was powerful and moving.

Born in England to wealthy Hebrew parents, Emilia Louise Aronson, who was often sickly, left school at thirteen. Later, when her first fiancée died, she suffered a debilitating breakdown and was sent to Australia in an effort to recover her health. Settled in Melbourne, Emilia met Charles Baeyertz, an Anglican bank manager. They married in October 1865 and had two children—one of whom was C.N. Baeyertz, who immigrated to New Zealand and became a famous linguist and patron of the arts.[73] Tragically, Charles Baeyertz was killed in a gun accident in 1871. Yet amid her searing loss, heaven's solace came. Emilia found hope, when all had seemed so hopeless.

In 1891, she published a slender memoir called *From Darkness to Light*, and its pages contain her testimony. It holds something of what she shared during her time with A.J. Gordon and the parishioners of Clarendon Street Church, during the very same year of her visit there.

"By an accident," she began—

> my beloved husband was taken from me...So terribly sudden was the blow that I could hardly realize that he had gone forever; and, oh, what a gulf separated us!—it seemed to me impassible.
>
> I knew he had died in the faith of Jesus [but] I was very bitter and hard in my grief, and felt that God had dealt cruelly in crushing me so, taking all the youth and brightness out of my life. It seemed impossible to live, and I felt nothing but the desire to be with my loved one again. Many a day I have laid on his grave in the damp, and prayed that God would take me; but God "while I was yet a long way off," took compassion, and raised up dear friends who showed me that only *in one way* could I ever hope to see my husband again. The desire to be a Christian now became so intense as to become a part of my life...I began to seek the Lord with all my might...
>
> One day I was reading the old, old story, when something

whispered to my soul, "He suffered all this for you," and the truth seemed to burst upon me like a flash of lightning. I had found the Saviour, *my* Saviour, and such a flood of love as came into my heart for Him I cannot describe. I went into my room and on my knees I sobbed aloud, not for sorrow this time, but for joy...

Looking back I see...there was always a want the Saviour alone can fill... Oh! that He may awaken you to a knowledge of this...Take this precious Saviour, and the moment you do so His glorious, beautiful life is yours, and He will be henceforth the strength of your life...[74]

In time, Emilia Baeyertz felt a call to religious and philanthropic work. Just as Elizabeth Fry had done in England two generations earlier, she began jail and hospital visits. She undertook Sunday School teaching, then "door-to-door evangelism in the Jewish community of Melbourne." She also became active in the YWCA. By 1880, she was conducting missions throughout South Australia, with reports of conversions in the hundreds. Now a noted Anglican evangelist, she undertook missions to America, Canada and Great Britain.[75]

When Emilia Baeyertz came to Clarendon Street Church, she had a transformative time of ministry. A.J. Gordon was deeply impressed with her "knowledge of the Hebrew Scriptures and usages," saying this gave her "a marked advantage in setting forth the Word of God." Especially "instructive and powerful" were her talks "upon Cain and Abel, upon the Passover, upon the Second Coming of Christ, and the Restoration of Israel." She was, Gordon stated, "clear, uncompromising and most tender in her setting forth of the way of life."[76]

Then too, many at Clarendon Street were "savingly converted" during these sermons, and many Christians were "helped and established." Gordon said he was profoundly grateful that "such a witness has been raised up." He wished Baeyertz "great success in her future missions," and prayed "that God will greatly use her, as in the past, to strengthen Christians" and to win the lost.[77]

Clarendon Street's welcome of Emilia Baeyertz was a telling symbol in its way—and a sign of things to come. For with the founding of the

Boston Missionary Training School, A.J. and Maria Gordon, with their
dedicated colleagues, sought to blaze new trails of opportunity for young
women as well as young men, among them disadvantaged students of
many ethnicities and impoverished circumstances. It was no easy task,
given strong opposition and financial challenges. Also, as seen above,
Gordon had seriously considered closing the school in the trying summer
of 1891.

But he and his colleagues resolved to shoulder the burden.

It was worth the doing.

* * *

After its first decade, Boston's new Missionary Training School had
much to be thankful for. Led by fine scholars and administrators, each
respected leaders, some one hundred and fifty students had taken courses
"in attendance for two years," while, as F.L. Chapell noted, "a thousand
to fifteen hundred have received some benefit from the evening classes."
About fifty students had entered the pastorate, and the same number had
entered the mission field.[78]

Everyone who passed through the school's doors would never have
had any education, were it not for the groundbreaking, persevering vision
of A.J. Gordon and H. Grattan Guinness—a vision taken up and shared by
an array of talented men and women, who concerted their gifts to make
this vision a reality.

In January 1901, "The Gordon Training School" was given prominent
notice through a half-page article published in *The Missionary Review
of the World*. The hallmark of this fine piece was its affirmation that
"The Gordon Training School" rightly honored the founding vision of
its namesake, A.J. Gordon.

"The thirteenth year of this useful school," this article began—

> opens Wednesday, October 9, 1901, in the Clarendon
> Street Baptist Church, Boston. It is undenominational
> and independent. The design is to give a free course of
> biblical and practical training to such men and women as
> have offered themselves to Christ, and who desire a better

equipment for His service, but whose age and attainments or other circumstances make impracticable a more extended course of study.

Rev. Emory W. Hunt has been elected president, to take the place of Rev. A.T. Pierson, who, since the death of the founder, Dr. A.J. Gordon, has been at the head. Dr. James M. Gray has been with the school from its beginning, and continues as instructor in the synthetic study of the Bible. Associated with him are Dr. W.H. Walker, Dr. Robert Cameron, Dr. A.C. Dixon, and others, together with a corps of special lecturers, including the retiring president, [Dr. Pierson, along with] Dr. C.I. Scofield, Dr. Harris of Toronto, and others.

We can safely commend this school for the purity of its doctrinal teaching, the helpfulness of its methods, and especially for the purity of its spiritual atmosphere. The spirit of its founder still lingers there...[79]

And twelve years after A.J. Gordon's passing, in July 1907, Maria Gordon herself wrote a brief article to mark the 18th anniversary of what was now called "the Gordon Bible and Missionary Training School." This anniversary, Maria said—

was observed on May 12th to 16th in the Clarendon Street Baptist Church, where the sessions of the school are held. The blessing of God abides on the school.

Forty-seven students attended during the past year, of whom 13 graduated, having completed the two years' course.

Seventy-five of the students have gone as missionaries to foreign lands, of whom some 40 are now actively engaged in the work. Thirty-three pastors are settled over parishes. Twenty-four city missionaries are doing rescue work in various stations, and as many pastors' assistants and assistant pastors and home mission workers are successfully filling the positions for which they were trained in the school.[80]

Kevin Belmonte

Maria Gordon's article was a powerful and poignant tribute to her husband's educational legacy. But it also pointed to a larger truth—one best understood by way of a question: how many future parishioners, and people served in the mission field, owed Boston's new Missionary Training School a debt beyond price? How many generations since have had abiding cause to say the same?

It was, and remains, a resplendent legacy.

Chapter Seventeen
Where the White Banner Flew

*[Dr. Gordon] has a profound sympathy for the fallen, and
established The Boston Industrial Home—of which he has
been the continual supporter and moving spirit ever since. It
is one of the most beneficent and useful institutions of the city.[1]*
—The Baptist Missionary Magazine

On Thursday, February 12, 1931, in the early years of the Great
Depression, H.J. Mahoney, editor of *The Cambridge Sentinel,* went to the
studios of WEEI at 182 Tremont Street, on the edge of Boston Common,
to give a 3 o'clock address in place of Cambridge Mayor Richard M.
Russell.[2]

Radio tubes crackled and warmed in the homes throughout greater
Boston as they tuned to station 590. As people listened, they heard a
moving and memorable tribute to a benevolent association that had been
a city institution for fifty-seven years: The Boston Industrial Home.

In his address, H.J. Mahoney recounted the history of this venerable
charity, and its good works. He began with a dash of wit.

"Because Mayor Russell," he said, "was busy at Beacon Hill Thursday,
your editor read his address over the radio at WEEI...The mayor is
arousing much *éclat* as a radio orator, and his proxy in this instance tried
to maintain the Russell standard." Mahoney then began reading the text
of Mayor Russell's tribute, saying: "one of the oldest and most useful
institutions...in Massachusetts, an association for social welfare both
ancient and honorable, [is] The Boston Industrial Home...an institution

of such high and proven purpose that it stands for a confident future when unquestioning trust is the one reliable cure for our present, and, let us hope, passing economic ills." This home, Mahoney continued—

> came into existence at the close of a deep religious awakening. At the time, one of the big problems was what to do [for those] without homes, friends, or money. Dr. A.J. Gordon, pastor of the Clarendon Street Baptist Church, had taken a leading part in the revival campaign. He gave to the movement his fine mind, his noble enthusiasm and his clear eloquence and, out of these energies—aided by the open-hearted help of others—a constructive program was devised...The present building, at the corner of Harrison Ave. and Davis St., Boston, was first occupied in the 1890s... Today, as never before...the Home provides a temporary refuge for those who reach out desperately for a sustaining hand...It acts as a torch to lighten the path of those whose hearts are crushed in losing their way in life...*Human friendship takes on a brighter glow...*
>
> Each year over three thousand men, and 1,500 women, are given succor at the Home, where a clean, lightsome, disciplined environment brightens the spirits...and fortifies them...At Christmas and Thanksgiving the cheer would gladden the heart of Dickens...Last Thanksgiving, four hundred and fifty men and women formed a restless line awaiting the signal when the tables burdened with food were ready...
>
> The Boston Industrial Home is custodian of a "Fresh Air Fund"...for children in the congested parts of the metropolitan area to be given a day either in the country or at the seashore during the hot summer days. It is a pleasure and inspiration to see [them] climb into a bus and know that they are going to have a day that will never be forgotten...
>
> The work of the Home is not exclusive. Its service is extended to all...whether residents of the city or not...The Home asks no questions as to race or creed, only the query: "Do you need help, and how best can we serve you?"[3]

Such was a window on the legacy and work of the Boston Industrial Home, as it was among residents of greater Boston in February 1931.

By 1934, the Home had its own broadcast radio program on WEEI, the "Silver Lining Hour," which aired on Thursday afternoons, bringing a faith-based message of hope for listeners.[4] For one memorable "Silver Lining Hour" broadcast, airing on sister station WNAC for March 25, 1932, five MIT collegians performed several classical music selections to benefit the Boston Industrial Home.[5]

Here, they continued a well-established tradition of support and volunteer work for the Home undertaken by students from their rival school, Harvard. Members of Harvard's Student Volunteer Committee had provided many items of winter clothing for residents of the Boston Industrial Home, and often traveled to the Home to assist in its work for a day.[6] Thus the Home had prominent recognition, strong community involvement, and was gratefully regarded by many.

But the earliest days of the Boston Industrial Home, in contrast, were times of great challenge, when no one knew if the Home would survive very long beyond its founding. A.J. Gordon never forgot those days, and what they taught him about the place of trust in God.

* * *

At the start, in 1874, the Boston Industrial Home was an institution much like the Salvation Army "shelters" known today; and as such, it was established "for the immediate relief of those out of work."[7] In concept it was a noble endeavor of faith; but numerous practical difficulties soon emerged.

Finding long-term, capable, superintendants and matrons to oversee the day to day needs of the men and women who came to the Home was the first such difficulty. As one account had it, these early superintendants and matrons "succeeded one another with ominous rapidity." This was a great discouragement to the Home's first Trustees, "resignation followed resignation," and "financial backing was withdrawn."[8]

Amid such a downward spiral and bleak outlook, responsibility was shifted, finally and entirely, upon A.J. Gordon's shoulders. As his son Ernest recalled, "For a term of years he carried almost alone the heavy weight of a work, the only assured fruit of which was the annually recurring deficit."[9] Undoubtedly, those in need were being helped, and the blessings of this relief work were clear—yet how much longer could it continue? It couldn't for much longer, running at a deficit and without a capable staff in place.

Gordon grew despondent. A sense of "deep disheartenment pressed heavily upon him. An undertaking promising, useful, necessary, was trembling on the edge of disruption." Burdened by this, he left the city one summer for a "vacation in the hill-country." He could discern no means of help for the Boston Industrial Home, and felt himself "driven into the arms of God."[10]

Every morning of that summer, "he withdrew to a quiet place in the woods." It became a place of solace, long remembered as "still, and sun dappled." There, Gordon "laid before the Lord the discouragements and the needs of the work."[11] Summer passed, and in early September, he returned to Boston.

Then, seated in his study one day after his return, he was "handed a note in unfamiliar writing, requesting an immediate interview." He answered the letter, and traveled to its address, the residence of an elderly gentleman in a fashionable quarter of the city.

Still, Gordon had never met his host; a man whom he later learned was "inordinately fond of his properties,"[12] wealthy, yet someone clearly in bad health.

When Gordon entered this home, he saw a man who was "dry, wizened, in skullcap, surrounded by a clutter of dust-covered documents and papers, a bottle of brandy at his left hand." Straightway, the elderly host came to his point. He had heard, during the summer, of the Boston Industrial Home, its difficulties, and its mission. That mission, he had come to believe, held potential, and "he wished, therefore, to make provision for it in his will." Dumbfounded, Gordon then heard his host say he wanted to hear suggestions about "looking toward the enlargement of the work, and the placing of it upon a secure basis."[13]

"It was the greatest lesson in faith I have ever had," Gordon said later. "From that day to this, I have prayed with the greatest assurance of God's intervention in practical matters."[14]

This unlikely interview was "the first in a series of events which resulted in the complete solution of this problem of many weary years."

The bequest from Gordon's host, when paid, amounted to over twenty thousand dollars—a princely sum worth well over $400,000 today. With such a gift Gordon, as President of the Boston Industrial Home, was able to form a strong cabinet "for the more efficient care of the institution, composed of men able, generous, [and] reliable." They served the home for nearly twenty years, or until the time of Gordon's passing.[15]

These leaders were prayerful as well, and in answer to their faithful petitions, "a superintendent of exceptional ability and consecration," a British émigré named T.D. Roberts, was brought unexpectedly to Gordon's notice. Not only did Roberts lead the ministry of the Home "with superior executive skill," but he also helped "found homes of a like character" in many Northern and Western cities.[16]

With such a fine team in place, the institution was soon "on a paying basis." By 1895, just under thirty-five thousand lodgings were provided annually, and about fifty thousand meals. The Home was, in the phrase of that time, "a successful rescue work,"—one where heaven's hope shone in Christ's gracious call to love and serve "the least of these," or those most in need of food, clothing, and shelter in Boston.

Briefly described, the mission of Boston Industrial Home was to provide temporary lodging and food for destitute men and women who were willing to work, and follow the practices of the Home, centered largely on chapel attendance and the teachings of faith, alcohol abstinence and recovery meetings.

Literacy training was also provided, with instruction in various trades and handicrafts, and teaching about personal hygiene. For those who were sick and in need of medical treatment, a physician and nurses were also on staff.

Guest lecturers and musicians were often there as well—invited with a view toward continuing education, recreation, and fellowship. The idea behind all this was to help whose who stayed in the Boston Industrial Home find hope, become self-sufficient, and be guided to gainful employment.[17] The Home fostered a sense of place where people in need could "seek strength and grace from God,"[18] learning how to chart a new course forward in life.

At the same time, the public was invited to purchase "tickets," eight for one dollar, that could be given to those in need, entitling them to "meals and lodgings in payment for work." Typically, this involved the cutting and delivery of kindling wood for stove and furnace fires, the packing and delivery of coal for the same purpose, along with laundry work, "machine stitching, or plain sewing done to order." Residents were also "hired out" for other kinds of household work by the day or hour, as needed in homes throughout Boston.[19]

During all this time, and to the end of his life, A.J. Gordon was a guiding spirit and driving force for the Boston Industrial Home. As his colleagues said in memorial resolutions following his death—

"He was, indeed, the central figure [in the work], being in a sense its founder, and always its devoted friend, giving to it unceasingly his time, his thought, his effort, and his prayers...We gladly concede that in service and sacrifice he has outstripped us all."[20]

Apart from Gordon's central role in founding the Boston Industrial Home, and setting it on a secure financial footing, the role of T.D. Roberts – the gifted superintendent mentioned above—holds a special place in the history of this institution. His story was remarkable, and had something very like a Dickensian quality about it—when the touch of grace was ever present.

To follow events in Roberts' life, and his time at the Boston Industrial Home, is to see one powerful way A.J. Gordon's philanthropic vision became reality—through circumstances no one expected. Part of Roberts' story unfolded in a setting of national prominence— the pages of *The New York Times*.

* * *

Thomas Roberts' earliest years, by his own account, were humble.

"I first saw the light of day," he wrote, on "November 5, 1849, in a little thatched cottage in the town of Penzance, county of Cornwall, England... being the ninth of a family of eleven children, seven boys and four girls." Tragically, it was a home touched by great sadness. Only eight of the eleven children born to his parents survived, and that was all Roberts ever said on the matter. Some wounds are too tender to say more.[21]

As to matters of faith, Roberts' parents were conscientious, if no more than nominally religious. His father had been raised in the Wesleyan

Church, while his mother "made no profession of Christianity." Yet they did "all in their power to give me an education, or to have me learn some useful profession." This had been done for Roberts' elder brothers; but he, by his own admission, "seemed deaf" to his parents' entreaties.[22] He was, as the old phrase had it, a headstrong colt who would not be gentled, or take to any good training.

When he was just ten years old, Roberts "started out to earn my own living." This was no need for this, he later said, "but having a spirit which my parents could not curb or control, I was bent on having my own way."[23] He took up smoking and drinking, young as he was, and frequented a tavern near to home. A cycle of false starts for finding a job followed, to no lasting purpose.

Then, young Roberts had a horrific accident. While watching a band play at an Esplanade, his hat blew away—only to be caught by a large Newfoundland dog. He tried to take the hat back, but the dog turned on him and attacked. "Had it not been for some gentlemen," Roberts recalled, "who broke their sticks and umbrellas over his back in driving him off, he would have killed me." As it was, Roberts "was nearly dead when they took me into the hotel [nearby], and sewed up my wounds." Taken home, he was confined to bed for nearly twelve months.[24]

At this time, young Roberts was much like those he would later help at the Boston Industrial Home, greatly in need of kind assistance and guidance. He found both in the doctor who tended him during his long recovery. This good physician, a family friend, thoughtfully allowed the boy to visit his "surgery," or place of practice.

"He owned a very fast horse," Roberts recalled, "a great jumper, and [he] delighted in following the fox-hounds across country. I, being very small and of light weight, used to be taken to the race-course to exercise this horse; and it was there I began to acquire my uncontrollable passion for horse-racing."[25]

The family doctor was a fine horseman himself, and "proved a good instructor" to young Roberts. At one time he went to London and asked the boy to exercise the horse, which he "did with a vengeance." It wasn't long before Roberts became "quite an expert in the saddle, by the uninterrupted practice."[26]

A career as a jockey soon followed. Roberts rode in many prominent races, "commencing when I rode for the Prince of Wales plate, weighing only seventy-two pounds." He kept racing until the year 1870, riding twice for the St. Buryon Steeple-chase, placing second both times. But a dangerous fall occurred when his horse stumbled, and once more brought a close brush with death. That accident "more than anything else," made Roberts, now twenty, decide to go to America.[27]

Once there, Roberts became a much-in-demand exercise rider and trainer for several prominent stables. One such stable-owner was Henry Winthrop Sargent, who lived at "Wodenethe," a beautiful home at Fishkill-on-the-Hudson. He showed Roberts special kindness.[28] Through Sargent's compassionate witness, Roberts came to faith, renouncing his rough, destructive habits of fight and drink.

"The arrow of conviction," Roberts said, "found a lodgment in my poor, troubled conscience [and] I recalled the years of my misspent life." At this, Sargent took the young man aside, and spoke earnestly with him. As Roberts remembered—

> Mr. Sargent cited to me an instance that morning…of a man who had been led astray by bad company, but who in after years had turned to the right and had become a successful and prosperous businessman; and then, with tears in his eyes, said, "Tom, I hope this will be the means of your salvation." I shook his hand and turned away from him, promising to go and shake hands with [a] man with whom I had [fought] and forgive him, which I did…
>
> The more I thought of my past, I fully realized how fast I was riding down, with a terribly loose rein, the hill of reckless disregard…and that if I did not put the brakes on…I should soon be at [a] precipice.[29]

That evening, at dusk, Roberts went to his room near the stable, and "poured out my heart to something or somebody. [I] had a vague idea of Jesus Christ coming into this world to save men, therefore, I prayed if there was a God, would he reveal himself to me." Traveling soon after with H.W. Sargent to his Boston home, Roberts experienced a deep and searching conversion.

Sargent became a second father. He took Roberts, now twenty-three, under his wing, introducing him to the young woman he would marry, and tutored him for hours at a time—purchasing several textbooks for the purpose. "I always felt," Roberts said later, "that it was his leniency, and the kind words he spoke…which turned the whole current of my life towards God."[30]

Roberts more than repaid Sargent's kindness. Several years later, as Sargent's health slowly gave way, Roberts kept vigil by his mentor's bedside for twenty-seven days and nights, scarcely leaving his bedside until Sargent died in his arms. And as long as Sargent's wife lived, Roberts kept a promise to him to "look after matters of the estate, as best I could, as long as Mrs. Sargent lived." She died in 1887.

Within a year of this, a new sphere of service beckoned through A.J. Gordon and the Boston Industrial Home. The man and his ministry had met.

* * *

As Christmas drew near in 1888, T.D. Roberts had only just begun work at the Boston Industrial Home. He decided to give those who were homeless, hungry, and without work a special gift for the holiday: a meal and after-dinner celebration to which poor children, most of all, would be invited.

The dinner was lavish in hospitality and good hope: a large Christmas tree stood in one corner, heavily laden with gifts provided by friends and benefactors. Just as Roberts and his co-workers wished, "poor children formed the larger part of a great audience that packed the room."[31] Anticipation grew, even as the aroma of good food filled the room. Roberts had a special surprise as well: he would enter the room dressed as Santa Claus. Cheers and fine bedlam ensued when he walked in. Going over to the Christmas tree, he was careful to put out the burning candle lights nearest him. He then began to regale the children, and hand out gifts.

But one candle was missed, and Roberts brushed against it.

In a thrice, and to the horror of all those watching, the glue and cotton batting of his costume ignited. He was "enveloped in a sheet of flame."[32]

Those nearest rushed to help, and they quickly pulled the costume away—but not before Roberts' "arms, back, face, and head were horribly scorched."[33] To ease his great pain he was placed under opiates, and taken to a nearby hospital.

The next day, *The New York Times* reported: "Superintendent T.D. Roberts of the Boston Industrial Temporary Home is dying, as the result of frightful burns received...while personifying Santa Claus."[34] As this story ran, people throughout the eastern U.S. gathered to pray. Doctors held out little hope.

But T.D. Roberts didn't die.

Incredibly, though it meant several months of slow, very painful recovery—his condition stabilized and improved. "There were," he later said, "special prayers for me in several of the churches in Boston and elsewhere, together with the best skill that could be obtained; and after three or four long months of anxiety, I recovered, with but few scars on my person to remind me of that terrible occasion."[35]

Roberts' recovery, with so little trace of his wounds, was a wonder to many—and as it unfolded, expressions of sympathy and condolence came from all over the country. These were things, Robert said movingly, "I shall never forget."[36]

And there was yet one more thing—for Roberts was given a tender grace during this crucial period of his recovery. "One night," he remembered—

> when I was lying between life and death, and the doctor and nurse were doing all they could for me, I heard the sobs of my dear wife and three little children in the adjoining room, as they were made aware of the fact that it would be only a few hours when I should succumb...
>
> But through it all I had a most blessèd experience...
>
> I saw all the sins of my past life rise before me as though written on a blackboard, and I stood, as it were, on the edge of a tremendous precipice. There seemed to be a ravine which was bottomless, out of which proceeded the blackness...Something seemed to be pushing me over this precipice.

I said, "Is it possible that, after all, Jesus Christ will not come to my assistance and deliver me from this terrible experience?"

...black clouds seemed to whirl up before me, and there was no light, I began to cry out to God, and prayed that Jesus would reveal himself to me and dispel the darkness. Just then a light seemed to light up the very heavens, and I saw a form distinctly, the like of which I had never seen before, and which I cannot describe for its beauty. I said, "Ah, Jesus, I knew you would come..."

How the words of the Psalmist came to my mind!

"Yea, though I walk through the valley of the shadow of death I will fear no evil, for thou art with me, thy rod and thy staff they comfort me."[37]

It was little wonder then, that A.J. Gordon had such regard for T.D. Roberts. When Roberts wrote a memoir of his life and work at the Boston Industrial Home, Gordon wrote a Foreword for the book, saying that since Roberts had been "identified with this philanthropic enterprise from the beginning," it was a distinct pleasure to be "commending this volume." He continued—

Mr. Thomas D. Roberts has put into form the story of the remarkable work now going on for many years in the [Boston Industrial] Home of this city. This work has solved the question as to what can be done to help the unemployed [and] homeless, and to put them again upon their feet. The Home has been a blessing to thousands. It has also been an object-lesson for the observation of those who, in every city, are trying to solve the hard question—

"What shall we do with that unhappy class who are without work, and without home or hope?"[38]

"The Home," Gordon concluded, "has aimed first at changing the heart, and then at employing the hands of those whom it has sought to rescue; and under God the writer of this book has been greatly instrumental in making this work signally successful."[39]

Nor was Gordon the only one to repose such trust in Roberts' leadership at the Boston Industrial Home. The Boston Police Department did as well. In fact, they presented him with a badge, and gave him special authority to give youth facing jail time a choice between jail and coming to the Boston Industrial Home. Beyond this, Roberts said, "Many have been brought to us at all hours of the night by police officers on the beat."[40]

* * *

And what, we might ask, did the Boston Industrial Home look like?

Near to T.D. Roberts' time, the main facility was a five-floor brick building, with large floor-to-ceiling windows, that fully filled the corner of Davis Street and Harrison Avenue. As one contemporary print shows, the Home also had a rooftop garden, making in effect a sixth floor to the Home—save that it was fenced and screened in—all the way around the edge of the building. This sixth floor was essentially an arboretum, ringed by small trees in planters at each of the strong wooden beams that supported the arboretum's roof. So the Boston Industrial Home had an on site urban park, to help with the raising of vegetables, and offer a green space with walkways.

Along the sidewalk, at the base of the Boston Industrial Home, was a long and narrow concrete enclosure used for storing firewood and coal. Men needing work were asked to deliver these items to homes nearby. They did so by teamster-style horse and wagon, even as trolleys passed at intervals on the streets beyond.

Behind the Boston Industrial Home's main building was a brownstone-like structure, used partly for living quarters, and partly for offices. Its windows looked out over a bustling city. Within, there were rooms where compassion beckoned.

It was a shelter the care-worn knew.

* * *

Aside from its coordination with the Boston Police Department, in later years the Boston Industrial Home was also ecumenical in its collaborative work. This was shown in a fine letter written by Catholic chaplain J.C. Hart, speaking of T.D. Roberts' successor, Oliver Elliot. The letter stated—

> I have made an arrangement with Mr. Oliver V. Elliot, Manager of the Boston Industrial Home, to furnish both men and women with food and lodging until employment can be found, and in cases of persons with willing hands, Mr. Elliot has proven himself a friend in need.

The Boston Industrial Home was a bright beacon in the heart of a great city. It provided food, lodging, and employment for tens of thousands of homeless men and women during its first fifty years of existence.

In 1907 alone, a night's lodging for 41,914 homeless men and women was provided, and a still larger number of meals for the hungry. 14,669 days' work of various kinds to those unemployed had also been furnished.[41] All this gives an idea of just how effective the Boston Industrial Home was.

Other accounts of the Boston Industrial Home within twenty-five years of A.J. Gordon's passing tell still more of how his vision led to changed lives.

One pamphlet, published in 1920, set out a moving vignette of one family that was transformed through the Boston Industrial Home's ministry. This story, written in 1918, was called "What Timely Sympathy Can Do." The names of the family involved remained discreetly anonymous.

"I remember distinctly my childhood home," the pamphlet's author wrote,

> beginning at three years of age. Our home was happy and my Dad and Mother great chums, who always took us out for little holidays.
>
> When I reached the age of 7 years I remember, I used to sit in mother's lap waiting for Dad, while my sister, 3 years younger, slept in her bed. It was night. Mother cried and I cried, too. Something was wrong, though I didn't understand then. Liquor had begun to take our father from us and Mother seemed helpless.

And then he came.

He was hurt and his head all cut and bloody. I wanted to help him and love him but my mother put me away, while she talked to him and tried to help him undress and get into bed, after washing him and bandaging his head.

Then night after night I would wait for Dad until I fell asleep, only to be awakened later to find him foul and dirty and intoxicated, holding on to the foot of the bed and using obscene language and profanity. In this way I learned the first profane words I can remember.[42]

Tragically, this young man continued, his father "used also at these times to attempt to beat Mother, but his maudlin condition made him unsuccessful. Once when he had Mother cornered, I got the stove poker and told him I would hit him if he didn't let Mother alone. This sunk into his drunken mind and touched him. He was good to us then for several days but it didn't last. Drink beckoned and he had not the strength to withstand it."[43]

At age eleven, the pamphlet's author said, "[my father] left us, after breaking open my bank, and I knew he would not come back after that. My mother took in some laundry for a minister and rented rooms and so managed to keep a home. I was sent to a private charitable school near Boston and taken from there when 13 years of age. I then went to work and gave my Mother my whole earnings for four years."[44]

As a young adult, the pamphlet's author said, "I found a letter addressed to me from Dad, asking if I would care to come and see him once more. He said he had been a good man for two years and was at The Boston Industrial Home, 17 Davis Street." Though there had been so many painful childhood scenes, he agreed, saying: "I hurried to Boston at once. My own Dad didn't know me, and when I told him I was his boy, we just hugged each other and I guess we both cried."[45]

In the time remaining for this visit, a grateful son listened as his father told him all that the Boston Industrial Home had done for him—

Dad took me out into the dining-room, of which he had been given charge, and told me his story. He had come to the Home on a Christmas Eve two years before, broken, coatless, his bare feet coming through the soles of his shoes, hungry and sick.

He was taken into the Home. Kindly hands and Christian charity, devoid of censure, caused him to be bathed and cleanly attired. Though long past supper-time, a good warm meal was given him, and the seed of Christ's teachings had been sown. After his terrible years of kicks and abuse, shuffling and stumbling, he had reached a haven.

...kindly words and patience and the words of salvation...in the Chapel brought him to a closer touch with our Master...[Dad] gave his heart and soul to God. It was hard, mighty hard at first, for he had to battle with his overpowering desire for drink.[46]

This grateful son, writing during World War I, closed with a sequel that would have rejoiced A. J. Gordon's heart. "Dad," this young man said,

is 64 years of age now and living with me. He has worked for two employers only in eighteen years, has bought each issue of Liberty Bonds, and owns a farm in Florida. Dad is a grand, lovable, Christian father and grandfather today and both he and I have reason to thank God Almighty that there was and still is a haven of earthly hope like the Boston Industrial Home for men and women whose troubles and trials are greater than they can bear without the grace of God... whose open doors constantly invite the broken wayfarer to a better life.[47]

* * *

Ninety-three years after the Boston Industrial Home was established, in 1967, it was still a vital part of the charitable community in Boston. At this time, its work and mission were chronicled by James Peters (Harvard, Class of 1960), as part of his research for a Master's Degree in City Planning at MIT.[48] His thesis was titled "Alternatives to Skid Row," and in this context, Peters wrote about the Boston Industrial Home in great detail.

Peters' thesis pointed to a telling truth.

Many rescue missions founded in the late 1800s no longer exist today. Some lasted only one generation, perhaps two. Few would have predicted that the Boston Industrial Home, given the formidable challenges at its inception, would be one among the few such philanthropic institutions to endure. Yet it did.

Nearly one hundred years after it was established, the Boston Industrial Home—so close to the heart of A.J. Gordon—still carried forward a deeply important mission: commending faith through compassion. Today, his devotion to service projects lives on at the school that bears his name, Gordon College, through endeavors like "Each 1 Counts," with involvement in "community servings" of meals in A.J. Gordon's former parish, Jamaica Plain, inner city initiatives, and community garden projects in and around the north shore of Massachusetts.

Many keepsakes survive from the Boston Industrial Home—papers of patrons and friends, books that chart its early history. One keepsake is a simple quatrain of verse, written with deep gratitude for the work of the Home—lines that likened comfort and shelter to a kind of music—

> *You ask where I found it, this peace which I have;*
> *Well, I'll tell you—it won't take me long—*
> *I was passing one night the Industrial Home,*
> *And was stopped by the sound of a song...*[49]

But of all such keepsakes, perhaps none is so eloquent as one photograph to survive the passing years. It shows a great flag set on the rooftop of the Home, caught by the wind. This ensign—white, with the home's name rendered in blue—could be clearly seen from far away: the banner for a haven of hope.

A place the homeless called home.

Chapter Eighteen
Gatherings in Summer

The "Northfield Meeting" of the Y.M.C.A. was held last night, to get a large Harvard delegation to go to the meeting this coming July. The Northfield Conference was started seven years ago, with over two hundred men in attendance. Each year more colleges have sent delegations, until last summer over five hundred men were present, representing one hundred and twenty-five colleges and universities, both American and foreign...Many prominent divines have been secured to [speak,] the most prominent of whom are: Rev. Wilton Merle Smith. D.D., of New York; Rev. Frank Bristol, D.D., of Chicago; President Gates, of Amherst; [and] Rev. A.J. Gordon, of Boston...[1]

—The Harvard Crimson,
22 April 1892

Apart from D.L. Moody, few were more closely associated with the famous Northfield Summer Conferences than A.J. Gordon. And no one felt more privileged by that storied association than he did.

Seeing these conferences grow from modest beginnings to annual gatherings known the world over brought deep gratitude to Gordon, who noted in 1893: "I have been here to every conference, at least during some part of the session, since they began [in 1880]. I was here when that first building [East Hall,] stood alone, and this field where we stand now was a rough and stony pasture."[2]

First hand, Moody's biographer and eldest son Will knew the many things A.J. Gordon's leadership and involvement meant, saying "Dr. Gordon's assistance at the Northfield conferences was of inestimable value."[3]

As shown above, D.L. Moody wholeheartedly agreed. "I cannot thank you enough," he had said one summer, when the whole charge of the conference went to Gordon, "for your great help at Northfield. All the letters I have got from there speak in the highest terms of your generalship. I know of no one who could have taken your place. *It will now answer the question, What is going to become of the work when I am gone?* May the Lord reward you a thousandfold."[4] High praise indeed.

*   *   *

What were these famous conferences like?

Ernest Gordon knew that story well, and wrote about the Northfield Summer Conferences in his father's biography. In 1896, when this book appeared, D.L. Moody was still living and the conferences were at the height of their influence.

"There are," Ernest Gordon said—

> few lovelier spots than Northfield. The broad Connecticut, flowing with many a sweeping bend between hills and rich intervals, the "sweet aisles of the wilderness" stretching beyond the town, and the long street lined with elms...like the clustered pillars of a church, meet overhead in green... The conferences here, which have come to fill so important a place in the current life of American Christianity, were first organized by Mr. Moody in 1880...
>
> For speakers and teachers the great globe itself is ransacked, the best men in the world-church being brought into service. Hither have come the courtly, piquant Henry Drummond from Edinburgh, A.T. Pierson, mighty in the Scriptures, Andrew Murray, the saintly mystic of South Africa, Andrew Bonar, John McNeill, F.B. Meyer, H.W. Webb-Peploe [of St. Paul's Cathedral, London], and more of equal

note...They preach to the preachers and lead the leaders of the people. Yet hundreds of laymen as well gather about them...These are brought into relation with missionaries and Christian workers...Finally, the wholesome inter-denominationalism of the place establishes the best bonds of Christian unity.[5]

As to the origin of the Northfield conferences themselves, the vision for them was suggested to D.L. Moody by an experience he had at Cleveland, Ohio, in November, 1879, when he was holding an evangelistic campaign in that city.[6]

One morning a gathering was held for prayer, and a brief opening address, on "Prayer for the Church," was made by Dr. H.B. Hartzler. "Mr. Moody sat immediately before me," says Dr. Hartzler. "He listened with bowed head. Suddenly he raised his head, flashed a glance at me as if struck with a thought, and then resumed his former position." As soon as the meeting was over he asked Dr. Hartzler to come to Northfield the next summer to hold a similar meeting, and on August 4, 1880, wrote him: "Inclosed you will find a circular that explains itself" (the call to the first conference). "I got a start toward it when in your city and you spoke at the convention held there about November 1st."[7]

The call was for "a convocation for prayer," to be held from September 1 to 10. "The object," Moody had written in a widely published open letter—

is not so much to study the Bible, (though the Scriptures will be searched daily for instruction and promises,) as for solemn self-consecration, and to plead God's promises, and to wait upon Him for a fresh anointment of power from on high.

Not a few of God's chosen servants from our own land and from over the sea will be present to join with us in prayer and counsel.

All ministers and laymen, and those women who are fellow-helpers and laborers together with us in the kingdom and patience of our Lord Jesus Christ, and, indeed, all

Christians who are hungering for intimate fellowship with God and for power to do His work, are most cordially invited to assemble with us.

It is hoped that those Christians whose hearts are united with us in desire for this new endowment of power, but who cannot be present in the body, will send us salutation and greeting by letter, that there may be concert of prayer with them throughout the land during these days of waiting.

D.L. Moody[8]

Not only was almost every state in the Union represented at this gathering, but Canada, England, Scotland, Wales, South Africa, Athens, Smyrna, Cappadocia, and other lands and cities helped increase attendance. Hundreds of letters and telegrams came pouring in, expressing widespread interest and sympathy with the object of the convocation.[9]

The purpose of the Northfield Conferences, as they came to be, was to foster a deeper commitment to the essentials of Orthodoxy, or, to use Richard Baxter's phrase—made famous by C.S. Lewis—"mere Christianity." The hope of this, as with the schools Moody founded, lay in his "grand object"—to prepare men and women "for true Christian life and service, and set them to work for Christ in whatever sphere of life and labor God might place them."[10]

These conferences were noted for their "catholicity," as a description given by Moody's Irish-born son-in-law, A.P. Fitt, reveals:

not a single truth held by evangelical Christianity has failed of due honor in the teaching from the Northfield platform. Not only so, but presentation has been effected through men of every branch of the universal church. A bishop may be followed by an unordained evangelist.

This means more than mere inter-denominationalism. While no sect or denomination is ever allowed to present the particular point or points of its difference, it is felt that each stands for certain truths held alike by all branches of evangelical Christianity. Hence, while no controversy arises to mar the sweetness of fellowship, there results a majestic harmony of affirmation. The value to constructive faith of this agreement...can hardly be overestimated. Northfield undoubtedly finds in this one great secret of its influence.

And in the last summer of his life, 1899, Moody re-affirmed this from the Northfield Conference platform: "The central idea of the Northfield Conference is Christian unity, and the invitation is to all denominations and to all wings of denominations; but it is understood that along with the idea of Christian unity goes the Bible as it stands. We seek at these meetings to find points of common belief."[11]

* * *

The Northfield Summer Conferences live on, as they were in Moody's time, through Dr. H.B. Wright of Yale—in a chapter he was asked to write for the book *Two Centuries of Christian Activity at Yale* (published by G.P. Putnam's Sons in 1901).

Wright, who died at forty-seven, was one of America's fine and accomplished young academics in the early twentieth century. He taught at Yale for nearly twenty years, earning his Ph.D. there, with graduate studies in Grenoble, France, and the University of Berlin, Germany. He was also a prolific author, writing "numerous historical and philosophical and religious works."[12]

That the Northfield Summer Conferences were a deep and guiding influence of Wright's college years shines in *Two Centuries of Christian Activity at Yale.* Taking up his pen in 1900, Wright set the stage by saying—

A half century ago, the Christian forces which influenced student life at Yale were practically all centred and operative within the college walls. Men learned little of the religious movements of the outside world during the four years of their residence...The college pastor was at the same time college preacher, and whatever was needed in a religious way to supplement his efforts was, as a rule, supplied by the members of the faculty.

But with the decline of the pastorate as a preaching office and the inception of the intercollegiate student movement, a new order of things began.

Little by little the steady pressure exerted by this movement for variety and living issues in the chapel sermon has made itself felt until to-day preachers of reputation from all over the country, college presidents, leaders of student and mission movements, and even Christian laymen coming in from the world of action, present weekly to the student body the problems of many different spheres of Christian life.

But beyond this, within the last decade and a half, the desire of Yale men to see and know more of what is going on in the religious world without, and to fit themselves for efficient service in that world has found expression in an annual pilgrimage of sometimes as many as a hundred or more Yale students for a ten days' conference with students of other colleges, at Northfield, Massachusetts.[13]

Wright had attended the "ten days' conference" several times, and drew on his recollections to describe what they were like. "As we near the ground," he said, "every spot has some bit of interest to the newcomer or awakens fond memories in the veteran of past conferences. [Places like] Round Top and Senior Glen recall those informal hours in the early morning or on a Sunday afternoon, when [Moody] the great evangelist, seated in his big armchair beneath the trees, answered informally the numberless questions of life and practice raised by the eager inquirers who sat at his feet."[14]

One place that held special significance was Stone Hall, "made memorable," as Wright observed, "by the first of the great addresses of Henry Drummond upon *The Greatest Thing in the World*, which awoke the college world of America in 1887." It stood near the center of the Northfield Seminary campus, and beyond were "those quiet Northfield hills with their undisturbed retreats in which many a man has wrestled out alone his life problems and gone forth to a career of usefulness."[15]

Wright also described what it was like to "enter the seminary grounds" once the conference sessions had already begun. As a carriage drew near,

> the buildings rise all about bright with college flags and college colors, while far above and crowning all, from the top of the great auditorium, floats the Stars and Stripes. On the steps of East Hall a group of Yale men are instructing their Harvard and Princeton friends in the intricacies of the fascinating game of "peel." From Marquand [Hall] down in the valley a college song is borne up faintly on the evening breeze, and when it dies away a sharp and stirring college cheer from another direction answers the arrival of some belated delegate to the conference.
>
> After a while a convent bell of unusual sweetness begins to toll slowly from the tower of East Hall, and instantly the songs and fun cease, the crowds about the buildings disperse, and little groups of men with their coats on their arms pass over through a field of standing grain to Round Top, a small knoll directly back of Mr. Moody's house.
>
> Here in the calm of the gathering twilight as the sun goes down in red and gold behind the hills, leaving the still waters of the Connecticut all aflame in the valley below, some man well known in the outside world talks frankly and fairly on the choice of a life work.[16]

It was amidst such scenes and associations, that college students for fifteen years had "gathered from all over the land, and, indeed, in recent years, from all lands," to discuss methods and to receive inspiration for efficient Christian work.[17]

Yale had been "vitally connected with the movement from the start." And Wright believed D.L. Moody was "greatly influenced in his decision to start these conferences by the cordial reception he met with at the hands of Yale and Princeton men when on an evangelistic mission to these colleges" in the 1880s. Wright took particular pride in knowing that of the two hundred and fifty students who gathered across the river at Mt.

Hermon, at Moody's invitation in 1886, for the launch of what became "the Student Volunteer Movement," seven collegians were Yale men.[18]

At the first Northfield Summer Conference, Moody, "with characteristic modesty," kept in the background, "but was forced to speak frequently at the request of the students." With the exception of 1892, when he was abroad in Europe and the Holy Land, and in 1893, when he conducted the great six month evangelistic campaign in Chicago during the World's Fair, he was always in attendance and "presided at the morning and evening platform meetings."[19]

Here, A.J. Gordon played a crucial role, for, as Will Moody remembered: "when [my father] was abroad in 1892, Dr. A.J. Gordon, of Boston, had charge of the meetings, and the following year, when the World's Fair Campaign engrossed all of Mr. Moody's energies, Dr. Gordon, assisted by H.M. Moore, again conducted the conference."[20]

What made these conferences, as conducted by Moody and Gordon, so memorable and lasting in their effects? H.B. Wright believed "the secret of the attractiveness of these conferences, and the ready response which they have met with from college men everywhere, are not far to seek."[21]

Northfield, Wright stated, stood "for a healthy, hearty, common-sense Christianity." To underscore this, he gave an example, saying: "it did not seem in the slightest incongruous that when President Patton of Princeton had finished his masterly and logical address on "Doubt" [at Northfield], the whole audience should burst spontaneously into applause. He had met a need in his hearers' religious life and they were not backward about showing it."[22]

In the same vein, Wright said "this great assembly of trained minds" annually "calls for and receives the best thoughts of the ablest preachers and evangelists of all denominations in America and England." A.J. Gordon was among this company of noted Christian leaders, and Wright remembered other famous names, including William Harper, President of the University of Chicago, Sir J.E. Kynaston Studd, later Lord Mayor of London, J.R. Mott, the future Nobel Prize Laureate, and missions pioneer J. Hudson Taylor.[23]

Some of what Gordon was asked to oversee in Moody's absence took place outside buildings like Stone Hall, for the "ten days at Northfield" were by no means "wholly confined to religious meetings." Afternoons were devoted "to recreation and athletics," in which there was "plenty of good-natured intercollegiate rivalry." There were "tennis tournaments and track meets," and Yale was "more than ordinarily successful on account of the large size of her delegation." There was also "a baseball series, generally ending in a final struggle between Yale and Princeton." Many famed college athletes attended the Northfield Summer Conferences, among them future football legend Amos Alonzo Stagg, who insured that "Yale's athletic interests have been well looked after."[24]

Stagg, who had attended the Northfield Summer Conference of 1888, penned his recollections of what it was like, saying memorably—

> Last Friday night Mr. Moody came over to see the Yale delegation at Hillside Cottage. He spoke to us on the Holy Spirit, and prayed with us; and asked us if we would like to be filled with the Spirit?
>
> Man by man we said we would. We knelt on our knees, and prayed to God that He would give us this power. We feel that we have received it. We are going back to Yale, and filled with the Spirit of God we intend to do a work there that will tell for the Master and in the Judgment Day. We don't know, many of us, why we came up here. Various were our objects, various our purposes. But we are here, and we have received a blessing. What are we going to do? We are going back to Yale a band of men consecrated to the Lord.
>
> To-night, an hour ago, we knelt together, and man by man we pledged ourselves to do personal work next year. We pledged ourselves to study up the Holy Scriptures this summer, and to do work this summer; that the fire that is within us may not burn out, and that when we get back to college we shall be ready to meet the enemy and to fight him on his own ground. We feel that we have a great work there in Yale to do. It is different from being here living in a holy atmosphere; but we feel that God is on our side, and with Him on our side we have nothing to fear.
>
> We pledge ourselves as a band to pray all summer long for the blessing of the Holy Spirit upon us and upon Yale,

and we know that we shall have that blessing. We trust that henceforth we shall not sing as we usually do, with the emphasis on the "*Yale*": "For God, for country, and for Yale"; but we shall sing: "For *God*, for country, and for Yale."[25]

Judging from Wright's account, there must also have been more than a few moments that recalled high jinks from A.J. Gordon's undergraduate days at Brown. Wright lumped these moments in with what he called "the social side" of the Northfield Summer Conferences, and such pranks involved things like "clandestine raids on the pantry, and on each others' quarters… the rivalry for possession of the big bell [used to start events] and in the flaunting of the college colors from the highest point on the grounds."[26]

Last, there was what Wright called "the patriotic side" of the Northfield Summer Conferences. This centered largely on "the afternoon and evening of the Fourth of July," which was "given over to a patriotic and intercollegiate celebration unparalleled elsewhere." Field day games were held in the afternoon, "with the regulation track and field events which call for skill," plus just enough of roustabout events like "the sack and potato races and the obstacle race, through the deceptive waters of the duck pond," which left "the final result to luck rather than to skill."[27]

On the evening of the 4th, places like "the great auditorium," became "one mass of college emblems and colors, each section occupied by the delegates of a certain college," which, at the time appointed, sang its college song and gave its college cheer. After this, a patriotic oration was given sometimes by Moody himself. Then the conference leader of music, say D.B. Towner, who had "led the singing at the conferences since 1887," was gently compelled "to respond to the call for [singing] *The Sword of Bunker Hill*," following which the festive audience adjourned "to the great bonfire on the auditorium grounds," where Yale would "initiate the other colleges into the mysteries of the Omega Lambda Chi dance."[28]

Taking all this in, Wright then offered his reflections on the life lessons Northfield Summer Conferences imparted. "To some," he said, "the conference as a whole undoubtedly means little more than a training school for methods of Christian work." However for him, and for "the generality of student delegates," it had "a greater and more important significance." Here, Wright was thinking especially of "those in the upper classes of a college who have just entered upon the critical and faith-challenging studies which must necessarily form part of a true student's education." To all such, Wright believed, "the great principles of the Christian faith are reiterated with a power which tells and which sets men thinking. The message of Northfield is the Ten Commandments preached in the spirit of the 13th of First Corinthians."[29]

Foundational faith was the hallmark of these gatherings, with "the emphasis laid on the Bible as the guide of life, the presentation of the claims of the ministry and missions, the appeal for consecrated laymen in every profession, [and] the utter absence of all denominationalism, or, better, the union of all denominations."[30]

In such a setting, collegians heard things lending a wider perspective of what it was like to think Christianly about lives of service, through meetings with leaders in prison relief, rescue mission work, and inner city charities. Meeting delegates from other cultures, like Japan—who had come from the Far East to be part of Northfield—reminded collegians from Yale how precious the privilege was of Bible study under well respected thought leaders. Yale delegates had only to board a train from nearby New Haven; delegates from Japan crossed an ocean and a continent to go deep in the things of God. To see faith mirrored in the eyes of their Japanese friends made a profound and lasting impression.

"All these things," H.B. Wright concluded, "combine to give the college man a better and a truer view of life and to lead him to think seriously upon his own place of work in the world."[31]

And Yale, Wright told his readers, owed "the Northfield conferences a peculiar debt of gratitude." During the years from 1890 to 1900 the Northfield delegation from New Haven, bringing together as it did, each year, "men of all classes and departments, of varied circumstances, with concentration of interests and singleness of purpose," did much to return these students to their university united in purpose and resolve to live for Christ.[32]

Northfield, Wright remembered, "even with a delegation of over a hundred," was a place where all university class lines were "broken down, and in a few days men come to know one another as they meet in the common dining-room and at the delegation meetings as would be well-nigh impossible at New Haven."[33]

The evening Yale delegation meetings held a special place for Wright, leaving "their impress most strongly upon the lives of individuals and upon Yale as a whole." Then, "every night of the ten days of the conference," the Yale delegation "met to gather up the results of the day and apply them." Scarcely a movement of recent years, Wright said, in which the men of Yale had "engaged for the improvement of the religious and moral life of the university which cannot be traced back to suggestions made or plans set on foot at these meetings."[34]

Down from the hilltops where Moody, A.J. Gordon, and other leaders spoke, Wright said that "eight hundred Yale men have come since 1886." Many went back to New Haven "to right wrongs of the past and to ally themselves more closely with the church and the [Young Men's] Christian Association." All, he said, "have felt a new force in their lives. The enthusiasm and consecration which they have brought with them have been contagious and have been a mighty leavening force for good in the Association, the church, and through them in Yale."[35]

* * *

If H.B. Wright memorably recreated what it was like to attend the Northfield Summer Conferences, A.J. Gordon's talks there were some of the best-remembered moments from the famous "ten day" event. These talks were later published for readers throughout America, and beyond.

The first such address was one Gordon gave in the summer of 1881, published in *Gems from Northfield*. To read this address is to hear something of his voice in settings like East Hall, or on the hill called Round Top. Here, Gordon said: "It refreshes me to remember that we have the Holy Spirit always with us. In the 9th chapter of Acts, and 31st verse, we read: *'Then had the churches rest throughout all Judea and Galilee and Samaria, and were edified; walking in the fear of the Lord, and in the comfort of the Holy Ghost...'*"[36] It is the Christian's privilege, Gordon stated, "to walk in the comfort of the Holy Spirit. We ought to have real, solid comfort when the Comforter is with us.[37]

To explain this truth memorably, Gordon told a story that mingled humor and winsome truth. It came from the Rev. William Jay of England, for many years a great friend of the reformer, William Wilberforce.

Jay had written a famous book called *Morning Exercises*, and in its pages, Gordon remembered, Jay spoke of

> a poor woman in his parish...one of the most distressed Christians he ever saw. She was always in trouble, [and] said to him:
>
> "Oh, Mr. Jay, if the Lord knew how much trouble I was going to cause Him, He wouldn't have had anything to do with me."
>
> [Jay] answered her that God *did know* what trouble we were going to cause Him, every one of us. However faithless and backsliding we were going to be, He knew it all from the beginning, *and yet He did have to do with us, and received us.* She wiped away her tears, and said: "Well, if the Lord does save me, He will never hear the last of it." And that should be the spirit of us all.[38]

After telling this moving story, Gordon said he wished "to say something on the subject of being filled with the Spirit, and its relation to our work in the world." A great many, he noted, "seem to think that being filled with the Spirit is something mysterious, intangible, and difficult to apprehend." Yet, Gordon said, "this cannot be so, because it is a command that we be thus filled, and God would not command anything so mysterious that we could not grasp it, apprehend it, undertake it." Moreover, the command to be filled with the Spirit was "just as much a command as that we should believe on the Lord Jesus Christ, and do works meet for repentance. We are to live," Gordon told the Northfield delegation, "in communion with the ascended Christ, and so drink in the power of the Spirit that we shall be filled. Only thus can we have power."[39]

Why was he insistent on this point of Christian teaching?

Gordon urged his listeners to consider something they might have missed. "You must have noticed," he said, "that there is no marked instance of great success on the part of Christ himself and the Apostles where we do not have the account prefaced by some such words as *being filled with the Holy Ghost.*" Here, Gordon offered a vivid reminder—

It was so when Peter came before the council. It was so when Stephen saw Jesus. It was so when Paul gave that awful rebuke—spoke those burning words to the sorcerer. All through the Acts of the Apostles, when anything signal or mighty is done, you have it prefaced with the remark, "being filled with the Holy Ghost." And I suppose it is just as true to-day. If we do anything great in the name of the Lord Jesus, it is because we are filled with the Spirit.[40]

Gordon's own experience in this regard had been striking. As James Francis, Gordon's later successor in at Clarendon Street Church recalled, and later told Nathan Wood, one evening he and several other young men who had met with Gordon thought to ask how the Spirit came to him.

Gordon answered: "I simply knelt and said, 'O God, Thou hast said by the lips of Jesus that Thou art more ready to give the Holy Spirit to them that ask Thee than we are to give good gifts to our children. *Father, I take Thee at Thy word.* I ask Thee in Jesus' name for the Holy Spirit.' Then I got up and went about my work."

At this, Francis and his friends said, "Was that all?"

"What more was necessary?" Gordon replied. "But I can say this, that from that hour, as I have gone about my parish, and to and from hospitals and meetings, it has often seemed that my feet hardly touched the sidewalk."[41]

* * *

To those listening in Northfield in 1881, Gordon spoke in much the same vein. Those who "made way for the Spirit to enter into them and fill them," he said, "are so filled with the Spirit that they drop seeds here and there and make the wilderness rejoice and blossom as the rose. They make even the desert become a garden, and they do it inevitably." Some Christians, he thought, have thus "done good without knowing it, without intending it [and] I don't know but that, if we were fully the Lord's, the greater part of the good we did would be that of which we were not cognizant. Service would overflow from us. That is the true idea, is it not, of the Christian?"[42]

To compliment these thoughts, Gordon spoke about two central facets of the Christian life. The first was conversion, which he described as something we receive—the gift of faith, the priceless bequest of God.

Yet the second facet, consecration, or the giving of self fully to God, was really the only thing "we have to give," as Paul of Tarsus said: *present your bodies a living sacrifice unto God.* In other words, Gordon explained, "Give your time, strength, intellect, heart, everything you have and are, to the Lord. If you give yourself, it doesn't matter what else you give. Your gold and silver will be sanctified. Give yourself utterly to God...Become indeed a temple of the Holy Ghost. Then shall you know what it is to be filled with the Spirit and you shall abound in every good work."[43]

* * *

In 1885, Gordon's visits to Northfield were so well regarded they were written into the early history of Northfield Seminary. Two visits that year were especially noteworthy.

The first took place on Thursday June 18, graduation day at the seminary. Gordon gave the parting address to the senior class, of sixteen members, in the new chapel of Marquand Hall. His commencement speech was a telling symbol of his commitment to the schools D.L. Moody founded.[44]

Then, in August 1885, the third Northfield Summer Conference was held. Present for the occasion were J.E. Kynaston Studd of London, and Dr. A.T. Pierson, whose address about foreign missions made a deep impression on all who heard it. Much of what he shared was later published in a book called *The Crisis of Missions.*[45]

A.J. Gordon was also there, and "spoke a number of times upon the ideal, possibilities, and factors of Christian life." His words were called "fresh every time they are heard," and were said to "deeply stir the hearts of those who listen." These views, *The Northfield Seminary Handbook* stated, "may by found in [Dr. Gordon's] books," released by D.L. Moody's publisher, F.H. Revell, and "in the monthly periodical, called *The Watchword,* that [Dr. Gordon] edits in Boston."[46]

* * *

One of A.J. Gordon's finest Northfield talks was later printed in *Select Northfield Sermons*, published in 1897, with talks given by H.W. Webb-Peploe, Prebendary of St. Paul's Cathedral, London, and missionary leader Andrew Murray, among others.

Speaking about the work of the Holy Spirit, Gordon said, "I believe that He is in the church in living power, [and] if you will only let Him, He will do things of which you hardly dream—in the management of the church and the raising of funds—but most especially in the preaching of the gospel." Only think, Gordon continued, "of how many things Christ promised: (1st) the Spirit was to show us things to come; (2nd) to bring all things to our remembrance, and (3rd) in the epistle to the Romans He has promised to help our infirmities. There is nothing we need that He has not promised to do for us; and His help is to me the most real experience."[47]

Gordon also said that when we live earnestly seeking the Holy Spirit's guidance, we are many times prompted by "just such a suggestion that could not have come from anywhere else except from God through the Holy Ghost."

Here, Gordon voiced a thought consonant with the teaching of Luke 12:12, where the Lord Jesus told his disciples what to expect when they were brought before authorities and asked to answer for the hope within them. "The Holy Spirit," Jesus said, "will teach you in that very hour what you ought to say."

To show what he meant, Gordon shared a deeply moving vignette from his own experience. Here, the Holy Spirit had prompted him, and when he yielded to that suggestion, a great blessing resulted that he, and many others witnessed first hand. "I was preaching one Sunday in my church," he said, "and it occurred to me to illustrate what I was saying by an anecdote which I had read long ago, and had quite forgotten until I went into the church that morning."

So Gordon told his parishioners at Clarendon Street Church a story connected with the famous Professor Blaikie of Edinburgh.

One day, Dr. Blaikie, called upon a student to recite. The student stood and held his book before him in his left hand.

At this, Blaikie said: *"Please take your book in your right hand."*

The student blushed and stammered, but kept his book in his left hand and went on reading, whereupon, the professor thundered at him:

"Young man, don't you know manners? Take that book in your right hand!"

The student stopped reading, paused, and then lifted the stump of his right arm, saying—

"I have no right hand, Professor."

The entire class was aghast. Dr. Blaikie, ashen-faced and instantly chastened, came over and put his arms around the student and begged his pardon.[48]

When Gordon finished telling this story, he spoke of the great lesson it held: "If you cannot take hold of Jesus Christ, He will take hold of you and lift you up."

As Gordon finished his sermon, a young man in the audience rose, and lifted up the stump of his right arm, saying—

"I am that very young man."

Gordon and everyone there marveled.

Quickly, and kindly, he asked the young man to please come to the pulpit, and in his own words he confirmed everything Gordon had shared.

"How did that illustration happen to flash into my mind that morning?" Gordon said. "The impression of the truth and force of what I had been saying about being taken hold of when we cannot take hold, was tremendous."

Gordon closed by re-affirming what he had experienced so indelibly: "May the Holy Spirit [help us to] learn that our strength is made perfect in weakness, our sovereignty is made victorious in surrender!"[49]

* * *

One of those who remembered A.J. Gordon's sojourns in Northfield well was J. Wilbur Chapman. A close friend of D.L. Moody, Chapman later wrote a famous hymn sharing the same melody with "Come, Thou Long Expected Jesus." Its title is given in the first line, and began—

Jesus, what a friend for sinners,
Jesus, Lover of my soul...[50]

As to Northfield, Chapman long remembered its association with prominent leaders "whom Mr. Moody was wise enough to call to his assistance and help."[51]

One of these was A.J. Gordon, "the honored pastor for so many years of the Clarendon Street Baptist Church in Boston. Mr. Moody relied much upon him," Chapman said, and often dwelt "upon his readiness to do any service, to take any place, to stand in any gap."[52]

Chapman wrote movingly of "Dr. Gordon's later ministry at Northfield," and in particular of "the evening baptism in the lake which has, since his death, been called after his name." These services, Chapman said—

> were of great solemnity. The assembled people, the soft singing in the eventide air, the majestic baptismal formula... [Dr. Gordon's] face as it had been the face of an angel, the broken waters, and the resurrection chant at the end— these things can never be forgotten by those who stood by the water's edge.[53]

But of all those to speak of Gordon's time in Northfield, none wrote better about its lasting influence than Ernest Gordon, who had witnessed his father's ministry there for much of his life. As a graduate of Harvard, Class of 1888, he knew how often his father was heard with great respect by scores of collegians from all over the world. Remembering this, he wrote—

> At the Northfield college conferences [father's] influence upon young men was always marked...Mr. Robert P. Wilder, the original and most prominent leader in the Student Volunteer Movement, since grown to such proportions, has declared in a recent letter that to A.J. Gordon and to J. Hudson Taylor he owes more for the development of his spiritual life than to any others, living or dead. [And] in later years, in addition to the addresses given at these college conferences, [father] spoke at various times at Yale,

Amherst, Rutgers, Mount Holyoke, Williams, at Princeton...
and at Brown, always with great acceptance.[54]

* * *

Gordon's long involvement with Northfield, and the student summer conferences, led D.L. Moody to call him to another famous undertaking: the great Chicago World's Fair mission of 1893, which lasted for six months, beginning on May 7th of that year.

In March, Moody had written a memorable letter to Gordon, setting out just what this "opportunity of a century" promised—

> My dear Dr. Gordon,
>
> I was away from Northfield as you know last year, & this year I want much to be there; but June & July I want to make as strong as possible.
>
> Now if you will go to Chicago *June* or *July* & give all the month, I will give you $1,000, & it will be a great favour to me. Can you not do it?
>
> We will have 300 students, & you will have as good a chance to work as you will ever have in your life—for we will not only have the students, but leading Christian people from all over the world--& you will speak to the nations.
>
> I hope you will take it a call from on High,
>
> Yours as Ever,
> D.L. Moody[55]

Gordon must have smiled on reading a letter that was more like a benign onslaught—but he knew his friend well, and knew Moody was right about the import of this new endeavor. He sent back word of acceptance. He and Maria then boarded a train west, and spent the month of July 1883 in Chicago.[56]

But Gordon did more than take part in the massive undertaking the Chicago World's Fair mission represented. He wrote at length about it, much as what we now call a "participant observer." Few records of the World's Fair were as richly detailed, and we are able to closely follow Gordon's ministry in the west as a result.

But his writings about the Chicago World's Fair mission were more than a travelogue. They were, in their way, a brief memoir of Moody. For as Gordon said in the opening of his first article for *The Watchword* magazine: "A man's work often furnishes the best character-sketch of himself which can possibly be drawn. We therefore give an outline of Mr. Moody's summer campaign in Chicago as a kind of full-length portrait of the evangelist himself."[57]

After he'd introduced his mission memoir, Gordon moved to a description of how the Chicago World's Fair outreach had been organized.

"Four of the largest churches," he said—

> in different parts of the city, are held for Sunday evenings and various week-evening services. Two theaters, "The Empire" and "The Haymarket," located in crowded centers, are open on Sundays, and the former on every week-night, and they are not infrequently filled to their utmost capacity while the gospel is preached and sung. Five tents are pitched in localities where the unprivileged and non-church-going multitudes live. In these services are held nightly, and as we have visited them we have found them always filled with such, for the most part, as do not attend any place of Protestant worship.[58]

This overview of venues and their purpose was impressive, but they weren't the extent of what Moody, Gordon, and others were undertaking.

"A hall in the heart of the city," he noted, "is kept open night after night, the services continuing far on to the morning hours."[59] This hall in the heart of city had a specific intent: a setting for ministry among alcoholics and prostitutes. They were among the most destitute of Chicago's people, and Moody had known their plight only too well in the days when, as a young man he ventured into the slums. Often at risk to his own life, and drawing down on his life savings, he had brought food, clothing, and coal for them and their families—sharing all the while of the faith that brought hope into his own life. He had hoped then that hope might become theirs. Now, forty years later, he had not forgotten the needs of these people or their families.

Among folk who had never known any kind of church, Moody had long since learned the value of word pictures, or vivid stories that brought heaven's hope near.

One fine anecdote came by way of C.H. Spurgeon, the great friend of both Gordon and Moody. One day, Mr. Spurgeon, Moody said—

> went into the country to spend time with a friend. This friend had a weathervane on his barn, and on the weathervane were the words "God is Love."
>
> "What do you mean by that?" said Spurgeon. "Do you mean that God's love is as changeable as the wind?"
>
> "Not at all," the friend was quick to explain, "I believe that God is love—whichever way the wind blows."[60]

Moody was no less adept at telling a story with appeal to a more educated audience, as with this vignette drawn directly from the life and letters of Alfred, Lord Tennyson. "The poet," Moody began—

> once asked an elderly lady if there was any news.
>
> "Why, Mr. Tennyson," she said, "there's only one piece of news that I know, and that is—Christ died for all men."
>
> At this, Tennyson told her:
>
> *"That is old news, and good news, and new news."*[61]

Gordon saw all this first hand, and it left a deep impression. What is more, it was of a piece with the kind of "home mission" work he and parishioners at Clarendon Street Church had done for many years.

* * *

Another facet of the Chicago World's Fair mission involved the Chicago Bible Institute that D.L. Moody had founded in 1886, the school known today as Moody Bible Institute. Gordon was asked to give daily lectures "for the instruction in the Bible of the students, Christian workers, ministers, missionaries, and others who wish to attend." The hall for these lectures seated 350 comfortably, and was "always filled." Along with Gordon, "there were thirty-eight preachers, evangelists, and singers, and others cooperating in the work." Moreover, their labors were "supplemented by an endless variety of house-to-house and highway-and-hedge effort by the 250 students in residence in the Institute."[62]

Gordon long recalled Moody's brief, pungent statement of the hopes he cherished for this great mission. "We shall beat the World's Fair!" Here, as Gordon knew, Moody was saying that of all the wonders the World's Fair could boast—modern marvels of technology, beautifully constructed venues, and the like—none could surpass the wonder, the matchless gift of faith. The gospel mission now underway was a great effort intended to do everything possible to commend faith to millions who would attend the World's Fair.

Gordon described it all, beginning with a flourish of Lincolnesque prose—

> With malice toward none and charity toward all, this is what [Moody] set out to do—to furnish such gospel attractions, by supplementing the churches and cooperating with them, that the multitudes visiting the city might be kept in attendance on religious services on Sunday instead of attending the Fair. So it has been. Mr. Moody estimates that from 30,000 to 40,000 people have been reached by his special Sunday evangelistic services.
>
> This, multiplied by seven days easily foots up about 100,000 brought weekly within reach of the gospel.
>
> The World's Fair has been closed on Sunday for want of attendance, but the religious services are daily growing. Every good opening for the gospel is readily seized. When Forepaugh's great circus tent had been set up in the city, Mr. Moody tried to secure it for Sunday. He was granted the use of it for a Sabbath morning service, but as the manager expected Sunday in Chicago to be a great harvest day, he reserved the tent on the afternoon and evening for his own

performances. Fifteen thousand people came to hear the simple gospel preached and sung at the morning service. The circus, however, was so poorly attended in the afternoon and evening that Sunday exhibitions were soon abandoned.

More than that, the manager said he had never been in the habit of giving performances on Sunday and should not attempt it again, and he offered, if Mr. Moody would appoint an evangelist to travel with him, to open his tent thereafter on Sundays for gospel meetings, and be responsible for all expenses. It was the same with the theaters. At first they declined to allow religious services on Sunday. Their performances on that day not having proved as successful as they anticipated, now Mr. Moody can hire almost any one which he wishes to secure.[63]

So the first part of Gordon's "Moody memoir" closed; but there was more to share, namely with those attending the Northfield Summer Conference of 1893. When Gordon went there, fresh on the heels of his time in Chicago, on the 1st of August 1893, "there was an eager desire to learn all about it." So he gave a morning address on "Mr. Moody's Work in Chicago."[64]

"You will remember," Gordon said, "that I came to this conference directly from Chicago, where I have been during the month of July assisting Mr. Moody as best I could in the great work…undertaken for that city in this centennial year."[65] The last Sunday he had been there, Gordon said, *The Chicago Inter-Ocean* newspaper "gave the largest attendance that could be counted on the Fairgrounds as less than 30,000. Mr. Moody estimated that on a recent Sunday there were gathered in connection with his evangelistic services 40,000 people, while the regular church services were also remarkably well attended."[66]

Seldom had the gospel received such a hearing, among so many, and here A.J. Gordon's kindred spirit with D.L. Moody came to the fore. He genuinely relished the unconventional nature of what had been undertaken, with the innovation and outside-the-box vision behind it all.

"Now I like the spirit in which [Mr. Moody,] our beloved friend and leader undertook this work," Gordon told his listeners—

Some said, "Let us boycott the Fair;" others said, "Let us appeal to the law and put in money enough to prosecute its managers and compel them to shut it up."

But our friend, Mr. Moody, said: "Now let us open so many preaching-places and present so many attractions that the people from all parts of the world will come and hear the gospel," and that is actually what has happened.[67]

Moody's foresight and perseverance yielded a sphere of influence that would be felt throughout the world. "This is what I often found to be true," Gordon said, "these congregations were made up of people from every part of the United States and Canada, and I may say from every part of the globe…a great mass of people brought together from every nation and every race in the world, and preachers are brought together who can speak to them in their own tongue. So it is a remarkable movement… all the world is present in Chicago, and being there, they come to hear the gospel. I consider it one of the most blessed triumphs of the grace of God."[68]

Then, taking aim squarely at those who had wrong-headedly clamored for bringing legal action against the World's Fair organizers, Gordon stated emphatically that Moody's strategy of engagement was best. The right way to win people over, he said, "is not by violence, not by law, not by threatening, but by a counter-attraction, *by offering something better.*"[69]

Indeed, Gordon concluded,

we may praise God that such advantage is being taken of this great occasion…We shall never again see such an event. I need not say that the Fair is magnificent; it is a dazzling alabaster city set on the lake. People are there from every part of the earth; and next to that architectural wonder, and the marvelous display of art and science and beauty of every sort, I consider that the most striking thing in that city to-day is the evangelistic work that is going on.[70]

* * *

Nor was Gordon the only clergyman who found the Chicago World's Fair mission transformative. He recalled one pastoral friend who had said: "I have had a new experience…in preaching to crowds of rough, dissolute, hardened men on the streets. I, who had been accustomed to a daintily carved pulpit, where the light came through stained glass windows, and where everything pleased the senses. I realized to-day, as never before, how Jesus must have felt as he preached to just such crowds of lost, wretched souls."[71] That Gordon shared this story, from so many that he might have told, said much about his own commitment to ministry beyond the safe confines of a local church. Far too often, many looked on a church as little than a spiritual social club. It was always meant to be more: in keeping with a rescue mission—better still a beacon for neighbors in time of need and in all seasons of life.

Apart from this, Gordon was himself deeply grateful for opportunities to speak to large gatherings at Moody's Chicago Bible Institute.

"I was there, giving Bible lectures each morning at nine o'clock," he said. "What surprised me in connection with that work was especially this: that room was filled at nine o'clock in the morning every day I was there; and mechanics, blacksmiths, and farmers were present in order to get the help for carrying on the work in the towns of the West from which they came."[72]

Also present were "quite a large number of theological students" who had come "to spend their vacations and take the lectures." Gordon also learned that there were more than a few "returned missionaries present, and quite a number of pastors from different parts of the country who had come for the lectures." Given these different groups, Gordon found himself consistently speak before "350 to 400 listeners in the class-room."[73]

What they told him left a lingering impression. "These men," he said, "were frank enough to say: 'This is just what we [need]; we have had the minute study of Greek and Hebrew, but we want more biblical study."[74]

* * *

Other impressions stayed with Gordon too, among them the way Moody vividly set an example of servant leadership for Chicago Bible Institute students. "One thing I would like to say in Mr. Moody's absence," Gordon told conference guests at Northfield—

> [and] I think it is a true test, according to Jesus Christ…of spiritual greatness, *that one is ready to take any place.*
>
> I was preaching one night in a hall in Chicago, on the first floor, where the people could flow in easily, and I looked through the open door and our friend Mr. Moody was out on the sidewalk, pulling men in while I was preaching.
>
> He brought them in and seated them, sometimes taking hold of them and urging them with considerable energy to get them in; and that sort of service…goes on repeatedly in that hall [one of the worst places in Chicago,] until two or three o'clock in the morning.[75]

Throughout their stay in Chicago, A.J. and Maria Gordon had lodgings at Moody's Chicago Bible Institute. During the four weeks they were there, Gordon preached in the city churches on Sunday mornings and evenings, and spoke at various inner-city meetings throughout the week. As stated above, he also lectured to an average of 350 students daily at the Bible Institute.[76] It was taxing, but he relished every moment.

At the same time, Moody was very well aware of Maria Gordon's gifts, saying: "We must utilize Mrs. Gordon while she is here."[77]

Just how that resolve from Moody unfolded is shown in a letter Maria wrote home to her children. "I have" she told them—

> been off speaking this P.M. at a Union Meeting for Ladies at Dr. Mather's church. Tomorrow I am advertised [to speak] at the Mother's Meeting [on] Chicago Ave. [Mr. Moody's church].
>
> Thursday evening I am to address a women's meeting at Mr. Shivera's Tent. And Friday to take charge of the noonday meeting at Willard Hall.
>
> So you will see that it takes all my time to prepare and

attend & rest after these meetings. Saturday night I took charge of the meeting at Bethseda Mission & Sunday was three hours at the Jail, & addressed two meetings. I will reserve for another letter an account of what Mr. Moody is planning for next week.[78]

Taking in all they had witnessed and been part of, the Gordons were awed by the massive venture that marked their time in Chicago.

"Truly," A.J. Gordon wrote home, "[Moody] is the Napoleon of the religious world. No such campaign was ever imagined. It matches the World's Fair...I thank God that I am counted worthy to be in it."[79]

* * *

Of the many times Gordon spoke at Northfield, none proved as meaningful as the August morning in 1894 when he preached on the resurrection of Christ.[80] "No one," said D.L. Moody, "who listened to [Dr. Gordon's] closing sermon in our new auditorium—to the largest audience ever assembled in Northfield, will forget that morning and the comforting message he delivered. As he talked to us for the last time, his theme was the resurrection...We were privileged to hear [his] voice, and that message... With the gathering [anew] in the hall will come the remembrance of [our] friend's face and the words *"I am the resurrection and the life."*[81]

Moody spoke again of this "valedictory" sermon after Gordon's unexpected passing in February 1895, saying: "Dear man—he has got home, and left a bright light behind him...We will have a memorial service [in Northfield] this summer, in the same place where he spoke on the resurrection."[82]

Few things are more poignant about A.J. Gordon's life than this. Moody, and many others, never forgot his stirring address on the resurrection, the centerpiece of faith. It was later reprinted in *Northfield Echoes*, a fitting book title indeed. If we would hear something of Gordon's voice as it then was, and know something of the spiritual wisdom God gave him—this address, and this subject, are the place to begin.

Gordon began by telling the collegians present to turn to Romans 8:11, which he then read out for them: *"But if the Spirit of Him that raised up Jesus from the dead dwell in you, He that raised up Christ from the dead shall quicken your mortal bodies by His Spirit that dwelleth in you."*[83]

Gordon then turned to *The Pilgrim's Progress,* one of the timeless masterworks of English literature. Gordon knew it from cover to cover, and quoted passages many times in his own books.[84] He could make Bunyan's text come alive as he spoke, vividly calling forth characters and scenes.

"You know," Gordon said, "how vividly [John] Bunyan personifies...events and incidents...He talks graphically about 'the terrible Captain Sepulchre and his standard-bearer, Corruption.' I think I hear those two talking over the situation on the night that Jesus Christ was buried. Corruption says to Sepulchre: 'Hold fast to that man in Joseph's tomb yonder! There is a rumor that he proposes to break forth from the grave; do not let him go till I can fasten upon him.'"

"But," Gordon continued—

> Corruption fails to touch Him during all those hours in the tomb, because it had been written, "Thou wilt not suffer Thine Holy One to see corruption." Then Hell from beneath cries out, "Hold fast to this man. If he comes out he will make a breach in the walls of death through which all the prisoners of Hades will escape." And, "he that hath the power of death, even the devil," exclaims in fright, "If thou let this man go, thou art not Satan's friend!"
>
> But vain the seal, and vain the watch, and vain the grip of death, and vain the doors of the tomb. As it began to dawn the first day of the week, there began to be a mighty stir in the sepulchre; terrible Captain Sepulchre tightens his grip, but in vain. "It was not possible that He should beholden of death."
>
> He rises. He lives, even as saith the Scripture: "For this cause Christ died and rose and revived that He might be Lord both of the living and of the dead.[85]

Beyond the shining images John Bunyan cast, Gordon told his listeners that Christians are heir to an ever-living hope—the resurrection's resplendent power. For benighted humanity, Christ comes a risen Savior—a truth "wonderfully divine," and "wonderfully human."[86]

Then Gordon asked, "And what proof does He give that He is risen?"

Pillars of scripture held the key, and Gordon paraphrased them beautifully. As he did, heaven's hope drew close—

> "Reach hither thy finger...behold My hands...reach hither thy hand, and thrust it into My side, and be not faithless but believing"...I am the same Jesus who was crucified, and these nail-prints are the proofs that I am the same and not another...a spirit hath not flesh and bones...I have a body like your own...Again He said to them: "Have ye any meat? And they gave Him a piece of a broiled fish and of an honeycomb. And He took it and did eat before them."[87]

Our Lord, Gordon said, was "wonderfully human," taking food just as we can; but, on the other hand, "wonderfully divine...passing through the closed doors where His disciples were assembled, as a ray of sunlight passes through a pane of glass...So like to men and yet so unlike! so earthly and yet so heavenly!"[88] Here indeed were bright emblems of faith—for there was none like unto the Savior.

* * *

Next, Gordon described the two-fold victory Jesus won through His resurrection. Remembering 2 Timothy 1:10, Gordon said Christ "abolished death," and "brought life and immortality to light."

He then used this verse as a point of departure to contrast hope, as set in the sayings of Plato, with teachings of the apostle Paul.[89] Here, Gordon's lifelong study of classical languages and literature served him well. He could quote copiously and insightfully from books by the ancient sage of Greece. These reflections would have been the more telling for the many collegians to whom he speaking on that summer morning in Northfield.

"Did not the philosophers bring immortality to light?" Gordon asked. So many believe. But in truth, there was a vast difference "between the immortality of faith and the immortality of philosophy."[90]

Plato stated, "I *hope* that the dead will live beyond the grave." Paul could say, "I *know* that the dead will live again this side of the grave." The difference, Gordon said, lay between a good hope and a blessèd assurance.

Elsewhere, Plato had written movingly of the close of life. "I hope," he said, "that when the body returns to the grave the soul will go forth like an uncaged eagle and soar away to realms of freedom and tranquility, forever free from the trammels and fetters of a material body."

Here was Plato's dream of immortality; and yet it was deeply poignant to acknowledge *that is all it was*. The hope of this dream went no further than the aspiration so beautifully expressed.

In contrast, Paul confirmed the hope given to every Christian in scripture: "the spirit that had been separated from the body a little while should go back and re-inhabit it and lift it up, and that body would be transfigured and glorified, and made like the body of Jesus Christ."[91]

In other words, Gordon said, Plato hoped for the immortality of the soul. Resurrection hope, through Christ, truly brought "the immortality of man—the whole man."[92] Then came one of the finest images Gordon ever conveyed.

"God," he said, "is not satisfied that the spirit should go out, and the body lie forever in the grave, but the two must be brought together, the sanctified body and the sanctified soul, remarried, after the long divorce of sin and death, in the wedlock of resurrection, never to be divorced again. That is our hope, and that is the hope of the gospel."[93]

* * *

Next, Gordon moved from a reflective contrast of Plato and Paul to thoughts about resurrection vis-à-vis the created world.

"Preachers say," he told his listeners, "that nature teaches the doctrine of the resurrection just as distinctly as the Scriptures. I say, yes, it does—as far as it goes."[94]

True enough, he said—

> the seed…dropped into the earth blooms to-morrow into a
> flower,—a beautiful type of resurrection. The day that sinks
> into night this evening, and is wrapped about in the shroud

of darkness, will rise to-morrow in resurrection beauty as it is led forth by the sun coming out of his chamber like a bridegroom, rejoicing as a strong man to run a race; and we have a new day, another type of the resurrection. And the year that is full of beauty and bloom will in a few months lie down in the sepulchre of winter and be wrapped about with the winding sheet of snow. But in the springtime it will revive again, and nature will be preaching "resurrection! resurrection!"[95]

These were beautiful images, Gordon knew, yet there would always be a somber truth for analogies of resurrection woven in nature.

"That flower that rose out of the [ground]," he said, "in a little while dies! The day that has had its resurrection, in a little while will lie down again in the sepulchre of night. The year that bursts into bloom which we call spring, will in a few months again return to the grave of ice. *There is no resurrection in nature that is not followed by death.*"[96]

But, Gordon said, we may find the resplendent glory of the true resurrection. There, amid the high hills of Northfield, he offered parting thoughts something like a doxology or hymn. Hundreds heard him say these words; thousands more would read them in the years to come—

O you that have laid away your loved ones, has one of you been able to open the door to bring them back? How you have wished that some fair morning you could go out and turn the key and usher them back, and introduce them into the world again!

But there is One that has the key, "Fear not, I am He that liveth and was dead, and behold I am alive forever more, and have the keys of death and of the grave." Thou art the King of Kings, O Christ, but Thou art also the King and Conqueror of death, and in a little while we shall hear Thy voice sounding down from heaven, *"Awake, and sing ye that dwell in the dust."*

And we will sing, as He calls us to Him.[97]

Chapter Nineteen
To See the Morningstar

And all the rest will come as certainly as the green
leaf comes in the springtime... May we remember...
and let it be with us as it was in the beginning...[1]
—A.J. Gordon

Wednesday, December 26, 1894 dawned fair but cold in the city of Boston. Winds grew brisk later that day, with an overnight forecast for rain or heavy snow. Grey clouds gathered.[2] In the evening, carriages travelled the narrow city streets, gas lamps lit each thoroughfare against a lowering sky. Passengers and pedestrians alike bundled warmly against the bitter wind and cold.

Still, hundreds braved the elements that evening to gather for a celebration at Clarendon Street Church—amid warmth inside, and bright chandelier lights. There, it was as though they had found a castle keep, and the conditions outside were just so much sound and inclement weather.

This was the more fitting an image, as the red brick and quarried stone of Clarendon Street Church lent grace and strength to its twin towers and buttresses, hallmarks of the American Gothic style that guided its designers.

And of course, December 26th fell within the twelve days of Christmas. For all who had come to mark an anniversary, it may have been a day of "bleak midwinter" without—but there was reverence for the King of Kings within.

A castle keep indeed.

* * *

The anniversary celebration of this December day was set to honor the twenty-fifth year of A.J. Gordon's pastorate at Clarendon Street Church.

As parishioners and invited guests arrived, they walked through a sanctuary that mingled black walnut woodwork and light frescoes. Well-placed aisles gave easy access to any of the church's two hundred pews, which could seat up to twelve hundred people. A grand organ graced the front of the sanctuary. When played, this powerful instrument lifted many an anthem heavenward in ways that could only be called majestic. Sacred song filled the air.[3]

Resounding music captured the joy of this anniversary celebration too, for Clarendon Street's pastor, by this time, was known throughout America as a gifted musician and composer of hymns.

The Christian Work newspaper described festivities that set the stage for this special evening. On December 26th, the paper stated—

> was celebrated the 25th anniversary of Dr. A.J. Gordon's pastorate. There was a very large reception in the auditorium from 5 until 6 o'clock for Dr. and Mrs. Gordon, and supper was served to 500 in the vestry. At the exercises in the evening, [several] addresses were made...[4]

The Congregationalist, another of Boston's leading religious magazines, also covered this event. It reported—

> A quarter of a century in a Boston pulpit is not a very rare thing in the history of this city, but today it is almost unique. Dr. A.J. Gordon of the Clarendon Street Baptist Church enjoys that distinction, and the church to which he has ministered so long has many honorable distinctions, one of them being that its contributions to missions have for years been the largest of any Baptist church in the country. Dr. Gordon's twenty-fifth anniversary was fitly celebrated...

leading ministers of other denominations sharing in the exercises…

Dr. Gordon has been and is the leader in many noble enterprises, some of which have world-wide influence…Few men in this generation have been so blessed as instruments in renewing souls through the Holy Spirit.

We earnestly join in the prayer that he may be spared to continue his ministry in the Clarendon Street Church for another twenty-five years.[5]

One tribute to Gordon, sent by letter, was from Edward Everett Hale, Minister of Boston's South Congregational Church; a distinguished author known throughout America for his classic novella, *The Man Without A Country*.

Hale was unable to attend the December 26th anniversary, and his Unitarian leanings were a faith tradition far different from the Baptist faith. But his respect for Gordon was very genuine, and fulsomely expressed. Hale stated—

We are all indebted to you for your loyal and constant service, in what you do yourself, and for what you stimulate others to do. And I am thankful that we have such good prospects for looking forward…for the same service to the kingdom—from you and your dear Mrs. Gordon.[6]

The Boston Journal, for its part, caught the essence of this anniversary event when it reported, on page one: "It is seldom, indeed, that a clergyman is the recipient of so affectionate and respectful congratulations from members of all denominations as Dr. Gordon received."[7]

Gordon, for his part, read from a fine letter to his parishioners, recounting much of what had taken place in and among them. His pastor's heart shone through: "In the name of the Lord I greet you, wishing you a blessed New Year, and praying that all grace may abound toward you, and that you may be *enriched in everything unto all bountifulness*."[8]

"Twenty-five years," he said, "have passed since I entered upon my pastorate among you." The fruit of "these years of labor and prayer and fellowship" were now "abundantly manifest." A church once "a little over three hundred at the beginning," now numbered eleven hundred.[9] It had nearly quadrupled in size.

Gordon was also heartened to recall "the habit of systematic and special giving," that had taken hold at Clarendon Street—so much so, that in the year 1894 the church had given "more than *twelve thousand dollars* to the cause of foreign missions alone," with "proportionate gifts" to other benevolent endeavors. This was a sum worth something like $300,000 in modern currency.[10] Little wonder, then, Gordon felt deep gratitude that such a true spirit of philanthropy, or "love of humanity," was now an integral part of Clarendon Street's way of life.[11]

Home missions work had also flourished among his parishioners. Gordon spoke gratefully of the "devoted band of our young people ... going out Sunday after Sunday to preach the gospel to non-churchgoers at the wharves and at the car-stables." They worked seven days a week by harbor docks and carriage stations. To have the hope of heaven brought near in this way was an instance of outside-the-box kindness, or unconventional charity. Nor were immigrant groups neglected, and Gordon felt a pastor's pride over the "self-denying work" many had undertaken to assist the Jewish and Chinese communities of Boston.[12]

Other home mission endeavors involved "the young men and young women of the Missionary Training School," who were carrying on "a most efficient and extended work in house-to-house visitation." Hundreds of non-churchgoers, Gordon said, "are reached, labored with, and prayed with every week." Clarendon Street Church was no longer what it was at the outset of Gordon's ministry there: an inward-looking congregation bent solely on genteel, fashionable, inner-circle expressions of faith. People in the many neighborhoods close to the church knew its people cared. Its doors were open and its parishioners going out—commending Christ through food, clothing, shelter, listening ears, and consolation.

Gordon thought to close with the apostle Paul's words to the Thessalonians: *"From you sounded out the word of the Lord...in every place your faith...is spread abroad."*[13]

And if such had been Gordon's "pastoral letter," many tributes were given to him, and his time of ministry at Clarendon Street. *The Outlook* magazine covered the 25th anniversary in detail—

> One of the most spiritually suggestive preachers in the Baptist denomination in the United States is Dr. A.J. Gordon, of the Clarendon Street Baptist Church...
>
> Dr. Gordon is well known on both sides of the Atlantic as a preacher and an author. On the 26th of December the twenty-fifth anniversary of his pastorate in Boston was celebrated.
>
> In the afternoon a reception was held, when hosts of friends came to offer their congratulations. Later a supper was served in the vestry, at which not only members of the church and friends of the pastor, but distinguished members of his own denomination and those who brought fraternal greetings from other churches, were present.
>
> In the evening appropriate services were held in the auditorium. Dr. Gordon's own hymn, "My Jesus, I Love Thee," was rendered, and friends spoke their cordial appreciation of the man and his work.
>
> Among those who took part were Dr. G.C. Lorimer, Dr. Murdoch, Dr. E.B. Webb, Dr. Hovey, of Newton Seminary, Dr. Arthur T. Pierson, and Joseph Cook... A host of others besides those present...unite in extending their congratulations to the pastor, and to the church which he has served so long and well.[14]

For his part, Gordon, with the pastoral manner so many knew, replied to the formal tributes he'd been given in "a brief speech, half humorous, half serious." With self-deprecating charm, he "rebutted" these tributes, choosing instead to heap praise on "his people and his splendid cabinet of deacons."[15]

"The growth of a tree is due," he said, "not to its own excellences, but to the excellence of the soil at its roots." His only merit, he roguishly insisted, lay in his "staying so long where God had placed him, and where conditions were so favorable."[16]

Gordon then moved to more serious reflections—and, in the language of scripture, sought to "remember the works of the Lord" (Psalm 77:11).

"In twenty-five years," he said gratefully, "we have never been under the shadow of impending mortgage; finances have been kept so remarkably in hand that I have often asked: *'How do you do it?'*" The answer, he insisted, lay with other gifted leaders at Clarendon Street: "Charles S. Butler, Charles S. Kendall, and Miles Standish." Their wise stewardship had made all the difference.[17]

He looked to others, among them "that worthy man," former Church Superintendent Eben Shute, recently passed away, "whose absence we [mourn], whose presence was such a benediction." He thought of Clarendon Street's sexton, "twenty-five years ever faithful," and the many church organists whose gifted hands moved "upon the organ keys... to make melody." Last, he thought of how church-wide singing was a hallmark of Clarendon Street, music "taken out of a little box," or the sole province of a hired quartet, "and given to the congregation." Each of these people, and moments, he counted a blessing.[18]

Gordon then began, as he said, "to speak familiarly." It was five or six years, he stated—

> after I began my ministry here [that] I became exceedingly cast down over the slow progress that to me appeared to be made in the church, forgetting that the church of Jesus Christ is builded together for an habitation of God for the Spirit. In my discouragement I said: *"Why not let Him do it, and let the fact of the presence of Jesus Christ in the midst of the church, and having all power in heaven and earth, prove itself?"*[19]

Here was the key for any good that occurred during his time at Clarendon Street. "If the Holy Ghost," Gordon said, "can only have men and women who are willing to be used, there is nothing that cannot be accomplished. Let me publicly say that when I awoke to this fact, and began to preach it, and called you to pray about it, and put myself into the power of the Holy Ghost—then began the real progress in this church."[20]

Gordon then spoke of "Mr. and Mrs. [T.D.] Roberts," and their ministry at the Boston Industrial Home. "I want to praise God on their behalf," he said, for "there has been established in this city a work, by which not only have thousands been brought to Christ, but has been copied all over the United States, and for this combination of industry and conversion as shown in the [Home,] I want to thank God, a great number who have been brought into this church can rise up and call this work blessèd."[21]

Clarendon Street's "work among the Chinese" was next in Gordon's hall of remembrance. "Perhaps," he reflected, "this is the best work of the church, having its own missionary in China, and twenty-five representatives in the church, all true as steel. One who has been with us has said to me, 'I have been twenty-five years in China, I have visited your work, and you have in Clarendon Street Church as flourishing a mission to China as I had in Hong Kong.'"[22]

Here Gordon warmed to his theme. "How shall I speak," he asked—

> of the evangelism in missions, the money given or the interest growing up? How shall I speak of the work among the benighted dwellers in our own land, and remind you that the heart of one of our deacons was drawn out to the stained Magdalenes of our city, and that for [former prostitutes] a place of refuge has been established?
>
> …then [recall] just a moment: there were days when we were nearly broken-hearted over the perils of our Congo mission; and in the darkest days our missionary training school was started, to prepare humble lay workers or anybody who felt the call to go.
>
> I cannot tell you *all* about it; you have heard how they have gone out two by two into the destitute parts of New England, where they sometimes find one or two Christians, sometimes no Christians. They have been begged to stay, they have not been able to come back to their studies. *You have the way all open to you, to reach the ends of the world, in these scores of young men and women who have proved that they can go into these communities.*[23]

Here Gordon paused and reflected on the great privilege he had known as Clarendon Street's pastor, through all these seasons of hope. He then said forthrightly that he was only too well aware of his shortcomings. That many good things had taken place, despite his failings, was genuinely humbling; a point he made with gentle, self-deprecating humor.

"Do not think," he said, "that I have ever learned the secret that I longed to know—how to exercise the executive talent. All this has been but the simple growth of a tree, a branch here, a little fruit there, not because the tree has any executive talent, but because it abides in the earth. Let a church abide in Christ and rest in the Holy Ghost, and all the rest will come as certainly as the green leaf comes in the springtime."[24]

What lay ahead? Gordon hoped after twenty-five years he rightly understood. "As we begin another quarter century," he said, "we do so with full hearts and bowed heads."[25]

These were but other names for consecration and holy resolve. What made the difference was not "great preaching, great organizing, [or] great magnificence of architecture," but rather this truth: save for God's gracious leading and provision "we are nothing, and can do nothing." When we honestly confess this, Gordon said, "then can we glorify His name."[26]

He then recited a beautiful apostolic call from scripture, Jude 1, verse 3 –

"May we remember that the faith was delivered unto the saints, and let it be with us as it was in the beginning, pure; and the Lord bless us all. Amen."[27]

* * *

Gordon had closed with a watchword that he and his fellow parishioners remain faithful for all the days that lay ahead. The record of Clarendon Street Church was not yet closed, and the call to remain faithful was one he, and they, should always be careful to follow.[28]

That evening, when he and his wife Maria returned home, Gordon sat with her, and both reflected on all that this special day had brought. Then, going over to a nearby bookshelf, he took down a biography he had been reading, and thumbed through its pages. Finding the page he wanted, he said to Maria: "Here is something which just expresses my feelings." The passage read—

[this] jubilee passed over very pleasantly in one way, but was to me at the same time very solemn and humbling. I see in the retrospect so much that was altogether imperfect, and so much that was left undone. But it was a great gathering, and most hearty on the part of all the friends who came…I had no idea that I had so many friends in so many parts, and that the Lord had been pleased to use me in so many ways.[29]

The next morning, in keeping with the twelve days of Christmas, children and grandchildren gathered about the family breakfast-table. Also present was Gordon's close friend A.T. Pierson, and, as Ernest Gordon recalled: "what raillery, what wit, what flow of anecdote [there was] that morning! Retort and repartee coruscated and sparkled."[30]

The new year, 1895, opened with a full "round of engagements." Everything looked as if A.J. Gordon was "entering upon another cycle of usefulness, even larger and more fruitful than the one just closed."[31]

* * *

Yet, Ernest Gordon said, there had been "indications of a coming break" in his father's health, like "a straining beam upon which additional pressure is being constantly placed."[32]

"When at Northfield last summer," said one close friend, Robert Cameron, in early 1895, "[Dr. Gordon] was very weary and worn out. He said to his good wife, in one of these tired moods, that as soon as he had finished his twenty-fifth year at Clarendon Street, they would go away together for a full year of rest." Several times, moreover, Gordon told Cameron "that his burdens were too heavy—that he must be relieved from the care of *The Watchword* [magazine,] and from the lectures at the Training School."[33] It was a clear sign of strain from overwork.

All this notwithstanding, Gordon's schedule in January 1895 was "continuous and intense." Concerned family members thought it was all too much for a man of fifty-eight to shoulder.[34]

Gordon seemed to know it too. "I must get out from under these burdens for a little," he would say. Yet when kind suggestions were offered, and plans for rest, "he could never be induced to stop."[35]

This had been a recurring struggle. "I sorrowfully own that I make many failures in the Christian life," he said, and it "has often been too much work."[36]

Then came lines that were at once somber and prescient: "I believe in the maxim of John Eliot: *'Prayer and pains through faith in Christ can do all things.'* Yes, if we only keep the two yoked together, and always moving with equal footstep. But let pains outrun prayer, and then comes an inevitable breakdown."[37]

Gordon faced a dilemma often in the way of someone with many gifts and abilities: to not say "no" to opportunities, and run the risk of spreading himself too thin. Here his caring nature, and what he regarded as his responsibilities, overrode the more considered judgment that he was shouldering too much.

He was indeed a man of few faults. No scandal, however slight, marred his personal life or ministry, and he was a devoted husband and father. No surviving account described him as even losing his temper. Yet as a minister, author, educator, editor, administrator, philanthropist, and speaker, he failed to think of himself as he should have—or follow the counsel of others to moderate his commitments. Too often, he pushed himself too hard.

So he kept to long scheduled events: "addresses at Philadelphia, at Newark, at the midwinter convention of Dr. [Charles] Cullis's church, at the conference of the Christian Alliance [in] Boston, at Mount Holyoke College, and two addresses in Rochester, N.Y." And all these commitments, Ernest Gordon remembered, with "church cares at home."[38]

On the evening of Monday, January 21st, Gordon attended the annual meeting of the Industrial Home, and went from there "to address the Young Men's Baptist Union on the subject of missions." All who heard him said he never spoke with more warmth of humor, "more captivating grace, [or] with greater earnestness;" but there were deep lines on his face, and those nearby "could clearly see that he was far from well."[39]

The next day, he was unable to leave his bed. A physician was called to the parsonage on 182 West Brookline Street, and a terse diagnosis given: influenza, "with tendencies to bronchitis."[40]

Gravely ill, Gordon endured the next several days "as in a blinding storm." His fever "became violent, and was accompanied with intermittent delirium." Night after night he suffered from insomnia. He complained of a "ceaseless storm, [with] incessant noise as of great raindrops on a windowpane," yet all the while, "the air outside was as still as an Indian summer."[41]

Then, "sudden bursts of blackness" came, which overwhelmed him "as if he were felled with a club to the ground."[42] During these "night hours," he sought comfort by whispering words from a hymn by John Angelus—

Jesus, Jesus, visit me;
How my soul longs after thee!
When, my best, my dearest friend,
Shall our separation end?

Gordon's physical suffering also brought emotional pain, an overwhelming "sense of isolation and desertion." On the night of Wednesday, January 30th, Gordon asked everyone to leave, to "be alone, and face to face with Jesus."[43]

This done, he voiced a heartrending "appeal for the presence and companionship of the Savior," offered with "strong crying and tears." It was, his family recalled, like "a Gethsemane prayer."[44]

Knowing the end was near, Gordon called Maria to his side, and asked that four hymns could be "sung by the people," in the event of his passing. One of them was "My Jesus, I Love Thee." Maria assured him this would be done, and he seemed to find some measure of relief.

The next morning his condition worsened. Sleeplessness had robbed him of what little strength he had left.

Toward evening, his doctor came in and thought to rouse him gently by asking, "Dr. Gordon, have you a good word for us to-night?" With a clear, full voice he answered, *Victory!*

This was his last audible word.

"It was as if," Ernest Gordon said, "after the typhoon-like sickness, he had passed the last range of breakers, and had been given a glimpse of the Eternal City gleaming beyond."[45]

* * *

Five minutes after midnight, on Saturday, February 2, 1895, A.J. Gordon "fell asleep in Jesus." Soon after, solemn tolling from the belfry of Clarendon Street Church let people know their pastor and friend was gone.

Ernest Gordon, who would so ably chronicle his father's life, wrote a deeply moving description of the moments just after his father's passing—

> The stars in the dark sky looked down...as the chamber door was closed upon the still form, tenantless now, "until the morning breaks, and the shadows flee away."[46]

In the days after A.J. Gordon's passing, thousands of condolence letters arrived at the parsonage at 182 Brookline Street—from places all over the world. Still others shared their reflections in magazine and newspaper articles.

None was more moving, or more heartfelt, than A.T. Pierson's long tribute in *The Missionary Review of the World* magazine. "The one leading occurrence of the month of February," Pierson said—

> not only to this REVIEW, with its editors and readers, but to the whole circle of evangelical believers, will be the death of Adoniram Judson Gordon, of Boston, Mass. At 3 o'clock on the morning of February 2d a telegraphic message was brought to the door of the editor-in-chief, with this brief announcement:
>
> "Dr. Gordon passed away at twelve-five, this morning."
>
> —ERNEST GORDON

> That message of nine words meant, to the writer of these lines, the departure of one of the dearest of friends and the most sympathetic and helpful of co-workers—a man who seemed as part of himself.
>
> It meant to the Clarendon Street Church of Boston the loss of a pastor who for twenty-five years had been a servant of servants to his brethren, while the master of all

by conceded supremacy in holiness, faith, and consecration. But, far beyond any narrow limits of personal friendship, church pastorate, or denominational connection, Dr. Gordon was a universal benefactor. No man of his generation has had more to do with the spiritual education of the Church in the direction of holding fast the faithful Word, pushing the lines of aggressive missions, and enthroning the Holy Spirit in His true seat in the Church.

In the previous issue, Charles H. Spurgeon and his world-wide work confronted the reader as he opened these pages. This month Adoniram J. Gordon fills the leading place—a remarkable coincidence. These two men died, each at the same age, their lives running strangely parallel in many things.

Both were Baptists and both leaders in their denomination on different sides of the Atlantic. Both were great preachers, emphasized the foundation truths of the Word of God and work of Christ, sought to build up a church on apostolic principles, and led in evangelism; both were editors and authors, and did grand service with the pen; both originated training schools for evangelists and Christian workers, etc.

The comparison might be carried much further were it needful or helpful; and we venture to add that, if Spurgeon were the best-loved man in Britain, Gordon was the best-loved man in America...Such a man has no successor.

When God made A.J. Gordon, He broke the mould.[47]

Joseph Cook, a leading figure in the famous "Boston Monday Lectureship"—chaired by Gordon for twelve years, with addresses published by Houghton Mifflin—gave a tribute to Gordon in the best tradition of these lectures, devoted to the intellectual heart of faith.[48] The *London Quarterly Review* had praised the Boston Monday Lectureship for "searching philosophical analysis," fine presentations from "a wide field of reading and observation," and the Lectureship's "noble loyalty" to "great Christian verities."[49]

All this was true, yet Cook's address was bittersweet, for it was presented at Park Street Church before a gathering of the Boston Monday Lectureship itself. Gordon had once led this forum. Now his legacy, intellect, and faith would be celebrated there. "If you wish to know Judson Gordon," Cook told his colleagues—

> read all the lyrics that he thought fit to give to the world, with music. He was highly gifted, and able to prepare music for his own hymns. Some of them, I have no doubt, will go down across many scores of years...
>
> Read Dr. Gordon in full. Read all his many books; several of them are religious classics...[Charles] Spurgeon a dozen other critics I could mention have spoken of Dr. Gordon's books in terms which one might think fulsome, if personal acquaintance with their value had not shown the merits of those writings so powerful, so quiet, so filled with the Spirit. I [have] read Dr. Gordon's volumes from end to end...[50]

Gordon's spirituality also left a marked impression with Cook, and he recalled how the people of Scotland had said, "when Dr. Pierson and Dr. Gordon made a tour as lecturers after the great World's Missionary Convention in London in 1888, 'Dr. Pierson inspired us. Dr. Gordon fed us.'"[51]

What fostered such sentiments among who heard Gordon speak? Cook thought he knew the why of it all: lifelong scholarship and close study of scripture. "Several times," he told those gathered for the Boston Monday Lectureship, "the cover had been worn off and replaced on [Dr. Gordon's] copy of the Greek New Testament." Here, Cook came to the heart of his address, saying—

> Dr. Gordon was the superior of most of us in spiritual insight. He was born with wonderful natural capacities in the direction of religious thought, emotion and intuition. He was a thinker, he was a philosopher; and he was a mystic also.
>
> He had a great head, a great heart. He was able to let a

bucket down very deeply into the wells of spiritual truth. I advise you to notice what crystalline waters he brought up, and to drink often from those fountains...[52]

There were many incidents Cook might have shared to illustrate what he had said above. But one aspect of Gordon's legacy, he knew, was a centerpiece of his friend's spiritual and intellectual gifts. "If I could choose," he said—

but one circumstance out of Dr. Gordon's life to show both his intellectual and his spiritual power, it would be the fact that over and over, by invitation of such men as President McCosh of Princeton and President Andrews of Brown University, for instance, he would visit our colleges, hold evangelistic services and go from room to room among the students for conversation on personal religion.

And you know who college students are.

I had rather face any audience I ever looked upon than go into students' rooms alone to converse on personal religion. But Dr. Gordon did this in Princeton and many other colleges, moving from apartment to apartment and always leaving behind him the atmosphere of heaven. [Students] felt that God was with him.[53]

Dr. Elisha Benjamin Andrews, President of Brown University, also treasured A.J. Gordon's friendship. As he reflected on his friend's life and work, memories of Gordon's remarkable rapport with collegians stood out.

"All who know about college affairs," Andrews remembered—

know that it is not every man—not even every good or every able man—who can touch the hearts of the student body; and in all my acquaintance I have never met many— there may have been two or three—who even began to have the power in this sort of work that Dr. Gordon had. He never came to us without bringing a blessing—never without a large blessing—never without leaving behind him a permanent blessing. Never did he speak a word in our student body without so impressing many a student heart that the impress of that lesson would abide forever.[54]

One especially meaningful tribute came from Dr. H. Grattan Guinness in London—the one person to whom Gordon owed the strongest inspiration to found the Boston Missionary Training School.

Guinness sought to comfort Maria Gordon, and cast blessing on the great friendship he had known with her husband—

Harley House,
London, Feb. 22, 1895

Beloved Sister:

If Jesus is not here but gone up to glory and to God, why should we wish your beloved one here? Is he not better where he is?

Yea, infinitely. No wasting, no stumbling, no lingering; he has *walked in* like Enoch, where his heart and treasure have long been.

You know it, God comfort you.

We sorrow, we rejoice with you. Now it is *well* with him. Now he sees face to face. Gone into a world of light—and we lingering—but soon to follow. Lo, the morning breaketh. *"Ecce Venit!"* No tears in that day—joy in the morning.

I think of your dear ones—of each of them—including the little pet [Theodora]—not fatherless, no, nor you a widow, while God is the father of the fatherless and the husband of the widow.

I cannot realize he has left us all. We are more pilgrims than ever, and heaven is nearer and Christ is dearer.

"Father I *will* that those whom thou hast given me be *with me, where I am,* that they may behold my glory." The only time *He* said, *"I will"* in prayer...Love said it.

Poor Boston—poor Clarendon Street [Church]. The Lord has taken away Moses—may he give Joshua.

The sun has set, may the moon rise on the darkness.

And now let none say *he is gone,* say rather, he has arrived. He has *touched* the shore we see in shadow, and beholds while we *believe.*

> With love to your children,
> Your sad, glad friend,
> H. Grattan Guinness[55]

Another deeply moving tribute came from D.L. Moody, by way of two letters that opened a window on his remarkable, enduring friendship with Gordon. The first letter is one of the finest Moody ever wrote, and should be read in its entirety—

Dallas, Texas,
Feb. 18, 1895

My dear Mrs. Gordon—

You are in my mind all of the time, and my thoughts constantly go out toward you and your children. I wish I could see you and tell you how much we all love you, and how very much we sympathize with you and all your family.

Dear man! none of us knew how much we loved him until he was gone. Northfield has never been stirred over anyone's death as it has been over his.

We shall miss him so much next summer. It is a great loss to us all; but how much he has gained! To think he has done his work *so* well and gone home! What joy must be his in the company of the saints redeemed.

And now I am going to tell you what is in my heart. I hope you will not be hurt at my writing to you about it; but I do want his dust to lie in Northfield, he seemed so large a part of it.

I believe Northfield will become a great resort for all coming time, and it seems to me his memory will be kept so much fresher in that place than in any other. If you will give your consent, I will select a suitable and quiet resting place.

It would be a great comfort to me to have him or his earthly house resting in that valley; and when our Lord returns, I would like to have him receive his glorified body in that place.

Next August, I want a memorial service for him in the Auditorium where he last spoke in Northfield, and where I last saw him. My wife joins me in sending much love to you and yours...

Your true friend,
D.L. Moody[56]

One day after Gordon sent this letter to Maria Gordon, Moody telegrammed a second letter to Dr. Robert Cameron, long a Gordon family friend. Cameron had cabled Moody asking for any recollections he might send, and from Dallas, Texas (where he'd been speaking) Moody dictated a long, detailed reply.

"My dear Mr. Cameron," Moody began—

As I thought of the personal help Dr. Gordon had been, and the many times he had responded to my request for some of his strong, helpful teaching, I felt that a tower of strength had been taken from our midst.

Many a young lady from the Northfield Seminary and young man from Mt. Hermon School will remember in years to come the strong, loving words of their friend, as they felt him to be.

Not only on special occasions were visits made to these schools, and most helpful addresses given; but many of the students remaining through the summer vacation felt the influence and benefit of his visits at these times.

At the college conferences in July, where the young men gather from different parts of the United States and some from foreign countries, the strong, manly utterances and Bible teachings made a deep impression on them. Again, in August, when the many Christian workers met together for teaching and refreshment, it was felt by the many who gathered in Northfield that *our friend who has now gone, was of himself enough to bring them to the place.*

He had been ready to help in any way, and when I was absent one summer in Great Britain, and at the time of the [World's] Fair had to be most of the summer in Chicago and could only be at the August conference part of the time, Dr. Gordon was the man whom all felt would guide wisely and would be able best to take the leadership.[57]

Moody also remembered how Gordon's sojourns in Northfield came at personal cost. "We realized," Moody said, "in these summer visits that there was devotion to the work and self-sacrifice as the time given to us there was taken from [Dr. Gordon's] own season of rest."

Beyond Northfield, Gordon had been part of Moody's ministry in Chicago. "Not least," Moody said, "we were privileged to cooperate with [Dr. Gordon] in the Bible Institute in Chicago, where young men and women are trained for Christian work. At two different times he has gone to help there, spending a month each time, the last occasion being at the time of the great [World's] Fair, when he not only gave his helpful lectures to the students in the mornings, but preached each evening to large audiences made up very much of the strangers in the city."[58]

Here, Moody saw Gordon in his true element, saying, "in the Institute with the students, the Bible was the book of books, and the truths of the gospel were presented in a clear and forcible way. Many who are now laboring as missionaries in home and foreign fields, will, I am sure, be better workers for the instruction and help of Dr. Gordon at our Institute."[59]

Over time, Moody told Robert Cameron, his friendship with Gordon deepened, and grew richer. "As year after year passed," he remembered, "and I knew our friend better, I have been impressed more and more with the clearness with which he presented the truth, and the spirit he showed in his life."[60]

Moody recalled the last conversation he had with Gordon also, saying: "the last talk I had with him was on the importance of having the fundamental doctrines of the Scriptures taught in our conference annually." Gordon's recurring theme of the Holy Spirit's work among believers also stood out. "For twelve years or more," Moody said, "each summer he had come to us, there had been a request that Dr. Gordon should preach on the Holy Spirit and each time that he did this, fresh blessing seemed to come."[61]

As his letter closed, Moody said that Gordon was for him a "son of thunder" in power, but also much like the disciple whom Jesus loved: "He held the truth, but he held it in love, and though I have known that at times he did not see things as someone else did, he had no harsh word to say."[62]

Moody's last words were a summation of the friendship he treasured in Gordon. "Thinking of him," Moody said, "the words that were applied to Daniel come to my mind, *O Man greatly beloved!*"[63]

A.J. Gordon could not have asked for finer parting words.

Nothing would have pleased him more.

* * *

And what is the measure of A.J. Gordon's legacy?

Part of it flowed from cradle-gifts, but also from conviction. As one prominent historian has observed, Gordon had a warm personality, and the "ability to maintain friendships across theological barriers." Others disagreed with him, "but they continued to like him as a person."[64]

As to conviction, from Jamaica Plain to years at Clarendon Street, Gordon believed faith taught the way of conciliation, in the context of "mere Christianity." Just two years into his time at Jamaica Plain, he had said, "Whatever brings the church into nearer accordance with the spirit of Christ and His gospel, whatever exalts the central and centralizing truths of our common faith, will do most toward promoting that unity for which we all hope and pray."[65] So long as he lived, Gordon showed "unity for missions could transcend theological and institutional boundaries." This, and his steadfast "refusal to separate social justice from evangelism," as with the abolition of slavery, are hallmarks posterity may always look to.[66]

In the Boston Missionary Training School, Gordon brought hope to anyone who felt called to mission work: women, the poor, and students of many ethnicities. He was a great pioneer in fostering opportunity through education.

Though a leading voice for foreign missions, Gordon also established vital inner-city ministries. The Boston Industrial Home was a beacon in this regard, and for decades after his passing. Nor should his work among Boston's Jewish and Chinese communities be forgotten, along with Clarendon Street's rescue work to help destitute women. All these came out of the transformative Moody meetings of 1877, with subsequent gospel gatherings Moody and Gordon led.[67]

Moreover, Gordon refused to separate home and foreign missions, and here his legacy is one that defies stereotypes. He worked "where he saw the Spirit leading—not where narrow theological parties thought he should go."[68]

Gordon also had a memorable bearing, as Nathan Wood once observed. He had "a robust figure, strong features and voice, and massive delivery," yet these were mingled with a "mystical withdrawal, [and] quiet inwardness—a personality at once reserved and genial, meditative and crusading."[69]

Those who knew him well saw these things.

John McElwain knew Gordon better than many. He recalled Gordon's profound sense of consecration, a willingness "to do anything God wanted him to do, to be anything God wanted him to be, and to suffer anything God wanted him to suffer—the giving up of his whole being, life and destiny to the will of God."[70]

And as his wife Maria knew best, Gordon cherished a high view of women in the church. Together they were, as he said, "a pretty good team," and many times, he gratefully deferred to her wisdom. Then too, his reading of scripture, and fidelity to it—with published writings such as "The Ministry of Women," did much to influence others regarding "women's divinely appointed rights."[71]

So it was that "a generation of women responded to Gordon's concern for the training of laywomen," and became students at the Boston Missionary Training School. In all these things, Gordon was well in advance of his time. A world we know, and may take for granted, was one he and Maria modeled long years ago—in their beliefs and practice. We owe them much.[72]

A.J. Gordon was a sterling ambassador for the faith.

As an educator, pastor, and prominent American Baptist—he shaped a generation of Christian workers "who witnessed to the world for Jesus Christ." Today the Boston Missionary Training School's heritage lives on in Gordon College and Gordon-Conwell Theological Seminary. Both schools keep their founder's memory alive.[73]

Yet Gordon's legacy goes beyond the two fine institutions bearing his name. World evangelization was a passion the last ten years of his life, and he was Chairman of the Executive Committee of the American Baptist Missionary Union, thus orchestrating "an era of expansion for Baptist missions." His long pastorate at Boston's Clarendon Street Church was a catalyst for that congregation to become "the leading Baptist fund-raiser and promoter of missions in New England." As a highly valued colleague of D.L. Moody, Gordon was one of the most able and admired evangelical mission advocates of his time.[74]

He faithfully burnished the many gifts God gave him—becoming a scholar, writer, educator, philanthropist, pastor, and leader of international renown. He was a dedicated husband and parent: all of his children later became admirable adults. Family and friends knew he had heard the ancient music of faith—and, in gratitude for all it meant, he edited four hymnals. At his passing, he was summoned to where that music had its beginning—the bright realm where it would always be heard—

I shall see the King in His beauty,
In the land that is far away...
To behold the Chief of Ten Thousand,
Ah! My soul this were joy...[75]

Chapter Twenty
Years Beyond

At last she sought out Memory, and they trod
the same old paths where Love had walk'd with Hope.[1]
—Alfred, Lord Tennyson

For many years after her husband's passing, Maria Gordon brought their shared vision forward through active involvement and ardent dedication to the Boston Missionary Training School—or as it was known at her passing in 1921, Gordon Bible College. To follow this era, if only for a chapter, seems most fitting, as A.J. Gordon knew best how much Maria had given to the founding of the school.

Other colleagues were F.L. Chapell, John McElwain and a young scholar, Nathan R. Wood—a future president of the college, and author of *A School of Christ,* which charted the history of Gordon Bible College for several decades. Wood's joining the school was most welcome, as he studied at Harvard (Class of 1898), Newton Theological Institute (Class of 1900), and also in Germany. He came from a family of distinguished academics. His father, Nathan E. Wood, was President of Newton, while his mother, Alice Boise Wood, was the first woman to graduate from the University of Chicago—where her father, James R. Boise, was Head of the Department of Greek, and a member of the Divinity School Faculty.[2]

Drawing on Nathan Wood's richly detailed book, it is possible to follow the school's development for yet another twenty-five years—from 1895 to 1920, and a relocation of the school to the Fenway in Boston.

* * *

Just after A.J. Gordon's passing, the Boston Missionary Training School was re-named the Gordon Missionary Training School, a name it retained until 1903. This story was featured in a November 1896 article in *The Record of Christian Work* magazine, founded by D.L. Moody and edited by his son, W.R. Moody.

"The Boston Missionary Training School," the article stated—

> was born seven years ago, through the divinely-inspired faith and labor of Rev. A.J. Gordon, D.D., who was its president until death, since which time his name has been given to the school that it might thus stand as a living memorial of him, and Rev. Arthur T. Pierson, D.D. has been elected to the presidency.
>
> Here is offered, to men and women alike, a two years' course of most Scriptural, most practical and most spiritual preparation, and it would be impossible for any honest soul to pass through this course of study without being wonderfully enriched thereby.[3]

One of the ways students at the Gordon Missionary Training School were enriched came from Maria Gordon herself. At Clarendon Street Church, she lectured to students each week on "Bible Reading," drawing on a lifetime of study. It was deeply gratifying as well for her to see at this time that "a considerable part of the enrolment was the number of women, largely from Clarendon Street Church, but from other churches also, who joined the forenoon classes to enrich their non-professional life and work." Indeed, this facet of the Gordon Missionary Training School was so predominant, that "it was even suggested once that it should be a ladies' School entirely." But, as F.L. Chapell noted wryly, "we have not as yet turned the gentlemen away, altho as might be expected, they have since been in the minority rather than in the majority."[4]

As ever, missionary endeavor was the central aspiration for students at the Gordon Missionary Training School, and one notice from the December 1899 issue of *The Intercollegian* reported that of the "the list of sailed volunteers reported to the office of the Student Volunteer Office since December 1, 1899," Miss Grace J. Raynor and Rev. Herbert W. Innis, of the Gordon Missionary Training School, had sailed for Africa.[5]

In October 1901 *The American Friend* magazine, a Philadelphia-based Quaker publication, reported on the missionary legacy that the Gordon Missionary Training School, young as it was, had already established. An article by E.B. Mendenhall explained how the GMTS had already earned a national reputation for service in the cause of faith.

In the autumn of 1889, Mendenhall said—

> the same year that Moody's Bible Institute was opened, the graciously gifted, but now lamented A.J. Gordon opened his "Boston Missionary Training School"; but which, since his death, is distinctively known as "The Gordon Missionary Training School," and is claimed to be among the first of its kind opened in this country. The prospectus of this school, issued for 1900, is peculiarly interesting, giving one a fair conception of the great sum total of its spiritual worth. Yet it has neither endowment nor pledged support, but is dependent upon the free will gifts of God's people.
>
> Of the nineteen members of its executive committee, five are women; and four of its twelve instructors are women also. "It is designed for men and women who have heard the call of God to engage in Christian service, but who, from age or other reasons, cannot pursue academic, collegiate or seminary courses"...
>
> From it 137 have gone out either as pastors, missionaries or evangelists—many of them women. *Some have laid down their lives in foreign fields—in Africa, the West Indies and India;* while others are proclaiming the way of salvation to the peoples of China, Japan and Assam.[6]

Moving beyond the honored roll of missionaries who trained at the GMTS, F.L. Chapell, chronicler of the school's earliest years, described another calling that soon became prominent among graduates. "It rather *surprises* us," he wrote for an official school report, "to find that about fifty men have gone into the pastorate, inasmuch as it was more particularly the mission field that was contemplated in the origin of the School. There have also been about fifteen wives of ministers on our lists."[7] Home missions, as a phrase of the time had it, offered a compelling call that many would answer in the years to come.

Humor doesn't often intrude into rather prim Victorian accounts from this time, but one aspect of student life at the Gordon Missionary Training School brought a knowing smile to those who read Nathan Wood's account of it.

There had been, Dr. Wood stated, "a poignant co-educational problem," recorded in "the minutes of the Executive Committee of the School on May 13, 1896." The subject of "courtship and marriage among the students" was discussed, and although no vote was taken, "all agreed that such proceedings should be discouraged." And if this was somehow deemed "an educational panacea," it utterly failed in its intended purpose. Wood must have smiled as he wrote: "It may be added that leaders of the later School," of whom he was one, "through many years, have not found the formula either...the cosmic processes of love and courtship seem still to be as resistless as the sunlight or the tides."[8]

Throughout this time, Clarendon Street Church "continued to realize its opportunity" in students from the GMTS, and gave "loyal support to the School, including free use of the Church vestry and other rooms." In return, many students joined the church or undertook "parish visitation and missionary work in Boston." They did so under John McElwain's capable direction, and over time, the lists of foreign and home missionaries, and evangelists, which adorned the vestry wall, "came largely from the student and alumni ranks of the Training School." It was, said Nathan Wood, "one of those arrangements in which both parties benefit."[9]

And if John McElwain supervised such student involvement with Clarendon Street Church, Maria Gordon was no less central to the mission of the GMTS in those first years after her husband's passing.

From the beginning, she had been the School Secretary, and after its first two years, Treasurer of the School. Her grateful colleagues always placed great value on her fine administrative skills, and her records were called "models of orderliness."[10] Of her it was said: "She knew what people ought to do, and planned to see that they did it, but was surprisingly forgiving if they didn't."[11] As a leader, she mingled kindness with guiding purpose.

At the same time, Maria Gordon devoted "motherly and masterful care" to the Carey Home for girls at the School, in the house next door to the parsonage at 182 West Brookline Street. Those training for missionary service, soon to become teachers, or perhaps pastor's wives, found her advice invaluable. She could speak from a depth of experience to all these callings, commending many practical insights along with spiritual wisdom.[12]

In the classroom, GMTS students saw Maria Gordon's gifts as well. Her teaching in its "first decade, and in the first part of the second," centered on "Bible reading, choral and individual." And for a time, she gave "chapter studies of the Old Testament." Still later, she was asked "to teach similar courses as Synthetic Bible Study—not exegetical, but practical and effectual." Last, as Nathan Wood said, "she was the dear friend" of younger co-workers, who "warmly remember her."[13] In a word, she'd been a mentor for him—imparting many things that stood him in good stead when he became president of the school some years later.

* * *

All these things brought cause for gratitude; yet by 1903 one pressing challenge could no longer be ignored: declining student enrollment. Nathan Wood described the dilemma by saying—

> except as an adjunct of [Clarendon Street Church] the School did not advance as so fine a group of leaders deserved. It was perhaps better as a School than in earlier years, but it did not grow. In 1903 the Graduating Class numbered six. In 1905 it was ten, three men and seven women...[14]

In the face of this unsettling trend, the administrators of the GMTS attempted "to find a building for the School which would attract more students, and perhaps to make it less an *appanage* [or adjunct] of an individual church and so to win the confidence of other churches." To secure funds for such a building, "letters were sent widely to possible givers with the appeal that such a building should be a memorial to A.J. Gordon."[15] But this yielded no immediate result.

Yet in time, one ultimately promising development did arise. As Nathan Wood recalled, one of the letters sent out relative "to securing a fund to perpetuate the memory of Dr. A.J. Gordon," was mailed "to a number of prominent brethren, among whom [was the] President of Newton Theological Institution."[16]

This was none other than Nathan Wood's father, Dr. Nathan E. Wood, and "in place of responding by letter," he visited two of the members of the GMTS Advisory Committee, and "opened the question of forming an affiliated relation" between Newton and the GMTS, or, as it was now called, the Gordon Bible and Missionary Training School. After "a prolonged interview," it was "deemed wise to hold a further conference" which might include others interested in the matter.[17]

An informal meeting was duly called, which yielded "a frank interchange of views." It closed with a consensus understanding that "the greatest liberty" should be granted the authorities of the Gordon Bible and Missionary Training School "to formulate, if deemed wise, any proposition that might look toward an affiliated relation between the two institutions."[18]

This turn of events had been unexpected, after letters had been sent out merely to secure funding for a school building. But as those involved thought more upon the matter, there were strong inducements to warrant an alliance for the Gordon Bible and Missionary Training School. Not least was the fact that Newton Theological Institution was the oldest Baptist seminary in America.[19] It could therefore lend widely acknowledged prestige, access to donor lists, and the possible use of facilities—to say nothing of the benefits of added staff and faculty.

Yet at this first juncture, the Executive Committee of the Training School hesitated. They could have moved quickly to build on the informal first meeting by "seeking the further friendly conference." But instead, following a motion by Professor J.M. Gray, it was decided to post a letter saying "we invite the authorities of Newton to formulate a definite statement of what is in their mind."[20]

As Nathan Wood the younger noted ruefully, "one would think that after long conference of the President, a leading Professor and the

Chairman of the Board of the Newton Seminary," and a subsequent "careful report," the Executive Committee "might have some idea of what the Newton authorities had in their mind."[21] Whatever the motive was for such caution, it yielded a perception that the Gordon Bible and Missionary Training School might not be an institution to partner with, after all.

Within a fortnight, the Newton Administration sent a letter saying—

> The Executive Committee of the Newton Theological Institution has devoted two evenings…to a full and careful consideration of the proposition in your advice…as to the affiliation of the Gordon Bible and Missionary Training School with the Newton Theological Institution and has voted to lay the whole matter upon the table.[22]

A door of promise had abruptly closed. The Executive Committee of the Gordon Bible and Missionary Training School now "began other efforts."[23]

This led, within a year, to discussions with Revere Lay College about a possible union, as "both schools needed reinforcement." These consultations proved far more fruitful and, as the two institutions agreed "in all points of view," Dr. Henry C. Graves, a "fervent and thoughtful President and Professor at Revere," was made Head Instructor of the united School, at Clarendon Street, "to plan and supervise the studies of the School," beside his own classes.[24]

One immediate result of this was the Gordon Bible and Missionary Training School gained "a few students" from Revere Lay College. And this was undoubtedly a help, as was the seasoned guidance Dr. Graves could now provide. For the next year, the school continued under this regime.

Meanwhile Nathan Wood the elder, President of Newton Theological Seminary, had not been idle. Although his leadership board had closed the door earlier on any thought of a merger with the Gordon Bible and Missionary Training School, he had not stopped thinking about it, and praying about it. Nor had leaders at the Training School like John McElwain, who understood that the union with Revere Lay College was at best a holding action—a temporary solution.

This context led, in January 1905, to the posting of "a proposal from representatives from Newton Center of an affiliation between Gordon Training School and Newton Theological Seminary."[25]

But just then, still another development came—one of seeming promise. Yet though it was well-intentioned, it muddied the waters for a while.

Events unfolded in this wise.

Dr. A.C. Dixon, the well-respected Pastor of nearby Ruggles Street Church, and President of the Gordon Bible and Missionary Training School, proposed in April 1905 that the school move from its current base at Clarendon Street Church to Ruggles Street Church. In support of this idea he gave four reasons. First, as President of the school he wished to give it more of his personal supervision. Second, he believed this would set the school on "a permanent and independent basis, and avoid affiliation with any other educational institution." Third, such a move would allow for financial support from the large Ford legacy bequeathed by Daniel Sharp Ford, who had been the wealthy publisher of the highly popular *Youth's Companion* magazine. Access to Ford legacy funds was not available apart from Ruggles Street Church. Fourth and last, Dr. Dixon's proposal included the provision of "dormitories for young women, and a house where young men could have room and board at a moderate price."[26]

On May 5, 1905, a formal letter from Ruggles Street Church tendered a "unanimous invitation to the Training School to occupy without charge any of the buildings that might be needed for the work."[27]

On its face, as Nathan Wood later observed, this scenario would have seemingly solved "all the [school's] problems at a stroke," and make any Newton affiliation unnecessary. However in the event, A.C. Dixon's proposal met a far different fate than the one intended. For as Nathan Wood wrote: *"The Gordon Executive Committee by unanimous vote rejected the offer."*[28]

The why of this was a story in itself.

For however well-intended, Dixon's offer would have changed the character the Gordon Bible and Missionary Training School greatly.

During his lifetime, A.J. Gordon had seen Clarendon Street Church as the natural home for his new school. So it had been through 1905, or for sixteen years. That heritage, that foundation, was not to be set aside lightly. As the leaders of the Gordon Executive Committee saw it, and stated in their formal reply to Dr. Dixon's proposal, he "had expressed a desire that the School might be transferred to his Church, *and become a branch of the work of that Church.*" Nathan Wood captured the consensus about this idea when he wrote years later: "What Dr. Gordon had joined together," they had no wish—even at the request of so good a man as Dr. Dixon—to "put asunder."[29]

A.C. Dixon was a man of fine character. Therefore, when he learned of the unanimous feeling of the Gordon Executive Committee, he received it with grace. Wishing for no dissension of any kind, he ultimately joined in the vote to reject the proposal he himself had brought forward. There was, in his mind, something to be said for collective wisdom, and also the pain any thought of severing relations with Clarendon Street Church would bring. A.J. Gordon had only been gone ten years. The school bore the stamp of his character and founding vision. In the end, such a step just wasn't to be taken.[30]

Within a year, a clearer perspective on things emerged. Dr. Dixon accepted a call to become the pastor of the church founded by D.L. Moody in Chicago, once called the Chicago Avenue Church, known today as The Moody Church. The Ruggles Street Church, for its part, continued friendly in its relations with the Gordon Bible and Missionary Training School. Near to the school as Ruggles Street was, many Gordon students in the future served in ministries the church offered. Still later, a Gordon alumnus would become pastor of Ruggles Street.[31]

But there was something more to consider, as Nathan Wood discerned.

"The striking fact," he wrote, "is that those in the Executive Committee who resisted any change in the doctrinal or educational policies, or the location of the School—and forced other members to go with them in order to avoid dissension—had in this vote upon [Dr.] Dixon's offer rejected an extraordinary opportunity, and the last opportunity, to keep the School as it was and had been."[32]

What did this mean? The upshot, as Wood believed, was "God answered their prayers, but not their preferences," for the Gordon Bible and Missionary Training School.

Witness to all this, and speaking from the perspective of one who later became president of the school, Wood stated that *"the time had come for a process which was to be not a transfer, but a transformation; not new funds, but a new founding; not a new building, but a new birth."*[33]

This new process commenced on October 8, 1907, and culminated on December 4, 1907, when "the Board of Trustees of the Newton Theological Institution...voted to consolidate the Gordon Bible and Missionary Training School with the Institution." From that time it was known as "the Gordon School of the Newton Theological Institution."[34]

This agreement stipulated that "all alumni and past students should be in the same relation to the School as before; [and] the School should be located in Boston." Further, an Administrative Committee of eleven was to be "nominated first by the Gordon Executive Committee, and thereafter by the Administrative Committee itself, and elected by the Newton Trustees." Last of all, this new Administrative Committee would "nominate all instructors, to be elected by the Newton Trustees, [while] the President of Newton should be a member [and] the Newton Trustees should be responsible for finance." The Administrative Committee, as envisioned, would include "distinguished ministers and laymen from both groups."[35]

For Nathan Wood the elder, this agreement marked the attainment of a goal he had long cherished, despite failing health. He would finish his Newton Presidency, serving to September 1, 1908, and "organize the new Gordon Faculty first."[36]

That much he could do.

Yet remarkably, his health, so long a source of worry, began to improve in tandem with his new responsibilities overseeing "the Gordon School of the Newton Theological Institution." For many years to come, he would "impart to generations of students [a] saintliness" kindred to that which A.J. Gordon, F.L. Chapell and John McElwain "had imparted to the early School."[37]

Space does not allow for a detailed overview of the years when the Gordon School of the Newton Theological Institution existed. But it did so until 1914, providing the secure finances and administrative leadership so greatly needed.

Beyond this, it was a source of gratitude for all that Maria Gordon's long involvement with the school continued, as she taught what was described as a "thorough elementary course in Synthetic Bible Study of the Old Testament." She, in turn, was deeply grateful to see her son, Arthur Hale Gordon, join the fold as an "able teacher of Homiletics [with] an excellent group of ministerial students to instruct." Educated at Boston Latin and Harvard, Class of 1893, Arthur Gordon was a very fine addition to the faculty.[38] Twenty-five years into the life of the school that A.J. Gordon founded, his family was closely involved with its life and work.[39]

Meanwhile, starting in 1911, Nathan Wood the younger became Dean of the Gordon School of the Newton Theological Institution. As he assumed his new duties, he was deeply grateful that his wife, Isabel Warwick Wood, had agreed to "organize and conduct a modern department of English and Literature." She had studied Pedagogy, English, and German at Brown University, earning her Bachelor and M.A. degrees there, and she would eventually became Dean of Faculty, a true pioneer in her field—as she had been at Brown, where she was "one of eleven young women" who formed the first class to complete the four years' course there.[40]

Greatly gifted, Isabel Wood soon established "a first-year course in College Rhetoric and a second-year course in Christian Literary Masterpieces," better known as a "Great Books" course of study today. And this, as her husband observed, marked "the quiet beginning of a religious-college policy." Where the school had centered mainly on training for service in missions and pastoral ministry, it would now retain these spheres of instruction, while steadily adding courses more in keeping with a traditional liberal-arts four-year course of undergraduate study.[41]

* * *

With so many fine developments in place, the school grew and flourished—leading ultimately to a decision in September 1914 on the part of the Gordon School trustees to fraternally part ways with the Newton Theological Institution. Their goal would be to establish "the Gordon Bible Institute." This was duly undertaken, and what Dean Wood called "the threefold founding" of the school was complete. By this he meant (1) the A.J. Gordon era commencing in 1889, (2) the era of the Gordon

School of the Newton Theological Institution (1908-1914), and (3) the establishment of the Gordon Bible Institute in 1914.[42]

As he thought about it all, the journey of the school hadn't always been easy, but through all the seasons of its life, he and other leaders felt God had opened doors and provided in ways that allowed A.J. Gordon's founding vision to continue.

And another time of flourishing lay just ahead.

* * *

That time of flourishing came in many ways through the philanthropy of Martha Dodge Frost. How she came to be part of the Gordon story was nothing short of remarkable. Dean Nathan Wood described it memorably, saying this series of events transformed her life, and "and brought a far-reaching advance in the life of the School."[43]

When Dean Wood first met her, Martha Frost was "an elderly but vigorous and intelligent lady [living] in her beautiful home in Belmont, a Boston suburb." Wood thought to visit her, seeking to widen a circle of friends for the school.[44]

Standing on the doorstep of Miss Frost's home, Wood felt a sense of "sudden, intense brief urgency of prayer." This, he believed, was prompted by the Holy Spirit. He drew comfort from that, as he had no acquaintance with Miss Frost, save for the fact she "belonged to the Church in the neighboring suburb of Arlington" where Wood's father had become pastor. Moreover, Miss Frost had not attended this church in years, and had not as yet met Wood's father. So the Spirit's prompting on her doorstep graced the start of this important visit.[45]

Miss Frost came to the door, and kindly invited Wood in. As he recalled, their "friendly talk" began with her statement that "she could not give anything, because she had just given twenty-five dollars to a local hospital." At this, Wood told her how the school never asked for any dollar amount, but sought friends; leaving it to them as to "whether and how much to give."[46]

They then talked about students, "their eagerness and ability, their sacrifices, and their widespread activities." Notably, Wood spoke of the gifted undergraduates who lived at the rooming house for young women at 592 Tremont Street—especially "the four [residing] in the front parlor, what brilliant girls they were, and what they lived on." Wood was grateful for this "happy hour-long conversation," and felt it "left a pleasant feeling, but nothing more [as] this Christian lady was not naturally a giver."[47] Still, because of the Holy Spirit's prompting at Miss Frost's door, Wood and his colleagues "continued to pray at home about her." Perhaps there was something at work here not readily apparent.

Just what that might have been seemed more remote when a week or two later a postcard came, saying *"Sorry I cannot give to so good a work. Martha D. Frost."*[48]

Two months went by. Still, prayers for Martha Frost continued.

Then one day, the telephone rang in Dean Wood's office, upon which the receptionist told him: "There is a lady here who wants to make a gift to the Gordon School." A visit thereafter soon revealed what had prompted this call.[49]

It seemed that Martha Frost, "lying awake nights, and sitting long days by her window," had thought about the Gordon students, and especially about the four girls "in the 592 parlor." She said she "wanted to give $10,000 at once, and to bequeath her house to the School." She then added: "if the School would be too large" to fit within the house, "could the Dean use it as official residence?"

Dean Wood was astounded. He began consulting with his administration colleagues as to next steps; but felt constrained to say initially that, humbled as he was by the noble offer of Miss Frost's home in Belmont, he believed it wouldn't be right for he and Mrs. Wood to "live in such a magnificent mansion, when the students were struggling for a living."[50]

So it was decided to make continuing visits to Miss Frost at discreet intervals, to see where future discussions might lead. All the while, Dean Wood and his colleagues would be prayerful, and leave "the Lord plenty of time to work."[51] Miss Frost was grateful, for her part, to meet with leaders who modeled Christian character in their dealings. The more she dealt with them, the more they did to earn her trust.

Martha Frost's life to his point had been one of wise stewardship. Though her investment advisers "were the officers of a Boston Trust Company," she made her own decisions. These officers told Dean Wood and his colleagues that "she was a remarkable investor; and had trebled her inheritance by wise investments."[52]

Now, with the advent on Dean Wood's appeal on behalf of Gordon Bible Institute, "she was estimating a new kind of investment, and was living in the atmosphere of an extraordinary adventure." Heretofore, she'd been someone who decided she "could not give anything because she had given twenty-five dollars to the local hospital." Now she was contemplating a gift that was "changing her whole Christian life."[53]

As this time continued, Miss Frost "asked for a list of some Gordon men, especially students in pastorates, and pored over the typed paragraphs" which told her something of their stories. Now, students training for pastoral ministry "became an equal presence in her mind with the young women who were her first interest." Soon she "offered very confidentially to buy any building in Boston which the Dean and Mrs. Wood might select, up to $100,000," and to remodel it.[54]

In modern currency, this was a gift worth something like $2 million dollars, plus whatever the re-modeling costs might entail—a truly munificent sum.

And so a search for a suitable property was undertaken, "in downtown Beacon Hill, the Hub of Boston, and among Back Bay hotels and churches;" but nothing was deemed suitable.

It was then that Isabel Wood had an inspired thought: "Let's ask Miss Frost instead to build a new building exactly right for her School!" Prayerfully, the Dean and Mrs. Wood put this to Miss Frost, whereupon she "happily acquiesced, and said she was herself 'coming to that conclusion!'"[55]

Dean Wood gave a moving summary of the next stage of this endeavor—

> with the help of real estate men, [looking over] the Charles River bank in Boston and Cambridge, and on Huntington Avenue; and in the new Fenway district, they found a location ideal for surroundings and transportation, facing the renowned Fenway park system, with the [Museum of Fine Arts], Simmons College, Harvard Medical School, and a dozen other such buildings around it, the Gardner

Venetian palace and Museum directly opposite it across Evans Parkway, and Symphony Hall, the Y.M.C.A. and other public buildings near it…

Trustees familiar with Boston properties regarded it as perfect.

And the price per square foot was, from the desire of three elderly New York City owners to [sell,] half of that asked and obtained around it. When we told Miss Frost about it, she rejoicingly agreed to buy it and build on it. *The things which were impossible with men were possible with God and Miss Frost.*[56]

At a Trustee's Meeting on July 1, 1915, Dean Wood "reported a gift of $75,000 from Miss Martha Frost, of Belmont, for the purpose of purchasing land and erecting such buildings as the Trustees might determine."[57]

And on July 8, still more good news came when it was learned that "Mrs. Elisha M. White of Framingham, Massachusetts, offered "whatever sum is necessary, approximately $10,000," for an Auditorium in connection with the building or buildings to be given by Miss Frost." These funds were soon re-directed for a library. The July 8 meeting also resulted in the appointment of a Building Committee, and on November 11, 1915 it was voted to purchase the land already described, 30 Evans Way, on which the future Frost Hall and auditorium would be built.[58]

The prestigious *American Architect* magazine, based in New York City, carried the story in December 1915: "The Gordon Bible Institute has taken title from the Henry Thompson estate to the site for the new building to be known as Frost Hall. This site is on the south side of the Tremont entrance to the Fenway."[59]

The firm of Kendall, Taylor & Co. were chosen as architects. H.H. Kendall, head of the firm, was designer of many public buildings in Boston, including the Memorial Library of the Boston Architectural Club, "one the largest and finest architectural libraries in the country." H.H. Kendall had been New England President of the American Association of Architects, and as a loyal Gordon Trustee was deeply interested in the success of the building.[60]

Frost Hall was to have an Italian Renaissance design. Its floor plans were drawn up by Dean and Mrs. Wood who, "by much experience knew the needs of the classes and students." Offices and classrooms were to be on the main floor, dormitories on the three floors above. A dining room, kitchen, heating plant and storerooms were slated for the basement floor. The new Chapel and White Library were to be sited just outside and to the rear of Frost Hall.[61]

One novel challenge connected with Frost Hall and its adjacent buildings was how to construct the nearby Chapel/Auditorium so as to avoid covering or obscuring any Frost Hall dormitory windows. This became a subject of prayer, and a solution came when Isabel Wood suggested that the Chapel/Auditorium might be constructed to be equal in height to the combined basement and main floors, but no higher. She also suggested that a large classroom be created in Frost Hall, "opening also as a gallery into the auditorium, and with stairways outside each end of the gallery from street floor to chapel floor." In no time at all, difficulties that had been a concern were overcome.[62]

There was also the matter of how to construct "deep-driven pile foundations" for the Chapel and the other buildings. The site for Frost Hall, "like all the Back Bay and Fenway from Boston Common Hill to Brookline Village, [was] filled-in land." It had been literally the "Back Bay" of Boston Harbor.[63]

As Dean Wood observed, "many of us knew it well. The father of Mrs. Wood's most intimate girl friend was the civil engineer who directed the moving of hills from Wellesley to the shallows of the Fenway."[64]

Further, as a young man himself, Dean Wood "had gone canoeing where now the Gordon buildings and the Art Museum stand, so that the Gardner Museum, across the narrow Tremont Entrance to the Fenway (now Evans Way), was literally not only in architecture but in lonely location, as one paddled around it, a Venetian palace, looking over the tide-flats as it would at low-tide in Venice. The Gordon pile and concrete foundations went down through more than twenty-five feet of such land to bedrock."[65] The construction of Frost Hall, with its adjacent buildings was thus something of an engineering marvel: truly a place of re-claimed and re-purposed land.

* * *

On a bright and sunny spring morning, Wednesday, April 5, 1916, "members of the Gordon Bible College Building Committee, the Faculty of the College, and the whole student body met on the lot purchased, and held an hour of prayer and song. Many fervent prayers of consecration and thanksgiving hallowed the very spot where the buildings were to arise." Taken together it was, Dean Wood recalled, "a solemn and memorable occasion. God was very near."[66]

As Dean Wood wrote of this years later, it came alive once more. Amid "trees of the Fenway as background [were] distant sounds of the city faint around us, the workmen with their pile-driving derricks encircling the crowd and looking in wonder at the unusual building operations, and the happy earnest worshippers." His last sentence seemed to say it all: "the foundations for those buildings went deeper than twenty-five feet, to the bedrock of eternity, in that hour."[67]

* * *

Aside from the stirring time of consecration for Frost Hall and the adjacent Gordon Bible College buildings, there was yet another challenge about this time for Dean Wood and his colleagues to weigh and consider. When he wrote about it for the official college history, some decades later, this particular scenario seemed, "as it were, from the Old Testament or the Book of Acts."[68] He explained it this way—

> A Boston Savings Bank had agreed to a $40,000 mortgage on Frost Hall and the land, but delayed while the title was made secure by agreements from all possible heirs to the land. Some of these lived on Nantucket, [and] that winter unprecedented cold isolated the Island in a frozen sea for many weeks.
>
> But while the loan waited for their signatures, [I felt] led to ask Dr. Cortland Myers, pastor of Tremont Temple, to go with him to talk with Miss Frost about the whole situation. [I did not wish] to ask for more [funds], after all that had been done by Miss Frost. And Dr. Myers was greatly gifted in such matters.

> While [I called on a friend] who was in her last illness, Miss Frost talked happily with [Dr. Myers] about Palestine, which they both loved…But before he left, Dr. Myers said to Miss Frost: *"This delay gives you opportunity to have Frost Hall dedicated without debt. Would you not rather do it?"*
>
> She said she would "think about it," for it was a sudden proposition.
>
> But a little later, she sent [me] word that she did not wish her building to be dedicated with a mortgage on it, and would give an additional $45,000 before the dedication. Only the one condition was made, that no mortgage should ever be placed on what she so joyfully gave without encumbrance. It was a sacrificial gift [as] the total amount was one-half of her entire property. All this took place while the unprecedented cold isolated Nantucket Island. But for that delay, there would undoubtedly have been a heavy burden of debt on the new property.[69]

Frost Hall's Italian Renaissance design shone throughout the building, but nowhere more memorably than its stately entrance. Atop four Tuscan columns of quarried granite, two on each side of the main door, was a frieze with the college name centered and inset, flanked by sculpted seashells and filigree—all intricate displays of the stonemason's art. Below the college name were words that bore witness to philanthropy: "Frost Hall – The Gift of Martha Dodge Frost." Just above the entryway frieze was a fine balcony, square cornered, with balusters carved to recall the amphorae of ancient Rome—symbols, in their way, of knowledge kept. Last, centered beneath each window on the second storey, crosses had been wrought in the aureate brickwork. Frost Hall was a center of learning hallowed by faith.

On Tuesday, April 3, 1917, Dedication Exercises for "the beautiful new home" of Gordon Bible College took place. Guests arrived by motorcar and trolley, and alighted at the entrance to the handsome new campus. While everyone looked forward to this festive occasion, there was a somber air about it too, for the Dedication Service took place on the day President Woodrow Wilson read before Congress the message which brought the United States into the First World War. Dean Wood was one among many hundreds who were grateful that in this troubled time, hope was a beacon in the reality of this new college.[70]

It was a time of reunion as well.

Dr. Cortland Myers of Tremont Temple, "who did most for the yearly support of the School and for its dedication without debt," gave an eloquent address. Though now elderly, Rev. M.R. Deming, the great friend of A.J. Gordon, and "one of the first founders in 1889," prayed the Dedication Prayer.[71]

Then, at a large, brief outdoor service after the Dedication, Colonel E.H. Haskell, a Trustee, raised an American flag on Frost Hall. He had presented its flag-pole as a gift, and in view of what took place that day with President Wilson's Declaration of War, everyone there was deeply moved.[72]

That evening, a Dedication Dinner was held in the chapel/auditorium, christened as "Gordon Hall." Its highlight was a talk by Maria Gordon, who had been asked to "speak for the past." She had only just retired from teaching, in 1914. But she, as everyone understood, had been there when Gordon Bible College was just a vision she, A.J. Gordon, and H. Grattan Guinness spoke of in their home.[73]

She stood, and shared things that only she knew—recalling faces now no more, hopes fondly cherished, and hundreds of lives transformed. She must have thought too of the future that was to be in this stately new setting: Frost Hall, Gordon Hall, and White Library. They were here, at last. They had become a reality.

At the heart of it all, Maria Gordon had been given a special grace: to glimpse a good future her beloved husband hadn't lived to see. Their vision was now entering a new chapter of its life and work. That brought a deep and renewing sense of blessing. It was one she carried with her for the rest of her life.

* * *

"But the story," as Nathan Wood remembered, "is not complete to some of us without the memory of the way in which her gift had transformed the life of Martha Frost." It is best to let Dr. Wood's thoughts here stand on their own—

She talked about the School. Its students and alumni were her children. She wanted all the news about it...She felt, and rightly, that she who had no literal descendants would continue through coming generations in many lands in the lives and work of ministers and missionaries going out from her building.

When she met the Gordon Committee at the Trust Company to make the final payments on her gift, and the Committee thanked her, she rose and with old-fashioned courtesy said,

"Gentlemen, it is I who thank you. You have immortalized my name."

[And I think of her] standing, in her old age, in the garden of her home.[74]

Seeds Martha Frost planted, for the kingdom, were to take root and flourish.

Not very long before this, another scenario representative of the life of Gordon Bible College had taken place. It centered on the creation of "the Gordon flag and seal." As Dean Wood phrased it, "this was more than a decorative matter. For both flag and seal were public statements of faith and policy."[75]

While traveling in England some years before, and in places on the Continent, Dean and Mrs. Wood had seen many emblems and crests that were heralds of faith. They remembered all they had seen when it came time to design the Gordon flag and seal. And so they envisioned "a central, crimson Roman cross." For both flag and seal, this cross was to be set in a shield of "a blue field of stars, with a monogram on the lower quarterings for J-C (Jesus Christ), and S.G.S. (Son of God, Savior)." Consultation with other administration colleagues and Trustees led to a revised design for both flag and seal that placed "the five glorious words of the Christian faith in a circle in the original Greek around the shield."[76]

Iesous Christos Theou Yios Soter
"Jesus Christ, Son of God, Savior"

"This phrase," said Dean Wood, "which comes down to us in its New Testament Greek from the early Christians, embodies in a few words the heart of the evangelical faith."[77]

From this time, Dean Wood said long years later in 1953, "Gordon publications have carried this proclamation of the Christocentric faith. The new building [Frost Hall,] has carried those words along its entire front for thirty-five years; and the present Administration, strong in faith and in publicity, has made them yet more widely known."[78] Under Dr. Wood's tenure, many superb scholars joined the college faculty—one of whom, to cite a case in point—was the Rev. C.W. Dunham of South Boston. *The Congregationalist and Advance* magazine reported on this; and gave a near view of the college's development during these years as well—

> Gordon Bible College, Boston, is to be congratulated on securing Rev. C.W. Dunham of Phillips...as Professor of Greek and New Testament Interpretation. Mr. Dunham was graduated from Williams College as salutatorian of the class of 1896, winning Phi Beta Kappa and the "Prize for Prizes," the latter being an award to the one winning the most prizes during his college course.
>
> In his senior year and the two following years he taught Greek at the North Adams High School, instructing in the same also at Auburn Seminary from which he was graduated in 1901, with a brilliant record for scholastic attainment.
>
> When he came to the pastorate of Phillips Church in September 1914, after successful pastorates over Presbyterian churches at Warrensburg and Mount Kisco, N.Y., he began teaching at Gordon Bible College; and the growth and claims of this institution now result in this new relationship...
>
> In his new position, in addition to his teaching [classical Greek], he will serve in the capacity of a Dean to the 185 students now at the college, 75 of whom are studying for the B.D. degree and the work of the ministry.[79]

Other gifted faculty colleagues C.W. Dunham knew included educator and author Margaret Slattery; Dr. A.Z. Conrad—also Pastor of Park Street Church, Boston—who held two doctorates (a Doctor of Divinity degree from Carleton College, and a Ph.D. from the University of the City of New York); and Dr. Edward Payson Drew, D.D. Yale.[80] Learning from such scholars led Dr. Emmet Russell, who earned two Harvard degrees before his studies at Gordon, to offer this testimonial: "After investigating personally and by catalogue several of the strongest theological schools in the United States, I chose Gordon because it has a spirit and a message which honor God as revealed in Jesus Christ, and which grip men with the reality of truth. I am glad that I came to Gordon. The standards of instruction and scholarship are as high and exacting as I have known."[81]

Russell also described his Gordon days for the *Harvard College Class of 1914* alumni magazine, saying: "My life at Gordon is very happy. We are like a big Christian family, and there is no life so rich as the Christian life. With all of our sociability and thought and work for the improvement of the world at Harvard, we missed the heart of it all, for all these things can abound in purity and lasting joy only when they are centered around the person of the Lord Jesus Christ."[82]

This reflected much the same spirit as Dean Wood's phrase that Gordon was "fearlessly, intelligently, openly evangelical."[83] As a college, it had committed itself to this ideal: "There is no reason why education and inquiry should not deepen and enlarge the faith of a young man or woman if they are conducted in the white light and the atmosphere of reality which are in Christ."[84]

As Frost Hall, Gordon Hall, and White Library opened their doors on the new Fenway campus, an advertisement ran nationwide for Gordon Bible College. Its words capture the essence of this new chapter in the life of the school.

"Gordon Bible College," the advertisement began—

> has entered a new period of development…The entrance requirement is now college preparation or its equivalent, and the curriculum includes eighty courses required for the varied needs of its students, [among these,] two courses in the Bible in English and Greek, fourteen in theology, psychology, ethics and apologetics, fourteen in rhetoric,

homiletics, and literature, twelve in history of Christianity, missions and comparative religion, and eleven in pedagogy, phonetics, evangelism, sociology, hygiene, stenography and expression.

The School of Theology and the School of Missions both report strong work already accomplished, and large plans for the coming year.[85]

And in tandem with this fine overview of Gordon Bible College was one description intended to complement all that had been said. The college, this description stated, was "National, Evangelical, Interdenominational, Vocational, Cultural. A school for the development of Christian leadership."[86]

These words were at once a mission statement, and a sterling affirmation. They embody the ethos Gordon College carries forward to this day.

Its heritage shines undimmed.

Afterword
The Sacred Isle

...but the generations following see it, and praise their memory.[1]

—A.J. Gordon

On a lovely day [Father] visited Iona, the center from which wide-reaching missionary impulses radiated in medieval times. The day at this shrine he counted one of the most inspiring of his life, and ever after St. Columba shared with [David] Brainerd and [William] Carey in his heart's affection.[2]

—Ernest Gordon

The last essay A.J. Gordon ever wrote was a long, reflective contribution to *The Missionary Review.*[3] Called "The Apostle Columba," it was perhaps the most poignant essay ever to come from his pen.

Something of Columba's pilgrimage called to Gordon across the centuries, tied to Columba's close association with Iona, an island off Scotland's western coast—"a bit of land, amid the lashing waters" of the sea.[4]

Scotland was the land of Gordon's ancestors, of Alexander Gordon, who'd suffered so much—war, imprisonment, indentured slavery, and exile—to at last find home a far ocean away. A.J. Gordon crossed that ocean and returned to his ancestral land. He walked its terrain.

To speak of this in his final essay was an emblem of finding a kindred spirit in Columba—whom he called "a saint of Hebraic earnestness."[5]

Certainly there was admiration, for Gordon described how Columba, with his fellow Celts, lived on "a dank, stern islet shrouded in Hebridean mists," laying "deep foundations for the blessing of mankind in the succeeding thirteen hundred years." Every spot, Gordon said, "where Scotch missionary feet have trod, are to him, at the last, debtor."[6] Alexander Gordon would have rejoiced over all of this—centuries on, his great-grandson made a return to Scotland he never could make.

A.J. Gordon's visit to Iona came in summer 1888, as he, his wife Maria, and his close friend A.T. Pierson were on their celebrated speaking tour in Scotland after the close of the historic London Centenary Conference.[7]

"I think," Gordon said, "the most sacred spot my feet have ever stood upon was in that little island of Iona on the coast of Scotland. There, one afternoon, with my friend, Dr. Pierson, I looked across to the green banks and fields of Scotland that were visible to the eye, and I was filled with wonder and astonishment."[8]

To give a vivid sense of what he felt during his visit to Iona, he drew on Journal entries that dated from this time.[9]

"The day of pilgrimage to this historic spot," he said—

> will ever stand as a marked day in my calendar…A thousand years before the Reformation [Columba] kept the primitive faith [at] a seminary for training his disciples in the Scriptures and in Divine communion, to fit them to be his co-laborers in the great work of carrying Christianity into Britain…Iona, therefore, [was] a fortress of the ancient faith, a stronghold of primitive Christianity…[10]

Gordon then described things he saw on this storied isle. He found poetry in the stone and the seascape. "Yonder," he said—

> within near sight, lies Staffa—with its wonderful Fingal's Cave. The tourist who has visited cathedral after cathedral on the Continent, and has become satiated with the voluble discourse of verger and guide, can here gaze in silence upon

one of God's cathedrals—built without sound of hammer or saw, but far surpassing all others in grandeur; for [as the Duke of Argyll has written,] "there is nothing like this great hall of columns standing round their ocean floor, and sending forth in ceaseless reverberations the solemn music of its waves."

Let a party sing *Old Hundred* as we did, beneath these arches of stone, and as its strains thunder and echo through the "long drawn aisle," let them tell me if they ever heard such majestic music before.[11]

Here, Gordon became deeply reflective. Something of this slender land, and its holy ways, lent wisdom. "Perhaps," he said, "we have something to learn of Columba...if we would be better missionaries."[12] He paused, and then explained what he meant by naming traits he admired in this Celtic saint.

Columba "deeply reverenced and profoundly studied the Holy Scriptures," Gordon observed; and "all traditions agree" in ascribing to him "a spirit of extraordinary prayerfulness."[13]

Gordon then looked to words about Columba written by Dr. John Smith, the author of the book, *Gaelic Antiquities*. Gordon set these words in his essay.

"It seems to have been Columba's invariable rule," Smith had written—

not to undertake any work nor engage in any business without having first invoked God. If about to officiate in any ministerial duty, he would first implore the Divine presence and aid to enable him to discharge it properly. If he himself or any of his friends were to go any whither, by land or by sea, their first care was to implore God to be propitious, and their last words at parting were solemn prayer and benediction.

If he administered medicines for the cure of any diseases, he accompanied them with prayer to God who healeth. If he administered even counsel or advice, he would attend it with a prayer to Him who disposeth the heart to listen, often accompanying that prayer with fasting. In seasons of danger and alarm, whether public or private, he always had recourse to prayer...[14]

*　*　*

The best things Gordon shared in his essay were a window on his life, and consecrated heart. Things he saw in Columba were part of *his* pilgrimage. They had shaped his times and seasons—with all the work God gave him to do.

And always, there was the blessèd hope. "Gazing," he said—

I shall see the King in His beauty, and all standing in blessed relationship to Him, He, the author and finisher of my faith; He the architect and builder of my life; He, the Origin and End of all my ways...

What reason will there be for praise when I stand with the Lamb upon Mount Zion, in company with those who have been redeemed...For, in the glorified Christ, all contradictions shall vanish, all mysteries be explained...[15]

And what of Gordon's work, and his legacy, in the retrospect?
Here too, there were ties to Columba.

"Remember," Gordon said, "that events are only truly great or insignificant in their final result...Recall how far-reaching the influence of Iona became."[16]

Living all his life far from Columba's isle "amid the lashing waters," Gordon's words and work themselves still speak—their influence is still widely felt—in tens of thousands of lives. We may be grateful for him, as he was for Columba.

Both men laid deep foundations of blessing—for all the years to follow.

Author's Note

A detailed view of A.J. Gordon's theology lies beyond the scope of this book, which has been written solely as an introductory narrative life.

Those who wish to explore A.J. Gordon's theology are encouraged to read the rich, definitive study written by Dr. S.M. Gibson, *A.J. Gordon: American Premillennialist* (University Press of America, 2001).

Beyond this, I would paraphrase Dr. Gordon and simply say—"If this little book should be to any in reading it, what it has been to the author in writing it…it will have served the end of its publication."

Works of A.J. Gordon

British and American Editions, and where they are housed in some of the world's finest repositories

1869 – *The Service of a Good Life: A Discourse Commemorative of the Life and Character of Richard Fletcher, Delivered by Request in the Clarendon Street Baptist Church, July 11, 1869,* by Adoniram Judson Gordon, D.D. (Boston: Gould and Lincoln, 1869). Housed at Yale University.

1872 – *In Christ, or The Believer's Union with His Lord,* by A.J. Gordon, (Boston: Gould and Lincoln, 1872). Housed at Princeton University.

1874 – *Congregational Worship,* by A.J. Gordon, (Boston: Young and Bartlett, 1874). Housed at Harvard University, Brown University, and Wellesley College.

1878 – *The Fiftieth Year: A Sermon, Preached on the Semi-Centennial Anniversary of the Clarendon Street Baptist Church, in Boston, October 21st, 1877,* by A.J. Gordon, (Boston: Printed for the Church, 1878). Housed at Harvard University.

1880 – *Grace and Glory: Sermons for the Life that Now Is, and That Which Is To Come,* by A.J. Gordon, (Boston: Howard Gannett, 1880). Housed at Harvard University and the University of Virginia.

God's Tenth, by A.J. Gordon, (Richmond, Virginia: Southern Baptist Convention, 188?). Housed at the University of North Carolina.

1882 – *The Ministry of Healing*, 3rd ed., by A.J. Gordon, (Boston: Howard Gannett 1882). Housed at Harvard University and Wellesley College.

In Christ, by A.J. Gordon, (London: Hodder and Stoughton, 1882). Housed at The Bodleian Library, Oxford University.

1883 – *The Holy Spirit in Missions*, by A.J. Gordon, (New York: Revell, 1883). Housed at Princeton University and Boston University.

The Two-Fold Life, by A.J. Gordon, (Boston: Howard Gannett, 1883). Housed at Harvard University and Brown University.

1884 – *The Two-Fold Life*, by A.J. Gordon, (London: Hodder and Stoughton, 1884). Housed at The Bodleian Library, Oxford University.

1888 – *Grace and Glory*, by A.J. Gordon, (London: Hodder and Stoughton, 1888). Housed at the University of Oxford, and catalogued in The British Museum.

1889 – *Ecce Venit: Behold He Cometh*, by A.J. Gordon, (New York: Revell, 1889). Housed at Yale University and The Library of Congress.

1890 – *Ecce Venit: Behold He Cometh*, (London: Hodder and Stoughton, 1890). Housed at Harvard, Boston College, and Saint Anselm College.

1891 – *The First Thing in the World*, by A.J. Gordon, (New York: Revell, 1891). Housed at Columbia University and Brown University.

The First Thing in the World, by A.J. Gordon, (London: Nisbet, 1891).

1892 – *Rest In Christ*, by A.J. Gordon, (London: Hodder and Stoughton, 1892).

1893 – *The Holy Spirit in Missions,* (London: Hodder and Stoughton, 1883). Boston College and McGill University Library (Canada).

1894 – *The Ministry of the Spirit,* by A.J. Gordon, (Boston: Am. Bapt. Pub. Soc., 1894). Housed at Harvard University and The University of Virginia.

Posthumous Works

1895 – *How Christ Came to Church,* by A.J. Gordon, (Philadelphia: American Baptist Publication Society, 1895). Housed at Harvard University, the University of Chicago, and Princeton Theological Seminary Library.

Elements of Christian Character, by A.J. Gordon, (Philadelphia: American Baptist Publication Society, 1895). Housed in The Library of Congress.

Risen with Christ: An Address on the Resurrection, by A.J. Gordon, (New York: Revell, 1895). Housed at Columbia University.

The Ministry of the Spirit, (London: Baptist Tract Society, 1895).

1896 – *Ecce Venit: Behold He Cometh,* by A.J. Gordon, (London: Hodder and Stoughton, 1896). Housed at Harvard University.

The Holy Spirit in Missions, 2nd ed., (London: Hodder and Stoughton, 1896).

How Christ Came to Church, (London: Baptist Tract Society, 1896).

1897 – *Yet Speaking: A Collection,* by A.J. Gordon, (New York: Revell, 1897). Housed at Columbia University and Brown University.

Yet Speaking: A Collection, by A.J. Gordon, (London: James Nisbet, 1897). Housed at Brown University, McGill University, and UMass Amherst.

1900 – *Ecce Venit: Behold He Cometh,* (London: Hodder and Stoughton, 1900). Housed at Harvard University, Boston College, and Saint Anselm College.

A.J. Gordon as Contributor

Uncle John Vassar, by T.E. Vassar, Introduction by A.J. Gordon, (New York: American Tract Society, 1879). Housed at Cornell University.

Christ Yet To Come: A Review of I.P. Warren's "Parousia of Christ," by Josiah Litch, Introduction by A.J. Gordon, (Boston: American Millennial Association, 1880). Housed at Harvard University.

The Life and Labors of Charles H. Spurgeon, by G.C. Needham, Introduction by A.J. Gordon, (Boston: D.L. Guernsey, 1883). Housed at Harvard University.

Steps and Studies, by G.B. Beck, 2nd ed., Introduction by A.J. Gordon, (Boston: Watchword Publishing Company, 1890). Housed at Columbia University.

Means and Ways, by T.D. Roberts, Introduction by A.J. Gordon, (Boston: J.H. Earle, 1892). Housed at Harvard University.

John Thomas: First Baptist Missionary to Bengal, Introduction by A.J. Gordon, (Halifax, Nova Scotia: Baptist Book and Tract Soc., 1893). Housed at Columbia University.

A.J. Gordon as an Editor

The Service of Song for Baptist Churches, ed. by A.J. Gordon and S.L. Caldwell, (Boston: Gould and Lincoln, 1871). Housed at Harvard University, Yale University, and Brown University.

The Vestry Hymn and Tune Book, ed. by A.J. Gordon, (Boston: H.A. Young & Co., 1872). Housed at Columbia University and Brown University.

The Coronation Hymnal, ed. by A.J. Gordon, and A.T. Pierson, (Philadelphia: Am. Bapt. Pub. Soc., 1894). Housed at Harvard University and Yale University.

About A.J. Gordon, by Ernest Gordon

Adoniram Judson Gordon: A Biography, by Ernest Gordon, (New York: Revell, 1896). Housed at Harvard University, Cornell University, Princeton Theological Seminary, and The Library of Congress.

Adoniram Judson Gordon: A Biography, (London: Hodder and Stoughton, 1896). Housed in The Bodleian Library, Oxford, University of Cambridge (U.K.), the National Library of Scotland, and Trinity College Library, Dublin, Ireland.

A.J. Gordon: A Timeline

1836 — A.J. Gordon was born in New Hampton, N.H. on Tuesday, April 19th.

1852 — June. AJG was converted and baptized in New Hampton, NH.

1853 — Autumn. AJG began studies at Colby Academy in New London, NH.

1856 — July. AJG completed his last term at Colby Academy
    — Fall. AJG began studies at Brown University (Providence, RI).

1860 — Summer. AJG graduated from Brown University.
    — Autumn. AJG began studies at Newton Theological School (Andover, MA).

1863 — Friday, June 12. AJG was ordained at Jamaica Plain Church (W. Roxbury, MA)
    — Wednesday, June 24. AJG graduated from Newton Theological School.
    — Tuesday, October 13, AJG married Maria Hale, of Providence, RI.

1869 — Dec. AJG bade farewell to his pastorate at Jamaica Plain Church
    — Dec. AJG began 25 years of ministry at Clarendon Street Church

1871— AJG joined the Exec. Comm. of the American Baptist Missionary Union, and became Chair of that Committee after 1888.

1872 — June. AJG's book, *In Christ,* was published.

1874 — AJG was appointed a Brown University Trustee, and served until 1888.
    — AJG published *Congregational Worship.* The Boston Industrial home is established.

1877 — winter. AJG befriended & worked closely with D.L. Moody, during Moody's great mission to Boston. 15 Feb., The Boston Industrial home is incorporated.

1878 — Wednesday, June 19. Brown University awarded AJG a D.D. degree.

— month. AJG became the Founding Editor of *The Watchword* magazine

1880 — Sept. 1. For 10 days, AJG attended the 1st Northfield Summer Conference

— late autumn/thru Dec. AJG published *Grace and Glory*

1883 — month. AJG published *The Ministry of Healing*

— Oct. 28. AJG spoke on "Preparation for Service" at The Inter-Seminary Alliance (inspiring Robert Wilder, a prime mover of The Student Volunteer Movement)

— month. AJG published *The Twofold Life*

— month. AJG & G.C. Needham published *The Life and Labors of Charles H. Spurgeon*

1886 — AJG addressed the Northfield Conf. when the Student Vol. Movement began

1888 — month. AJG was elected a Fellow of Brown University, & served until 1895.

— June. Gordon attends the World's Missionary Conference in London, and thereafter began a speaking tour of Scotland with A.T. Pierson.

1889 — Wed., Oct. 2. The Boston Missionary Training School, founded by AJG, opened.

— Sept 1. AJG published *Ecce Venit*

— month. AJG was profiled in the British book, *The Christian Portrait Gallery,* marking his appearance a Christian leader of international renown.

1891 — April. AJG published *The First Thing in the World*

1892 — July 2-13. AJG led the Northfield Summer Conference in D.L. Moody's absence

1893 — April. AJG published *The Holy Spirit in Missions*

— summer. AJG again led the Northfield Summer Conf. in D.L. Moody's absence

1894 — Sept. AJG & A.T. Pierson published *The Coronation Hymnal*

— Dec. 26. Clarendon St. Baptist Church honored 25 years of AJG's pastorate.

1895 — Saturday, February 2. Death of A.J. Gordon.

— Aug. AJG's book *How Christ Came to Church* was published.

1897 — Nov. AJG's book, *Yet Speaking,* was published.

Appendix

from the Funeral Tribute for A.J. Gordon given by Dr. Elisha Benjamin Andrews, President of Brown University[1]

I do not conceive it to be profitable that I should say very much to you on a solemn occasion like this, for I stand here in official relation, and even were I to speak personally of the knowledge I had of the man, that would take a great deal more time than I have any right to occupy.

Dr. Gordon was a graduate of Brown University. He graduated in the class of 1860, and was looked upon as the light of that class. He was very dearly beloved, not only by the men in that class who entered the Christian ministry, but also by those whose lines of work were remote.

Quite early in his ministry to this congregation, he was chosen to be a member of the Governing Board of Brown University, and I cannot tell you how faithful he has always been in that relation. He was always faithful, not only in attending the meetings whenever possible—and the occasions when it was not possible were very few—but in attending to the matters that were brought before the Board from time to time. He always showed an uncommon grasp of commercial matters from one year's session to another, and I felt very proud of Dr. Gordon. He was engaged in spiritual matters, but he was never so much engaged in them that he was not able to take up any matter of temporal detail, and I believe the men most immersed in business with him also respected him the most and felt a sort of pride in him because of this signal ability in matters of temporal detail.

Not to speak further upon this, I wish now to tell you of a line of Dr. Gordon's activity, of which very few have been aware, even in this church—even those very intimate with him. He was accustomed to tear himself away and run down to Brown University for a single day to their services. On these occasions it was often absolutely indispensable that he should come back to Boston for some duty, and then fly back to Providence.

All who know about college affairs know that it is not every man—not even every good or every able man—who can touch the hearts of the student body; and in all my acquaintance I have never met many—there may have been two or three—who even began to have the power in this sort of work that Dr. Gordon had. He never came to us without bringing a blessing—never without a large blessing—never without leaving behind him a permanent blessing. Never did he speak a word in our student body without so impressing many a student heart that the impress of that lesson would abide forever.

Endnotes

Frontispiece epigraph quotes

1   A.J. Gordon, *In Christ* (London: Hodder & Stoughton, 1882), 126.

2   E.B. Gordon, *Adoniram Judson Gordon* (London: Hodder & Stoughton, 1909), 200. See also *Great Pulpit Masters: A.J. Gordon*, ed. by Arthur Gordon, with an Introduction by N.R. Wood, (New York: Revell, 1951), 148.

Prologue – A Man of Many Parts

1   no author, "All Praised Him," *Boston Globe*, February 11, 1895, 10. This Prologue subtitle is taken from a description of A.J. Gordon given by Dr. Thomas Askew in the 2011 documentary film, "A School of Christ."

2   Alice Rosalie Parker, "Rev. A.J. Gordon, D.D.," *The Granite Monthly*, March 1895, 127. For the earliest publisher's notice of the release of Ernest Gordon's biography, see *The Publishers Weekly*, July 4, 1896, 27.

3   no author, *The Harvard University Catalogue, 1888-89*, 316. See also C.H. Moore and D.C. Torrey, *The Harvard Index for 1887-88*, 99.

4   no author, *The Outlook* magazine, July 18, 1896, 163.

5   no author, *The Literary World*, March 6, 1897, 71.

6   no author, *The Publishers Weekly*, July 4, 1896, 27.

7   no author, *The Publishers Weekly*, July 4, 1896, 27.

8   E.B. Gordon, *Adoniram Judson Gordon* (London: Hodder & Stoughton, 1909), 200.

9   E.B. Gordon, *Adoniram Judson Gordon* (London: Hodder & Stoughton, 1909), 196-197.

10   no author, *General Catalogue of Officers and Students of Mount Holyoke College, 1837-1911*, 50. See also *Proceedings of the New Hampshire Historical Society*, v. 2, 1895, 4. Here General H.L. Porter and Alice Rosalie Porter are listed as "Resident Members" of The New Hampshire Historical Society.

11   Alice Rosalie Porter, "Rev. A.J. Gordon, D.D.," *The Granite Monthly,* March 1895, 128.

12   Alice Rosalie Porter, "Rev. A.J. Gordon, D.D.," *The Granite Monthly,* March 1895, 132.

13   Alice Rosalie Porter, "Rev. A.J. Gordon, D.D.," *The Granite Monthly,* March 1895, 132.

14   Alice Rosalie Porter, "Rev. A.J. Gordon, D.D.," *The Granite Monthly,* March 1895, 131. Italics added.

15   Alice Rosalie Porter, "Rev. A.J. Gordon, D.D.," *The Granite Monthly,* March 1895, 134.

16   Alice Rosalie Porter, "Rev. A.J. Gordon, D.D.," *The Granite Monthly,* March 1895, 129.

17   Alice Rosalie Porter, "Rev. A.J. Gordon, D.D.," *The Granite Monthly,* March 1895, 134. Italics added.

Chapter One – Upon the Blue Hills

1   E.B. Gordon, *Adoniram Judson Gordon* (London: Hodder & Stoughton, 1909), 199. Citation edited.

2   E.B. Gordon, *Adoniram Judson Gordon* (London: Hodder & Stoughton, 1909), 11.

3   R.W. Emerson, *Poems* (Boston: Houghton Mifflin, 1895), 139.

4   L.P. Dolliver, *Lineage Book,* v. 18 (Harrisburg: Daughters of the American Revolution, 1904), 240-241.

5   E.B. Gordon, *Adoniram Judson Gordon* (London: Hodder & Stoughton, 1909), 14.

6   S.M. Gibson, *A.J. Gordon: American Premillenialist* (Lanham: University Press of America, 2001), 2.

7   E.S. Stearns, W.F. Whitcher, et al, *Genealogical and Family History of New Hampshire,* v. 2, (New York: Lewis Publishing Co., 1908), 802. There is a connection between Alexander Gordon and the lineage of this biography's author—whose Scottish ancestor, Micum McIntire, also fought against Cromwell. Like Alexander Gordon, Micum McIntire was a Scottish prisoner of war transported to America as a slave. Both served in the Scottish army, and were caught up in a conflict that eventually brought them to America. Micum McIntire's story is recounted on page 79 of *The William and Mary College Quarterly,* (Williamsburg: William and Mary College, 1941).

8   no author, *Proceedings of the Massachusetts Historical Society,* vol. 61, (Boston: Published by the Society, 1928), 25.

9   no author, *Proceedings of the Massachusetts Historical Society,* vol. 61, (Boston: Published by the Society, 1928), 26.

10   no author, *Proceedings of the Massachusetts Historical Society,* vol. 61, (Boston: Published by the Society, 1928), 26-27.

11 no author, *Proceedings of the Massachusetts Historical Society,* vol. 61, (Boston: Published by the Society, 1928), 25. See also David Dobson, *Scottish Emigration to Colonial America* (Athens: University of Georgia Press, 2004), 35-36.

12 E.S. Stearns, W.F. Whitcher, et al, *Genealogical and Family History of New Hampshire,* v. 2, (New York: Lewis Publishing Co., 1908), 802. See also Barbara Rimkunas, *Exeter: Historically Speaking* (Charlestown, South Carolina: History Press, 2008), 40.

13 E.S. Stearns, W.F. Whitcher, et al, *Genealogical and Family History of New Hampshire,* v. 2, (New York: Lewis Publishing Co., 1908), 802.

14 S.M. Gibson, *A.J. Gordon: American Premillenialist* (Lanham: University Press of America, 2001), 2.

15 F.H. Kelley, *Reminiscences of New Hampton, N.H.* (Worcester, Mass: Charles Hamilton, 1889), 94.

16 C.S. Lewis, from Jerry Root, and Wayne Martindale, eds., *The Quotable Lewis* (Wheaton, Illinois: Tyndale, 1989), 148.

Chapter Two – Yet Another Music

1 E.B. Gordon, *Adoniram Judson Gordon* (London: Hodder & Stoughton, 1909), 11. Citation edited.

2 E.B. Gordon, *Adoniram Judson Gordon* (London: Hodder & Stoughton, 1909), 179.

3 H.H. Vail, *A History of the McGuffey Readers* (Cleveland: Burrows, 1911), 33.

4 A.J. Gordon, "The Chameleon Guinea," *The Watchword,* July 1882, 228.

5 R.C. Morgan, ed., "Rev. A.J. Gordon, D.D.," *The Christian Portrait Gallery,* (London: Morgan & Scott, 1889), 107.

6 A.J. Gordon, "Separation and Service," *Great Pulpit Masters* (New York: Revell, 1951), 96.

7 A.J. Gordon to Maria Gordon, 14 August [1864], a letter in the A.J. Gordon Papers, Jenks LRC, Gordon College.

8 E.B. Gordon, *Adoniram Judson Gordon* (London: Hodder & Stoughton, 1909), 19.

9 "yarns and heavy cloth" are described as products of the Gordon Woolen Mill on page 155 of *The New Hampshire Business Directory for 1868,* (Boston: Briggs & Co., 1868). And that A.J. Gordon was called "Judson" by his family, when young, is stated in S.M. Gibson, *A.J. Gordon: American Premillenialist* (Lanham: University Press of America, 2001), 1.

10 A.J. Gordon, "Teach Me and Lead Me," *The Watchword,* March 1891, 58.

11 A.J. Gordon, "Taken Into Partnership," *The Watchword,* April 1891, 86.

12 Maria Hale to Harriet Hale, 10 August 1862, a letter in the A.J. Gordon Papers, Jenks LRC, Gordon College.

13 S.M. Gibson, *A.J. Gordon: American Premillenialist* (Lanham: University Press of America, 2001), 4.

14 E.B. Gordon, *Adoniram Judson Gordon* (London: Hodder & Stoughton, 1909), 200.

15 S.M. Gibson, *A.J. Gordon: American Premillenialist* (Lanham: University Press of America, 2001), 3.

16 E.B. Gordon, *Adoniram Judson Gordon* (London: Hodder & Stoughton, 1909), 20.

17 lines from the 1st verse of A.J. Gordon's hymn, "The King In His Beauty," composed in 1893. See A.J. Gordon, *Hymns* (Boston: Gordon College of Theology and Missions, 1949), 9.

18 E.B. Gordon, *Adoniram Judson Gordon* (London: Hodder & Stoughton, 1909), 20.

19 E.B. Gordon, *Adoniram Judson Gordon* (London: Hodder & Stoughton, 1909), 20.

20 E.B. Gordon, *Adoniram Judson Gordon* (London: Hodder & Stoughton, 1909), 20. Citation edited.

21 E.B. Gordon, *Adoniram Judson Gordon* (London: Hodder & Stoughton, 1909), 20.

22 E.B. Gordon, *Adoniram Judson Gordon* (London: Hodder & Stoughton, 1909), 20.

23 see the biography of Adelaide Pierce Bailey given on page 86 of *The Register of the Malden Historical Society,* (Lynn: F.S. Whitten, 1912). Colby Academy is now Colby-Sawyer College.

24 E.B. Gordon, *Adoniram Judson Gordon* (London: Hodder & Stoughton, 1909), 21.

25 E.B. Gordon, *Adoniram Judson Gordon* (London: Hodder & Stoughton, 1909), 21.

26 E.B. Gordon, *Adoniram Judson Gordon* (London: Hodder & Stoughton, 1909), 21. See also S.M. Gibson, *A.J. Gordon: American Premillenialist* (Lanham: University Press of America, 2001), 8.

Chapter Three – The Business of a Scholar

1 A.N. Marquis, ed., *Who's Who of New England: A Biographical Dictionary* (Chicago: Marquis & Co., 1909), 1100. Citation edited.

2 G.G. Bush, *The History of Education in New Hampshire* (Washington: Government Printing Office, 1898), 77.

3 G.G. Bush, *The History of Education in New Hampshire* (Washington: Government Printing Office, 1898), 77.

4 G.G. Bush, *The History of Education in New Hampshire* (Washington: Government Printing Office, 1898), 77.

5 G.G. Bush, *The History of Education in New Hampshire* (Washington: Government Printing Office, 1898), 77.

6 H.K. Rowe, A Centennial History, 1837-1937, Colby Academy (New London: Colby College, 1937), 71.

7 H.K. Rowe, A Centennial History, 1837-1937, Colby Academy (New London: Colby College, 1937), 71.

8 H.K. Rowe, A Centennial History, 1837-1937, Colby Academy (New London: Colby College, 1937), 77-78.

9   H.K. Rowe, A Centennial History, 1837-1937, Colby Academy (New London: Colby College, 1937), 77.

10   H.K. Rowe, A Centennial History, 1837-1937, Colby Academy (New London: Colby College, 1937), 77-78.

11   H.K. Rowe, A Centennial History, 1837-1937, Colby Academy (New London: Colby College, 1937), 77-78.

12   H.K. Rowe, A Centennial History, 1837-1937, Colby Academy (New London: Colby College, 1937), 78-79.

13   H.K. Rowe, A Centennial History, 1837-1937, Colby Academy (New London: Colby College, 1937), 82-83.

14   H.K. Rowe, A Centennial History, 1837-1937, Colby Academy (New London: Colby College, 1937), 83.

15   H.K. Rowe, A Centennial History, 1837-1937, Colby Academy (New London: Colby College, 1937), 82-83.

16   S.M. Gibson, *A.J. Gordon: American Premillenialist* (Lanham: University Press of America, 2001), 10.

17   E.B. Gordon, *Adoniram Judson Gordon* (London: Hodder & Stoughton, 1909), 22.

18   S.M. Gibson, *A.J. Gordon: American Premillenialist* (Lanham: University Press of America, 2001), 11.

19   E.B. Gordon, *Adoniram Judson Gordon* (London: Hodder & Stoughton, 1909), 21.

20   E.B. Gordon, *Adoniram Judson Gordon* (London: Hodder & Stoughton, 1909), 21.

21   see Alice Rosalie Porter, "Rev. A.J. Gordon, D.D.," *The Granite Monthly*, March 1895, 128. See also page 12 of *A.J. Gordon: American Premillenialist,* by S.M. Gibson, (Lanham, Maryland: University Press of America, 2001).

22   see "Religious Intelligence," an article in *The Watchman* magazine, 13 June 1878: 4; also see the article, "More About Academies," in *The Watchman* magazine, 7 October 1886: 4. See also H.K. Rowe, A Centennial History, 1837-1937, Colby Academy (New London: Colby College, 1937), 315. In 1860, "Dr. A. J. Gordon '56, delivered the Commencement] oration" at Colby.

23   H.K. Rowe, A Centennial History, 1837-1937, Colby Academy (New London: Colby College, 1937), 266-267.

24   no author, *The Watchman* magazine, January 7, 1904, 2.

Chapter Four – University Years

1   select lines from the hymn, "Alma Mater," see no author, *Songs of Brown University*, (New York: Hinds, Noble & Eldredge, 1908), 2.

2   this information on the founding of Brown University is given online at: http://www.brown.edu/about/history

3   R.A. Guild, *The History of Brown University* (Providence: Providence Press Company, 1867), frontispiece engraving.

4   E.B. Gordon, *Adoniram Judson Gordon* (London: Hodder & Stoughton, 1909), 23.

5   E.B. Gordon, *Adoniram Judson Gordon* (London: Hodder & Stoughton, 1909), 23.

6   Francis Wayland, *A Memoir of the Life and Labors of the Rev. Adoniram Judson, D.D.* (Boston: Phillips, Sampson, and Company, 1853.

7   no author, *The Catalogue of Brown University: 1858*, (Providence: Knowles, Anthony & Co., 1858), 11. Here Gordon, a member of the Junior Class, is listed as living in "44 U.H."

8   E.B. Gordon, *Adoniram Judson Gordon* (London: Hodder & Stoughton, 1909), 31.

9   E.B. Gordon, *Adoniram Judson Gordon* (London: Hodder & Stoughton, 1909), 24. See also page 172 of *The Life and Correspondence of Thomas Arnold*, v. 1, by A.P. Stanley, (London: Fellowes, 1844).

10 E.B. Gordon, *Adoniram Judson Gordon* (London: Hodder & Stoughton, 1909), 25.

11 E.B. Gordon, *Adoniram Judson Gordon* (London: Hodder & Stoughton, 1909), 26.

12 E.B. Gordon, *Adoniram Judson Gordon* (London: Hodder & Stoughton, 1909), 26.

13 E.B. Gordon, *Adoniram Judson Gordon* (London: Hodder & Stoughton, 1909), 26-27.

14 E.B. Gordon, *Adoniram Judson Gordon* (London: Hodder & Stoughton, 1909), 27.

15 E.B. Gordon, *Adoniram Judson Gordon* (London: Hodder & Stoughton, 1909), 27.

16 E.B. Gordon, *Adoniram Judson Gordon* (London: Hodder & Stoughton, 1909), 27-28.

17 E.B. Gordon, *Adoniram Judson Gordon* (London: Hodder & Stoughton, 1909), 28.

18 E.B. Gordon, *Adoniram Judson Gordon* (London: Hodder & Stoughton, 1909), 28.

19 E.B. Gordon, *Adoniram Judson Gordon* (London: Hodder & Stoughton, 1909), 27.

20 E.B. Gordon, *Adoniram Judson Gordon* (London: Hodder & Stoughton, 1909), 28. See also John Todd, *Index Rerum* (Northampton: Hopkins, Bridgman, and Co., 1856), 6-8.

21 A.J. Gordon, "Untitled Citation," *The Watchword*, December 1891, 317.

22 E.B. Gordon, *Adoniram Judson Gordon* (London: Hodder & Stoughton, 1909), 27.

23 A.J. Gordon, "Untitled Introductory Article," *The Watchword*, December 1891, 309. See also page 164 of *The Writings of Henry David Thoreau: Familiar Letters*, ed. by F.B. Sanborn, (Boston: Houghton Mifflin, 1906).

24 from page 34 of *Yet Speaking*, by A.J. Gordon, (New York: F.H. Revell, 1897).

25 E.B. Gordon, *Adoniram Judson Gordon* (London: Hodder & Stoughton, 1909), 27.

26 Thomas Fuller, *The Holy and Profane States* (Boston: Little, Brown and Company, 1864), 97.

27 Thomas Fuller, *The Religio Medici and Other Writings* (London: J.M. Dent, 1906), 12.

28 E.B. Gordon, *Adoniram Judson Gordon* (London: Hodder & Stoughton, 1909), 36.

29 A.J. Gordon, "Untitled Introductory Article," *The Watchword*, January 1890, 1.

30 S.M. Gibson, *A.J. Gordon: American Premillenialist* (Lanham: University Press of America, 2001), 16.

Chapter Five – There is the Fair Vision

1   William Wordsworth, *Poetical Works* (London: Moxon, Son, & Co., 1870), 65.

2   E.B. Gordon, *Adoniram Judson Gordon* (London: Hodder & Stoughton, 1909), 31-32.

3   no author, *National Register of Historic Places: College Hill Historic District, Providence, Rhode Island,* (Providence: College Hill Grant Study, 1959), 7.60i. Online at: http://www.preservation.ri.gov/pdfs_zips_downloads/national_ pdfs/providence/prov_college-hill-hd.pdf

4   S.M. Gibson, *A.J. Gordon: American Premillenialist* (Lanham: University Press of America, 2001), 115.

5   L.A. Jewett, *The Jewett Family in America* (Rowley, Mass: The Jewett Family Assoc. of America, 1913), 172.

6   no author, *Calendar of the Correspondence of George Washington,* v. 3, (Washington: Government Printing Office, 1915), 2132.

7   S.M. Gibson, *A.J. Gordon: American Premillenialist* (Lanham: University Press of America, 2001), 115-116.

8   S.M. Gibson, *A.J. Gordon: American Premillenialist* (Lanham: University Press of America, 2001), 115. See also Thomas A. and Jean M. Askew, *A Faithful Past* (Wenham: Gordon College, 1988), 19.

9   Harriet Johnson Hale to Maria Hale Gordon, 23 January 1865, a letter in the A.J. Gordon Papers, Jenks LRC, Gordon College.

10 all information here on Elizabeth Comstock is given in E.T. James and J.W. James, *Notable American Women: A Biographical Dictionary,* v. 1, (Cambridge: Harvard University Press, 1971), 369.

11 S.M. Gibson, *A.J. Gordon: American Premillenialist* (Lanham: University Press of America, 2001), 116.

12 S.M. Gibson, *A.J. Gordon: American Premillenialist* (Lanham: University Press of America, 2001), 115-116. See also Thomas A. and Jean M. Askew, *A Faithful Past* (Wenham: Gordon College, 1988), 19.

13 Maria Hale Gordon to Isaac Hale, 24 August 1889, a letter in the A.J. Gordon Papers, Jenks LRC, Gordon College.

14 E.B. Gordon, *Adoniram Judson Gordon* (London: Hodder & Stoughton, 1909), 116-117. See also Thomas A. and Jean M. Askew, *A Faithful Past* (Wenham: Gordon College, 1988), 19.

15 Maria Gordon to A.J. Gordon, n.d., a letter in the A.J. Gordon Papers, Jenks LRC, Gordon College.

16 S.M. Gibson, *A.J. Gordon: American Premillenialist* (Lanham: University Press of America, 2001), 15-16. See also E.B. Gordon, *Adoniram Judson Gordon* (London: Hodder & Stoughton, 1909), 31 and 36.

17 no author, *The Outlook* magazine, September 26, 1896, 582.

18 E.B. Gordon, *Adoniram Judson Gordon* (London: Hodder & Stoughton, 1909), 31-32.

19 S.M. Gibson, *A.J. Gordon: American Premillenialist* (Lanham: University Press of America, 2001), 16.

Chapter Six – Jamaica Plain

1   E.B. Gordon, *Adoniram Judson Gordon* (London: Hodder & Stoughton, 1909), 42. Citation edited.

2   E.B. Gordon, *Adoniram Judson Gordon* (London: Hodder & Stoughton, 1909), 40. Emphasis added.

3   E.B. Gordon, *Adoniram Judson Gordon* (London: Hodder & Stoughton, 1909), 40.

4   E.B. Gordon, *Adoniram Judson Gordon* (London: Hodder & Stoughton, 1909), 40.

5   James Pike, ed., *History of the churches of Boston...Baptist and Presbyterian* (Boston: Ecclesia Pub. Co., 1883), 64.

6   E.B. Gordon, *Adoniram Judson Gordon* (London: Hodder & Stoughton, 1909), 40.

7   Baron Stow and Samuel F. Smith, eds., *The Psalmist: A New Collection of Hymns* (Philadelphia: American Baptist Publications, 1850), 501. See also no author, *The Clifton Chapel Collection of Psalms* (Clifton Springs: Henry Foster, 1881), 234.

8   R. Pollan, C. Kennedy, et al, *The Jamaica Plain Preservation Study* (Boston: Boston Landmarks Commission, 1983), 32.

9   James Pike, ed., *History of the churches of Boston...Baptist and Presbyterian* (Boston: Ecclesia Pub. Co., 1883), 64.

10 E.B. Gordon, *Adoniram Judson Gordon* (London: Hodder & Stoughton, 1909), 34.

11 E.B. Gordon, *Adoniram Judson Gordon* (London: Hodder & Stoughton, 1909), 34.

12 E.B. Gordon, *Adoniram Judson Gordon* (London: Hodder & Stoughton, 1909), 34.

13 A.J. Gordon, "The Harvest and the Harvesters," *The Watchword*, May 1891, 114.

14 A.J. Gordon, "The Harvest and the Harvesters," *The Watchword*, May 1891, 114.

15 E.B. Gordon, *Adoniram Judson Gordon* (London: Hodder & Stoughton, 1909), 34.

16 E.B. Gordon, *Adoniram Judson Gordon* (London: Hodder & Stoughton, 1909), 43.

17 Robert and Samuel Wilberforce, *The Life of William Wilberforce*, v. 4, (London: John Murray, 1838), 290.

18 E.B. Gordon, *Adoniram Judson Gordon* (London: Hodder & Stoughton, 1909), 43.

19 E.B. Gordon, *Adoniram Judson Gordon* (London: Hodder & Stoughton, 1909), 43.

20 E.B. Gordon, *Adoniram Judson Gordon* (London: Hodder & Stoughton, 1909), 44.

21 A.J. Gordon, "Good News," *The Watchword*, October 1885, 166.

22 E.B. Gordon, *Adoniram Judson Gordon* (London: Hodder & Stoughton, 1909), 40-41.

23 E.B. Gordon, *Adoniram Judson Gordon* (London: Hodder & Stoughton, 1909), 41.

24 E.B. Gordon, *Adoniram Judson Gordon* (London: Hodder & Stoughton, 1909), 43.

25 E.B. Gordon, *Adoniram Judson Gordon* (London: Hodder & Stoughton, 1909), 214. Italics added.

26 E.B. Gordon, *Adoniram Judson Gordon* (London: Hodder & Stoughton, 1909), 214-215. Punctuation inserted.

27 "in-tim-ay" is a Latin word meaning "cordial." See E.B. Gordon, *Adoniram Judson Gordon* (London: Hodder & Stoughton, 1909), 43.

28 E.B. Gordon, *Adoniram Judson Gordon* (London: Hodder & Stoughton, 1909), 43.

29 E.B. Gordon, *Adoniram Judson Gordon* (London: Hodder & Stoughton, 1909), 44.

30 A.J. Gordon, "The Christian Unity Society," *The Congregational Review*, July 1865, 405.

31 Dora Greenwell, *The Patience of Hope* (Boston: Ticknor and Fields, 1862), 116-117.

32 A.J. Gordon, "Untitled Introductory Article," *The Watchword*, June 1880, 161-162.

33 E.B. Gordon, *Adoniram Judson Gordon* (London: Hodder & Stoughton, 1909), 44-45.

34 E.B. Gordon, *Adoniram Judson Gordon* (London: Hodder & Stoughton, 1909), 45.

Chapter Seven – Clarendon Street

1 James Pike, ed., *History of the churches of Boston...Baptist and Presbyterian* (Boston: Ecclesia Pub. Co., 1883), 38.

2 E.B. Gordon, *Adoniram Judson Gordon* (London: Hodder & Stoughton, 1909), 45. See also page 93 of *The Jewett Family Year Book of 1911*, (Rowley, The Jewett Family of America, 1911), which confirms that Ernest Gordon was born on March 2, 1867.

3 E.B. Gordon, *Adoniram Judson Gordon* (London: Hodder & Stoughton, 1909), 46.

4 E.B. Gordon, *Adoniram Judson Gordon* (London: Hodder & Stoughton, 1909), 46.

5 E.B. Gordon, *Adoniram Judson Gordon* (London: Hodder & Stoughton, 1909), 46.

6 E.B. Gordon, *Adoniram Judson Gordon* (London: Hodder & Stoughton, 1909), 46.

7 E.B. Gordon, *Adoniram Judson Gordon* (London: Hodder & Stoughton, 1909), 46.

8 A.J. Gordon, "This Month Shall be To You," *The Watchword*, January 1886, 239-240.

9 E.B. Gordon, *Adoniram Judson Gordon* (London: Hodder & Stoughton, 1909), 189.

10 E.B. Gordon, *Adoniram Judson Gordon* (London: Hodder & Stoughton, 1909), 188-189.

11 E.B. Gordon, *Adoniram Judson Gordon* (London: Hodder & Stoughton, 1909), 189.

12 E.B. Gordon, *Adoniram Judson Gordon* (London: Hodder & Stoughton, 1909), 189-190. Italics added.

13 A.J. Gordon, *How Christ Came To Church: The Pastor's Dream, A Spiritual Autobiography* (Philadelphia: American Baptist Publication Society, 1896), 18.

14 Marion Howard, "Rev. A.J. Gordon, D.D.," *The Granite Monthly*, March 1892, 89.

15 Marion Howard, "Rev. A.J. Gordon, D.D.," *The Granite Monthly*, March 1892, 89.

16 Marion Howard, "Rev. A.J. Gordon, D.D.," *The Granite Monthly*, March 1892, 89.

17 Marion Howard, "Rev. A.J. Gordon, D.D.," *The Granite Monthly*, March 1892, 90.

18 Marion Howard, "Rev. A.J. Gordon, D.D.," *The Granite Monthly*, March 1892, 90.

19 A.J. Gordon, *How Christ Came To Church: The Pastor's Dream, A Spiritual Autobiography* (Philadelphia: American Baptist Publication Society, 1896), 52.

20 A.J. Gordon, *How Christ Came To Church: The Pastor's Dream, A Spiritual Autobiography* (Philadelphia: American Baptist Publication Society, 1896), 52-53.

21 A.J. Gordon, *How Christ Came To Church: The Pastor's Dream, A Spiritual Autobiography* (Philadelphia: American Baptist Publication Society, 1896), 53.

22 A.J. Gordon, *How Christ Came To Church: The Pastor's Dream, A Spiritual Autobiography* (Philadelphia: American Baptist Publication Society, 1896), 53.

23 A.J. Gordon, *How Christ Came To Church: The Pastor's Dream, A Spiritual Autobiography* (Philadelphia: American Baptist Publication Society, 1896), 53.

24 A.J. Gordon, *How Christ Came To Church: The Pastor's Dream, A Spiritual Autobiography* (Philadelphia: American Baptist Publication Society, 1896), 53.

25 A.J. Gordon, *How Christ Came To Church: The Pastor's Dream, A Spiritual Autobiography* (Philadelphia: American Baptist Publication Society, 1896), 53.

26 A.J. Gordon, *How Christ Came To Church: The Pastor's Dream, A Spiritual Autobiography* (Philadelphia: American Baptist Publication Society, 1896), 53.

27 A.J. Gordon, *The Fiftieth Year: A Sermon Preached on the Semi-Centennial Anniversary of the Clarendon Street Baptist Church* (Boston: Printed for the Church, 1878).

28 A.J. Gordon, *The Fiftieth Year: A Sermon Preached on the Semi-Centennial Anniversary of the Clarendon Street Baptist Church* (Boston: Printed for the Church, 1878), 3-4.

29 A.J. Gordon, *The Fiftieth Year: A Sermon Preached on the Semi-Centennial Anniversary of the Clarendon Street Baptist Church* (Boston: Printed for the Church, 1878), 3-4.

30 A.J. Gordon, *The Fiftieth Year: A Sermon Preached on the Semi-Centennial Anniversary of the Clarendon Street Baptist Church* (Boston: Printed for the Church, 1878), 4.

31 A.J. Gordon, *The Fiftieth Year: A Sermon Preached on the Semi-Centennial Anniversary of the Clarendon Street Baptist Church* (Boston: Printed for the Church, 1878), 14-15.

32 Cambridge Chronicle, Volume XXIX, Number 1, 3 January 1874.

33 A.J. Gordon, *The Fiftieth Year: A Sermon Preached on the Semi-Centennial Anniversary of the Clarendon Street Baptist Church* (Boston: Printed for the Church, 1878), 15.

34 see among others, "The Clarendon Street Church Seriously Damaged," *The Boston Globe*, January 5, 1874; see also Henry Ward Beecher, ed., *The Christian Union*, January 14, 1874, 34; *The Indianapolis News*, January 5, 1874; *The Alexandria Gazette* (Virginia), January 5, 1874; *The Knoxville Weekly Chronicle* (Tennessee), January 7, 1874; and *The Kingston Daily Freeman* (Kingston, New York), January 5, 1874.

35 no author, "A Baptist Church In Boston Partially Burned," *The New York Times*, Monday, January 5, 1874.

36 A.J. Gordon, *The Fiftieth Year: A Sermon Preached on the Semi-Centennial Anniversary of the Clarendon Street Baptist Church* (Boston: Printed for the Church, 1878), 15-16.

37 A.J. Gordon, *The Fiftieth Year: A Sermon Preached on the Semi-Centennial Anniversary of the Clarendon Street Baptist Church* (Boston: Printed for the Church, 1878), 17.

38 no author, A History of the Rowe Street Baptist Church (Boston: Gould and Lincoln, 1858), 6.

39 E.B. Malcom, *Malcom-Cox with Allied Families: A Genealogical Record* (Gladstone, Oregon: privately printed 1982), 29.

40 A.J. Gordon, *The Fiftieth Year: A Sermon Preached on the Semi-Centennial Anniversary of the Clarendon Street Baptist Church* (Boston: Printed for the Church, 1878), 17.

41 see, for example, *The Atlantic Monthly*, v. 18, (Boston: Ticknor and Fields, 1866); see also *The North American Review*, v. 105, (Boston: Ticknor and Fields, 1867).

42 Kathryn Ledbetter, *Tennyson and Victorian Periodicals* (Burlington: Ashgate Publishing, 2007), 173. Tennyson's "two-volume American collection appeared on 7 July 1842...Ticknor paid Tennyson $150...this resulted in the first payment to any British author before 1852."

43 A.J. Gordon, *The Fiftieth Year: A Sermon Preached on the Semi-Centennial Anniversary of the Clarendon Street Baptist Church* (Boston: Printed for the Church, 1878), 18.

44 A.J. Gordon, *The Fiftieth Year: A Sermon Preached on the Semi-Centennial Anniversary of the Clarendon Street Baptist Church* (Boston: Printed for the Church, 1878), 18-19.

45 A.J. Gordon, *The Fiftieth Year: A Sermon Preached on the Semi-Centennial Anniversary of the Clarendon Street Baptist Church* (Boston: Printed for the Church, 1878), 22.

46 A.J. Gordon, *The Fiftieth Year: A Sermon Preached on the Semi-Centennial Anniversary of the Clarendon Street Baptist Church* (Boston: Printed for the Church, 1878), 22.

47 A.J. Gordon, *The Fiftieth Year: A Sermon Preached on the Semi-Centennial Anniversary of the Clarendon Street Baptist Church* (Boston: Printed for the Church, 1878), 23.

48 A.J. Gordon, *The Fiftieth Year: A Sermon Preached on the Semi-Centennial Anniversary of the Clarendon Street Baptist Church* (Boston: Printed for the Church, 1878), 23-24.

49 James Pike, ed., *History of the churches of Boston...Baptist and Presbyterian* (Boston: Ecclesia Pub. Co., 1883), 38.

50 James Pike, ed., *History of the churches of Boston...Baptist and Presbyterian* (Boston: Ecclesia Pub. Co., 1883), 38.

51 James Pike, ed., *History of the churches of Boston...Baptist and Presbyterian* (Boston: Ecclesia Pub. Co., 1883), 39.

52 E.B. Gordon, *Adoniram Judson Gordon* (London: Hodder & Stoughton, 1909), 69-70.

53 E.B. Gordon, *Adoniram Judson Gordon* (London: Hodder & Stoughton, 1909), 70.

54 E.B. Gordon, *Adoniram Judson Gordon* (London: Hodder & Stoughton, 1909), 70.

55 E.B. Gordon, *Adoniram Judson Gordon* (London: Hodder & Stoughton, 1909), 70-71.

56 E.B. Gordon, *Adoniram Judson Gordon* (London: Hodder & Stoughton, 1909), 71.

57 "The Pilgrim's Place and Promise," from *Great Pulpit Masters: A.J. Gordon* (New York: Revell, 1951), 149.

58 A.J. Gordon, "Individual Responsibility Growing Out of Our Perils and Opportunities," *National Perils and Opportunities: The Discussions of the General Christian Conference Held in Washington, D.C. December 7-9, 1887, Under the Auspices of the Evangelical Alliance for the United States* (New York: Baker & Taylor, 1887), 381-382.

59 A.J. Gordon, "Individual Responsibility Growing Out of Our Perils and Opportunities," *National Perils and Opportunities: The Discussions of the General Christian Conference Held in Washington, D.C. December 7-9, 1887, Under the Auspices of the Evangelical Alliance for the United States* (New York: Baker & Taylor, 1887), 379.

60 A.J. Gordon, "Individual Responsibility Growing Out of Our Perils and Opportunities," *National Perils and Opportunities: The Discussions of the General Christian Conference Held in Washington, D.C. December 7-9, 1887, Under the Auspices of the Evangelical Alliance for the United States* (New York: Baker & Taylor, 1887), 382.

61 E.B. Gordon, *Adoniram Judson Gordon* (London: Hodder & Stoughton, 1909), 71.

62 E.B. Gordon, *Adoniram Judson Gordon* (London: Hodder & Stoughton, 1909), 71.

63 E.B. Gordon, *Adoniram Judson Gordon* (London: Hodder & Stoughton, 1909), 71.

64 E.B. Gordon, *Adoniram Judson Gordon* (London: Hodder & Stoughton, 1909), 71-72.

65 E.B. Gordon, *Adoniram Judson Gordon* (London: Hodder & Stoughton, 1909), 73.

66 E.B. Gordon, *Adoniram Judson Gordon* (London: Hodder & Stoughton, 1909), 73.

67 E.B. Gordon, *Adoniram Judson Gordon* (London: Hodder & Stoughton, 1909), 73.

68 Epictetus, *The Works of Epictetus* (Boston: Little, Brown, and Co., 1866), 67.

Chapter Eight – To Hear a New Song

1 A.G. Stacy, *The Service of Song* (St. Louis: Southwestern Book and Pub. Co., 1871), 95. See also A.J. Gordon, *Congregational Worship* (Boston: Young and Bartlett, 1874), 120. Last, see R.S. Willis, *Our Church Music* (New York: Dana and Co., 1856), 16. Willis attended Yale, and studied music in Germany under Felix Mendelssohn. He composed the music for "It Came Upon A Midnight Clear." See also "From the Archives: Richard Storrs Willis," published by Yale at: http://music.yale.edu/2011/09/02/from-the-archives-richard-storrs-willis/

2 A.J. Gordon, *Congregational Worship* (Boston: Young and Bartlett, 1874), 58. Italics added.

3   A.J. Gordon, *Congregational Worship* (Boston: Young and Bartlett, 1874), 65-66. Italics added.

4   A.J. Gordon, *Congregational Worship* (Boston: Young and Bartlett, 1874), 3.

5   A.J. Gordon, *Congregational Worship* (Boston: Young and Bartlett, 1874), 3.

6   A.J. Gordon, *Congregational Worship* (Boston: Young and Bartlett, 1874), 3.

7   A.J. Gordon, *Congregational Worship* (Boston: Young and Bartlett, 1874), 3.

8   A.J. Gordon, *Congregational Worship* (Boston: Young and Bartlett, 1874), 4.

9   S.M. Gibson, *A.J. Gordon: American Premillenialist* (Lanham: University Press of America, 2001), 54.

10   S.M. Gibson, *A.J. Gordon: American Premillenialist* (Lanham: University Press of America, 2001), 54.

11   S.M. Gibson, *A.J. Gordon: American Premillenialist* (Lanham: University Press of America, 2001), 56.

12   S.M. Gibson, *A.J. Gordon: American Premillenialist* (Lanham: University Press of America, 2001), 56.

13   A.J. Gordon, *Grace and Glory* (New York: Revell, 1880), 1.

14   A.J. Gordon, *Grace and Glory* (New York: Revell, 1880), 2.

15   A.J. Gordon, *Grace and Glory* (New York: Revell, 1880), 3.

16   A.J. Gordon, *Grace and Glory* (New York: Revell, 1880), 4.

17   A.J. Gordon, *In Christ* (London: Hodder & Stoughton, 1882), 126.

18   A.J. Gordon, *Grace and Glory* (New York: Revell, 1880), 6.

19   A.J. Gordon, *Grace and Glory* (New York: Revell, 1880), 151.

20   A.J. Gordon, *Grace and Glory* (New York: Revell, 1880), 151.

21   A.J. Gordon, *Grace and Glory* (New York: Revell, 1880), 151.

22   C.H. Spurgeon, *Autobiography*, v. 4, (London: Passmore and Alabaster, 1900), 177.

23   D.L. Robert, "The Legacy of Adoniram Judson Gordon," *The International Bulletin of Missionary Research* (October 1987), 176.

24   this dollar conversion comes via the website Measuring Worth, at: https://www.measuringworth.com/uscompare/relativevalue.php
See also D.L. Robert, "The Legacy of Adoniram Judson Gordon," *The International Bulletin of Missionary Research* (October 1987), 176.

25   D.L. Robert, "The Legacy of Adoniram Judson Gordon," *The International Bulletin of Missionary Research* (October 1987), 177.

26   D.L. Robert, "The Legacy of Adoniram Judson Gordon," *The International Bulletin of Missionary Research* (October 1987), 177. Guinness was awarded a Doctor of Divinity degree in 1889. See page 100 of *Catalogue...of Brown University*, (Providence: Snow & Farnham, 1889).

27   D.L. Robert, "The Legacy of Adoniram Judson Gordon," *The International Bulletin of Missionary Research* (October 1987), 177.

28   D.L. Robert, "The Legacy of Adoniram Judson Gordon," *The International Bulletin of Missionary Research* (October 1987), 177.

29 D.L. Robert, "The Legacy of Adoniram Judson Gordon," *The International Bulletin of Missionary Research* (October 1987), 177.

30 D.L. Robert, "The Legacy of Adoniram Judson Gordon," *The International Bulletin of Missionary Research* (October 1987), 177.

31 D.L. Robert, "The Legacy of Adoniram Judson Gordon," *The International Bulletin of Missionary Research* (October 1987), 177.

32 D.L. Robert, "The Legacy of Adoniram Judson Gordon," *The International Bulletin of Missionary Research* (October 1987), 177.

33 D.L. Robert, "The Legacy of Adoniram Judson Gordon," *The International Bulletin of Missionary Research* (October 1987), 177.

34 A.J. Gordon, "The Overflow of Missions," The Missionary Review of the World, March 1893, 170.

35 D.L. Robert, "The Legacy of Adoniram Judson Gordon," *The International Bulletin of Missionary Research* (October 1987), 177.

36 E.B. Gordon, *Adoniram Judson Gordon* (London: Hodder & Stoughton, 1909), 250. See also D.L. Robert, "The Legacy of Adoniram Judson Gordon," *The International Bulletin of Missionary Research* (October 1987), 179. Italics added.

37 E.B. Gordon, *Adoniram Judson Gordon* (London: Hodder & Stoughton, 1909), 348.

38 E.B. Gordon, *Adoniram Judson Gordon* (London: Hodder & Stoughton, 1909), 348.

39 E.B. Gordon, *Adoniram Judson Gordon* (London: Hodder & Stoughton, 1909), 348-349.

40 E.B. Gordon, *Adoniram Judson Gordon* (London: Hodder & Stoughton, 1909), 349.

41 E.B. Gordon, *Adoniram Judson Gordon* (London: Hodder & Stoughton, 1909), 349.

42 E.B. Gordon, *Adoniram Judson Gordon* (London: Hodder & Stoughton, 1909), 349.

43 E.B. Gordon, *Adoniram Judson Gordon* (London: Hodder & Stoughton, 1909), 348.

44 E.B. Gordon, *Adoniram Judson Gordon* (London: Hodder & Stoughton, 1909), 349-350.

45 A phrase used by A.N. Rowland one page 345 of James Hastings, J.A. Selbie, et al, *The Dictionary of Christ and the Gospels* v. 2, (Edinburgh: T & T. Clark, 1908). This phrase is also used as early as 1846, by the Rev. Uriah Clark. See "Purity of Hope," an article in the April 18, 1846 issue of *The Universalist Union* (New York: Universalist Union Press, 1846), 354.

46 E.B. Gordon, *Adoniram Judson Gordon* (London: Hodder & Stoughton, 1909), 350.

47 E.B. Gordon, *Adoniram Judson Gordon* (London: Hodder & Stoughton, 1909), 350.

48 E.B. Gordon, *Adoniram Judson Gordon* (London: Hodder & Stoughton, 1909), 350.

49 E.B. Gordon, *Adoniram Judson Gordon* (London: Hodder & Stoughton, 1909), 350-351.

50 E.B. Gordon, *Adoniram Judson Gordon* (London: Hodder & Stoughton, 1909), 347-348.

51 E.B. Gordon, *Adoniram Judson Gordon* (London: Hodder & Stoughton, 1909), 351.

52 E.B. Gordon, *Adoniram Judson Gordon* (London: Hodder & Stoughton, 1909), 351.

53   E.B. Gordon, *Adoniram Judson Gordon* (London: Hodder & Stoughton, 1909), 351-352.

Chapter Nine – The Heart of the Matter

1   *The Boston Globe,* as cited in *The Literary World: A Review of Current Literature,* March 1873, end pages. Citation edited.

2   June 1872 is the earliest posting of a publication notice the author has been able to find for *In Christ.* Gordon's Preface is dated April, 19, 1972, but it would have taken some little time for the book to come through the press. See page 11 of the June 1872 issue of *The Religious Magazine and Monthly Review,* (Boston: L.C. Bowles, 1872).

3   A.J. Gordon, *In Christ* (London: Hodder & Stoughton, 1882), iii.

4   E.B. Gordon, *Adoniram Judson Gordon* (London: Hodder & Stoughton, 1909), 82.

5   see the advertisement for *In Christ* in the first pages of the Oct. 1872 issue of *Bibliotheca Sacra,* (New Haven: Judd and White, 1872).

6   from page 15 of *Church History of the Government of Bishops and Their Councils,* by Richard Baxter (London: John Kidgell, 1680). "I am a Christian," Baxter said, "a Meer Christian." I am "of no other religion" than "that by which Christ and the apostles was left."

7   A.J. Gordon, *In Christ* (London: Hodder & Stoughton, 1882), iii.

8   A.J. Gordon, *In Christ* (London: Hodder & Stoughton, 1882), iii-iv.

9   A.J. Gordon, *In Christ* (London: Hodder & Stoughton, 1882), iii-iv.

10   A.J. Gordon, *In Christ* (London: Hodder & Stoughton, 1882), 126.

11   see page 11 of *In Christ,* by A.J. Gordon, (London: Hodder & Stoughton, 1882).

12   see pages 9-10 of *In Christ,* by A.J. Gordon, (London: Hodder & Stoughton, 1882). This quote is in paragraphs, and emphasis added.

13   see page 605 of *An Exposition of All the Books of the Old and New Testaments,* vol. 5, by Matthew Henry, (London: W. Baynes, 1806).

14   A.J. Gordon, "Wisdom from the Old Divines," *The Watchword,* October 1883, 6.

15   A.J. Gordon, *In Christ* (London: Hodder & Stoughton, 1882), 109.

16   A.J. Gordon, *In Christ* (London: Hodder & Stoughton, 1882), 110.

17   A.J. Gordon, *In Christ* (London: Hodder & Stoughton, 1882), 110.

18   see the advertisement for *In Christ* in the first pages of the Oct. 1872 issue of *Bibliotheca Sacra,* (New Haven: Judd and White, 1872).

19   A.J. Gordon, *In Christ* (London: Hodder & Stoughton, 1882), 13-14.

20   A.J. Gordon, *In Christ* (London: Hodder & Stoughton, 1882), 30-31. Here, Gordon cites a passage from Coleridge's *Aids to Reflection.* See S.T. Coleridge, *The Complete Works of Samuel Taylor Coleridge,* v. 1 (New York: Harper, 1884), 303n.

21 A.J. Gordon, "Untitled Introductory Article," *The Watchword*, November 1890, 309. See also page 185 of *The Complete Works of Samuel Taylor Coleridge*, v. 6, ed. by W.G.T. Shedd, (New York: Harper, 1884).

22 A.J. Gordon, *In Christ* (London: Hodder & Stoughton, 1882), 189.

23 A.J. Gordon, *In Christ* (London: Hodder & Stoughton, 1882), 129n. See also page 60 of *The Journal of George Fox*, v. 1, (London: Cash and Smith, 1852). Here, the relevant passage reads: "and the Lord answered, 'That it was needful I should have a sense of all conditions, how else should I speak to all conditions!' and in this I saw the infinite love of God."

24 E.B. Gordon, *Adoniram Judson Gordon* (London: Hodder & Stoughton, 1909), 36.

25 A.J. Gordon, *In Christ* (London: Hodder & Stoughton, 1882), 129n. Gordon's citation of Rutherford is attributed to Rutherford on page 67 of *Select Sentences, or Excellent Passages from Eminent Authors*, no author attributed, (New York: W. Barlas, 1809). It is also attributed to Rutherford far earlier on page 369 of *The Works of Augustus Toplady*, v. 4, (London: Printed for the Proprietors, 1794).

26 C.S. Lewis, *Mere Christianity* (New York: HarperCollins, 2001), 133.

27 A.J. Gordon, *In Christ* (London: Hodder & Stoughton, 1882), 60.

28 E.B. Gordon, *Adoniram Judson Gordon* (London: Hodder & Stoughton, 1909), 36.

29 A.J. Gordon, *In Christ* (London: Hodder & Stoughton, 1882), 70.

30 A.J. Gordon, *In Christ* (London: Hodder & Stoughton, 1882), 84.

31 A.J. Gordon, *In Christ* (London: Hodder & Stoughton, 1882), 17.

32 A.J. Gordon, *In Christ* (London: Hodder & Stoughton, 1882), 17.

Chapter Ten – Chansons du Rédempteur

1 E.B. Gordon, Adoniram Judson Gordon (London: Hodder & Stoughton, 1909), 194.

2 K.W. Osbeck, *101 More Hymn Stories* (Grand Rapids: Kregel Publications, 1985), 40-41.

3 see the back cover text of E.L. Blumhofer, *Her Heart Can See: The Life and Hymns of Fanny J. Crosby* (Grand Rapids: Eerdmans, 2005).

4 all biographical information in this paragraph is from G.E. Weeks, *W. Spencer Walton* (London: Marshall Brothers, 1907).

5 all biographical information about Sir Joseph Barnby is taken from pages 130-131 of *The Dictionary of National Biography: Supplement*, v. 1, ed. by Sidney Lee, (New York: Macmillan, 1901).

6 A.J. Gordon, ed., *The Vestry Hymn and Tune Book* (Boston: H.A. Young, 1872), 284. See also the Library of Congress webpage: http://www.loc.gov/jukebox/recordings/detail/id/1349/

7   Disc. of Am. Hist. Recordings, s.v. "Victor 16007 (Black label (popular) 10-in. double-faced)," acc. Jan. 8, 2016, http://adp.library.ucsb.edu/index.php/object/detail/9836/Victor_16007.

8   E.B. Gordon, *Adoniram Judson Gordon* (London: Hodder & Stoughton, 1909), 194 & 180.

9   E.B. Gordon, *Adoniram Judson Gordon* (London: Hodder & Stoughton, 1909), 180.

10 A.J. Gordon, "The Concealed Enemy," *The Watchword*, October 1883, 4.

11 Ola Winslow, *John Bunyan* (New York: The Macmillan Company, 1961), 11.

12 A.J. Gordon, "The Holy Spirit in the Church," *The Watchword*, November 1891, 283.

13 E.B. Gordon, *Adoniram Judson Gordon* (London: Hodder & Stoughton, 1909), 200.

14 A.J. Gordon, "The New Name—The Lamb," *The Watchword*, December 1878, 39.

15 A.J. Gordon, "Untitled Introductory Article," *The Watchword*, November 1883, 25.

16 A.J. Gordon, "Untitled Introductory Article," *The Watchword*, November 1883, 25.

17 E.B. Gordon, *Adoniram Judson Gordon* (London: Hodder & Stoughton, 1909), 181.

18 E.B. Gordon, *Adoniram Judson Gordon* (London: Hodder & Stoughton, 1909), 194.

19 E.B. Gordon, *Adoniram Judson Gordon* (London: Hodder & Stoughton, 1909), 194.

20 E.B. Gordon, *Adoniram Judson Gordon* (London: Hodder & Stoughton, 1909), 194.

21 E.B. Gordon, *Adoniram Judson Gordon* (London: Hodder & Stoughton, 1909), 194.

22 E.B. Gordon, *Adoniram Judson Gordon* (London: Hodder & Stoughton, 1909), 194.

23 E.B. Gordon, *Adoniram Judson Gordon* (London: Hodder & Stoughton, 1909), 194-195.

Chapter Eleven – Messages of Grace

1   no author, "Madison-Avenue Baptist Church: Reopening of the Edifice…," *The New York Times*, December 31, 1877. Citation edited.

2   A.J. Gordon, as quoted in, "Madison-Avenue Baptist Church: Reopening of the Edifice…," *The New York Times*, December 31, 1877.

3   A.J. Gordon, as quoted in, "Madison-Avenue Baptist Church: Reopening of the Edifice…," *The New York Times*, December 31, 1877.

4   A.J. Gordon, as quoted in, "Madison-Avenue Baptist Church: Reopening of the Edifice…," *The New York Times*, December 31, 1877.

5   A.J. Gordon, *Yet Speaking: A Collection* (New York: F.H. Revell, 1897), 6.

6   George MacDonald, as quoted in *Great Pulpit Masters: A.J. Gordon* (New York: Revell, 1951), 31-32. See also page 96 of George MacDonald, "The Carpenter," in *Good Words*, (London: Strahan & Co., 1872).

7   S.M. Gibson, *A.J. Gordon: American Premillenialist* (Lanham: University Press of America, 2001), 94. Here, Gibson states: "[Gordon] took his model from

Moravian missions and the Pietists of Germany, in addition to H. Grattan Guinness and Charles Haddon Spurgeon."

8   Count Zinzendorf, as quoted in *Great Pulpit Masters: A.J. Gordon* (New York: Revell, 1951), 38. See also page 239 in David Lyle Jeffrey, ed., *English Spirituality in the Age of Wesley* (Vancouver: Regent College Publishing, 2000). Here, Wesley's complete translation and abridgement of Zinzendorf's hymn is given.

9   *Great Pulpit Masters: A.J. Gordon* (New York: Revell, 1951), 129. Italics added.

10   *Great Pulpit Masters: A.J. Gordon* (New York: Revell, 1951), 35-36, 46, 73, 79, 88, 124, 127.

11   A.J. Gordon, "Wisdom from the Puritans," *The Watchword*, December 1883, 51.

12   Warren Wiersbe, ed., *Classic Sermons on the Love of God* (Kregel, 1998), 125-134.

13   *Great Pulpit Masters: A.J. Gordon* (New York: Revell, 1951), 43. Italics added.

14   no author, *The Publishers' Weekly*, March 27, 1886, 454. *Grace and Glory* was published in London by Hodder and Stoughton in 1888.

15   A.J. Gordon, *Grace and Glory* (New York: Revell, 1886). 346. Emphasis added.

16   A.J. Gordon, *Grace and Glory* (New York: F.H. Revell, 1897), 28.

17   A.J. Gordon, "Christ Crucified, the Power of God," *The Watchword*, November 1885, 190.

18   A.J. Gordon, *Grace and Glory* (New York: F.H. Revell, 1897), 354.

19   A.J. Gordon, "Untitled Introductory Article," *The Watchword*, April 1879, 113.

20   A.J. Gordon, "Your Labor Is Not In Vain," *The Watchword*, January 1890, 2.

21   A.J. Gordon, *Grace and Glory* (New York: F.H. Revell, 1897), 175.

22   A.J. Gordon, "Threefold Sonship: An Address Given at Northfield, August 1885," *The Watchword*, December 1885, 215.

23   A.J. Gordon, *Grace and Glory* (New York: F.H. Revell, 1897), 37-38.

24   A.J. Gordon, *Grace and Glory* (New York: F.H. Revell, 1897), 85.

25   C.S. Lewis, *Mere Christianity* (New York: HarperCollins, 2001), 155.

26   A.J. Gordon, "Christ Our Righteousness," The Watchword, March 1882, 131-132.

27   no author, *The Bookseller*, October 9, 1889, 1107. See also R.C. Morgan, ed., "Rev. A.J. Gordon, D.D.," *The Christian Portrait Gallery* (London: Morgan & Scott, 1889), 106-109.

28   See the Preface for *The Christian Portrait Gallery* (London: Morgan & Scott, 1889), wherein it is stated: "The portraits and biographic sketches contained in this volume have appeared in 'The Christian', by the readers of which they have been highly appreciated." This is confirmed in Wheaton College's online catalogue listing for this book, at: http://buswell.worldcat.org/title/christian-portrait-gallery-containing-over-one-hundred-life-like-illustrations-with-biographic-sketches/oclc/500819494

R.C. Morgan is confirmed as the founder and editor of 'The Christian' newspaper on page 1211 of *Who's Who 1906: An Annual Biographical Dictionary*, (London: Adam and Charles Black/New York: Macmillan, 1906).

29 no author, *The Bookseller*, October 9, 1889, 1107.

30 no author, *The Scot's Magazine*, Dec. 1889 – May 1890, 397.

31 R.C. Morgan, ed., "Rev. A.J. Gordon, D.D.," *The Christian Portrait Gallery* (London: Morgan & Scott, 1889), 107.

32 R.C. Morgan, ed., "Rev. A.J. Gordon, D.D.," *The Christian Portrait Gallery* (London: Morgan & Scott, 1889), 108.

33 R.C. Morgan, ed., "Rev. A.J. Gordon, D.D.," *The Christian Portrait Gallery* (London: Morgan & Scott, 1889), 108.

34 R.C. Morgan, ed., "Rev. A.J. Gordon, D.D.," *The Christian Portrait Gallery* (London: Morgan & Scott, 1889), 108.

35 R.C. Morgan, ed., "Rev. A.J. Gordon, D.D.," *The Christian Portrait Gallery* (London: Morgan & Scott, 1889), 108.

36 R.C. Morgan, ed., "Rev. A.J. Gordon, D.D.," *The Christian Portrait Gallery* (London: Morgan & Scott, 1889), 108.

37 R.C. Morgan, ed., "Rev. A.J. Gordon, D.D.," *The Christian Portrait Gallery* (London: Morgan & Scott, 1889), 108.

38 R.C. Morgan, ed., "Rev. A.J. Gordon, D.D.," *The Christian Portrait Gallery* (London: Morgan & Scott, 1889), 108.

39 J.B. Houser, "A.J. Gordon, D.D.," *The Pulpit Treasury*, Feb. 1887, 623.

40 J.B. Houser, "A.J. Gordon, D.D.," *The Pulpit Treasury*, Feb. 1887, 623.

41 J.B. Houser, "A.J. Gordon, D.D.," *The Pulpit Treasury*, Feb. 1887, 623.

42 J.B. Houser, "A.J. Gordon, D.D.," *The Pulpit Treasury*, Feb. 1887, 623.

43 J.B. Houser, "A.J. Gordon, D.D.," *The Pulpit Treasury*, Feb. 1887, 623.

44 A.J. Gordon, "If Ye Continue In My Word," *Great Pulpit Masters* (New York: Revell, 1951), 136.

45 A.J. Gordon, "If Ye Continue In My Word," *Great Pulpit Masters* (New York: Revell, 1951), 136.

46 A.J. Gordon, "Rest and Welcome," *The Watchword*, July 1882, 217.

47 J.B. Houser, "A.J. Gordon, D.D.," *The Pulpit Treasury*, Feb. 1887, 623.

48 no author, "Under the Rose," *The Boston Sunday Globe*, June 19, 1892.

49 J.B. Houser, "A.J. Gordon, D.D.," *The Pulpit Treasury*, Feb. 1887, 623.

50 J.B. Houser, "A.J. Gordon, D.D.," *The Pulpit Treasury*, Feb. 1887, 623.

51 A.J. Gordon, "Voices from Our Dead President's Grave," *The Watchword*, November 1881, 32.

52 A.J. Gordon, "Voices from Our Dead President's Grave," *The Watchword*, November 1881, 32-33.

53 A.J. Gordon, "Untitled Article," *The Watchword*, March 1882, 134.

54 J.B. Houser, "A.J. Gordon, D.D.," *The Pulpit Treasury*, Feb. 1887, 624.

55 T. DeWitt Talmage, D.D., was as famous and prominent a religious figure as America knew in the late 1800s. "In 1869 he went to the Central Presbyterian Church in Brooklyn, where he drew immense crowds because of his eloquence and his showmanship. His sermons were published weekly by a syndicate in over 3,000 newspapers." See "Talmage, T. DeWitt," a scholarly article published by Northern Illinois University Libraries at: http://www.ulib.niu.edu/badndp/talmage_t.html

56 T. DeWitt Talmage, ed., "Rev. A.J. Gordon, D.D.," *The Christian Herald*, 11 November 1886, 706.

57 All information in this paragraph is taken from Moses King, ed., "The Christian Herald," *King's Handbook of New York City* (Boston: Moses King, 1893), 632. See also G.M. Marsden, *Fundamentalism and American Culture* (New York: Oxford University Press, 2006), 84. Here, Marsden reports that by 1910, *The Christian Herald* had a circulation of "about a quarter of a million."

58 J.B. Houser, "A.J. Gordon, D.D.," *The Pulpit Treasury*, Feb. 1887, 624.

59 J.B. Houser, "A.J. Gordon, D.D.," *The Pulpit Treasury*, Feb. 1887, 624.

60 J.B. Houser, "A.J. Gordon, D.D.," *The Pulpit Treasury*, Feb. 1887, 624.

61 J.B. Houser, "A.J. Gordon, D.D.," *The Pulpit Treasury*, Feb. 1887, 624.

62 J.B. Houser, "A.J. Gordon, D.D.," *The Pulpit Treasury*, Feb. 1887, 624.

Chapter Twelve – Well Remembered Days

1 A.J. Gordon, as quoted in, "Madison-Avenue Baptist Church: Reopening of the Edifice...," *The New York Times*, December 31, 1877.

2 no author, *The Missionary Review*, January 1914, 9-10.

3 W.R. Moody, *The Life of Dwight L. Moody* (London: Morgan and Scott, 1900), 258.

4 J.W. Chapman, *The Life and Work of Dwight L. Moody* (Philadelphia: International Publishing Co., 1900), 197.

5 The precise dates for the start and close of Moody's mission to Britain are: June 17, 1873 to July 21, 1875. See D.W. Bebbington's essay "D.L. Moody and Ira Sankey, in *The Oxford Dictionary of National Biography*.

6 the date of January 28, 1877 is confirmed in B.J. Evensen, *God's Man for the Gilded Age* (Oxford: Oxford University Press, 2003), 172. See also "Words of Parting," an article on the Boston Tabernacle Meetings, in *The Boston Daily Globe*, 30 April 1877. Also, Boston's notoriety as "the Athens of America" dates from far back into the 19th century. It appears, for example, in George Rose, *The Great Country: Impressions of America* (London: Tinsley Bros., 1868), 253.

7 the proximity of Moody's tabernacle to Clarendon Street Church is stated on page 19 of Dana L. Robert's article, "Adoniram Judson Gordon, 1836-1895: Educator, Preacher, and Promoter of Missions," in *Mission Legacies: Biographical*

Studies of Leaders of the Modern Missionary Movement, ed. G.H. Anderson, (Maryknoll, New York: Orbis Books, 1994).

8   E.B. Gordon, *Adoniram Judson Gordon* (London: Hodder & Stoughton, 1909), 95.

9   This citation, with all the quotes and information given in the preceding paragraphs, is taken from E.B. Gordon, *Adoniram Judson Gordon* (London: Hodder & Stoughton, 1909), 95.96.

10 See Dale Suderman's review article, "Moody, the Media, and the Birth of Modern Evangelism," in *Books & Culture,* archived online at: http://www.booksandculture.com/articles/webexclusives/2004/january/040105.html?paging=off

Here it is stated: "Seventy-eight local churches organized the Boston campaign in the winter of 1877. The two competing local newspapers made Moody a headline event with daily transcripts of his sermons on their front pages. Unitarians kept their distance, but a wide range of Congregationalists, Episcopalians, Methodists, and Baptists united behind Moody. The Tremont Tabernacle, with seating for 7,000 souls was built in the shadow of A.J. Gordon's Baptist Church. When attendance flagged, special trains offering free or half-price fares brought in small-town and rural folks to fill the seats. By the conclusion, a million people had attended the revival, and 6,000 new converts were reported."

11 B.J. Evensen, *God's Man for the Gilded Age* (Oxford: Oxford University Press, 2003), 168, 173, 178 & 179.

12 Elias Nason, *Lives of the Eminent American Evangelists Dwight Lyman Moody and Ira Sankey* (Boston: B.B. Russell, 1877), 205. Monetary conversion was done via the website "Measuring Worth," at: https://www.measuringworth.com/uscompare/relativevalue.php

13 Elias Nason, *Lives of the Eminent American Evangelists Dwight Lyman Moody and Ira Sankey* (Boston: B.B. Russell, 1877), 205.

14 Elias Nason, *Lives of the Eminent American Evangelists Dwight Lyman Moody and Ira Sankey* (Boston: B.B. Russell, 1877), 205 & 207.

15 Elias Nason, *Lives of the Eminent American Evangelists Dwight Lyman Moody and Ira Sankey* (Boston: B.B. Russell, 1877), 207. See also "Eben Tourjée," an article posted online by New England Conservatory, at: ttp://necmusic.edu/archives/eben-tourjée

16 Elias Nason, *Lives of the Eminent American Evangelists Dwight Lyman Moody and Ira Sankey* (Boston: B.B. Russell, 1877), 207.

17 S.M. Gibson, *A.J. Gordon: American Premillenialist* (Lanham: University Press of America, 2001), 63.

18 S.M. Gibson, *A.J. Gordon: American Premillenialist* (Lanham: University Press of America, 2001), 63.

19 S.M. Gibson, *A.J. Gordon: American Premillenialist* (Lanham: University Press of America, 2001), 63.

20 S.M. Gibson, *A.J. Gordon: American Premillenialist* (Lanham: University Press of America, 2001), 63-64.

21 A.J. Gordon, "The Faith Element in Missions," *The Missionary Review of the World,* October 1891, 733. Citation edited.

22 S.M. Gibson, *A.J. Gordon: American Premillenialist* (Lanham: University Press of America, 2001), 64.

23 S.M. Gibson, *A.J. Gordon: American Premillenialist* (Lanham: University Press of America, 2001), 51.

24 S.M. Gibson, *A.J. Gordon: American Premillenialist* (Lanham: University Press of America, 2001), 51.

25 S.M. Gibson, *A.J. Gordon: American Premillenialist* (Lanham: University Press of America, 2001), 51.

26 Maria Gordon, "Pastor A.J. Gordon," *The Record of Christian Work,* April 1897, 104.

27 Maria Gordon, "Pastor A.J. Gordon," *The Record of Christian Work,* April 1897, 104.

28 Maria Gordon, "Pastor A.J. Gordon," *The Record of Christian Work,* April 1897, 104.

29 Maria Gordon, "Pastor A.J. Gordon," *The Record of Christian Work,* April 1897, 104.

30 S.M. Gibson, *A.J. Gordon: American Premillenialist* (Lanham: University Press of America, 2001), 51.

31 Maria Gordon, "Pastor A.J. Gordon," *The Record of Christian Work,* April 1897, 104-105.

32 E.B. Gordon, *Adoniram Judson Gordon* (London: Hodder & Stoughton, 1909), 96.

33 A.J. Gordon, as quoted in E.B. Gordon, *Adoniram Judson Gordon* (London: Hodder & Stoughton, 1909), 96-97.

34 D.L. Moody, *Northfield Echoes,* v. 3 (East Northfield: E.S. Rastall, 1896), 11-12.

35 D.L. Moody, as quoted in Elias Nason, *The American Evangelists* (Boston: Lothrop & Co., 1877), 217-218. Edited and paraphrased.

36 S.M. Gibson, *A.J. Gordon: American Premillenialist* (Lanham: University Press of America, 2001), 64.

37 S.M. Gibson, *A.J. Gordon: American Premillenialist* (Lanham: University Press of America, 2001), 64.

38 S.M. Gibson, *A.J. Gordon: American Premillenialist* (Lanham: University Press of America, 2001), 64.

39 S.M. Gibson, *A.J. Gordon: American Premillenialist* (Lanham: University Press of America, 2001), 64.

40 S.M. Gibson, *A.J. Gordon: American Premillenialist* (Lanham: University Press of America, 2001), 64-65.

41 S.M. Gibson, *A.J. Gordon: American Premillenialist* (Lanham: University Press of America, 2001), 65.

42 S.M. Gibson, *A.J. Gordon: American Premillenialist* (Lanham: University Press of America, 2001), 65.

43 S.M. Gibson, *A.J. Gordon: American Premillenialist* (Lanham: University Press of America, 2001), 65.

44 S.M. Gibson, *A.J. Gordon: American Premillenialist* (Lanham: University Press of America, 2001), 65.

45 S.M. Gibson, *A.J. Gordon: American Premillenialist* (Lanham: University Press of America, 2001), 65.

46 S.M. Gibson, *A.J. Gordon: American Premillenialist* (Lanham: University Press of America, 2001), 65.

47 J.W. Chapman, *The Life and Work of Dwight L. Moody*, (Toronto: Bradley-Garretson Co. Ltd., 1900), 445. Citation edited.

48 J.W. Chapman, *The Life and Work of Dwight L. Moody*, (Toronto: Bradley-Garretson Co. Ltd., 1900), 445. Italics added.

Chapter Thirteen – Among Collegians

1   see the article, citation edited, "The College Y.M.C.A," in the 23 February 1885 edition of *The Harvard Crimson*, archived online at: http://www.thecrimson.com/article/1885/2/23/the-college-y-m-c-a/

2   E.B. Gordon, *Adoniram Judson Gordon* (London: Hodder & Stoughton, 1909), 149.

3   E.B. Gordon, *Adoniram Judson Gordon* (London: Hodder & Stoughton, 1909), 149.

4   E.B. Gordon, *Adoniram Judson Gordon* (London: Hodder & Stoughton, 1909), 150-151.

5   J.H. Moorhead, *Princeton Seminary in A00000000000000000merican Religion and Culture* (Grand Rapids, Eerdmans, 2012), 302. Wilder was then Secretary of Princeton's "Foreign Mission Society." He would have been most likely to record Gordon's visit to Princeton in early 1884. Wilder entered Princeton in 1881—but his graduation, which would have taken place in 1885—was delayed a year, to 1886, because of illness.

6   E.B. Gordon, *Adoniram Judson Gordon* (London: Hodder & Stoughton, 1909), 153.

7   E.B. Gordon, *Adoniram Judson Gordon* (London: Hodder & Stoughton, 1909), 155-156.

8   E.B. Gordon, *Adoniram Judson Gordon* (London: Hodder & Stoughton, 1909), 153.

9   E.B. Gordon, *Adoniram Judson Gordon* (London: Hodder & Stoughton, 1909), 154.

10 E.B. Gordon, *Adoniram Judson Gordon* (London: Hodder & Stoughton, 1909), 154.

11 E.B. Gordon, *Adoniram Judson Gordon* (London: Hodder & Stoughton, 1909), 154.

12 E.B. Gordon, *Adoniram Judson Gordon* (London: Hodder & Stoughton, 1909), 154.

13 E.B. Gordon, *Adoniram Judson Gordon* (London: Hodder & Stoughton, 1909), 154.

14 E.B. Gordon, *Adoniram Judson Gordon* (London: Hodder & Stoughton, 1909), 157.

15 E.B. Gordon, *Adoniram Judson Gordon* (London: Hodder & Stoughton, 1909), 157. See also page 333 of the May 1897 issue of *The Church Missionary Review*, where it is stated: "Dr. Gordon was closely associated with Mr. Moody, and he took a special delight in the Student Volunteer Movement, which had its birth during the Conference of 1886. Mr. Robert P. Wilder, indeed, the original and prominent leader in that movement, has stated that he owes more to Dr. Gordon and Mr. Hudson Taylor for the development of his own spiritual life than to any others."

16 no author, *The Journal of Education*, March 5, 1885, 1885), 153.

17 see the march 2, 1886 issue of *The Harvard Crimson*, posted online at: http://www.thecrimson.com/article/1886/3/2/college-y-m-c-a-the/

18 see the march 2, 1886 issue of *The Harvard Crimson*, posted online at: http://www.thecrimson.com/article/1886/3/2/college-y-m-c-a-the/

19 J.F. Tyler, *The Harvard College Class of 1877 Secretary's Report* (Cambridge: Riverside Press, 1897), 29.

20 no author, *Harvard Alumni Bulletin*, vol. 25, n0. 3, (Boston: The Harvard Bulletin, Inc., 1922), 79.

Chapter Fourteen – Athens and the Arena

1   no author, *Our Day: A Record and Review*, May 1888, 425.

2   M.L. Bendroth, *Fundamentalists in the City* (New York: Oxford University Press, 2005), 39. See also "Rum, Romanism, and Evangelism…" an article by M.L. Bendroth in *Church History* (Sept. 1, 1999).

3   M.L. Bendroth, *Fundamentalists in the City* (New York: Oxford University Press, 2005), 51.

4   M.L. Bendroth, *Fundamentalists in the City* (New York: Oxford University Press, 2005), 86.

5   M.L. Bendroth, *Fundamentalists in the City* (New York: Oxford University Press, 2005), 86.

6   M.L. Bendroth, *Fundamentalists in the City* (New York: Oxford University Press, 2005), 45.

7   no author, *Our Day: A Record and Review*, May 1888, 425-426.

8   see "Rum, Romanism, and Evangelism: Protestants and Catholics in Late-Nineteenth-Century Boston," an article by M.L. Bendroth in the September 1, 1999 issue of the academic journal, *Church History*, online at: https://www.highbeam.com/doc/1G1-65541577.html

9   no author, *Our Day: A Record and Review,* May 1888, 426. Italics added.

10   see "Rum, Romanism, and Evangelism: Protestants and Catholics in Late-Nineteenth-Century Boston," an article by M.L. Bendroth in the September 1, 1999 issue of the academic journal, *Church History,* online at: https://www.highbeam.com/doc/1G1-65541577.html

11   see "Rum, Romanism, and Evangelism: Protestants and Catholics in Late-Nineteenth-Century Boston," an article by M.L. Bendroth in the September 1, 1999 issue of the academic journal, *Church History,* online at: https://www.highbeam.com/doc/1G1-65541577.html

12   no author, *Our Day: A Record and Review,* May 1888, 426. See also page 88 of *Bench and Bar of the Commonwealth of Massachusetts,* v. 1, by W.T. Davis, (Boston: Boston History Co., 1895); and see page 50 of *The Class of 1885, Harvard College: Secretary's Report,* (Cambridge: For the Class University Press, 1910), which reads: "I was appointed messenger of the Judges of the Municipal Court of Boston. I held this position until October, 1886, when I became a student in the office of Judge George Z. Adams."

13   no author, *Our Day: A Record and Review,* May 1888, 426.

14   no author, *Our Day: A Record and Review,* May 1888, 426.

15   M.L. Bendroth, *Fundamentalists in the City* (New York: Oxford University Press, 2005), 87.

16   George Batten, *Directory of the Religious Press of the United States,* (New York: George Batten, 1892), 58. The relevant entry reads: "The Watchword. Undenominational; monthly; 32 pages, 8x10 inches; subscription, $1 a year; circulation, 2,850; distribution scattered; established 1878; A.J. Gordon, D.D., editor; The Watchword Publishing Co., publishers, 120 Tremont street."

17   A.J. Gordon, "Promises Proved," *The Watchword* magazine, May 1885, 58.

18   A.J. Gordon, "Of His Fullness," *The Watchword* magazine, May 1885, 8.

19   A.J. Gordon, "Of His Fullness," *The Watchword* magazine, May 1885, 8-9.

20   A.J. Gordon, "The Pleasure of the Lord Shall Prosper In His Hand," *The Watchword* magazine, May 1885, 48.

21   A.J. Gordon, "One Another," *The Watchword* magazine, May 1885, 50.

22   A.J. Gordon, "Justified by Faith," *The Watchword,* November 1883, 27.

23   John Aikman Wallace, on page 270 of *Carmina Sanctorum,* ed. by R.D. Hitchcock, L.W. Mudge, et al, (New York: Barnes & Co., 1885).

24   A.J. Gordon, July 1885 issue of *The Watchword* magazine, July 1885, 95.

25   A.J. Gordon, *The Watchword,* July 1885, 95-96.

26   A.J. Gordon, "Wisdom from the Puritans," *The Watchword,* December 1883, 52.

27   A.J. Gordon, "Untitled Introductory Article," *The Watchword,* March 1886, 1.

Chapter Fifteen – Toward A Distant Shore

1   Maria Gordon & A.J. Gordon, *Journal of Our Journey*, ed. John Beauregard (Wenham: Gordon College, 1989), 8.

2   Maria Gordon & A.J. Gordon, *Journal of Our Journey*, ed. John Beauregard (Wenham: Gordon College, 1989), 8.

3   see the Tuesday 6 March 1883 edition of *The Sydney Morning Herald*, at: http://trove.nla.gov.au/ndp/del/article/28373802

4   see the Tuesday 6 March 1883 edition of *The Sydney Morning Herald*, at: http://trove.nla.gov.au/ndp/del/article/28373802

5   see the article, "The New Steamship Pavonia: The Latest Edition to the Cunard Fleet of Ocean Steamers," in the September 25, 1882 *New York Times*, online at: http://query.nytimes.com/mem/archive-free/pdf?res=9A01E7D61E3EE433A25756C2A96F9C94639FD7CF

6   see the Tuesday 6 March 1883 edition of *The Sydney Morning Herald*, at: http://trove.nla.gov.au/ndp/del/article/28373802

7   see the article, "The New Steamship Pavonia: The Latest Edition to the Cunard Fleet of Ocean Steamers," in the September 25, 1882 *New York Times*, online at: http://query.nytimes.com/mem/archive-free/pdf?res=9A01E7D61E3EE433A25756C2A96F9C94639FD7CF

8   see the article, "The New Steamship Pavonia: The Latest Edition to the Cunard Fleet of Ocean Steamers," in the September 25, 1882 *New York Times*, online at: http://query.nytimes.com/mem/archive-free/pdf?res=9A01E7D61E3EE433A25756C2A96F9C94639FD7CF

9   see the article, "The New Steamship Pavonia: The Latest Edition to the Cunard Fleet of Ocean Steamers," in the September 25, 1882 *New York Times*, online at: http://query.nytimes.com/mem/archive-free/pdf?res=9A01E7D61E3EE433A25756C2A96F9C94639FD7CF

10   Maria Gordon & A.J. Gordon, *Journal of Our Journey*, ed. John Beauregard (Wenham: Gordon College, 1989), 79.

11   Maria Gordon & A.J. Gordon, *Journal of Our Journey*, ed. John Beauregard (Wenham: Gordon College, 1989), 79.

12   Maria Gordon & A.J. Gordon, *Journal of Our Journey*, ed. John Beauregard (Wenham: Gordon College, 1989), 79.

13   Maria Gordon & A.J. Gordon, *Journal of Our Journey*, ed. John Beauregard (Wenham: Gordon College, 1989), 79-80.

14   Maria Gordon & A.J. Gordon, *Journal of Our Journey*, ed. John Beauregard (Wenham: Gordon College, 1989), 80.

15   Maria Gordon & A.J. Gordon, *Journal of Our Journey*, ed. John Beauregard (Wenham: Gordon College, 1989), 80.

16 Maria Gordon & A.J. Gordon, *Journal of Our Journey*, ed. John Beauregard (Wenham: Gordon College, 1989), 80.

17 Maria Gordon & A.J. Gordon, *Journal of Our Journey*, ed. John Beauregard (Wenham: Gordon College, 1989), 80.

18 Maria Gordon & A.J. Gordon, *Journal of Our Journey*, ed. John Beauregard (Wenham: Gordon College, 1989), 80. Italics added.

19 Maria Gordon & A.J. Gordon, *Journal of Our Journey*, ed. John Beauregard (Wenham: Gordon College, 1989), 80-81.

20 Maria Gordon & A.J. Gordon, *Journal of Our Journey*, ed. John Beauregard (Wenham: Gordon College, 1989), 81.

21 Maria Gordon & A.J. Gordon, *Journal of Our Journey*, ed. John Beauregard (Wenham: Gordon College, 1989), 81.

22 Maria Gordon & A.J. Gordon, *Journal of Our Journey*, ed. John Beauregard (Wenham: Gordon College, 1989), 77.

23 E.B. Gordon, *Adoniram Judson Gordon* (London: Hodder & Stoughton, 1909), 183-184.

24 Maria Gordon & A.J. Gordon, *Journal of Our Journey*, ed. John Beauregard (Wenham: Gordon College, 1989), 83.

25 Maria Gordon & A.J. Gordon, *Journal of Our Journey*, ed. John Beauregard (Wenham: Gordon College, 1989), 83.

26 Maria Gordon & A.J. Gordon, *Journal of Our Journey*, ed. John Beauregard (Wenham: Gordon College, 1989), 8-10.

27 Maria Gordon & A.J. Gordon, *Journal of Our Journey*, ed. John Beauregard (Wenham: Gordon College, 1989), 11.

28 Maria Gordon & A.J. Gordon, *Journal of Our Journey*, ed. John Beauregard (Wenham: Gordon College, 1989), 11.

29 Maria Gordon & A.J. Gordon, *Journal of Our Journey*, ed. John Beauregard (Wenham: Gordon College, 1989), 11.

30 D.L. Robert, "The Legacy of Adoniram Judson Gordon," *The International Bulletin of Missionary Research* (October 1987), 177. Monetary conversion comes via the website Measuring Worth: https://www.measuringworth.com/uscompare/relativevalue.php

31 T.A. Askew, "Gordon, A(doniram) J(udson)," in *The Biographical Dictionary of Christian Missions*, ed. by G.H. Anderson, (Grand Rapids: Eerdmans, 1999), 251. "In 1888 Dr. and Mrs. Gordon sailed to England to attend the Centenary Conference, convened to mark roughly 100 years of Protestant missionary work. The Centenary Conference was the most representative Anglo-American missions conference to date, and 139 mission societies from around the world sent representatives. At the conference, A. J. Gordon gained an international reputation as apologist for the missionary enterprise." –D.L. Robert, "The

Legacy of Adoniram Judson Gordon," *The International Bulletin of Missionary Research* (October 1987), 177.

32 D.L. Robert, "The Legacy of Adoniram Judson Gordon," *The International Bulletin of Missionary Research* (October 1987), 177.

33 E.B. Gordon, *Adoniram Judson Gordon* (London: Hodder & Stoughton, 1909)., 231-232.

34 A.J. Gordon to Clarendon Street Church, 19 June 1888, a letter in the A.J. Gordon Papers, Jenks LRC, Gordon College.

35 S.M. Gibson, *A.J. Gordon: American Premillenialist* (Lanham: University Press of America, 2001), 96.

36 S.M. Gibson, *A.J. Gordon: American Premillenialist* (Lanham: University Press of America, 2001), 96.

37 no author, "Home Religious Chronicle," *The Watchman* magazine, May 24, 1888, 4.

38 S.M. Gibson, *A.J. Gordon: American Premillenialist* (Lanham: University Press of America, 2001), 96.

39 S.M. Gibson, *A.J. Gordon: American Premillenialist* (Lanham: University Press of America, 2001), 96.

40 S.M. Gibson, *A.J. Gordon: American Premillenialist* (Lanham: University Press of America, 2001), 96.

41 James Johnston, ed., *Report of the Centenary Conference* (London: Nisbet & Co., 1889), 486.

42 C.H. Spurgeon, ed., *The Sword and Trowel*, September 1882, 493.

43 the seating capacity of Metropolitan Tabernacle is given at: http://www.victorianweb.org/art/architecture/churches/46.html

44 C.H. Spurgeon, *Autobiography*, v. 4, (London: Passmore & Alabaster, 1900), 177. Italics added.

45 G.C. Needham, *Charles H. Spurgeon: His Life and Labors* (Boston: D.L. Guernsey, 1884), vii.

46 G.C. Needham, *Charles H. Spurgeon: His Life and Labors* (Boston: D.L. Guernsey, 1884), viii.

47 G.C. Needham, *Charles H. Spurgeon: His Life and Labors* (Boston: D.L. Guernsey, 1884), viii.

48 G.C. Needham, *Charles H. Spurgeon: His Life and Labors* (Boston: D.L. Guernsey, 1884), ix.

49 E.B. Gordon, *Adoniram Judson Gordon* (London: Hodder & Stoughton, 1909), 229-230.

50 E.B. Gordon, *Adoniram Judson Gordon* (London: Hodder & Stoughton, 1909), 231.

51 E.B. Gordon, *Adoniram Judson Gordon* (London: Hodder & Stoughton, 1909), 231.

52 E.B. Gordon, *Adoniram Judson Gordon* (London: Hodder & Stoughton, 1909), 231.

53 E.B. Gordon, *Adoniram Judson Gordon* (London: Hodder & Stoughton, 1909), 231.

54 Maria Gordon & A.J. Gordon, *Journal of Our Journey*, ed. John Beauregard, (Wenham: Gordon College, 1989), 173-174.

55 E.B. Gordon, *Adoniram Judson Gordon* (London: Hodder & Stoughton, 1909), 231.

56 E.B. Gordon, *Adoniram Judson Gordon* (London: Hodder & Stoughton, 1909), 231.

57 E.B. Gordon, *Adoniram Judson Gordon* (London: Hodder & Stoughton, 1909), 231. See also S.M. Gibson, *A.J. Gordon: American Premillenialist* (Lanham: University Press of America, 2001), 97.

58 E.B. Gordon, *Adoniram Judson Gordon* (London: Hodder & Stoughton, 1909), 231

59 E.B. Gordon, *Adoniram Judson Gordon* (London: Hodder & Stoughton, 1909), 232.

60 E.B. Gordon, *Adoniram Judson Gordon* (London: Hodder & Stoughton, 1909), 232.

61 D.L. Robert, "The Legacy of Adoniram Judson Gordon," *The International Bulletin of Missionary Research* (October 1987), 177.

62 S.M. Gibson, *A.J. Gordon: American Premillenialist* (Lanham: University Press of America, 2001), 98.

Chapter Sixteen – The School In Bowdoin Square

1 Harriet Chapell, in F.L. Chapell, *Biblical and Practical Theology* (Philadelphia: Harriet Chapell, 1901), iv. See page 385 of *The Mount Holyoke* magazine, (South Hadley: Mount Holyoke College, 1902): "[Class of] '88. Harriet Chapell...will spend some time...attending to business connected with the publishing of her father's works. Her permanent address will be Flemington, New Jersey."

2 Orlando Leach, *The Biographical Record, Yale University, Class of 1860* (Boston: The Fort Hill Press, 1906), 81-83. See also page 47 of *Rochester Theological Seminary: General Catalogue, 1850 to 1910*, (Rochester: E.R. Andrews, 1910). See also "Commencement Week at Yale," a Friday, July 31, 1863 article where F.L. Chapell is listed among the graduates of the Class of 1860. This article appears online at: http://www.nytimes.com/1863/08/02/news/commencement-week-yale-alumni-meeting-graduating-class-orations-orators.html

3 the name "Boston Missionary Training School" was used consistently by A.J. Gordon's son Ernest, and also by Gordon's most authoritative biographer, Dr. S.M. Gibson. The BMTS later became The Gordon Bible and Missionary Training School – see N.R. Wood, *A School for Christ* (Boston: Halliday Lithograph Corp., 1953). 26.

4 N.R. Wood, *A School of Christ* (Boston: Halliday Lithograph Corp., 1953), 16.

5 "The Degree of Doctor of Divinity" was awarded to Guinness by Brown University in 1889, see page 100 of *Catalogue of the Officers and Students of Brown University 1889-1890*, (Providence: Snow & Farnham, 1890). See also page 18 of Dr. Harry Guinness, *Not Unto Us* (London: Regions Beyond Missionary Union, 1908). Here, Dr. Guinness wrote of H. Grattan Guinness: "In the following year, 1889, [my father] returned once more to the States, preaching

wherever he went. As one visible result of these visits, two Bible schools sprang into existence. One in Minneapolis president over by Dr. Henry Mabie, who subsequently became the distinguished Secretary of the American Baptist Missionary Union,—the second at Clarendon Street, Boston, *under the guidance of the late Dr. A.J. Gordon, a friend and admirer of my father, and himself one of the noblest of men.* These Bible schools have gone on ever since, and accomplished a valuable work." Italics added. Interestingly, Dr. Harry Guinness named one of his sons Gordon, one very much suspects to honor A.J. Gordon.

6   D.H. Bays, ed., The Foreign Missionary Enterprise at Home (Tuscaloosa: University of Alabama Press, 2003), 139.

7   W.H. Brackney, P.S. Fiddes, eds., *Pilgrim Pathways: Essays in Baptist History in Honor of B.R. White,* (Macon, Georgia: Mercer University Press, 1999), 312. Here, this chronology is confirmed by Gordon scholar, Dr. S.M. Gibson.

8   S.M. Gibson, *A.J. Gordon: American Premillenialist* (Lanham: University Press of America, 2001), 132-133. [Bowdoin Square Church] purchased the two prostitution houses in the neighborhood and changed their use, establishing a "Young Men's Institute in one of them which would provide lodging, religious training, and Biblical instruction for working men of the city."

9   E.B. Gordon, *Adoniram Judson Gordon* (London: Hodder & Stoughton, 1909), 269.

10 see also AJ. Gordon's 24 May 1889 letter to Dr. Alvah Hovey, housed in the Alvah Hovey Papers at The Trask Library, Andover-Newton Theological Seminary, Newton Centre, Massachusetts. In this letter, Gordon stated that H. Grattan Guinness had said to him: "Why not make a recruiting station for missionaries out of your Institute?"

11 M.L. Bendroth, *Fundamentalists in the City* (New York: Oxford University Press, 2005), 94. See also page 777 of the 30 July 1889 Board of Alderman Report, in *Proceedings of the City Council of Boston,* (Boston: Rockwell and Churchill, 1890): which writes of the "Tabernacle Young Men's Institute," as belonging to "the owners of the estate known as the Bowdoin Square Baptist Church, on Bowdoin Square and Chardon Street."

12 no author, *The Baptist Missionary Magazine,* October 1889, 388.

13 no author, "Progress of Missions—Monthly Bulletin: United States," *The Missionary Review of the World,* November 1889, 880.

14 no author, "Board of Alderman Report," in *Proceedings of the City Council of Boston,* July 1889, 777.

15 B.O. Flower, ed., *The Arena* (Boston: The Arena Pub. Co., 1891), xxxii. See also no author, "Board of Alderman Report," in *Proceedings of the City Council of Boston,* July 1889, 777.

16 B.O. Flower, ed., *The Arena* (Boston: The Arena Pub. Co., 1891), xxxii. See also no author, "Board of Alderman Report," in *Proceedings of the City Council of Boston,* July 1889, 777.

17 B.O. Flower, ed., *The Arena* (Boston: The Arena Pub. Co., 1891), xxxii. See also no author, "Board of Alderman Report," in *Proceedings of the City Council of Boston*, July 1889, 777.

18 B.O. Flower, ed., *The Arena* (Boston: The Arena Pub. Co., 1891), xxxii. See also no author, "Board of Alderman Report," in *Proceedings of the City Council of Boston*, July 1889, 777.

19 E.B. Gordon, *Adoniram Judson Gordon* (London: Hodder & Stoughton, 1909), 272-273.

20 E.B. Andrews "A.J. Gordon: A Career Consecrated and Crowned," in *Our Day* magazine, March 1895, 144-146.

21 E.B. Gordon, *Adoniram Judson Gordon* (London: Hodder & Stoughton, 1909), 272-273. See also S.M. Gibson, *A.J. Gordon: American Premillenialist* (Lanham: University Press of America, 2001), 16.

22 values have been determined via "Measuring Worth," online at: https://www.measuringworth.com/uscompare/relativevalue.php

23 see page 61 of the January 1897 *Missionary Review of the World*, v. 10, no. 1, (New York: Funk & Wagnalls, 1897).

24 N.R. Wood, *A School of Christ* (Boston: Halliday Lithograph Corp., 1953), 15.

25 Harriet Chapell, from the Publisher's Note in F.L. Chapell, *Biblical and Practical Theology* (Philadelphia: Harriet Chapell, 1901), iv.

26 see pages 234-235 of *General Catalogue of Bates College and Cobb Divinity School*, (Lewiston, Maine: Bates College, 1915).

27 see page 61 of the January 1897 *Missionary Review of the World*, v. 10, no. 1, (New York: Funk & Wagnalls, 1897).

28 see page 7 of the Saturday, April 25, 1903 issue of *The Cambridge Tribune*, v. 26, no. 8. Archived online at: http://cambridge.dlconsulting.com/cgi-bin/cambridge?a=d&d=Tribune19030425-01.2.50

29 no author, *Twenty-Third Annual Report of the State Board of Charity of Massachusetts*, (Boston: Wright & Potter, 1902), 228.

30 no author, *Annual Report of the New England Moral Reform Society: Talitha Cumi Maternity Home*, (Boston: Fort Hill Press, 1907), 5.

31 no author, *The Congregationalist and Advance*, January 3, 1918, 12.

32 D.L. Robert, "The Legacy of Adoniram Judson Gordon," *The International Bulletin of Missionary Research* (October 1987), 179-180.

33 E.B. Gordon, *Adoniram Judson Gordon* (London: Hodder & Stoughton, 1909), 341-342.

34 E.B. Gordon, *Adoniram Judson Gordon* (London: Hodder & Stoughton, 1909), 263-265.

35 E.B. Gordon, *Adoniram Judson Gordon* (London: Hodder & Stoughton, 1909), 266-267.

36 E.B. Gordon, *Adoniram Judson Gordon* (London: Hodder & Stoughton, 1909), 267.

37 E.B. Gordon, *Adoniram Judson Gordon* (London: Hodder & Stoughton, 1909), 269.

38 E.B. Gordon, *Adoniram Judson Gordon* (London: Hodder & Stoughton, 1909), 269.

39 E.B. Gordon, *Adoniram Judson Gordon* (London: Hodder & Stoughton, 1909), 269.

40 E.B. Gordon, *Adoniram Judson Gordon* (London: Hodder & Stoughton, 1909), 269.

41 E.B. Gordon, *Adoniram Judson Gordon* (London: Hodder & Stoughton, 1909), 273.

42 no author, *The Student Volunteer,* March 1895, 120.

43 E.B. Gordon, *Adoniram Judson Gordon* (London: Hodder & Stoughton, 1909), 345.

44 no author, "Monthly Bulletin," *The Missionary Review of the World,* February 1891, 158.

45 E.B. Gordon, *Adoniram Judson Gordon* (London: Hodder & Stoughton, 1909), 345.

46 E.B. Gordon, *Adoniram Judson Gordon* (London: Hodder & Stoughton, 1909), 345.

47 E.B. Gordon, *Adoniram Judson Gordon* (London: Hodder & Stoughton, 1909), 346.

48 E.B. Gordon, *Adoniram Judson Gordon* (London: Hodder & Stoughton, 1909), 345.

49 E.B. Gordon, *Adoniram Judson Gordon* (London: Hodder & Stoughton, 1909), 345.

50 *The Merriam-Webster Medical Dictionary* (Springfield: Merriam-Webster Inc., 1995), 137.

51 E.B. Gordon, *Adoniram Judson Gordon* (London: Hodder & Stoughton, 1909), 345. Italics added.

52 E.B. Gordon, *Adoniram Judson Gordon* (London: Hodder & Stoughton, 1909), 273.

53 E.B. Gordon, *Adoniram Judson Gordon* (London: Hodder & Stoughton, 1909), 274.

54 E.B. Gordon, *Adoniram Judson Gordon* (London: Hodder & Stoughton, 1909), 274.

55 D.L. Robert, "The Legacy of Adoniram Judson Gordon," *The International Bulletin of Missionary Research* (October 1987), 179.

56 N.R. Wood, *A School of Christ* (Boston: Halliday Lithograph Corp., 1953), 16-17.

57 F.L. Chapell, "Dr. Gordon and the Training School," in *The Watchword,* February 1895, 61.

58 D.L. Robert, "The Legacy of Adoniram Judson Gordon," *The International Bulletin of Missionary Research* (October 1987), 179.

59 F.L. Chapell, "Dr. Gordon and the Training School," in *The Watchword,* February 1895, 61.

60 Robert Cameron, ed., "Announcement," *The Watchword,* October 1895, 185.

61 no author, "Women's Baptist Foreign Missionary Society of the West: Chicago," in the November 1896 issue of *The Helping Hand* (Boston : Woman's Baptist Missionary Society, 1896), 17.

62 F.L. Chapell, "Dr. Gordon and the Training School," in *The Watchword,* February 1895, 61-62.

63 F.L. Chapell, "Dr. Gordon & the Training School," *The Watchword,* Feb.-March 1895, 62. Here Chapell stated: "As we glance over the records we find that 25 have gone to foreign lands, 15 are in the ministry, 20 have entered largely and very successfully into evangelistic work, more than 20 are in home and city missions and church work, while some 15 are in educational institutions of a

higher grade, besides a large number still in the School, but entering somewhat into work or anticipating soon going abroad."

64 D.L. Robert, "The Legacy of Adoniram Judson Gordon," *The International Bulletin of Missionary Research* (October 1987), 179-180.

65 D.L. Robert, "The Legacy of Adoniram Judson Gordon," *The International Bulletin of Missionary Research* (October 1987), 180.

66 D.L. Robert, "The Legacy of Adoniram Judson Gordon," *The International Bulletin of Missionary Research* (October 1987), 180.

67 A.J. Gordon, "The Ministry of Women," *The Missionary Review of the World*, December 1894, 911.

68 D.L. Robert, "The Legacy of Adoniram Judson Gordon," *The International Bulletin of Missionary Research* (October 1987), 180.

69 A.J. Gordon, "A Hebrew Phophetess," *The Watchword*, August 1891, 212.

70 Maria Gordon, "Women As Evangelists," *Northfield Echoes* (East Northfield: The Conference Book Store, 1894), 151.

71 Maria Gordon, "Women As Evangelists," *Northfield Echoes* (East Northfield: The Conference Book Store, 1894), 151. Emphasis added.

72 A.J. Gordon, "The Ministry of Women," *The Missionary Review of the World*, December 1894, 920.

73 G.A.K. Baughen. 'Baeyertz, Charles Nalder', from the Dictionary of New Zealand Biography. Te Ara - the Encyclopedia of New Zealand, updated 2-Sep-2013 URL: http://www.TeAra.govt.nz/en/biographies/2b1/baeyertz-charles-nalder

74 E.L. Baeyertz, *From Darkness to Light* (Toronto: Hill & Weir, 1891), 6-7.

75 John Walker, "Baeyertz, Emilia Louise," *Australian Dictionary of Evangelical Biography*, this biographical essay is archived online at: http://webjournals.ac.edu.au/ojs/index.php/ADEB/article/view/1318/1315 See also G.A.K. Baughen. 'Baeyertz, Charles Nalder', from the Dictionary of New Zealand Biography. Te Ara - the Encyclopedia of New Zealand, updated 2-Sep-2013 URL: http://www.TeAra.govt.nz/en/biographies/2b1/baeyertz-charles-nalder

76 A.J. Gordon, "A Hebrew Phophetess," *The Watchword*, August 1891, 212.

77 A.J. Gordon, "A Hebrew Phophetess," *The Watchword*, August 1891, 212.

78 N.R. Wood, *A School for Christ* (Boston: Halliday Lithograph Corp., 1953), 27-28.

79 A.T. Pierson, D.L. Pierson, et al, *The Missionary Review of the World*, January 1901, 781.

80 Maria Gordon, as quoted in *The Missionary Review of the World*, July 1907, 543.

Chapter Seventeen – Where The White Banner Flew

1 no author, *Baptist Missionary Magazine*, March 1895, 66. See also D.L. Robert, "The Legacy of Adoniram Judson Gordon," *The International Bulletin of Missionary Research* (October 1987), 176 - "[A.J.] Gordon began the Boston

Industrial Temporary Home as a shelter for the unemployed, often alcoholic, homeless men. In exchange for work at a woodpile that provided fuel for Boston's poor, the homeless received food and lodging. Despite financial and other difficulties, the industrial home became a fixture of Boston social service in the late nineteenth century."

2   R.M. Russell & H.J. Mahoney, *Cambridge Sentinel*, Saturday, February 14, 1931, 8.

3   R.M. Russell & H.J. Mahoney, *Cambridge Sentinel*, Saturday, February 14, 1931, 8. Italics added.

4   no author, "News WEEI Briefs," *The Microphone* newspaper, June 23, 1934, 11.

5   see the article "Radio Broadcast Given Tonight be Club Musicians," on page 1 of the Friday, 25 March 1932 edition of "The Tech" newspaper, the "Official Undergraduate News Organ of Massachusetts Institute of Technology," v. 52, no. 19, (Cambridge: Massachusetts Institute of Technology, 1932).

6   see the article, "Boston Missions," from the 12 March 1895 edition of *The Harvard Crimson*, archived online at: http://www.thecrimson.com/article/1895/3/12/boston-missions-two-delegations-will-go/
     See also the article, "Delegations to Boston Missions," from the 19 March 1895 edition of *The Harvard Crimson*, archived online at: http://www.thecrimson.com/article/1895/3/19/delegations-to-boston-missions-the-mission/
     See also the article, "Student Volunteer Committee," from the 28 February 1895 edition of *The Harvard Crimson*, archived online at: http://www.thecrimson.com/article/1895/2/28/student-volunteer-committee-the-committee-on/

7   E.B. Gordon, *Adoniram Judson Gordon* (London: Hodder and Stoughton, 1909), 106. See also page 15 of *A Directory of the Charitable and Beneficent Organizations of Boston*, (Boston: Williams & Co., 1880), which confirms 1874 as the date when the Boston Industrial Temporary Home was established.

8   E.B. Gordon, *Adoniram Judson Gordon* (London: Hodder and Stoughton, 1909), 106-107.

9   E.B. Gordon, *Adoniram Judson Gordon* (London: Hodder and Stoughton, 1909), 107.

10   E.B. Gordon, *Adoniram Judson Gordon* (London: Hodder and Stoughton, 1909), 107.

11   E.B. Gordon, *Adoniram Judson Gordon* (London: Hodder and Stoughton, 1909), 107.

12   E.B. Gordon, *Adoniram Judson Gordon* (London: Hodder and Stoughton, 1909), 107.

13   E.B. Gordon, *Adoniram Judson Gordon* (London: Hodder and Stoughton, 1909), 107.

14   E.B. Gordon, *Adoniram Judson Gordon* (London: Hodder and Stoughton, 1909), 108.

15 E.B. Gordon, *Adoniram Judson Gordon* (London: Hodder and Stoughton, 1909), 108.

16 E.B. Gordon, *Adoniram Judson Gordon* (London: Hodder and Stoughton, 1909), 108.

17 no author, *A Directory of the Charitable and Beneficent Organizations of Boston*, (Boston: Williams & Co., 1880), 52.

18 T.D. Roberts, *Means and Ways* (Boston: J.H. Earle, 1892), 110.

19 no author, *A Directory of the Charitable and Beneficent Organizations of Boston*, (Boston: Williams & Co., 1880), 52.

20 E.B. Gordon, *Adoniram Judson Gordon* (London: Hodder and Stoughton, 1909), 108.

21 T.D. Roberts, *Means and Ways* (Boston: J.H. Earle, 1892), 17.

22 T.D. Roberts, *Means and Ways* (Boston: J.H. Earle, 1892), 17.

23 T.D. Roberts, *Means and Ways* (Boston: J.H. Earle, 1892), 18.

24 T.D. Roberts, *Means and Ways* (Boston: J.H. Earle, 1892), 19-20.

25 T.D. Roberts, *Means and Ways* (Boston: J.H. Earle, 1892), 21.

26 T.D. Roberts, *Means and Ways* (Boston: J.H. Earle, 1892), 22.

27 T.D. Roberts, *Means and Ways* (Boston: J.H. Earle, 1892), 24-25.

28 no author, *The Cultivator and Country Gentleman*, February 2, 1882, 93.

29 T.D. Roberts, *Means and Ways* (Boston: J.H. Earle, 1892), 37.

30 T.D. Roberts, *Means and Ways* (Boston: J.H. Earle, 1892), 71.

31 see page 4 of the 25 December 1888 edition of *The New York Times*, archived online at: http://query.nytimes.com/mem/archive-free/pdf?res=9502EFDD163BE033A25756C2A9649D94699FD7CF

32 see page 4 of the 25 December 1888 edition of *The New York Times*, archived online at: http://query.nytimes.com/mem/archive-free/pdf?res=9502EFDD163BE033A25756C2A9649D94699FD7CF

33 see page 4 of the 25 December 1888 edition of *The New York Times*, archived online at: http://query.nytimes.com/mem/archive-free/pdf?res=9502EFDD163BE033A25756C2A9649D94699FD7CF

34 see page 4 of the 25 December 1888 edition of *The New York Times*, archived online at: http://query.nytimes.com/mem/archive-free/pdf?res=9502EFDD163BE033A25756C2A9649D94699FD7CF

35 T.D. Roberts, *Means and Ways* (Boston: J.H. Earle, 1892), 73.

36 T.D. Roberts, *Means and Ways* (Boston: J.H. Earle, 1892), 73.

37 T.D. Roberts, *Means and Ways* (Boston: J.H. Earle, 1892), 73-74.

38 A.J. Gordon, as quoted in T.D. Roberts, *Means and Ways* (Boston: J.H. Earle, 1892), 9-10.

39 A.J. Gordon, as quoted in T.D. Roberts, *Means and Ways* (Boston: J.H. Earle, 1892), 10.

40   T.D. Roberts, *Means and Ways* (Boston: J.H. Earle, 1892), 105-106, & 97.

41   W.R. Moody, ed., *The Record of Christian Work* magazine, April 1908, 243.

42   no author, "What Timely Sympathy Can Do: A Testimony Given by Dad's Son," pages 1-2, part of The Blackwell Family Papers housed at Harvard University Library, and posted online at: http://pds.lib.harvard.edu/pds/view/50672683?n=5

43   no author, "What Timely Sympathy Can Do: A Testimony Given by Dad's Son," pages 2-3, part of The Blackwell Family Papers housed at Harvard University Library, and posted online at: http://pds.lib.harvard.edu/pds/view/50672683?n=5

44   no author, "What Timely Sympathy Can Do: A Testimony Given by Dad's Son," page 3, part of The Blackwell Family Papers housed at Harvard University Library, and posted online at: http://pds.lib.harvard.edu/pds/view/50672683?n=5

45   no author, "What Timely Sympathy Can Do: A Testimony Given by Dad's Son," page 4, part of The Blackwell Family Papers housed at Harvard University Library, and posted online at: http://pds.lib.harvard.edu/pds/view/50672683?n=5

46   no author, "What Timely Sympathy Can Do: A Testimony Given by Dad's Son," pages 4-5, part of The Blackwell Family Papers housed at Harvard University Library, and posted online at: http://pds.lib.harvard.edu/pds/view/50672683?n=5

47   no author, "What Timely Sympathy Can Do: A Testimony Given by Dad's Son," pages 6-7, part of The Blackwell Family Papers housed at Harvard University Library, and posted online at: http://pds.lib.harvard.edu/pds/view/50672683?n=5

48   James Peters' MIT Master's Thesis is archived online at: https://dspace.mit.edu/bitstream/handle/1721.1/71088/25919558-MIT.pdf?sequence=2

49   T.D. Roberts, *Means and Ways* (Boston: J.H. Earle, 1892), 113.

Chapter Eighteen – Gatherings in Summer

1   see the 22 April 1892 issue of *The Harvard Crimson* at: http://www.thecrimson.com/article/1892/4/22/y-m-c-a-meeting-the/
See also the 2 March 1893 issue of *The Harvard Crimson*, which reported that Dr. A.J. Gordon was scheduled to speak in Harvard's Holden Chapel at 6:45pm on Thursday evening, March 30th. A notice for this service, scheduled as "the last vesper service of the year," was also given on page 4 of the Saturday, March 25, 1893 issue of *The Cambridge Chronicle*.

2   A.J. Gordon, as quoted in H.B. Hartzler, *Moody In Chicago*, (New York: Revell, 1894), 72. See also page 25 of *Handbook of the Northfield Seminary...*, by H.W.,

Rankin, (New York: Revell, 1889), where it is stated: "The meetings of this first conference, last[ed] through the first ten days of September 1880..."

3   W.R. Moody, *The Life of Dwight L. Moody*, (London: Morgan & Scott, 1900), 258.

4   D.L. Moody, as quoted in E.B. Gordon, *Adoniram Judson Gordon* (London: Hodder and Stoughton, 1909), 174-175.

5   E.B. Gordon, *Adoniram Judson Gordon* (London: Hodder and Stoughton, 1909), 173-174.

6   P.D. Moody & A.P. Fitt, *The Shorter Life of D.L. Moody: Two Volumes In One* (Chicago: The Bible Institute Colportage Assoc.,1900), 51.

7   P.D. Moody & A.P. Fitt, *The Shorter Life of D.L. Moody: Two Volumes In One* (Chicago: The Bible Institute Colportage Assoc.,1900), 51.

8   P.D. Moody & A.P. Fitt, *The Shorter Life of D.L. Moody: Two Volumes In One* (Chicago: The Bible Institute Colportage Assoc.,1900), 51-52.

9   P.D. Moody & A.P. Fitt, *The Shorter Life of D.L. Moody: Two Volumes In One* (Chicago: The Bible Institute Colportage Assoc.,1900), 52.

10   P.D. Moody & A.P. Fitt, *The Shorter Life of D.L. Moody: Two Volumes In One* (Chicago: The Bible Institute Colportage Assoc.,1900), 15.

11   D.L. Moody, as quoted in W.R. Moody, *The Life of Dwight L. Moody*, (London: Morgan & Scott, 1900), 426.

12   no author, "Dr. H.B. Wright Dead, Professor at Yale," *The Meriden Morning Record*, Friday, December 28, 1923, 1.

13   H.B. Wright, J.B. Reynolds, et al, *Two Centuries of Christian Activity at Yale* (New York: G.P. Putnam's Sons, 1901), 241-242.

14   H.B. Wright, J.B. Reynolds, et al, *Two Centuries of Christian Activity at Yale* (New York: G.P. Putnam's Sons, 1901), 242.

15   H.B. Wright, J.B. Reynolds, et al, *Two Centuries of Christian Activity at Yale* (New York: G.P. Putnam's Sons, 1901), 242.

16   H.B. Wright, J.B. Reynolds, et al, *Two Centuries of Christian Activity at Yale* (New York: G.P. Putnam's Sons, 1901), 242-243.

17   H.B. Wright, J.B. Reynolds, et al, *Two Centuries of Christian Activity at Yale* (New York: G.P. Putnam's Sons, 1901), 243.

18   H.B. Wright, J.B. Reynolds, et al, *Two Centuries of Christian Activity at Yale* (New York: G.P. Putnam's Sons, 1901), 243-244.

19   H.B. Wright, J.B. Reynolds, et al, *Two Centuries of Christian Activity at Yale* (New York: G.P. Putnam's Sons, 1901), 244.

20   W.R. Moody, *The Life of Dwight L. Moody*, (London: Morgan & Scott, 1900), 324.

21   H.B. Wright, J.B. Reynolds, et al, *Two Centuries of Christian Activity at Yale* (New York: G.P. Putnam's Sons, 1901), 245.

22   H.B. Wright, J.B. Reynolds, et al, *Two Centuries of Christian Activity at Yale* (New York: G.P. Putnam's Sons, 1901), 245.

23 H.B. Wright, J.B. Reynolds, et al, *Two Centuries of Christian Activity at Yale* (New York: G.P. Putnam's Sons, 1901), 245. See also pages 7-8 of D.L. Pierson, ed., *Northfield Echoes* (1894), stating Prof. W.R. Harper taught at the "Students Conference" of 1888.

24 H.B. Wright, J.B. Reynolds, et al, *Two Centuries of Christian Activity at Yale* (New York: G.P. Putnam's Sons, 1901), 246.

25 Amos Alonzo Stagg, as quoted in *College Students at Northfield* ed. by T.J. Shanks, (New York: Revell, 1888), 271-272.

26 H.B. Wright, J.B. Reynolds, et al, *Two Centuries of Christian Activity at Yale* (New York: G.P. Putnam's Sons, 1901), 246-247.

27 H.B. Wright, J.B. Reynolds, et al, *Two Centuries of Christian Activity at Yale* (New York: G.P. Putnam's Sons, 1901), 247.

28 H.B. Wright, J.B. Reynolds, et al, *Two Centuries of Christian Activity at Yale* (New York: G.P. Putnam's Sons, 1901), 247.

29 H.B. Wright, J.B. Reynolds, et al, *Two Centuries of Christian Activity at Yale* (New York: G.P. Putnam's Sons, 1901), 247-248.

30 H.B. Wright, J.B. Reynolds, et al, *Two Centuries of Christian Activity at Yale* (New York: G.P. Putnam's Sons, 1901), 247.

31 H.B. Wright, J.B. Reynolds, et al, *Two Centuries of Christian Activity at Yale* (New York: G.P. Putnam's Sons, 1901), 248.

32 H.B. Wright, J.B. Reynolds, et al, *Two Centuries of Christian Activity at Yale* (New York: G.P. Putnam's Sons, 1901), 248-249.

33 H.B. Wright, J.B. Reynolds, et al, *Two Centuries of Christian Activity at Yale* (New York: G.P. Putnam's Sons, 1901), 249.

34 H.B. Wright, J.B. Reynolds, et al, *Two Centuries of Christian Activity at Yale* (New York: G.P. Putnam's Sons, 1901), 249-250.

35 H.B. Wright, J.B. Reynolds, et al, *Two Centuries of Christian Activity at Yale* (New York: G.P. Putnam's Sons, 1901), 251.

36 A.J. Gordon, "Our Source of Power," in *Gems from Northfield,* ed. by T.J. Shanks, (Chicago: Revell, 1881), 203.

37 A.J. Gordon, "Our Source of Power," in *Gems from Northfield,* ed. by T.J. Shanks, (Chicago: Revell, 1881), 203.

38 A.J. Gordon, "Our Source of Power," in *Gems from Northfield,* ed. by T.J. Shanks, (Chicago: Revell, 1881), 203-204. Italics added.

39 A.J. Gordon, "Our Source of Power," in *Gems from Northfield,* ed. by T.J. Shanks, (Chicago: Revell, 1881), 205.

40 A.J. Gordon, "Our Source of Power," in *Gems from Northfield,* ed. by T.J. Shanks, (Chicago: Revell, 1881), 205.

41 See *Great Pulpit Masters: A.J. Gordon,* Introduction by N.R. Wood, (New York: Revell, 1951), 11. Italics added

42 A.J. Gordon, "Our Source of Power," in *Gems from Northfield*, ed. by T.J. Shanks, (Chicago: Revell, 1881), 206-207.

43 A.J. Gordon, "Our Source of Power," in *Gems from Northfield*, ed. by T.J. Shanks, (Chicago: Revell, 1881), 208-209.

44 H.W. Rankin, *Handbook of the Northfield Seminary...* (New York: Revell, 1889), 41-42.

45 H.W. Rankin, *Handbook of the Northfield Seminary...* (New York: Revell, 1889), 42-43.

46 H.W. Rankin, *Handbook of the Northfield Seminary...* (New York: Revell, 1889), 43.

47 A.J. Gordon, "The Holy Spirit's Relation to the Church and to the World," in *Select Northfield Sermons*, (Chicago: BICA, 1897), 126.

48 A.J. Gordon, "The Holy Spirit's Relation to the Church and to the World," in *Select Northfield Sermons*, (Chicago: BICA, 1897), 127.

49 A.J. Gordon, "The Holy Spirit's Relation to the Church and to the World," in *Select Northfield Sermons*, (Chicago: BICA, 1897), 128.

50 J.W. Chapman, "Our Great Saviour," *Victorious Life Hymns* (Philadelphia: Sunday School Times Co., 1919).

51 J.W. Chapman, *The Life and Work of Dwight L. Moody,* (Toronto: Bradley-Garretson Co. Ltd., 1900), 196-198.

52 J.W. Chapman, *The Life and Work of Dwight L. Moody,* (Toronto: Bradley-Garretson Co. Ltd., 1900), 196-198.

53 J.W. Chapman, *The Life and Work of Dwight L. Moody,* (Toronto: Bradley-Garretson Co. Ltd., 1900), 196-198.

54 E.B. Gordon, *Adoniram Judson Gordon* (London: Hodder & Stoughton, 1909), 157.

55 S.M. Gibson, *A.J. Gordon: American Premillenialist* (Lanham: University Press of America, 2001), 200. Punctuation added.

56 S.M. Gibson, *A.J. Gordon: American Premillenialist* (Lanham: University Press of America, 2001), 200.

57 A.J. Gordon, as quoted in H.B. Hartzler, *Moody In Chicago* (New York: Revell, 1894), 62.

58 A.J. Gordon, as quoted in H.B. Hartzler, *Moody In Chicago* (New York: Revell, 1894), 62-63.

59 A.J. Gordon, as quoted in H.B. Hartzler, *Moody In Chicago* (New York: Revell, 1894), 63.

60 D.L. Moody, as quoted in C.F. Goss, *Echoes From The Pulpit* (Hartford: Worthington & Co., 1900), 259.

61 Alfred, Lord Tennyson, as quoted in Hallam Tennyson, *Alfred, Lord Tennyson: A Memoir*, v. 1, (London: Macmillan, 1898), 218.

62 A.J. Gordon, as quoted in H.B. Hartzler, *Moody In Chicago* (New York: Revell, 1894), 63.

63   A.J. Gordon, as quoted in H.B. Hartzler, *Moody In Chicago* (New York: Revell, 1894), 63-64.

64   A.J. Gordon, as quoted in H.B. Hartzler, *Moody In Chicago* (New York: Revell, 1894), 69.

65   A.J. Gordon, as quoted in H.B. Hartzler, *Moody In Chicago* (New York: Revell, 1894), 69.

66   A.J. Gordon, as quoted in H.B. Hartzler, *Moody In Chicago* (New York: Revell, 1894), 69-70.

67   A.J. Gordon, as quoted in H.B. Hartzler, *Moody In Chicago* (New York: Revell, 1894), 70.

68   A.J. Gordon, as quoted in H.B. Hartzler, *Moody In Chicago* (New York: Revell, 1894), 71.

69   A.J. Gordon, as quoted in H.B. Hartzler, *Moody In Chicago* (New York: Revell, 1894), 71. Italics added.

70   A.J. Gordon, as quoted in H.B. Hartzler, *Moody In Chicago* (New York: Revell, 1894), 71.

71   A.J. Gordon, as quoted in H.B. Hartzler, *Moody In Chicago* (New York: Revell, 1894), 154-155.

72   A.J. Gordon, as quoted in H.B. Hartzler, *Moody In Chicago* (New York: Revell, 1894), 172.

73   A.J. Gordon, as quoted in H.B. Hartzler, *Moody In Chicago* (New York: Revell, 1894), 172.

74   A.J. Gordon, as quoted in H.B. Hartzler, *Moody In Chicago* (New York: Revell, 1894), 172-173.

75   A.J. Gordon, as quoted in H.B. Hartzler, *Moody In Chicago* (New York: Revell, 1894), 175. Italics added.

76   S.M. Gibson, *A.J. Gordon: American Premillenialist* (Lanham: University Press of America, 2001), 202.

77   S.M. Gibson, *A.J. Gordon: American Premillenialist* (Lanham: University Press of America, 2001), 202.

78   S.M. Gibson, *A.J. Gordon: American Premillenialist* (Lanham: University Press of America, 2001), 202. Punctuation added.

79   A.J. Gordon, letter, July 14, 1893, housed in the A.J. Gordon Papers, Jenks LRC, Gordon College.

80   A.J. Gordon, "The Resurrection," *The Record of Christian Work*, April 1916, 212. Monday, August 6th is given as the date of this address.

81   "Letter from D.L. Moody," *The Watchword*, February 1895, 56.

82   D.L. Moody, as quoted in L.W. Dorsett, *A Passion for Souls* (Chicago: Moody Press, 1997), 371.

83   A.J. Gordon, "The Resurrection," in D.L. Pierson, ed., *Northfield Echoes* (East Northfield: The Conference Bookstore, 1894), 537.

84   Among many places, Gordon cites Bunyan memorably in the pages of *In Christ* (London: Hodder and Stoughton, 1882), 189. See also pages 151-152 of *Great Pulpit Masters: A.J. Gordon*, Introduction by N.R. Wood, (New York: Revell, 1951).

85   A.J. Gordon, "The Resurrection," in D.L. Pierson, ed., *Northfield Echoes* (East Northfield: The Conference Bookstore, 1894), 539-540.

86   A.J. Gordon, "The Resurrection," in D.L. Pierson, ed., *Northfield Echoes* (East Northfield: The Conference Bookstore, 1894), 540.

87   A.J. Gordon, "The Resurrection," in D.L. Pierson, ed., *Northfield Echoes* (East Northfield: The Conference Bookstore, 1894), 540.

88   A.J. Gordon, "The Resurrection," in D.L. Pierson, ed., *Northfield Echoes* (East Northfield: The Conference Bookstore, 1894), 540.

89   A.J. Gordon, "The Resurrection," in D.L. Pierson, ed., *Northfield Echoes* (East Northfield: The Conference Bookstore, 1894), 542-543.

90   A.J. Gordon, "The Resurrection," in D.L. Pierson, ed., *Northfield Echoes* (East Northfield: The Conference Bookstore, 1894), 542-543.

91   A.J. Gordon, "The Resurrection," in D.L. Pierson, ed., *Northfield Echoes* (East Northfield: The Conference Bookstore, 1894), 543.

92   A.J. Gordon, "The Resurrection," in D.L. Pierson, ed., *Northfield Echoes* (East Northfield: The Conference Bookstore, 1894), 543.

93   A.J. Gordon, "The Resurrection," in D.L. Pierson, ed., *Northfield Echoes* (East Northfield: The Conference Bookstore, 1894), 543.

94   A.J. Gordon, "The Resurrection," in D.L. Pierson, ed., *Northfield Echoes* (East Northfield: The Conference Bookstore, 1894), 547.

95   A.J. Gordon, "The Resurrection," in D.L. Pierson, ed., *Northfield Echoes* (East Northfield: The Conference Bookstore, 1894), 547.

96   A.J. Gordon, "The Resurrection," in D.L. Pierson, ed., *Northfield Echoes* (East Northfield: The Conference Bookstore, 1894), 547.

97   A.J. Gordon, "The Resurrection," in D.L. Pierson, ed., *Northfield Echoes* (East Northfield: The Conference Bookstore, 1894), 548. Italics added.

Chapter Nineteen – To See The Morningstar

1   no author, *The Watchword* magazine, February 1895, 70.

2   no author, *The Brooklyn Eagle* newspaper, Wednesday, December 26, 1894, 10.

3   S.M. Gibson, *A.J. Gordon: American Premillenialist* (Lanham: University Press of America, 2001), 48.

4   no author, "untitled notice for A.J. Gordon's 25th Anniversary at Clarendon Street," *The Christian Work* newspaper, January 3, 1895, 11.

5   no author, *The Congregationalist* magazine, January 3, 1895, 5.

6   Edward Everett Hale to A.J. Gordon, 5 Jan. 1895, a letter in the A.J. Gordon Papers, Jenks LRC, Gordon College.

7   no author "Tribute to Gordon," *The Boston Daily Journal*, December 26, 1895, 1.

8   A.J. Gordon, "Pastoral Letter," in *The Watchword*, February 1895, 68.

9   A.J. Gordon, "Pastoral Letter," in *The Watchword*, February 1895, 68.

10 a monetary conversion done via "Measuring Worth," at: https://www.measuringworth.com/uscompare/relativevalue.php

11 A.J. Gordon, "Pastoral Letter," in *The Watchword*, February 1895, 68.

12 A.J. Gordon, "Pastoral Letter," in *The Watchword*, February 1895, 68.

13 A.J. Gordon, "Pastoral Letter," in *The Watchword*, February 1895, 68.

14 no author, "Dr. Gordon's Twenty-Fifth Anniversary," *The Outlook* magazine, January 12, 1895, 64-65.

15 E.B. Gordon, *Adoniram Judson Gordon* (London: Hodder & Stoughton, 1909), 367.

16 E.B. Gordon, *Adoniram Judson Gordon* (London: Hodder & Stoughton, 1909), 367.

17 A.J. Gordon, "25th Anniversary Sermon," in *The Watchword*, February 1895, 69. Italics added.

18 A.J. Gordon, "25th Anniversary Sermon," in *The Watchword*, February 1895, 69-70.

19 A.J. Gordon, "25th Anniversary Sermon," in *The Watchword*, February 1895, 70. Italics added.

20 A.J. Gordon, "25th Anniversary Sermon," in *The Watchword*, February 1895, 70.

21 A.J. Gordon, "25th Anniversary Sermon," in *The Watchword*, February 1895, 70.

22 A.J. Gordon, "25th Anniversary Sermon," in *The Watchword*, February 1895, 70.

23 A.J. Gordon, "25th Anniversary Sermon," in *The Watchword*, February 1895, 70. Italics added.

24 A.J. Gordon, "25th Anniversary Sermon," in *The Watchword*, February 1895, 70.

25 A.J. Gordon, "25th Anniversary Sermon," in *The Watchword*, February 1895, 70.

26 A.J. Gordon, "25th Anniversary Sermon," in *The Watchword*, February 1895, 70.

27 A.J. Gordon, "25th Anniversary Sermon," in *The Watchword*, February 1895, 70.

28 E.B. Gordon, *Adoniram Judson Gordon* (London: Hodder & Stoughton, 1909), 367.

29 E.B. Gordon, *Adoniram Judson Gordon* (London: Hodder & Stoughton, 1909), 368.

30 E.B. Gordon, *Adoniram Judson Gordon* (London: Hodder & Stoughton, 1909), 368.

31 E.B. Gordon, *Adoniram Judson Gordon* (London: Hodder & Stoughton, 1909), 368.

32 E.B. Gordon, *Adoniram Judson Gordon* (London: Hodder & Stoughton, 1909), 368-369.

33 Robert Cameron, "Untitled Tribute to A.J. Gordon," *The Watchword*, February 1895, 29b.

34 E.B. Gordon, *Adoniram Judson Gordon* (London: Hodder & Stoughton, 1909), 369.

35 E.B. Gordon, *Adoniram Judson Gordon* (London: Hodder & Stoughton, 1909), 369.

36 A.J. Gordon, "If Ye Continue In My Word," *Great Pulpit Masters* (New York: Revell, 1951), 143.

37 A.J. Gordon, "If Ye Continue In My Word," *Great Pulpit Masters* (New York: Revell, 1951), 143.

38 E.B. Gordon, *Adoniram Judson Gordon* (London: Hodder & Stoughton, 1909), 369.

39 E.B. Gordon, *Adoniram Judson Gordon* (London: Hodder & Stoughton, 1909), 369.

40 E.B. Gordon, *Adoniram Judson Gordon* (London: Hodder & Stoughton, 1909), 369. The address of the Clarendon Street Baptist Church parsonage is confirmed on page 860 of the Nov. 1891 issue of *The Missionary Review of the World*, (New York: Funk & Wagnalls Company, 1892). A.J. Gordon was a Contributing Editor to this publication.

41 E.B. Gordon, *Adoniram Judson Gordon* (London: Hodder & Stoughton, 1909), 369.

42 E.B. Gordon, *Adoniram Judson Gordon* (London: Hodder & Stoughton, 1909), 369-370.

43 E.B. Gordon, *Adoniram Judson Gordon* (London: Hodder & Stoughton, 1909), 370.

44 E.B. Gordon, *Adoniram Judson Gordon* (London: Hodder & Stoughton, 1909), 370.

45 E.B. Gordon, *Adoniram Judson Gordon* (London: Hodder & Stoughton, 1909), 370.

46 E.B. Gordon, *Adoniram Judson Gordon* (London: Hodder & Stoughton, 1909), 371.

47 A.T. Pierson, "A.J. Gordon, D.D.," in *The Missionary Review of the World*, April 1895, 295.

48 Joseph Cook, "Dr. Gordon as a Preacher, A Career Consecrated and Crowned: Address by Joseph Cook in Park St. Church, Boston, February 4, 1895, in the Boston Monday Lectureship, of which Dr. Gordon was for Twelve Years Chairman," *The Watchword*, February-March 1895, 54.

49 See advertisements given for "Joseph Cook's Boston Monday Lectures" on page 95-96 of *The Great Debate* (Boston: Houghton Mifflin, 1886). Here it is stated: *"For searching philosophical analysis, for keen and merciless logic, for dogmatic assertion of eternal truth in the august name of science such as thrills the soul to its foundations, for widely diversified and most apt illustrations drawn from a wide field of reading and observation, for true poetic feeling, for a pathos without any mixture of sentimentality, for candor, for moral elevation, and for noble loyalty to those great Christian verities which the author affirms and vindicates, these wonderful [Boston Monday] Lectures stand forth alone amidst the contemporary literature of the class to which they belong."* —The London Quarterly Review.

50 Joseph Cook, "Dr. Gordon as a Preacher, A Career Consecrated and Crowned: Address by Joseph Cook in Park St. Church, Boston, February 4, 1895, in the Boston Monday Lectureship, of which Dr. Gordon was for Twelve Years Chairman," *The Watchword*, February-March 1895, 54.

51 Joseph Cook, "Dr. Gordon as a Preacher, A Career Consecrated and Crowned: Address by Joseph Cook in Park St. Church, Boston, February 4, 1895, in the Boston Monday Lectureship, of which Dr. Gordon was for Twelve Years Chairman," *The Watchword*, February-March 1895, 54.

52 Joseph Cook, "Dr. Gordon as a Preacher, A Career Consecrated and Crowned: Address by Joseph Cook in Park St. Church, Boston, February 4, 1895, in the Boston Monday Lectureship, of which Dr. Gordon was for Twelve Years Chairman," *The Watchword*, February-March 1895, 54.

53 Joseph Cook, "Dr. Gordon as a Preacher, A Career Consecrated and Crowned: Address by Joseph Cook in Park St. Church, Boston, February 4, 1895, in the Boston Monday Lectureship, of which Dr. Gordon was for Twelve Years Chairman," *The Watchword*, February-March 1895, 54.

54 E.B. Andrews "A.J. Gordon," in *Our Day* magazine, March 1895, 144-145.

55 H. Grattan Guinness letter to Maria Gordon, in *The Watchword*, February 1895, 46-47.

56 D.L. Moody letter to Maria Gordon, in *The Watchword*, February 1895, 44. Punctuation added.

57 "Letter from D.L. Moody," *The Watchword*, February 1895, 55-56. Italics added.

58 "Letter from D.L. Moody," *The Watchword*, February 1895, 56.

59 "Letter from D.L. Moody," *The Watchword*, February 1895, 56.

60 "Letter from D.L. Moody," *The Watchword*, February 1895, 56.

61 "Letter from D.L. Moody," *The Watchword*, February 1895, 56.

62 "Letter from D.L. Moody," *The Watchword*, February 1895, 56.

63 "Letter from D.L. Moody," *The Watchword*, February 1895, 56-57.

64 D.L. Robert, "The Legacy of Adoniram Judson Gordon," *The International Bulletin of Missionary Research* (October 1987), 180.

65 A.J. Gordon, "The Christian Unity Society," *The Congregational Review*, July 1865, 405.

66 D.L. Robert, "The Legacy of Adoniram Judson Gordon," *The International Bulletin of Missionary Research* (October 1987), 180.

67 D.L. Robert, "The Legacy of Adoniram Judson Gordon," *The International Bulletin of Missionary Research* (October 1987), 176.

68 D.L. Robert, "The Legacy of Adoniram Judson Gordon," *The International Bulletin of Missionary Research* (October 1987), 180.

69 from page 13 of N.R. Wood's Introduction to *Great Pulpit Masters: A.J. Gordon*, (New York, Revell, 1951).

70 from page 14 of N.R. Wood's Introduction to *Great Pulpit Masters: A.J. Gordon*, (New York, Revell, 1951).

71 G.M. Mardsen, *Fundamentalism and American Culture* (Oxford University Press, 1982), 83. Here Marsden writes: "Like [Wendell] Phillips and [Jonathan] Blanchard, he [Gordon] also championed the legal recognition of the rights of women." And here, Marsden directs the reader to Gordon's December 1894 *Missionary Review* article, "The Ministry of Women." On page 911 of that article, Gordon states: "Here, then, we take the starting point for the discussion. This prophecy of Joel, realized at Pentecost, is the Magna Charta of the Christian

Church. It gives to woman a status in the Spirit hitherto unknown. And, as in civil legislation, no law can be enacted which conflicts with the constitution, so in Scripture we shall expect to find no text which denies to woman her divinely appointed rights in the New Dispensation." And on page 919 of this same article, Gordon cites Edward Irving with approbation and concurrence: "The famous Edward Irving speaks thus pointedly on this subject: "Who am I that I should despise the gift of God, because it is in a woman, whom the Holy Ghost despiseth not?...That women have with men an equal distribution of spiritual gifts is not only manifest from the fact (Acts 2; 18:26; 21:9 ; 1 Cor. 11:3, etc.), but from the very words of the prophecy of Joel itself, which may well rebuke those vain and thoughtless people who make light of the Lord's work, because it appeareth among women, *I wish men would themselves be subject to the Word of God, before they lord it s0 over women's equal rights in the great outpouring of the Spirit* (Irving's Works, v, 555)."

72   D.L. Robert, "The Legacy of Adoniram Judson Gordon," *The International Bulletin of Missionary Research* (October 1987), 180.

73   D.L. Robert, "The Legacy of Adoniram Judson Gordon," *The International Bulletin of Missionary Research* (October 1987), 176.

74   D.L. Robert, "The Legacy of Adoniram Judson Gordon," *The International Bulletin of Missionary Research* (October 1987), 176.

75   A.J. Gordon, quoted in N.R. Wood, *A School for Christ* (Boston: Halliday Lithograph Corp., 1953), 15. These are the first two lines of verse 1 and verse 2 of Gordon's hymn, "The King in His Beauty," published in 1893.

Chapter Twenty – Years Beyond

1   *The Poetical Works of Alfred Tennyson* (Boston: Houghton Mifflin, 1885), 591.

2   no author, "Death Notice for Alice Boise Wood," *The University of Chicago Magazine*, June 1919, 309.

3   W.R. Moody, ed., "The Gordon Missionary Training School," *The Record of Christian Work*, November 1896, 325.

4   N.R. Wood, *A School of Christ* (Boston: Halliday Lithograph Corp., 1953), 27.

5   no author, "Sailed Volunteers," *The Intercollegian*, June 1900, 217.

6   E.B. Mendenhall, "The Christian Workers' Training School," *The American Friend*, October 17, 1901, 991. Italics added.

7   N.R. Wood, *A School of Christ* (Boston: Halliday Lithograph Corp., 1953), 27-28.

8   N.R. Wood, *A School of Christ* (Boston: Halliday Lithograph Corp., 1953), 28.

9   N.R. Wood, *A School of Christ* (Boston: Halliday Lithograph Corp., 1953), 29.

10   N.R. Wood, *A School of Christ* (Boston: Halliday Lithograph Corp., 1953), 33.

11   N.R. Wood, *A School of Christ* (Boston: Halliday Lithograph Corp., 1953), 33-34.

12   N.R. Wood, *A School of Christ* (Boston: Halliday Lithograph Corp., 1953), 33.

13   N.R. Wood, *A School of Christ* (Boston: Halliday Lithograph Corp., 1953), 34.

14   N.R. Wood, *A School of Christ* (Boston: Halliday Lithograph Corp., 1953), 35.

15   N.R. Wood, *A School of Christ* (Boston: Halliday Lithograph Corp., 1953), 36-37.

16   N.R. Wood, *A School of Christ* (Boston: Halliday Lithograph Corp., 1953), 37.

17   N.R. Wood, *A School of Christ* (Boston: Halliday Lithograph Corp., 1953), 37.

18   N.R. Wood, *A School of Christ* (Boston: Halliday Lithograph Corp., 1953), 38.

19   N.R. Wood, *A School of Christ* (Boston: Halliday Lithograph Corp., 1953), 39.

20   N.R. Wood, *A School of Christ* (Boston: Halliday Lithograph Corp., 1953), 40.

21   N.R. Wood, *A School of Christ* (Boston: Halliday Lithograph Corp., 1953), 40.

22   N.R. Wood, *A School of Christ* (Boston: Halliday Lithograph Corp., 1953), 40-41.

23   N.R. Wood, *A School of Christ* (Boston: Halliday Lithograph Corp., 1953), 41.

24   N.R. Wood, *A School of Christ* (Boston: Halliday Lithograph Corp., 1953), 41-42.

25   N.R. Wood, *A School of Christ* (Boston: Halliday Lithograph Corp., 1953), 43.

26   N.R. Wood, *A School of Christ* (Boston: Halliday Lithograph Corp., 1953), 43-44.

27   N.R. Wood, *A School of Christ* (Boston: Halliday Lithograph Corp., 1953), 44.

28   N.R. Wood, *A School of Christ* (Boston: Halliday Lithograph Corp., 1953), 43-44.

29   N.R. Wood, *A School of Christ* (Boston: Halliday Lithograph Corp., 1953), 45.

30   N.R. Wood, *A School of Christ* (Boston: Halliday Lithograph Corp., 1953), 45.

31   N.R. Wood, *A School of Christ* (Boston: Halliday Lithograph Corp., 1953), 45-46.

32   N.R. Wood, *A School of Christ* (Boston: Halliday Lithograph Corp., 1953), 46.

33   N.R. Wood, *A School of Christ* (Boston: Halliday Lithograph Corp., 1953), 46. Italics added.

34   N.R. Wood, *A School of Christ* (Boston: Halliday Lithograph Corp., 1953), 46-47.

35   N.R. Wood, *A School of Christ* (Boston: Halliday Lithograph Corp., 1953), 47.

36   N.R. Wood, *A School of Christ* (Boston: Halliday Lithograph Corp., 1953), 47.

37   N.R. Wood, *A School of Christ* (Boston: Halliday Lithograph Corp., 1953), 47.

38   "Arthur Hale Gordon," *Harvard College Class of 1893: Secretary's Fifth Report* (Cambridge: Crimson Printing Co., 1913), 76.

39   N.R. Wood, *A School of Christ* (Boston: Halliday Lithograph Corp., 1953), 47.

40   N.R. Wood, *A School of Christ* (Boston: Halliday Lithograph Corp., 1953), 53. See also *The Catalogue of Brown University, 1894-1895* (Providence: Remington & Co., 1895), 211 & 220.

41   N.R. Wood, *A School of Christ* (Boston: Halliday Lithograph Corp., 1953), 53.

42   N.R. Wood, *A School of Christ* (Boston: Halliday Lithograph Corp., 1953), 79.

43   N.R. Wood, *A School of Christ* (Boston: Halliday Lithograph Corp., 1953), 81.

44   N.R. Wood, *A School of Christ* (Boston: Halliday Lithograph Corp., 1953), 81.

45   N.R. Wood, *A School of Christ* (Boston: Halliday Lithograph Corp., 1953), 81.

46   N.R. Wood, *A School of Christ* (Boston: Halliday Lithograph Corp., 1953), 81.

47   N.R. Wood, *A School of Christ* (Boston: Halliday Lithograph Corp., 1953), 81.

48   N.R. Wood, *A School of Christ* (Boston: Halliday Lithograph Corp., 1953), 81. Italics added.

49 N.R. Wood, *A School of Christ* (Boston: Halliday Lithograph Corp., 1953), 81-82.

50 N.R. Wood, *A School of Christ* (Boston: Halliday Lithograph Corp., 1953), 82.

51 N.R. Wood, *A School of Christ* (Boston: Halliday Lithograph Corp., 1953), 82.

52 N.R. Wood, *A School of Christ* (Boston: Halliday Lithograph Corp., 1953), 82.

53 N.R. Wood, *A School of Christ* (Boston: Halliday Lithograph Corp., 1953), 82-83.

54 N.R. Wood, *A School of Christ* (Boston: Halliday Lithograph Corp., 1953), 83.

55 N.R. Wood, *A School of Christ* (Boston: Halliday Lithograph Corp., 1953), 83.

56 N.R. Wood, *A School of Christ* (Boston: Halliday Lithograph Corp., 1953), 83-84.

57 N.R. Wood, *A School of Christ* (Boston: Halliday Lithograph Corp., 1953), 85.

58 N.R. Wood, *A School of Christ* (Boston: Halliday Lithograph Corp., 1953), 85-86.

59 no author, "Building News: Massachusetts," *The American Architect* (New York: Architectural & Building Press, Inc., 1915), 10.

60 no author, "The Boston Architectural Club," *The Architectural Forum*, July 1922, 27. See also N.R. Wood, *A School of Christ* (Boston: Halliday Lithograph Corp., 1953), 86.

61 N.R. Wood, *A School of Christ* (Boston: Halliday Lithograph Corp., 1953), 89-90.

62 N.R. Wood, *A School of Christ* (Boston: Halliday Lithograph Corp., 1953), 90.

63 N.R. Wood, *A School of Christ* (Boston: Halliday Lithograph Corp., 1953), 91.

64 N.R. Wood, *A School of Christ* (Boston: Halliday Lithograph Corp., 1953), 91.

65 N.R. Wood, *A School of Christ* (Boston: Halliday Lithograph Corp., 1953), 91.

66 N.R. Wood, *A School of Christ* (Boston: Halliday Lithograph Corp., 1953), 91.

67 N.R. Wood, *A School of Christ* (Boston: Halliday Lithograph Corp., 1953), 91-92.

68 N.R. Wood, *A School of Christ* (Boston: Halliday Lithograph Corp., 1953), 92-93.

69 N.R. Wood, *A School of Christ* (Boston: Halliday Lithograph Corp., 1953), 93-94. Italics added.

70 N.R. Wood, *A School of Christ* (Boston: Halliday Lithograph Corp., 1953), 97.

71 N.R. Wood, *A School of Christ* (Boston: Halliday Lithograph Corp., 1953), 97-98.

72 N.R. Wood, *A School of Christ* (Boston: Halliday Lithograph Corp., 1953), 98.

73 N.R. Wood, *A School of Christ* (Boston: Halliday Lithograph Corp., 1953), 98.

74 N.R. Wood, *A School of Christ* (Boston: Halliday Lithograph Corp., 1953), 99.

75 N.R. Wood, *A School of Christ* (Boston: Halliday Lithograph Corp., 1953), 84-85.

76 N.R. Wood, *A School of Christ* (Boston: Halliday Lithograph Corp., 1953), 84-85.

77 N.R. Wood, *A School of Christ* (Boston: Halliday Lithograph Corp., 1953), 49.

78 N.R. Wood, *A School of Christ* (Boston: Halliday Lithograph Corp., 1953), 85.

79 no author, "From Pastorate to Professorship," *The Congregationalist and Advance*, Apr 1, 1920, 454, & the June 24, 1920 issue, 846.

80 In April 1934, Dr. E.P. Drew addressed Harvard students "Hindrances to Christian Belief," a talk covered in *The Harvard Crimson*, on April 24, 1934. See http://www.thecrimson.com/article/1934/4/24/drew-to-speak-to-evangelists-pspeaking/

81 "Gordon College of Theology and Missions," an advertisement in *The Congregationalist*, June 30, 1921, page facing title page.

82 Emmet Russell, "Untitled Class Letter," *Harvard College Class of 1914*, (Cambridge: The University Press, 1921), 222.

83 N.R. Wood, Introduction to the *Catalog of Gordon Bible College* (Boston: Gordon Bible College, 1916). See also page 612 of *The Harvard Alumni Bulletin*, March 31, 1921, which states: "Emmet Russell, LL.B. '19, was married recently in Arlington, Mass., to Miss Amy M. Dyer. Russell will graduate from the Gordon Bible School, Boston, in June, and will then enter the Baptist ministry. His home address is 17 Bickford St., Roxbury, Mass."

84 N.R. Wood, *A School of Christ* (Boston: Halliday Lithograph Corp., 1953), 103.

85 D.L. Pierson, ed., "Gordon Bible College," *The Missionary Review of the World*, November 1916, 874.

86 no author, "Gordon Bible College advertisement," *The Missionary Review of the World*, August 1916, page after Table of Contents.

Afterword – The Sacred Isle

1   A.J. Gordon, "Grace and Reward," *Great Pulpit Masters* (New York: Revell, 1951), 123.

2   see page 232 of *Adoniram Judson Gordon*, by E.B. Gordon, (London: Hodder & Stoughton, 1909).

3   that Gordon's essay on Columba was "one of the last acts" his writing life is confirmed in a note from A.T. Pierson, on page 251 of the April 1895 issue of *The Missionary Review*.

4   A.J. Gordon, "The Apostle Columba" in *The Missionary Review*, April 1895, 247.

5   A.J. Gordon, "The Apostle Columba" in *The Missionary Review*, April 1895, 247.

6   A.J. Gordon, "The Apostle Columba" in *The Missionary Review*, April 1895, 248.

7   E.M. Bacon, ed., *Men of Progress*, (Boston: New England Magazine, 1896), 876. See also page 731 of the October 1888 issue of *The Missionary Review of the World*, (New York: Funk & Wagnalls, 1888). Here it is stated: "the following letter [dated July 28, 1888] will show what [Dr. Pierson] and his greatly beloved co-laborer, Dr. A.J. Gordon, of Boston, are doing, and have been doing, in Scotland, since the London Conference closed."

8   A.J. Gordon, "The Holy Spirit in Missions," *Report of the First International Convention of the Student Volunteer Movement* (Boston: T.O. Metcalf, 1891), 12.

9   A.J. Gordon, "The Apostle Columba" in *The Missionary Review*, April 1895, 248.

10 A.J. Gordon, "The Apostle Columba" in *The Missionary Review*, April 1895, 248. Gordon originally wrote these journal entries in the third person. But here, for a sense of immediacy, they're given in the first person.

11 A.J. Gordon, "The Apostle Columba" in *The Missionary Review*, April 1895, 249. Gordon had originally written these journal entries in the third person. But here, to create a sense of immediacy, they're rendered in the first person.

12   A.J. Gordon, "The Apostle Columba" in *The Missionary Review*, April 1895, 250.

13   A.J. Gordon, "The Apostle Columba" in *The Missionary Review*, April 1895, 250.

14   A.J. Gordon, "The Apostle Columba" in *The Missionary Review*, April 1895, 251.

15   "The Pilgrim's Place and Promise," from *Great Pulpit Masters: A.J. Gordon* (New York: Revell, 1951), 149.

16   A.J. Gordon, "The Apostle Columba" in *The Missionary Review*, April 1895, 248.

Appendix

1   E.B. Andrews "A.J. Gordon," in *Our Day* magazine, March 1895, 144-146.

CPSIA information can be obtained
at www.ICGtesting.com
Printed in the USA
BVHW03*0907051018

529170BV00014B/12/P

9 781512 799736